MW00636986

Geocriticism and Spatial Literary Studies

Series Editor
Robert T. Tally Jr.
Texas State University
San Marcos, TX, USA

Geocriticism and Spatial Literary Studies is a new book series focusing on the dynamic relations among space, place, and literature. The spatial turn in the humanities and social sciences has occasioned an explosion of innovative, multidisciplinary scholarship in recent years, and geocriticism, broadly conceived, has been among the more promising developments in spatially oriented literary studies. Whether focused on literary geography, cartography, geopoetics, or the spatial humanities more generally, geocritical approaches enable readers to reflect upon the representation of space and place, both in imaginary universes and in those zones where fiction meets reality. Titles in the series include both monographs and collections of essays devoted to literary criticism, theory, and history, often in association with other arts and sciences. Drawing on diverse critical and theoretical traditions, books in the Geocriticism and Spatial Literary Studies series disclose, analyze, and explore the significance of space, place, and mapping in literature and in the world.

Atsuko Sakaki

Train Travel as Embodied Space-Time in Narrative Theory

palgrave
macmillan

Atsuko Sakaki
University of Toronto
Toronto, ON, Canada

ISSN 2578-9694   ISSN 2634-5188   (electronic)
Geocriticism and Spatial Literary Studies
ISBN 978-3-031-40547-1   ISBN 978-3-031-40548-8   (eBook)
https://doi.org/10.1007/978-3-031-40548-8

© The Editor(s) (if applicable) and The Author(s), under exclusive licence to Springer Nature Switzerland AG 2023
This work is subject to copyright. All rights are solely and exclusively licensed by the Publisher, whether the whole or part of the material is concerned, specifically the rights of translation, reprinting, reuse of illustrations, recitation, broadcasting, reproduction on microfilms or in any other physical way, and transmission or information storage and retrieval, electronic adaptation, computer software, or by similar or dissimilar methodology now known or hereafter developed.
The use of general descriptive names, registered names, trademarks, service marks, etc. in this publication does not imply, even in the absence of a specific statement, that such names are exempt from the relevant protective laws and regulations and therefore free for general use.
The publisher, the authors, and the editors are safe to assume that the advice and information in this book are believed to be true and accurate at the date of publication. Neither the publisher nor the authors or the editors give a warranty, expressed or implied, with respect to the material contained herein or for any errors or omissions that may have been made. The publisher remains neutral with regard to jurisdictional claims in published maps and institutional affiliations.

This Palgrave Macmillan imprint is published by the registered company Springer Nature Switzerland AG.
The registered company address is: Gewerbestrasse 11, 6330 Cham, Switzerland

Paper in this product is recyclable.

For Stéphane Laframboise, who gave me a new lease on life,
and
Brett de Bary, who breathed life into this project

ACKNOWLEDGMENTS

For the past 15 years or so, I have concerned myself with the question of how novelistic discourse represents the way the body navigates space that is occupied with things, over time that is not absolute but immanent. The genre of modern prose fiction is often taken to be transparent, scientific, and static due to its publication format (printed and mass-produced text), mode of reading (silent and solitary reading), use of vernacular language (for the nation of imagined homogeneity), and narrative agency (either third person for observation or first person for confession). In my 1998 *Recontextualizing Text: Narrative Performance in Modern Japanese Fiction*, my consideration was how relations between narrative roles (narrator, narratee, narrated) are formed and transformed within a text. In my 2015 *The Rhetoric of Photography*, I moved on to consider the space beyond the frame of representation, and the relation between image and text. Since 2016, I have been considering sports as image, spectacle, and experience. Along the line, however, the present project—on the train journey as a passenger's body's experience of space-time—somehow overtook the sports project, not unlike an express train hurtling past a train stopped at a station. I apologize to my research assistants hired for the other project—Kristopher Poulin-Thibault, Edwin Michielsen, Sooyun (Clara) Hong, and Gianmarco Bocchi for this delay.

Without the intention of writing a book on the subject, in 2013 I revisited Kurahashi Yumiko's *Kurai tabi* (Blue Journey) for the nth time (the first having been for my 1992 PhD dissertation). In a chapter of *The Father-Daughter Plot* (University of Hawai'i Press, 2001), edited by Rebecca Copeland and Esperanza Ramirez-Christensen, I had

investigated how Kurahashi's anti-novel has failed to make the cut for the
literary canon, unlike major works by Abe Kōbō or Ōe Kenzaburō, other
intellectual writers of Japan who happened to be male. Along the way, I
examined the controversy sparked by the literary critic Etō Jun's accusation that Kurahashi had plagiarized Michel Butor's *La Modification*. I of
course refuted Etō's claim, but I did not compare the two texts beyond
the points of comparison made by Etō. In 2013, I thought of collating the
two narratives that share the storyline of the railway journey from a modern capital (Paris or Tokyo) to an ancient capital (Rome or Kyoto) for the
American Comparative Literature Association's 2014 conference at the
University of Toronto, where I organized a 12-paper seminar entitled
"'Where Were You Then?' 'Wish You Were Here' 'Same Place, Different
Time': Rhetoric of Sharing and Separation across Time or Space." My
own paper, "From Second Person to Third Person: A Sad Young Man/
Woman on a Train En Route to the Cultural Other," centering on Butor,
Kurahashi, and Marcel Dechamp's *Sad Young Man on the Train*, was then
accepted again for the International Comparative Literature Association's
2016 meeting at the University of Vienna. It was rejected for the conference's proceedings, however, and with that, and for other reasons touched
upon later, the paper sank into the depths of my computer—until April
2019, when Brett de Bary at Cornell University invited me to speak at the
Society of the Humanities and East Asia Program.

At that time, I had at hand a few finished yet unpublished papers, and
consulted Brett on those ideas, along with mentioning this newish idea
about the second-person narrative and train journey, still amorphous, pulsating yet lurking in the dark. Brett gently yet firmly pushed me toward
presenting the new project. After a few attempts to resist in favor of a safer
option, I agreed to prepare a new paper which, though extended from the
aforementioned ACLA/ICLA paper, would shift the central focus to
Tawada Yōko, an author on whom Brett and a few of her PhD students
had long been working. Until then I had been a novice reader of that
author: during a year-long sabbatical in 2014, I had undertaken a "binge-
reading" of Tawada's fiction, with which I had remained unacquainted
despite its enthusiastic reception among my peers in modern Japanese literature. It was then that I had read Tawada's *Yōgisha no yakō ressha*
(Suspects on the Night Train), which, like *Blue Journey*, is a second-person
narrative set on a train, and the thought of throwing it into conversation
with Kurahashi's anti-novel had germinated in the interim. An emphasis
on Tawada's book in my ensuing talk at Cornell, entitled "'It's Not 'I,'

It's 'You': Second-Person Narratives on the Train in Butor, Kurahashi, and Tawada," formed a prototype of Chap. 6 of this book.

It was an audacious move for me to make, but in the end it was most productive. The Tawada specialists in the audience, including Paul McQuade, Jean-Jacques Aupiais, and Brett, responded to my talk with great enthusiasm, and I received inspiring questions and suggestions from other attendees as well, such as Andrea Mendoza, Andrew Campana, and Marie-Claire Vallois. I also thank all who provided hospitality and set me up in a good frame of mind prior to the talk, including Joshua Young, Aya Saiki, and Aki Tanaka, as well as Paul. Their collective collegial warmth and nurturing propelled me to an intellectual cloud nine, where I dreamed up an idea—namely, that there was a book to be written on the subject.

I must add that something even more fundamental was brought about by this visit to Ithaca. Because I had failed to successfully nurture, challenge, and inspire future generations of scholars as an academic advisor of PhD students who had in most cases ended up disavowing the profession, the field, or a working relationship with me, I was contemplating unplugging myself—perhaps by leaving the field, perhaps in some more radical way. The exhilarating experience of intellectual exchange with the people I met at Cornell enabled me to change gears and to redefine myself as a critical reader, thinker, and writer, roles in which I could contribute to knowledge and critical thought, and connect with the like-minded, by keeping on producing my own work.

Not long thereafter, I decided to write a book on the space-time of train journeys as a trope in narratology. In order to put the project in motion and complete it, I needed some momentum and then time off from other responsibilities. I drafted a grant proposal, on which Linda Hutcheon was so kind as to offer thoughtful comments and generous moral support. The result was that the Scholars-in-Residence Program at Jackman Humanities Institute at the University of Toronto (Director Alison Smith), organized and managed by Angela Esterhammer and Ira Wells, offered a month-long research platform and funding support to hire five undergraduate students to participate in the first stage of the research on this project in May 2020. The Centre for Comparative Literature (Acting Director Ann Komaromi) then offered a SIG grant and the Work-Study Program at the University of Toronto made funds available, enabling me to hire research assistants in summer 2020.

I was fortunate to receive excellent research assistance from a number of students over the span of this project: Joelle Nazzicone, Michelle Smith,

Rachel Gerry, and Benjamin Bandosz. The five upper undergraduate students under the Scholars-in-Residence Program in May 2020 also assisted: Carlos Arceo, Kornelia Drianovski, India James-Licher, Victoria McIntyre, and Jane Yearwood. Carlos and Kornelia continued through that summer under different arrangements. Two research assistants were hired with the SIG grant: Joseph Klemens and Nisarg Patel. And finally, Aliju Kim helped as well.

In 2021, the Literature and Critical Theory Program Students' Union (Communications Coordinator Neve Ostry Young, President Maia Harris) of Victoria College at the University of Toronto invited me to deliver a keynote at their 3rd Annual Undergraduate Academic Conference, "Perceptions on the Passage of Time." On March 12, I presented "Swinging Between 'You' and 'I': Time Embodied and Embodying Time in Second-Person Railway Journey Narratives," a version of the Cornell paper on Butor, Kurahashi, and Tawada adjusted to the theme of the conference. It was a fantastic experience, with an energetic Q and A session with attendees who included some of my research assistants, out of which the project gained more fuel and speed.

Unfortunately, my applications for larger research grants that would have given me a leave of absence to complete the book fell through, one after another, for two years in a row. I thank Irmela Hijiya-Kirschnereit, Linda Hutcheon, Thomas Lamarre, Brett de Bary, Akira Mizuta Lippit, and other respected peers and forerunners who encouraged me to stay on track with the project, expressing their faith in its value and in my ability to complete it.

I am immensely grateful to the Department of East Asian Studies (Interim Chair Thomas Keirstead for approving the request, and Chair Janet Poole for arranging the teaching replacements) and the Centre for Comparative Literature (Director Jill Ross for releasing me from graduate teaching) for granting me an unpaid semester of leave that I needed in winter 2022 to combine with a half-sabbatical in fall 2021 and thereby be free of teaching and administrative duties.

I was exceptionally fortunate to be able to enlist Victoria R. M. Scott for copyediting my draft chapters. Her meticulous and sensitive editing, impeccable professionalism, and such great attention to my comments, plaints, and meandering thoughts were simply priceless. She was the ideal and irreplaceable traveling companion through the journey of intense writing and rewriting. I cannot describe how mesmerizing that process was for the seven months of writing, from September 2021 until May 2022. It was a special time that I wouldn't change for anything.

A cornucopia of workplace friends inspired me as I wrote, whether with their daringly interdisciplinary approaches to literature and art or their unflagging faith in the validity of close reading: Meng Yue, Yurou Zhong, Johanna Liu, the late Vincent Shen, Graham Sanders, Linda Feng, Neil ten Kortenaar, the late Roland Le Huenen, Barbara Havercroft, Antje Budde, Veronika Ambros, Julie LeBlanc, Alison Syme, John Ricco, John Zilcosky, Angelica Fenner, John K. Noyes, and James Cahill, among others. I am also grateful to the administrators of the department and the center for their explicit and implicit help and support: Natasja VanderBerg, Norma Escobar, Paul Chin, Aphrodite Gardiner, and Bao Nguyen.

I thank the University of Toronto Libraries, especially the John P. Robarts Research Library, Cheng Yu Tung East Asian Library, Victoria University's E. J. Pratt Library, St. Michael's College's John M. Kelly Library, Trinity College's John W. Graham Library, Media Commons (now gone, unfortunately), and also the Resource Sharing/InterLibrary Loan department, as well as the libraries that participate in this program for loans of needed materials.

I was able to step outside my comfort zone with this project, in no small part thanks to the moral support for my general intellectual orientation received from the Association for Literary Urban Studies, Fringe Urban Narratives, and Mobility Humanities.

This book is a personal triumph as well, since I experienced major medical challenges between 2017 and 2022. I am happy to express my gratitude to the people who enabled me to get through all the difficult processes involved: Dr. Stéphane Laframboise, the surgeon and also the doctor in charge of chemotherapy, and her team of doctors, including Dr. Randi Shaul, nurses, and other staff members (including Sharon) at Princess Margaret Hospital from March 2017 through September 2022; nurses at Toronto General Hospital (Lorna, Jane, Henry, Janet, Henk, Jana) who took exceptional and loving care of me after surgery in April 2017; nurses at Princess Margaret Hospital (including Ashley) who conducted chemotherapy from May to November 2017; Dr. Michael Milosovic with his team of doctors and radiation therapists (including Colin) at Princess Margaret Hospital for treatment from August to September 2017 and for follow-ups through February 2023; Ms. Kara Semotiuk at Zane Cohen Centre at Mount Sinai Hospital for investigating and certifying in 2017 that I am not genetically challenged for higher probability of recurrence of cancer; my former family doctor at Mount Sinai Hospital's Family Medicine, Dr. Vivian Trinh, for first insisting I should take medical exams which led to the detection of the disease and then offering periodical counseling sessions; Dr. Zhaoxin (Vito) Zou, my current family doctor at the same clinic, for seeing me through the last stage of the five-year run after the completion of chemotherapy; Ms. Lynne Kutsukake for watching over me ever since the diagnosis through the long process at just right distance, not intervening but letting me know she's there if I need any help; Dr. Cheryl Jaigobin at Toronto Western Hospital for pushing me toward surgery without hesitation; Dr. Maria Cino at Toronto Western Hospital for affirming my recovery from cancer despite the unfavorable odds, for scientific reasons; and staff members at About the Wig Salon & Accessories Boutique at Princess Margaret Hospital and the Look Good Feel Better Program, for ensuring no one should notice anything odd about my appearance and in the meantime also enjoyed fashion. At the university in 2017, Andre Schmid, chair of the Department of East Asian Studies, and Jill Ross, director of the Centre for Comparative Literature, were most sympathetic when I confided in them about my health situation and asked for their understanding should I fail to deliver my best while continuing to carry my usual teaching workload. I will always be especially grateful to Yuanfang Zhang, Wen Yin (Elaine) Cheng, and Na Sil Heo, who agreed to reprise their TAships for EAS209, the core course I was then teaching for a second year in a row; though they did not know it at the time, as a team they helped me manage to get through the fall 2017 semester. And Arisa Yamazaki and Satoru Miyata at NC Salon, for listening attentively and responding with care, despite the long interruption when I did not have any hair, and for the super-fashionable extremely short haircuts they provided right before and after chemotherapy.

Apparently that was not enough of a challenge, for another medical calamity befell me, in the form of macular degeneration in my right eye in February 2019. I thank doctors in residence at Toronto Western Hospital, for saving my right eye from going blind with the disease by swiftly conducting injections of Eylea; Ms. Yana Klebanov at Shoppers Drug Mart at Toronto Western Hospital, for setting up enrollment at Eylea Q so that the high expenses of the eye injections would be fully covered; and Dr. Erik Yeo and Ms. Susan Jenkins at Toronto General Hospital for keeping an eye on my thrombosis since 2007.

The final stretch of preparation of the manuscript for publication coincided with another emergency, this time with my left eye, and with my residence being flooded and evacuated. Many offered professional and kind help between December 2022 and May 2023, including Dr. Fatimah Gilani at Toronto Retina Institute and my real estate agent Jackie Green.

Last but never least, I am grateful to Allie Troyanos, the executive editor for literature at Palgrave Macmillan, for supporting this project, steadfastly staying with it for the months of consideration and peer review, and making it possible to publish this book in the Geocriticism and Spatial Literary Studies series that I contacted as my first and only choice. Thanks also go to the series editor, Robert T. Tally, Jr., for his enthusiasm about including this book in the series, of which I am a longtime fan. I cannot thank the anonymous reviewer enough for unconditionally supporting the project. Finally, I am grateful to the production team at Springer, led by Sasikala Thopu, V. Vinodh Kumar, and Brian Halm, for bringing this book to completion. This is literally a dream come true.

I thank my parents and ancestors for giving me the resilient mind with which to live to write this book while faced with adversities and am especially grateful to my mother and grandmother for joyous memories of traveling on railways in Japan and in Europe. None of us drives a car, and thus we have been reliant on and grateful for public transportation systems, especially trains. This book is a small token of appreciation and celebration of travels by rail.

Toronto, Ontario, Canada   Atsuko Sakaki
May 2023

CONTENTS

Introduction: The Train as Embodied Space-Time, with Case Studies of *The Lady Vanishes*, *The Narrow Margin*, and *Night Train*

Marcel Duchamp's *Jeune homme triste dans un train* (*Sad Young Man in a Train*, 1911–1912) indicates that the train the featured man is in, itself invisible in the picture, is not only moving forward as it should but also swaying left and right. The collection catalogue of Peggy Guggenheim Venice that owns this painting reads:

> Duchamp's primary concern in this painting is the depiction of two movements, that of the train in which we observe the young man smoking and that of the lurching figure itself. The forward motion of the train is suggested by the multiplication of the lines and volumes of the figure, a semi-transparent form through which we can see windows, themselves transparent and presumably presenting a blurred, "moving" landscape. The independent sideways motion of the figure is represented by a directionally contrary series of repetitions.[1]

The advancement of technology aims for less sway and more drive. Train rides, however, cannot be reduced to exploitations of the speed of their linear movement from the departure point to the destination. These journeys are not simply utilitarian but are assemblages of many minor disturbances that pull the passenger in diverse directions: pastimes (reading, listening, smoking, eating, drinking, sleeping, reminiscing,

© The Author(s), under exclusive license to Springer Nature Switzerland AG 2023
A. Sakaki, *Train Travel as Embodied Space-Time in Narrative Theory*, Geocriticism and Spatial Literary Studies,
https://doi.org/10.1007/978-3-031-40548-8_1

people-watching, or watching the scenery go by); irregular stimuli such as a jolt at a station; the comings and goings of other passengers or a visit from the ticket inspector or other service providers; and random reflections on matters not necessarily related to the trip presently being taken.

Considered this way, the sidelong movement of the train may be comparable to the various sides of a passenger's subjectivity. Its transformation is not as regulated or linear, like the route of the railway, but as incidental and digressive, like the lurching of the train. Thus occur paradigmatic complications of a journey that is primarily designed to be syntagmatic, portrayed with multiple vertical and horizontal lines, as in Duchamp's painting. Temporal variations of the linear chronology parallel spatial ones (sideways and forward). Remembrances and predictions—and flashbacks and flashforwards—are mingled with each other and with present occurrences, while differences and repetitions further obfuscate the sense of geometrically striated space-time.

* * *

Let us start with Michel Foucault's well-known definition of the train, in his essay on "Heterotopia," as "other spaces" that are "places ... in which the real emplacements, all the other real emplacements that can be found within culture, are simultaneously represented, contested and inverted" (Foucault 2008, 17):

> A train is an extraordinary bundle of relations because it is something through which one passes, it is also something by means of which one can go from one point to another, and then it is also something that passes by. (Foucault 2008, 16; 2004, 14)

This sentence appears inside quotation marks in Foucault's essay, as an aside within his discussion of "emplacements," of which the train is merely an example. Though he does not elaborate on the train, my focus here is on how the train is seen as a "bundle of relations."[2]

According to Foucault, the train's distinction begins with the fact that it is not seen as an entity, infrastructure, or tangible material presence. Rather, it is seen as a "bundle" that is inherently composite, heterogeneous, and contingent, and specifically as a bundle of "relations" that are formed among a *human subject* ("one"), a *thing* ("something"), and a *space-time* (suggested in the words "through" and "passes," and indicated in the words "from," "to," and "point"). These three elements are not presented as though their arrivals are chronologically arranged, their significances hierarchically ranked, or even their presences differentiated from one another. Instead, they are working in consortium to make the "train" come into being as a "relation" one way or another. The subject, thing, or space-time does not preexist either of the other two elements but is formed as such only through interaction with them. It matters little whether or not the human subject is utilizing the thing in order to navigate space more rapidly or spend time more productively. It is not instrumentality or purposiveness but a relationality that matters in this formulation. Moreover, this relationality is not single but a "bundle" of three relations among the subject, the thing (in this case the train), and the space(-time). To describe each relation in terms of the human subject's role, there can be (1) someone who moves inside the thing, (2) someone who moves across space by means of the thing, and (3) someone outside the thing, static in space themselves, who observes the thing that is mobile.

It is usually the second and third of these relations that are highlighted in discussions of how the train, as a technological device, has served the promotion of modernity. In both these cases, the subject, the thing, and the space-time are clearly differentiated from one another. In Foucault's first relation, however, in which the train is "something through which one passes," the relation among the three elements is distinctly different. First, the space is envisioned within the thing (the train) rather than outside it. Second, the human subject (passenger) is mobile within the thing, rather than being a passive recipient (as in the second case) or observer (as in the third case) of the movement induced by the thing (the train). The subject, such as Duchamp's sad young man in a train, is therefore not necessarily static and is not contrasted with the train's mobility. Thus, the train in the first relation acquires attributes of an interior space while simultaneously being an exterior space.[3]

The train both shields human subjects from the exterior space by means of the roofs and walls of the carriages and allows them to engage in new spatial practices outside their usual interior spaces (home, school, workplace, or other regular haunts). Michel de Certeau characterizes the former capacity of the train:

Only a rationalized cell travels. A bubble of panoptic and classifying power, a module of imprisonment that makes possible the production of an order, a closed and autonomous insularity—that is what can traverse space and make itself independent of local roots. (de Certeau 1984, 111)

Meanwhile, Louis Althusser has encapsulated the latter capacity of the train as follows, illustrating what we recognize as Foucault's first relation against his second and third relations while not explicitly stating this:

> [T]he idealist philosopher is a man who, when he catches a train, knows from the outset the station he will be leaving from and the one he will be arriving at; he knows the beginning [*origine*] and end of his route, just as he knows the origin and destiny of man, history and the world.
>
> The materialist philosopher, in contrast, is a man who always catches "a moving train," like the hero of an American Western. A train passes by in front of him: he can let it pass [*passer*] and nothing will happen [*se passe*] between him and the train; but he can also catch it as it moves. This philosopher knows neither Origin nor First Principle nor destination. He boards the moving train and settles into an available seat or strolls through the carriages, chatting with the travellers. He witnesses, without having been able to predict it, everything that occurs in an unforeseen, *aleatory* way, gathering an infinite amount of information and making an infinite number of observations, as much as the train itself as of the passengers and the countryside which, through the window, he sees rolling by. In short, he records *sequences* [*séquences*] *of aleatory encounters*, not, like the idealist philosopher, ordered successions [*conséquences*] deduced from an Origin that is the foundation of all Meaning, or from an absolute First Principle or Cause. (Althusser 2006, 277–78)

In "the materialist philosopher's" non-preordained, non-purposive, and non-linear travel by rail, the passenger's dynamic engagement with space-time, human subjects, and things is most essential.

The ambiguity, fluidity, and potentiality of the train in this first relation among the human subject, the thing, and the space-time are what drive the narratives of railway journeys that I discuss in this book. These three elements are not independent of but affect and transform one another. The first relation can be further broken down into (a) *affordances*, or relations in which the subject uses a space-time and things in it; (b) *movements*, or relations in which the subject and/or thing navigate(s) a space-time; and (c) *rhythms*, or relations that the thing and/or subject creates with space-time.

I propose to read the train as a lived/experienced space-time, extending Henri Lefebvre's term "experienced/lived space" (*l'espace vécu*) and informed by Edmund Husserl's notion of "immanent time" (*die erlebte Zeit*), which is time experienced, as distinct from the "absolute time" (*die absolute Zeit*) outside the (human) experience normatively imagined in chronology. The train here is thus of an elaborate and malleable structure in which human subjects' choreographed and incidental movements occur, in relation both to other subjects and to things and phenomena. Indeed, the train is imagined here as a stage, in which linear temporality—the very notion on which the train schedule is predicated—is not validated but complicated by multiple trajectories, variable pace, and fluctuating frequencies, and in which geometrical space both warps due to variable uses and negotiations and leaps by means of haunting memories. The stable, solid, and sovereign modern subject dissolves and becomes a performative, amorphous, and porous presence that is susceptible to the environment.

1 THE TRAIN AND THE RAILROAD IN MODERNITY STUDIES

In addition to the work of Foucault and de Certeau, who explained why the train matters within the context of studies of urban space, I cite the obvious two of the several important considerations of the train. Wolfgang Schivelbusch's meticulous study of the infrastructure of the passenger train carriage and Georg Simmel's sociologically informed conceptualization of intra-city public transportation (including the train) are both seminal works that have spawned many further reflections on the subject.

In Japanese literary studies, from which much of my present study springs, Alisa Freedman (2011), James A. Fujii (1999), and Barbara Thornbury (2014, 2020) have produced groundbreaking and monumental works about intra-city commuter train/public transportation and its daily, recurrent, and mundane experience. Through thorough source studies and conceptualization, their analyses expose the banality and precarity of everyday life encapsulated in the space-time of the commuter train, and reveal symptoms of the modern age. Their historically informed studies of the train shed light on documented facts and literary narratives inspired by known circumstances, such as tragic and traumatic incidents of suicide by rail (an extreme case of the third Foucauldian relation between the train and human subject) and sexual crime exploiting the congestion and anonymity within the train (another extreme relation that a human subject can develop with the train). Benjamin Fraser and Steven D. Spalding's extensive studies of the railroad worldwide (Fraser and Spalding 2012, Spalding and Fraser 2012), situated in cultural and literary histories, are both informative and highly inspiring. Meanwhile, Seth Jacobowitz (2015) has placed the railway in the definition of the modern sense of time, alongside other systems, such as the postal service and the telegraph, that also promote speed, homogeneity, and convenience at the cost of other values. In a similar vein, there are studies of British railways fiction edited by Adrienne E. Gavin and Andrew F. Humphries (2015) and of South American railway fiction by Sarah M. Misemer (2010). These scholarly contributions belong to the field of studies of modernity, of which the train/railway is an indispensable facet. Their historical significance, therefore, cannot be overestimated.

Keeping this existing scholarship in mind has served me well in this book, which seeks to unharness the potentials of the long-distance train ride under its specific material conditions for the mutual warping of space, time, and subjectivity. Yet I do not propose the present volume as a study of modernity, a regime that has established and promoted geometrical cartography, chronological temporality, and autonomous identity. Instead, what follows is a study of mobility in literature. Literary mobility studies, or mobility studies in the humanities, have thrived in recent years. In this field, illuminating discussions have appeared considering the three essentials of the subject, thing, and space-time—and the three relations of affordances, movements, and rhythms—vis-à-vis the human subject's relations with a number of different vehicles. Lynne Pearce (2016) on the automobile journey and Una Brogan (2022) on bicycle rides are among the prominent examples in this field. Their work benefits from interdisciplinary studies of mobility across the fields of human geography, tourism studies, and qualitative ethnography, while remaining firmly anchored in literary studies not only because their corpora are works of literature but, more importantly, because their work is not about the story (content) and its historical backdrop but about the *discourse* (form).

This is the intellectual path I follow in this book—namely, that of the train in literature, beyond the setting for a story, as in traditional literary studies, and beyond the train as a product of and an instrument for the modern age. How is the train as "embodied space-time" narrated in literary and cinematic discourse? This is what I have thought through. In what follows, I situate this project at the intersection of two recent trends in narrative studies and in studies of space.

Space-Time in Narrative Studies Before and After the "Spatial Turn"

The narrative has, by default, been considered to be temporally oriented, to be studied in terms of chronological and causal sequences of events and situations. To take a seminal theorist as an example, Gérard Genette, in his *Narrative Discourse* (1980), lists five key concepts, of which three are time-oriented—"Order," "Frequency," and "Duration," each of which determines the relation between story time and discourse time[4]—with the fourth, "Voice," being related to subjectivity, and the fifth, "Mood," being about distance and perspective, and thus about spatially measured subjectivity. The overwhelming attention to time as the central gauge in the narrative form had obliterated the importance of space, an element that had been reduced to a mere setting in the background, necessary yet irrelevant to the consideration of narrative discourse. In classical (structuralist) narratology, even the term "scene" was about temporality, denoting the slowest speed at which a narrative represents events (as opposed to a "summary" the fastest speed). This imbalance was addressed by Mikhail Bakhtin, who proposed the concept of "chronotope" and considered the performative nature of the narrative text, in which spatiality is as essential as it is in pictures.

Post-classical (post-structuralist) narratology/narrative studies have endeavored to de-neutralize the terms and concepts in structuralist narratology, and have made progress in the reconsideration of narrative subjectivity (taking into account its identity markers of race, gender, and ethnicity, among other modalities). In addition, the increased consideration of non-textual narratives—cinema, TV, new media—has evoked serious investigation of space, enacting and enacted by bodies and things. More generally, the humanities have endured a conversion termed the "spatial turn," since which space has been afforded increased attention in the humanities. Exploiting this tendency in narrative studies over the past few decades, the present volume considers the three aforementioned relations of affordances, movements and rhythms. Thus, in my study, "scene" is less about the time spent in a narrative representing events and unfolding situations than about a coordination of human bodies and things in temporally invested space, as in a "scene" in the performing arts.

The "Narrative Turn" in Space-Oriented Social Sciences

Geography, ethnography, mobility studies, and tourism studies are among the fields in the social sciences that study traveling by rail as important. These space-oriented disciplines have endured what is termed the "narrative turn," or a shift toward paying increased attention to the observing subject's experience in the social sciences. This shift entails qualitative rather than quantitative analysis, emphasis on the process of research (rather than the final results of the research), and a representational preference for the narrative.

Instead of scientific or putatively neutral third-person account of places that are objectified as static, finite, and delineated, scholars in these disciplines have been choosing to explicitly situate the human subject = traveler = researcher's position in the space that is not only their object of study but also a part of the circumstances in which their study develops. The researchers/travelers are themselves part of the space, and thus are under its effects. Instead of purporting to present a transparent description of fixed and finite space, they admit their own susceptibility to their natural and social environment and present their observations not as absolute but as relative, made from a first-person actant's perspective, based on the fully fleshed experience of the space.

David Bissell and George Revill are trailblazing theorists on the train who are informed by phenomenology, human geography, affect studies, mobility studies, and experience-based tourism studies. They have eloquently narrated passenger experience on the train in terms of multi-sensorial sensations and how they are experienced, registered, documented, and conceptualized. I have kept their pointers in mind when discussing literary and cinematic narratives of the train as experienced space-time.

My own work here thus stands at the intersection of post-spatial-turn narratology and the post-narrative-turn, space-oriented social sciences (geography, mobility studies, ethnography, tourism studies). It has benefited from and complements the recent accomplishments in the former (with an emphasis on space rather than on history), and the latter (a new direction for this space-oriented discipline that highlights human experience of the space and its registration in discourse).

2 THE TRAIN IN THE GENRE OF MYSTERY

In the following subsections, I offer a close reading of three mystery films in which the train is not just a setting for a story to unfold in, but a formative element of emplotment. In the genre of mystery, a perfect coordination of the plot and storytelling is crucial, which makes the genre an ideal model for consideration of the relationship between the train as experienced space-time and the narrative discourse that makes such space-time happen. Opportunity and means—two of the conditions for a crime to be committed (the other, of course, being motive)—engage with the three elements described earlier: human subjects/bodies (of victims and perpetrators); things (not only the train, but also objects to be stolen, tools to be employed, pieces of evidence present in the space); and space-time (access to the crime site when the coast is clear, alibis to be verified, escape from imminent danger). Taking advantage of the railways' connectivity and porosity, with multiple stops en route that allow passengers to board and disembark at different stations, the train offers a perfect setting for crime fiction, in which key players and relevant materials must enter and escape from the space-time. In the meantime, the relative finitude of the train carriage's space and the train ride's time encloses the criminal act, giving some direction to the investigation.

Because the narrative register of films is more show than tell (especially in films without voice-over, such as those chosen here), mystery films displays those elements which matter to the criminal act, yet make them look innocuous among irrelevant details to suspend their discovery until the investigation. More generally, the genre requires a tight connection between plot and setting, and between plot and the art of storytelling, as mentioned earlier. For these reasons, the thrillers analyzed below are ideal for elucidating important questions asked in this book, thus setting the standard for my procedure in later chapters, in which non-mystery narratives are discussed. Clear articulation of the relations between human subjects' bodies, things, and space-time is a key for crime fiction, so engaging with Alfred Hitchcock's *The Lady Vanishes* (1938), Richard Fleischer's *The Narrow Margin* (1952), and Jerzy Kawalerowicz's *Pociąg* (*Night Train*, 1959) will effectively set this book's conceptual orientation. Although there are many other mysteries that are set on a train, or that at least start out on one,[5] these three best suit my purpose because they are not so much about *who* the perpetrator is as about *where* the victim is hidden, *how* to prevent the crime from being committed (or how to protect the

potential victim from the potential perpetrators), and *how* to find the culprit on the run. Thus, each narrative focuses less on the person (as an
autonomous individual) than on the affordances within and movements
across the space-time (so that where and when are not presented separately but inform each other).

All three works are film noir, which involves not only a monochromatic
color scheme but both opacity about the crime and investigation and
ambiguity in the characterization. In film noir, the roles are not clearly and
stably assigned to characters but are elusive and transferrable, which further complicates their relationships with space-time: the investigator is
often not neutral but involved in the story. Although this proclivity of film
noir has often been considered in terms of the characterization or the
interiority of the detective (desires, emotions, temptations, hesitations,
surrenders), and thus as a part of the story (content), here it supports my
attention to bodies in space-time, since the detective is not guaranteed to
be of an analytical mind or in the neutral position but can be a body susceptible to circumstances that are loaded with things and conditions of
space-times.

As already mentioned, the focus in this study is on how the train functions in the narrative discourse as a space-time experienced by passengers
who share it both with other people and with things. However, in my
analysis of the three films in the mystery genre, I need to probe certain
nooks of their plots more deeply than a focus on discourse would otherwise require; space-time is experienced differently by human subjects of
varied physical conditions (height, agility, flexibility), contingent circumstances (tired, in haste, bored, sleepy), lifestyle preferences (has tea in the
afternoon, eats lightly while traveling, prefers a lower bed), acquired skills
and knowledge (able to open locked doors without a key, able to operate
the locomotive, informed about the train schedule), and roles (potential
or actual perpetrators, their collaborators, potential or actual victims, ama-
teur or professional detectives, curious onlookers or innocent bystanders).
These contingencies must be considered in terms of the discourse, even
though some of them may seem to belong in the realm of the story.

"The Lady Vanishes" (1938)

Alfred Hitchcock's *The Lady Vanishes* is mainly about the disappearance
from a transcontinental European long-distance train of a passenger by the
name of Miss Froy (played by May Whitty), who introduces herself to

other characters as an English governess and music teacher returning home after six years of service in the fictive country of Bandrika in Central Europe. Her disappearance is claimed only by an incidental female co-passenger, Iris (Margaret Lockwood), while all the other passengers whom Iris knows have seen Miss Froy deny having seen her. An acclaimed brain surgeon, Dr. Hartz, who happens to be on board, attributes this conflict to an accident Iris suffered earlier, on her head while on the train platform. Among the passengers and staff members, only Gilbert (Michael Redgrave)—a self-proclaimed ethnomusicologist and a third-class passenger—trusts Iris and joins forces with her searching for the missing lady.

My focus here is primarily on two peripheral characters—a duo of Englishmen traveling together, Caldicott (Naunton Wayne) and Charters (Basil Radford), who are anxious to arrive at Victoria Station, London, without delay so that they will not miss the "Test Match" in Manchester, an important cricket event they are keen to watch in support of Team England. Forced to stay at the inn overnight because of snow delay, they regret having earlier missed their train in Budapest (4:56)[6] due to Charters insisting on standing still while it proceeded to pull out of the station, to show respect for what he thought was the Hungarian national anthem (but what in fact was, according to Caldicott, Liszt's *Hungarian Rhapsody*) being played at the station. Already troubled by this coercion of human sentiment by the unforgiving timetable of the machine, they are determined to make their tightened schedule succeed for their own purposes as monomaniacal fans of cricket.

Charters and Caldicott are positioned to play a crucial role once aboard the train, as eye witnesses to the existence of Miss Froy. They are seen having tea in the dining car, at the table across the aisle from Iris and Miss Froy. The two parties do not acknowledge each other until Miss Froy realizes that she and Iris have no sugar pot on their table, and asks for sugar from the two men (30:45). Sugar cubes are abundant on the other table, where Caldicott and Charters are simulating a cricket match, with a cube representing each player. They are visibly bemused by the interruption, though they oblige and, with a frown and direct stare at Miss Froy, put the cubes back in the pot and pass it to her. Iris recalls this brief but memorable interaction (38:10) after all the passengers in Miss Froy's compartment deny having ever seen her. Although the two Englishmen are not involved in the kidnapping plot, they, too, say they have never laid eyes on Miss Froy because Charters has overheard Iris declare in the corridor that she will stop the train if that becomes necessary to prove that Miss Froy exists, has vanished from sight, and should be still on the train (38:55),[7] which he shares with Caldicott. Determined to avoid any further complication of the train journey that a criminal investigation might cause, they decide to deny having seen Miss Froy, despite Iris's desperate efforts to refresh their memories with details of their earlier encounter (40:00). The sequence of events involving Caldicott and Charters makes it clear that, for them, the train is nothing but a medium of transportation for moving from the departure station to the destination (Foucault's second relation of the subject, the thing, and the space) as quickly, conveniently, and uneventfully as possible. To their dismay, the frustrated Iris, demanding a thorough investigation, pulls an emergency brake (51:56) to stop the train for ten minutes.

For Gilbert, in contrast, who has become an incidental co-investigator of the mystery, the interim to be spent on the train offers an invaluable opportunity to get to know the heroine, Iris, and possibly win her heart by helping her—time well spent, indeed, and space well explored, in the process of the search for the lady who has vanished. For Gilbert the train is not a medium but a space-time in which he and Iris—perfect strangers, Gilbert a funny troublemaker and Iris betrothed to another man—become a team under contingent circumstances to solve the mystery of Miss Froy's disappearance.

The railway journey does not remain empty space-time in the film. Some of the scenes encapsulate the loss of transparency about the train. While seated across the table from the heroine in the dining car, the lady who is about to vanish writes her surname with her right index finger on the fogged windowpane (30:35) because the whistling sounds and shrieks of the wheels prevented the heroine from hearing it when they verbally introduced themselves to each other. The train interior is thus presented as both visually and aurally dense, not transparent; the voices of the humans engaged in conversation are muffled by the noise of the machine, while the transparent window glass becomes opaque with moisture to offer an incidental writing pad. Later, when Iris is seated at the same table, this time with Gilbert, the camera faces the window squarely so that the screen shows "FROY" (48:59), on the dewy windowpane. The camera position thus enables the viewer to see the letters before Iris does when she momentarily shifts her eye from Gilbert to the window (50:55), and tries to call Gilbert's attention to this piece of evidence that the lady existed (51:50)—except that it, too, disappears as the train pierces a tunnel.

The windowpane can also hold and display something that would stick to its surface on the other side of the glass: when a cook throws trash out the window on the transitional area between the second- and third-class carriages, Gilbert, who is standing there smoking, sees a teabag stick for a moment to the outside surface of the window—the Herman's teabag (53:55) that Miss Froy had produced from her handbag and asked the waiter to have the kitchen brew for her instead of the house brand, as shown in the scene of her with Iris in the dining car (29:08) and as recalled by Iris (49:45). This scene, which validates Iris's claim for Gilbert, also confirms the materiality of the glass windowpane. It is not an immaterial partition between the interior and exterior spaces or a neutral screen through which a person inside can see landscape in the exterior space. Rather, it exists as a thing itself, and is affected by humidity and temperature.

The materiality of the train interior is further illustrated in a sequence in which Iris and Gilbert peek into one compartment after another looking for the couple into whose second-class compartment Miss Froy had almost stumbled, while walking with Iris to the dining car earlier, due to a jolt from the train and their compartment's sliding door not being secured (28:09). At that time, the man in the compartment (Cecil Parker) had promptly shut the door and pulled the shades down over its top glass portion and over the two windows facing the corridor on either side of the door. This moment demonstrates the complex composition of the compartment, which can be publicly accessible but can also be kept private through the operation of the shades, just as a theatrical stage can be opened or closed to an audience through the operation of its curtains, along the Brechtian "fourth wall," a divide between spectacle and spectator. In the present case, the couple, who are in an extramarital relationship, are traveling together under the pretense of being married. While the woman (Linden Travers), who wants the man to divorce his wife and marry her, is more than eager to display their intimacy, the man is anxious to hide it as well as he can. The compartment's glass windows and the shades precisely embody their conflicting desires. Indeed, when Iris finds them and asks them to verify Miss Froy's existence, the man denies having seen her in order to avoid any public role in the investigation, whereas the woman later declares to Iris and Gilbert that she has indeed seen Miss Froy (44:15)—only to falsely confirm even later that the replacement for her (whose arrival is arranged by the perpetrators) is the same lady she had seen (47:17), after having been told by the man that any exposure at this point would foil their plan for his divorce rather than facilitate it.

The complexity of the carriage interior is further illustrated when Iris and Gilbert pursue a likely accomplice of Ms. Froy's kidnapper into the train's storage car, which is behind the third-class carriage. The man in question is an illusionist who disappears into and reappears out of his props to dodge his pursuers and get the better of them. In this sequence, the viewer is shown a backstage part of the train that is normally closed to passengers, and is thus reminded of the loaded and potentially expansive space of the train, whose streamlined appearance is deceptive.

The camera also capitalizes on the contiguity of the passenger's compartments and the landing area in the sequence in the landing space where Iris and Gilbert position themselves on opposite sides, watching for Miss Froy possibly getting off at an interim station. The camera first closes up to show each of them and what they see (he watches the platform, she the back side with no platform), then slides sideways horizontally along the exterior of the train to reveal the unwed couple's compartment, in which they are talking about their relationship and the prospect of his divorce and their marriage. The man's equivocal attitude frustrates her, as is evident in a close-up of her hands as she nervously files her painted nails.[8] The investigating heroine's anxiety and the secretive woman's frustration constitute a chiasmus in terms of their positions vis-à-vis temporality: whereas Iris would stop the train to solve the mystery—a determination that may be driven not only by her sense of justice but also, unwittingly, by her desire to prolong her journey so as to delay her undesired wedding as long as possible—the other woman wants to move quickly with her plans to marry the man she loves. These contrastive temporalities create a push-and-pull not in the plot (their lives are not causally related) but in the physics of rhetoric.

Spatially, this sequence confirms both the contiguity of the divided spaces and the heterogeneity of the narrative perspectives. The camera then moves to the interior of the couple's compartment from the side wall, showing a landscape picture between two shelves on which their belongings rest. The presence of such a horizontally elongated picture—or, alternatively, a mirror—common in mid-twentieth-century European trains,[9] suggests how visually oriented the train compartment is. In addition to the landscape across the windowpane, passengers can see a painted landscape or a reflection of themselves and the interior of the compartment. The space is saturated with objects of visual desire, not unlike the

1 INTRODUCTION: THE TRAIN AS EMBODIED SPACE-TIME, WITH CASE...   15

cinema—the screen showing other image-making devices and their products, while the gaze may focus not only on the screen but also elsewhere. Voyeurism is encouraged and vigilance is ubiquitous, whether of villains or of investigators.

Under just such a vigilant gaze of Gilbert from one side of the landing area, a fully bandaged person on a stretcher is carried on board the train. This corroborates Dr. Hartz's earlier remark that he is expecting a serious patient to embark at a station en route whom he will then accompany to a hospital near another station, where he will operate on them. At the next stop, the fully bandaged patient is brought down and transferred to the ambulance under Dr. Hartz's direction, in an exact reversal of the sequence at the previous station. According to the conspirators' plan, the original "patient" was to be replaced by Miss Froy. However, Miss Froy has been re-replaced by the original patient, just in time, by the accompanying "nun" who betrays Dr. Hartz and conspires with Iris and Gilbert. She does not drug them, as instructed by the doctor, and lets them unwrap the bandaged Miss Froy. When the train begins to pull out of the station, Iris and Gilbert think that they can safely continue their journey, with Miss Froy now restored to them. However, the viewer knows that Dr. Hartz has already removed the bandages from the patient's face while in the ambulance, learned that the second switch took place, and ordered that the carriages containing Iris, Gilbert, Miss Froy, and the nun (as well as the two Englishmen and the unwed couple, all of whom were in the dining car) be delinked and diverted to a branch line.[10]

This delinking process is shown on the screen, to confirm the physicality of the operation and the materiality of the train. If we had taken it for granted that the train carriages are contiguous, we are now reminded of the possibility of structural disjointing that must be manually accomplished by a railway worker. This human labor is further emphasized by showing two working hands operating the locomotive, a component not usually seen in railway journey narratives.[11] Moreover, the expectation of contiguous space in the form of more carriages is visually smashed when Gilbert opens the door of the first-class carriage and sees with his own eyes that there is nothing connected to it—there is no floor onto which he can step.

The next step Gilbert takes and its consequences are revealing of the experienced space (Lefebvre) or of space's inseparability from bodies and time. Gilbert surmises that the two Englishmen will be in the dining car (and thus still with them on this deviated course) because it is tea time—time informs space with the likelihood of a particular kind of people being in a certain place at a certain time according to their everyday routines. Gilbert's report of what has happened to the train is met with denial by the Englishmen, who have left their belongings in their first-class compartment which thus simply should not be gone. In their view, their status quo—their established practices and their belongings—is not the result but the cause of the stability of their compartment. This reveals a distinct consciousness of body-space or somatope: for them, their physical existence and activity define space. They need to see their first-class carriage's absence for themselves to come to the admission that this is an emergency—an emergency in which the dining car they are in has been delinked from the rest of the train and is running in a direction other than the predetermined route.

The villains (and the married man traveling with his mistress) are killed in a gunfight. Miss Froy, who confesses to Iris and Gilbert that she is indeed a spy and leaves the code with Gilbert, vanishes into the forest of her own free will. Eventually, the train leaves the scene at speed. After a brief insertion showing a vessel at sea, suggesting that the surviving passengers cross the English Channel to Dover, the scene jumps to Victoria Station, where their train arrives. There is a scene of the interior of a compartment, shot from outside the window, in which Iris looks in a mirror hung on a side wall while Gilbert stands at the door, looking at and talking to her (1:31:51). This scene shows many reflective surfaces, ranging from the exterior window, mirror, and glass windows on each side of the compartment door to the corridor window looking out onto the platform and the windows of another train on the other side of the platform. The palimpsest of windows is a configuration that is also seen in the next two films discussed, suggesting the affinity between cinematic photography and the train in terms of profuse reflection and the illusion of transparency.

These scenes and many others from *The Lady Vanishes* compel us to rethink the characterization of the train as instrumental to and embodying modernity—a regime that prioritizes velocity, efficiency, and transparency over all else. An alternative understanding of the train may not erase its normative portrayal, yet it plays a variation on it, to complicate the relationship between the train as space-time and the passengers who experience it.

"The Narrow Margin" (1952)

Dubbed the best B-movie or the best film noir by some, Richard Fleischer's *The Narrow Margin* (1952) takes place almost in its entirety on the west-bound transcontinental express passenger train from Chicago to Los Angeles (stopping only at Kansas City, La Junta, and Albuquerque). Whereas *The Lady Vanishes* is titled according to a character and an event involving her, the title of *The Narrow Margin* is spatial and could be taken literally as well as figuratively, suggesting its potential for theorization. At the beginning of the film, a moving train is seen and heard while the credits appear in several frames on the screen. There is little background to the train. This austerity is also in stark contrast to the beginning of *The Lady Vanishes*, in which an aerial view of expanded surroundings is shown against a piece of orchestral music. Whereas the Hitchcock movie is oriented toward an exotic atmosphere that is visually and aurally aestheticized, the Fleischer film is firmly focused on the materiality of the train itself, so the image and sound are not decorations but aspects that matter in themselves.

The story of *The Narrow Margin* begins at the Chicago station, where two men disembark from a train that has just arrived from Los Angeles. Through their conversation in a taxi from the Chicago station, the viewer learns that they are detectives from the Los Angeles Police Department who are in Chicago to escort a key witness in a murder back to Los Angeles. The witness is Mrs. Neall, the widow of the murder victim, who was a mob boss. One of the detectives (Gus Forbes, played by Don Beddoe) leaves the platform to get the taxi. The other, identified later as Detective Sergeant Walter Brown, played by Charles McGraw (hereafter Brown, as he is mostly addressed in the storyworld), asks a redcap to keep their luggage and put it in Car 10, Rooms A and B—adjacent rooms with a lockable door between them, as seen later—on the return train to Los Angeles. The redcap reminds him that that train will leave in an hour, which Brown is keenly aware of (1:35). He stays alert to the spatial-temporal point that he occupies at any given moment, as he needs to in his profession, and as the mystery genre requires of a main character. Station announcements are also heard, about the train that has just arrived and a train that will soon leave—the Central Pacific, Train Number 5, Gold West Limited, from Track D—indicating the multiplicity of trains arriving at and departing from this station. On the level of narrative discourse, this scene establishes how not only visual but aural effects—especially spoken words—deliver rich information in this cinematic narrative.

The next sequence is the only one outside the railway system in this film. The two detectives visit the apartment of Mrs. Neall (Marie Windsor). It turns out that they have been followed: Forbes is shot dead as he leads the way down the stairs from Mrs. Neall's second-floor apartment, by a man in a fur-trimmed coat whose intended victim was Mrs. Neall. The killer, Densel (Peter Virgo), suffers one of Brown's counter-shots but escapes by car. (It is later revealed that he flies out of Chicago to catch the same return train to LA at the La Junta station.)[12] Brown laments his colleague's death yet has to carry on without delay. He and Mrs. Neall take the same taxi back to the station in time to catch the return train to LA.

What needs to be remembered in this sequence, in our context, is the music. The sound of instrumental jazz is heard from the second floor in the stairwell the two detectives climb (3:33), confirming the permeability of sound from a confined space into a semi-public space.[13] The music is coming from the record player in Mrs. Neall's apartment, which she packs and carries with her. She is thus carrying a piece of her private acoustic space into the semi-public space of the train compartment to make herself at home—and, in effect, at risk. The problem with how sound crosses space from her private compartment (Room B) to the adjacent one (Room A, occupied by Brown) is reiterated twice during their train ride: first, when Brown reprimands her for playing the record and risking disclosure of her presence, which he is hiding from their pursuers (46:15); and second, when Brown's room is intruded upon in his absence by Densel and his associate Kemp (David Clarke), and the sound from the adjacent room (59:40) triggers their confrontation with and eventual killing of Mrs. Neall. The earlier sequence in the Chicago apartment building thus foreshadows the later development. As mentioned above, music in this film is part of the diegetic sound, not an aesthetic layer attached to the film discourse for the viewer. (In *The Lady Vanishes* music performs both roles.) In *The Narrow Margin*, music is firmly contained in the storyworld, where it complicates the division between spaces that are visually and tactilely shielded from each other—though both these divisions are negotiable, as will be discussed later.

Though the film's discourse time skips eventless hours in its story time, its order of events is more or less the same as in the story time: the viewer learns what happens as the story unfolds (with some exceptions, discussed later). Brown, the protagonist, is alert and capable, yet he is not a consistent focalizer. Rather than assuming his point of view, the camera tends to feature his figure in the frame of the screen. Furthermore, because the camera leaves his viewpoint at times, some events are known to the viewer when they happen unbeknownst to Brown. There is also one distinct leap in the discourse that withholds an important detail from the viewer, thus creating suspense.

An example of the viewer's knowledge superseding the protagonist's occurs in the sequence leading up to the departure of the LA train from the Chicago station. The camera features a scene in Brown's absence of two men (later named Kemp and Yost) with another man, behind the newspaper counter just outside the station entrance, who is completing a conversation on the telephone. Having hung up the phone, this man informs Kemp and Yost that Densel could not accomplish his task, and that he will fly out of Chicago to join them later. (Densel's name is new to the viewer, who has to figure out that he must be the killer of Forbes, which makes these three men adversaries of Brown and Mrs. Neall.) Yost tells Kemp that he will meet him "in the club car," indicating that the two are to ride the train in search of Mrs. Neall. The camera then stays with Kemp on the concourse, showing him looking at Brown and making eye contact with him, both when standing in line for entry to the platform and on the platform, on the way to their respective carriages on the train. Brown thus senses that Kemp is following him and veers behind a vendor's cart. After losing sight of Brown, however, Kemp glimpses him walking through the corridor toward his compartment. Once Brown has entered his compartment, Car 10, Room A, he watches out the window and sees Kemp speaking with a conductor. Upon checking with Mrs. Neall, who has already settled into the adjacent Room B,[14] Brown peeks out her window to confirm that Kemp is boarding the train (18:20). Kemp appears soon after with the conductor, claiming that his bag may have been mistakenly placed in Room A, and searches the room for it.

The occasion when the viewer is kept uninformed of what has already happened occurs when Kemp returns later and forces his entry into Brown's room with a metal tool, while Brown is in conversation with a female passenger, Ann Sinclair (Jacqueline White), in the club car. Kemp also checks the adjacent room (unlocked at this time), which caught his attention during his previous visit, but it turns out to be empty, to his disappointment and to the viewer's relief. As the viewer learns later, Mrs. Neall has evacuated the room in time to hide herself and all her belongings in the ladies' washroom down the corridor. Her escape is not shown on the screen—only her return with Brown is. This is one of the few places where the story and the discourse part ways with each other, and it is done for a reason. In this film without a voice-over narrator, this manipulation of the narrative order creates the effect of escalating suspense, since the viewer does not know that Mrs. Neall has already left her room and may hold their breath while wondering whether Kemp will find her there. The viewer, in short, is not omniscient. Although the viewer may see some things that Brown does not see (such as the scene of Kemp and Yost at the Chicago station), there are other things that the viewer does not know which Brown does know (such as Mrs. Neall's leaving her room before Kemp's forced entry, which Brown anticipates will occur).

These intricacies of visual storytelling exploit the space-time of the train and its surroundings (e.g., stations) effectively, so that the plot and the setting reciprocally and non-hierarchically sustain each other. To reiterate my point, space and time are not separate factors but work in coordination as space-time: space is temporally invested. Kemp, who is not aware of this, says to Densel, who is newly arrived on the train when they go to Car 10, Rooms A and B, that he has already searched Room B and that the room was—and thus he thinks *is*—unoccupied. But as Densel tells him, "That's yesterday" (59:37); space is different at different times, as bodies move, vacating and reoccupying the "same" space variantly invested by time. Indeed, with the second visit, they hear the sound of jazz discussed earlier, and find Mrs. Neall, whom Densel kills.

The way passengers navigate the train cars is crucial in the narrative formation of the film. In an earlier scene where Brown goes to the club car, and sits across a table from a woman (who later introduces herself as Ann Sinclair) just because the seat is empty. Kemp is seated on the sofa behind Brown's chair, so Brown watches Kemp's reflection on the glass windowpane to keep an eye on him. Brown loses sight of Kemp when Ann accidentally spills her drink on Brown's trousers and they begin to talk, and then he sees in the window's reflection that Kemp is gone (21:15). This foreshadows the later, more crucial scene in which Brown follows Densel's movements in Ann's room as they are reflected in the window-pane of the train parked alongside theirs, from the adjacent room occupied by Ann's son Tommy and his nurse.

This incident with Ann in the club car and Brown's subsequent encounter with an obese man (later known as Sam Jennings, played by Paul Maxey) in the narrow corridor and his difficulty in passing Jennings are the reasons that Kemp has a few extra minutes to search Rooms A and B of Car 10 for Mrs. Neall or any trace of her, though to no avail, as discussed earlier. Brown's first encounter with Jennings here foreshadows later incidents, and also reveals spatial practices that the structure of the train helps to form. First, the corridor is constricted, designed for two persons of slimmer frame than Jennings to barely be able pass each other, so if one of them is larger, it may be necessary to find a place to let the other pass. As in this crucial scene, this spatial constriction therefore moderates the pace at which time flows. In hindsight, the viewer will realize that since Brown already knows Mrs. Neall is not in her compartment, his hurry must be to escort her safely back to her room after Kemp searches it. To accomplish this, Brown must verify that Kemp has left Car 10 and also make sure that Kemp does not see him. This helps the viewer understand why Brown, realizing that Kemp is walking toward him, tries to hide from him.[15]

Here, the specifics of the corridor structure are decisive. Brown manages to pass Jennings only because they are in the section where the corridor is on the curve,[16] allowing a little more space to pass each other[17] and blocking the view of those walking in the corridor as it meanders. Thus, Brown at first cannot see Kemp coming, but sees him once he is in a straight section of the corridor. Brown then retreats behind the curve lest Kemp spot him, and looks for somewhere to hide before Kemp emerges around the curve. However, behind Brown, Jennings is still walking in the corridor and thus blocking Brown's possible retreat. Fortunately, he finds a compartment door that is unlocked, and slides into it (23:50).[18] It is there that he meets a juvenile boy Tommy (Gordon Gebert) on the lower bed and a middle-aged woman on the upper berth, whom Brown takes to be the boy's mother (later identified as his nanny, Mrs. Troll, played by Queenie Leonard). Naturally they are surprised and ask who Brown is and why he is there. Brown fakes having made a mistake and leaves once he gathers the corridor is clear, then goes to the ladies' washroom to escort Mrs. Neall to her room.

The boy, however, is astute enough to deduce that Brown was lying because their compartment (Room C, with the adjacent Room D) is next to the "day class" (the third-class car with unpartitioned upright seats only) and therefore cannot be mistaken for another compartment with a door. This is the beginning of Brown's having to navigate occasional appearances in the corridor of Tommy, who suspects him of being a "train thief." This throws a curveball into Brown's management of the train as a space-time. Small and light, yet excitable and ready to announce to the rest of the passengers that Brown is a train robber, the challenge Tommy poses to Brown is entirely different from that posed by Jennings. Brown is seen lifting the boy to comical effect to elude other passengers' suspicions in one scene (31:34). As narrow as the corridor may be, it is public enough to produce spatial practices and form social relations. Later, for instance, when Jennings is escorting Kemp under arrest to the storage room beyond the club car, they try to let an approaching female passenger pass them by stepping back slightly into the unlocked door to a compartment—which happens to be Densel's, thus causing the serious consequence of Jennings being taken hostage by him.

The compartments are also materially conditioned, which contributes to the formation of the narrative discourse as well as the story. Brown is hiding Mrs. Neall in Room B of Compartment 10, but he has to hide the fact that he is hiding her there. Thus, when Kemp first inspects Brown's Room A under the pretense of looking for his lost bag, as mentioned earlier, and casts a suspicious eye on the locked door to the adjacent room, Brown must improvise and tell the conductor who has accompanied Kemp that his companion has been held up in Chicago, so that Brown does not need the adjacent room any longer. Brown even asks for a refund, to which the conductor responds that he will contact the office at the next station, Kansas City, to see what he can do. This is all to make Kemp believe that the adjacent room is empty.

But this information is then transferred from Kemp to Jennings, who shares a table with Kemp in the dining car. Brown sees the two men talking from his own table, shared with Ann, which makes him become suspicious of Jennings (34:15).[19] Jennings immediately acts upon this information, approaching Brown to ask whether he might move into the adjacent room. Brown, of course, cannot accept the request, so he says that he has decided to keep the adjacent room to himself, at which an infuriated Jennings cites the discomfort of sleeping on the upper berth of a bunk bed, given his large frame.

Another conductor's remark that there is no rule against a passenger keeping an extra room, as long as it is paid for, confirms the unequal and liquid space of the train carriages. The physically same space can be experienced differently, depending on the money one can afford, one's physical condition, and one's wish for greater or lesser space. Space is social and somatic. At the same time, the way that one conversation leads to another, and that one spatial consideration leads to another, propels production or suspension of an event and situation—and, in the narrator-less narrative of

The Narrow Margin, creates heteroglossia/multivalency. Conversations inaudible across the screen to the viewer or to another character in the storyworld may be seen at distance, triggering speculation about relations between the characters having a conversation, whether Brown seeing Kemp and Jennings talking together or Kemp seeing Brown and Ann conversing.[20]

The aforementioned inequality is also revealed the next day: when Brown catches sight of Kemp leaving his room to use the men's washroom for morning grooming, he enters it to look for a telegraph he saw Kemp reading earlier. He has no trouble gaining entrance because Kemp's room has no lockable door, being separated from the corridor only by a curtain. Drawing the curtain for invisibility, Brown inspects Kemp's belongings, finds the telegraph in a pocket of his jacket, reads it, and puts it back just in time. During the process, the camera shifts to show Kemp finishing using the sink and making way for the next passenger in line—another instance in which the viewer's knowledge supersedes Brown's. This shot not only creates suspense for the viewer, who is anxious to see Brown leave Kemp's room before he returns, but also prepares the viewer for a later washroom scene in which Brown and Kemp fight. This occurs when Brown stops Kemp from following Ann—whom Kemp suspects must be Mrs. Neall—as she leaves the club car where they both were (Brown was at the glass door, watching them). Brown hides in a curtained space beside the men's washroom, lets Ann pass by, and then grabs Kemp from behind and throws him into the washroom. After the fistfight, Brown arrests Kemp and leaves him with Jennings, who is then revealed to be a special agent on the railroad.

Soon afterward, however, the inequality of space serves Kemp well. When Jennings, with the handcuffed Kemp, lets an approaching female passenger pass them by backing slightly into a compartment whose door is unlocked, as previously mentioned, the camera, from the interior of this compartment, focuses on the door being pushed open, and reveals the fur trim of a coat hanging there, thus announcing to the viewer that the killer of Forbes is back in the story.[21] Densel drags Jennings (and the linked Kemp) into his room and releases Kemp; the two then handcuff Jennings and lock him in Densel's compartment while they search for Mrs. Neall. It is crucial that Densel's is a first-class compartment, so that this process is completed in private and kept secret without anyone else seeing it happening.

The viewer is already aware that Densel is the killer's name, and that he has flown out of Chicago. Brown is informed of Densel's departure from Chicago much later, through a telegraph in reply to the one he sends from the La Junta station's Western Union telegraph and cable office to the LA District Attorney's office, asking about Densel after learning his name from reading the telegraph Kemp received on the train.

The reply from the DA, which reaches Brown while the train is en route to Albuquerque (the next station after La Junta), is shown on the screen superimposed on the image of train wheels turning at top speed. Since the information itself is not new to the viewer, the director's priority rests on the visual effects of its presentation, which results in one of the most elaborate sequences of moving images in this film. First, the screen shows Mrs. Neall filing her nails (55:48),[22] then replaces the image of the nail file's oscillation in her hand with the similarly repetitive back-and-forth motion of the train's wheels (the camera modifies the size of the file and that of the wheels so that they both look prominent within the frame of the screen). It is against the backdrop of this image of the wheels that the excerpts from the telegraph emerge on the screen. The viewer then sees Brown reading the telegraph and slowly tearing it into small pieces in the club car. He seems to look out the window and notice something, yet the next moment he is approached by the conductor, who blocks the viewer's sight of the window and tells Brown that neither Kemp nor Jennings is in the storage room, where they both should be. As Brown gets up and leaves the club car with the conductor, the screen reveals an automobile outside the window keeping pace with the train (56:37). The viewer can thus surmise that this must be what caught Brown's eye.

In the next scene, Brown is standing at the open window in the landing area, watching the car (56:48). Asking the conductor if any new passengers boarded at La Junta, and being informed that four compartments are newly occupied, Brown orders inspection of those rooms (which leads to the release of Jennings). He also orders that a message to be dropped from the train to the highway patrol to intercept the suspicious car. No moment is wasted in the storytelling, yet the images are elaborately knit. Even as the real-time unfolding of events accelerates in the story, the narrative does not sacrifice the aesthetic visual effect of superimposing the exterior (the speeding car) on the interior (Brown's concerned look) across the window here, thereby launching a visual pattern that is repeated frequently toward the climax of the film.

The first-class compartments (such as Brown's, Densel's, Tommy's, and Ann's) in *The Narrow Margin* do not have window or glass openings to the corridor, nor do the first-class compartments in *The Lady Vanishes*.[23] There is not even a peephole in the door to the corridor. Therefore, neither the outsider nor the insider can see who is behind the closed door, creating secrecy and suspense beyond ambience, and allowing some consequences to happen while suspending others. Thus, the co-conspirator Yost's visit to Brown's compartment, to unsuccessfully try to bribe him into releasing Mrs. Neall to him, is announced not by any sight of his figure but through the turn of the door knob, which Brown notices from inside (26:13).[24] There is no glass window on the door between the adjacent rooms of the same compartment, either, so that Mrs. Neall is fooled when Densel says he is Brown and opens the door to her killer.

The ensuing sequence is not only crucial in the story but a pinnacle of the ingenious use of the train's space-time in the narrative. After killing Mrs. Neall, Densel and Kemp search her belongings for the document they are after, and only then realize she was a policewoman posing as Mrs. Neall. Their realization happens simultaneously with Brown's, by way of alternating scenes between "Mrs. Neall's" room (with her body, Densel and Kemp) and Ann's room (with Ann and Brown). The two processes of revelation coincide here to thrilling effect. Kemp's earlier hunch that Ann is Mrs. Neall, wrongly founded on the seeming friendliness between Ann and Brown, proves to be correct (1:04:45). Brown learns at this time that Ann, whom he has been protecting from being "wrongly" identified and targeted, is indeed not an irrelevant bystander but the real Mrs. Neall (1:02:29). The viewer learns this along with Brown, and may feel as misled as the detective. The viewer may also share Brown's renewed and more acute concern about her safety due to seeing that Densel, also learning her identity simultaneously, will now be after her. The camera switches back and forth between the two scenes set in two compartments that are neither too distant nor too dissimilar from each other, effectively synchronizing the two storylines. This combination of parallel storytelling and the proximity and similarity of the two spaces intensifies the inseparable coordination of space-time in the film's discourse, while escalating the urgency in the storyworld both of Densel's hunt for Ann[25] and of Brown's protection of her.

There is a window facing the outside in each compartment,[26] however, and this plays an imperatively important role. As mentioned earlier, Brown peers out the window to see Kemp boarding the train at the Chicago

station. Kemp, in contrast, looks in from the platform of the La Junta station to watch Brown and Ann talking to each other. Brown visits Ann's
room to warn her about the present danger, and while waiting for her to
return from Tommy's room next to hers, he raises the shade and looks out
the window at the car speeding along beside the train. His concerned face
is then seen from outside the window, while it reflects the car farther out
(59:13).[27]

There are other instances in which the glass's reflexivity is essential. As
mentioned earlier, Brown keeps an eye on Kemp's whereabouts in the
club car by looking at the window reflection. This is followed by a number
of similar scenes that superimpose the interior and exterior across the windowpane, their appearance more frequent toward the climax. When
Densel holds Ann, or the real Mrs. Neall, at gunpoint in her room, Brown
is in Tommy's adjacent room. Densel threatens to kill Ann if Brown
unlocks the door between the two rooms and enters Ann's room. At this
critical moment, Brown notices that the interior of Ann's room is reflected
in the windowpane of another train that is parked on the parallel track,
since their train has been stopped by Kemp drawing the brake (1:06:25)
because the time for their pickup by the car has come.

The unscheduled stop of the train creates the climax in *The Narrow
Margin* as it does in *The Lady Vanishes*. From the interior, with the lights
off at Brown's request to the conductor, the detective's face in the window reflection looms larger than the scene of Densel and Ann in the adjacent room reflected in the windowpane of the second train outside
(1:07:18). Owing to the immobility of both trains and the parallel positioning of their windows, Brown can see Densel's position vis-à-vis Ann.
Hearing Brown falsely tell Ann through the door to retrieve the document
they are after from the medicine cabinet, Densel immediately walks to the
cabinet himself, leaving Ann's side for a moment. Brown seizes the chance
to break the barrier of the door, shoot Densel, and rescue Ann.[28] The
ingenuity of Brown's use of the window reflection is foreshadowed by
scenes in which his awareness of reflections is imprinted on the viewer's
mind through repetition.[29]

When the train arrives at the Los Angeles station, the platform is
crowded with newspaper writers who are covering the trial. Jennings uses
his large frame to block them from entering the carriage while Brown
escorts Ann onto the platform through another door, and then through
the downsloping exit from the platform (as captured by a camera positioned at a higher point in the station). There[30] they are met by the police,

who offer them a ride to allow Ann to remain incognito. However, Ann—
or, rather, the real Mrs. Neall—declares that she will no longer hide. It is
as if she becomes a new person once she is in an exterior space and in the
new phase of the game, having had enough of hide-and-seek while on the
train. Thus, the change of space-time triggers a change in personality,
action of choice, and plot development, not the other way around. The
human subjects do not precede or supersede the material conditions of
their surroundings. Rather, the human subjects are formed, informed, and
transformed by "affordances," or their use of things in space-time.

"Night Train" (Pociąg, 1959)

Pociąg (Night Train, 1959), directed by Jerzy Kawalerowicz, is often considered a masterpiece well before its time. The entire story takes place on
and around the northbound passenger train between the Łódź (Lodz)
Fabryczna station and the terminus on the Baltic coast (likely the Gdynia
Główna station). There are many similarities between this film and the
preceding two, yet there is also a noteworthy difference: the role of passengers other than main characters is formative in Night Train, whereas
they are simply space-fillers, provided for realistic effects, in The Lady
Vanishes and The Narrow Margin. For this reason—or as a cause of this—
space inside the train in Night Train looks much more crowded, and,
more importantly, each peripheral character receives a few seconds of
close-up from the camera. Thus, the public nature of the train interior is
more obvious than in the other two films.

   The film begins with an aerial view of a river of people walking in two
opposing directions, about eighteen persons wide, in a vast flat space that
turns out to be a station. There is no separate lane for the two directions,
so everyone is going either upward or downward in the frame of the
screen, which shows the horizontal space vertically, often dodging or running into others walking in the opposite direction. The space is thus not
striated but smooth, yet the flow of people is thick, constant, and variously
paced. A piece of jazz is heard, a tune from "Moon Rays" by Artie Shaw,
covered by the singer Wanda Warska (who only hums), with a solo trum-
pet and drums (all the creators of which, including the original composer,
are credited as the bird's-eye view is seen and the music heard). The music
ceases after the first scene but returns four times during the course of the
film. Three times are when a female character (the heroine [34:06], the
flirtatious next-door passenger, midway joined by Marta [38:43], or the

female conductor [1:22:19]) stands at a window, half looking at the land-scape outside and half looking at her own reflection in the windowpane, while evidently deep in thought. The other time is in the closing sequence at the terminus.[31] The background music is thus always related to the transaction between the train's (or the viewing subject's)[32] interior and the exterior spaces, with the screen capturing the liminal space.

No character is seen listening to or playing music, unlike the tune in *The Lady Vanishes* or the jazz recording listened to by Mrs. Neall in *The Narrow Margin*.[33] Other than the tune that opens the film, no background music or ambient sound is heard throughout *Night Train*: all the other sounds are "diegetic,"[34] such as train whistles and noise of the wheels' friction, voices of passengers and staff members, and other sounds caused by human subjects' activities or things' states within the storyworld.

The camera then moves on to show an area with two platforms with two parked trains, and a third train slowly moving farther right, where there is no platform. One of the parked trains then pulls out of the platform, moving upward within the frame of the screen. Once it has vacated the space, people cross the rails between the two platforms toward the remaining train. As in common in Eastern Europe, there seems to be no bridge or underpass by which to reach the platform. Though this depiction is thus realistic, it also confirms, pursuant to the opening shot, the contiguity of the space to be navigated: although each section of the visible space, such as rails and platforms, has its own function, it is not only technically possible but socially accepted for human subjects to cross it as they see fit and use it in any way that works for them. This sets up a later crucial sequence that exhibits a similar spatial aesthetic.

As captured in the bird's-eye view described earlier, the human crowd is not streamlined—a characteristic that is exemplified when the camera rests at ground level and focuses on a man in a suit and dark sunglasses (later identified as Jerzy, a surgeon, played by Leon Niemczyk). He keeps bumping into other passengers as he walks toward the train—the last crash being with a young man (later identified as the heroine's persistent ex-boyfriend, played by Zbignew Cybulski), standing and looking vaguely into the first-class carriage, who exchanges a stare with Jerzy. The primary impression that this sequence creates is that of Jerzy's mysteriousness and absentmindedness. Jerzy then tells the female conductor at the door to the first-class carriage that he has forgotten his ticket and that he is "exhausted," which partially accounts for his lack of attention to his surroundings. When she asks which compartment he has booked, he says he cannot remember. During their conversation, the conductor greets other first-class passengers and confirms their compartments by number. Jerzy will have to wait for the train's departure to purchase a ticket for a berth left unclaimed by a pre-booked passenger "who would be me."

The detail of this negotiation becomes crucial later in the plot, but what is noteworthy in the present context is that the space of each compartment is strictly allocated to each passenger or each pair (a space defines a human subject, a human subject defines a space), and that there is nevertheless a slim chance for contingency plans. This is comparable to the case of Room B, Car 10, in *The Narrow Margin*, which may or may not be available for another passenger (such as Jennings) because its ostensible vacancy has to be alternately emphasized (when the pursuers are around) and down-played (when the space has to be maintained for Mrs. Neall, who is hiding there). The relation between human bodies and their spaces is thus controlled, yet that control may be loosened by any unexpected turn of events (such as someone failing to catch the train and leaving a booked berth open) and at administrators' discretion.

Jerzy boards the train, and the camera stays on the platform until he reappears in the corridor (located on the platform side of the carriage) and, following another passenger standing there, buys a newspaper from a vendor on the platform through an open corridor window. This transaction is not merely circumstantial but leads to a rumor—about a wife-murderer at large, reported on the front page of the paper—spreading among first-class passengers, who do not know each other beyond their immediate companions but who bond during the ride through gossiping. These seemingly innocuous actions around the train encapsulate how spatial practices can develop in the space-time of the train—which is public space shared with a limited number of strangers who spend an extended period of time together.

The next moment the screen shows a close-up of a man running across the rails toward the platform. He barely catches the train, already in motion, grabs the door, and then enters. Later, when this character is identified as the murderer in the news, the viewer realizes that he has deliberately waited until the last minute to board so as to minimize his chances of being found on the train. At this point, his function in the plot is merely to inspire the aforementioned ex-boyfriend of the heroine to board the train the same way. Up to this point, he may have been simply looking for her, knowing she is leaving by the train, but he is now pursuing her on the same train—except that she is in first class and he is in second. When the ex-boyfriend spots his beloved, Marta (Lucyna Winnicka), in the corridor of the adjacent car, also looking out a window, he leans out his window and smiles and waves to her, at which she appears dismayed and looks away. Besides suggesting a complication of the romantic relationship between the two characters, this scene confirms the physical contiguity of the two carriages in distinct classes, and also the contiguity between the interior space and the exterior walls of the train. The space is smooth and yet striated at the same time.

The ex-boyfriend repeatedly exploits the smoothness and defies the striation of space across classes on the train. He attempts to reach Marta three times by various methods. First, he is denied entry to the first-class carriage through its locked but half-glass door by the female conductor (20:10). To hear what he has to say, she retrieves the key from the conductor's office. When she unlocks the door, he asks her to deliver a note to Marta (more on the consequence of this later). He thus permeates the barrier by way of a medium. In his second attempt, while the train is paused at an interim station, he descends to the platform and finds Marta alone at the window to her compartment, where he grabs her hand and pleads for the restoration of their relationship (30:25). Agitated by her firm refusal, he then bangs her right hand, with a bracelet on her wrist, violently and repeatedly against the exterior wall of the carriage,[35] shouting, and then softly and lovingly holds her hand in both of his and pulls it to his face, whispering to her.[36] The contact of hands across the open window exploits the porosity of the barrier between the interior and exterior spaces.

In his third attempt, seeing through the half-glass door that Marta is standing alone in the transitional area between the two carriages, he crawls the exterior walls of the moving train and grabs the sill of an open window near Marta's location (34:37). This scene may be choreographically inspired by the way that Gilbert in *The Lady Vanishes* reaches the compartment in which the bandaged Miss Froy is kept hidden, except that the two scenes are cinematographically contrastive: Gilbert's efforts are shown on the screen because the camera is behind Iris, who leans out the window Gilbert has exited and watches over him from behind (1:11:25 or 1:12:43), whereas Marta's ex-boyfriend in *Night Train* disappears from the frame and reappears clinging to the windowsill near Marta, leaving his action to the viewer's imagination.[37]

Though the ex-boyfriend's action catches Marta off guard, the viewer has spotted him lurking behind the half-glass door and then disappearing, and thus can anticipate his approach. The viewer is granted more knowledge than a given character in many other scenes as well, due to the film's multiplicity of perspective, with the focalizer shifting in scene after scene. The film also exploits the complexity of the train's interior space, which, with its barriers and vantage points, both enables and delimits passengers' and staff members' ability to view and hear at any given moment, thereby alternately empowering and disempowering them in relation to each other.

Marta's ex-boyfriend threatens to jump to his death if she does not yield to his entreaty to get back together with him, and fakes the beginning of this reckless action. When Marta is drawn as close to him as he hoped, he pops his head in the window, grabs her, and tries to force a kiss on her. Rejecting it, Marta pushes him away, making him disappear again from the frame (except for his hands on the windowsill). This sequence, which may be taken to demonstrate his passion and enhance a romantic dramatization, confirms, in my context, the ambiguous structure of the train carriages, which are divided by class and thus striated, yet are physically connected. It is possible, though difficult and dangerous, for a determined passenger to reach the next carriage by means of the exterior walls. Space inspires human subjects with options of action, while human subjects exploit or succumb to spatial conditions.

The train's striated contiguity is essential to another storyline in *Night Train*, namely, the hide-and-seek regarding the murderer, who initially had a first-class ticket that he sold at the station to Marta, who wanted seclusion. This transaction happens off screen and is only told as an analepsis (after the fact) on screen by Marta, who thus owns more knowledge of relevant circumstances than is dispensed to the viewer. What she has not known until this moment, which the viewer has known, is that he is on board. Thus, the witness character and the viewer each possesses half the picture, which helps the mystery continue for a while and then be resolved at the right moment.[38] Marta makes eye contact with the fugitive hiding behind a hung overcoat, and recognizes him (59:14), while visiting her ex-boyfriend in the second-class carriage after Jerzy's arrest.[39] The murderer's decision to cover his tracks by giving up his berth in a first-class compartment, which he had reserved in his real name,[40] thus does not protect him from the police after all. Precisely because of the contiguity of the two carriages, he is seen by Marta, who becomes suspicious of him. Why would he give up a first-class berth to hide behind an overcoat hanging in a second-class compartment? She reports her discovery to the police investigating Jerzy, who has been arrested because he was in the first-class compartment targeted by the police for the murderer's occupancy, in berth no. 16. Marta explains that Jerzy's assigned berth was not originally no. 16 but no. 15, which he had given to Marta. The female conductor remembers this and corroborates it, which in effect clears Jerzy of suspicion.

The contiguity of the train space also contributes to creating a climax in the sequence of the search for the murderer through the train. By the time Marta takes two of the officers to the spot where she saw the murderer, he has already disappeared. As one of the officers returns to the conductor's office in which his superior is holding Jerzy, the superior (sergeant) decides to conduct a thorough search for the murderer, who should still be somewhere on the train. Just as Iris and Gilbert search the train for Miss Froy in *The Lady Vanishes,* so a search is launched here, though perhaps with a more palpable thrill; the object of the search is not a person apparently missing for an unknown reason[41] but the perpetrator of a confirmed and publicized crime (murder), which makes the purpose and validity of the search much clearer in *Night Train.* There is also a contrast in the emotion that the searchers feel about the person they wish to find: a concern about the well-being of Miss Froy in *The Lady Vanishes* (finding her would be a relief), versus condemnation of the murderer in *Night Train* (finding him would be exaltation with justice served, as turns out to be the case).

The hunt for the fugitive is first launched by one police officer (in plain clothes) and the eyewitness Marta, later joined by the sergeant who received the report from another police officer of the disappearance of the fugitive. The officer opens one after another sliding door to the second-class compartments (which have a glass top half equipped with a window shade and do not lock, similar to the ones in *The Lady Vanishes*) and turns on the light inside (by this time it is well past midnight) to reveal various activities, including but not limited to sleeping. This sequence is shot from the corridor, with the camera more or less assimilating the policeman's gaze into the compartments, physically transmitting his expectation and disappointment repeatedly. In the process, the policeman and Marta are joined by a few passengers who learn that the police are looking for a murderer and follow them out of curiosity.

Meanwhile the murderer passes the conductor's office and enters the first-class carriage. The search group then takes the same route. At this point, the camera switches its position, no longer leading the chasers or representing their point of view, but letting them pass the camera by in the landing area and then following them. The new position of the camera in this sequence represents the curious bystanders' point of view/outlook. First-class passengers who have been talking in the corridor since Jerzy's arrest join the police as the search continues through the train. Another camera shows the murderer from his front, objectifying him, as he dashes through the corridor of another carriage and tries but fails to open the door to the emergency brake, which is locked. He then opens a door to the exterior, muffles a woman who tries to stop him, breaks the glass window from outside to pull the emergency brake inside the protected corner, and jumps out of the stopped train into a wide open space, where dawn is about to break. In this sequence, the camera switches between the fugitive's viewpoint and no specific character's, the latter only to inform the viewer of what is happening with the fugitive, just as an extradiegetic narrator would do in textual narratives.

Many people jump off the train and run after the fugitive into the field outside. Thus, the climax occurs while the train is stopped off its regular schedule, just as in *The Lady Vanishes* where the delinked carriages are diverted into a forest where a shooting takes place,[42] and in *The Narrow Margin* where Kemp stops the train by pulling the emergency brake for the scheduled exit, while Brown, helped by the immobility of the train, watches Densel's movements from next door. Each climax happens while the train is at an emergency stop in the middle of nowhere, in a segment of time other than the absolute/chronological time represented by the railway timetable. As the story thickens, so does the space-time, no longer (if ever) transparent or homogenous.

There is no gunfight in *Night Train*, however; most of the chasers are ordinary citizens, unarmed train passengers who are excited to become part of the dramatic hunt for the criminal. Unlike the Englishmen or the couple having an extramarital affair in *The Lady Vanishes*, who do not wish to get involved in the search for Miss Froy, or the passengers who are kept out of the search for and protection of Mrs. Neall in *The Narrow Margin*, these passengers in *Night Train* (not only main characters but others, too) are full of curiosity and willingness to get involved in other people's affairs. This is not necessarily for a noble reason, however, as is visually encapsulated in the next scene. When the murderer is caught up with, the camera suddenly assumes a bird's-eye view, showing many bodies swarming a single body in the center that becomes submerged and invisible (1:08:54). Here, the opening scene is to be recollected, with its swarm of people striding across the open space of the wide platform, shown on the screen through the camera's bird's-eye position. In contrast to this opening scene, in which humans are moving to and fro, in this scene their move-ment is firmly centripetal, consolidating their density toward the center point where the hunted man has been tracked down and is now being assaulted by the mass of chasers.[43]

The camera then returns to ground level, showing the faces of the chas-ers, mostly passengers who, having loosened their grip on the criminal, are suddenly silent after the intense mobbing[44]—except for one, who agitat-edly continues to kick and curse the murderer. The merciless attack is quietly but resolutely stopped by Marta's ex-boyfriend (1:09:35). The murderer then makes eye contact with Marta (1:11:37), standing among the crowd. For a few seconds they each stare at the other, represented in alternating close-ups. Marta becomes tearful, probably because she real-izes how irrevocably she can alter another human's fate, even when he deserves the punishment and when she is determined to do the right thing. And this realization may have another consequence, a possibility that I will consider shortly.

Let us get back on the night train and go backward in the story time, which mostly progresses along with the discourse time, as in the two other mystery films discussed here. Having considered the contiguity of space in and around the train, I now turn to the interior space of the compartment. Jerzy and Marta are incidental companions in a two-bed compartment. As mentioned earlier, Jerzy has forgotten to bring his ticket to a first-class berth. As the train leaves the station, the female conductor informs him that compartment 15/16 has remain unclaimed. He purchases two tickets to have the whole compartment for himself. Yet the ticket for no. 16 has already been sold by the fugitive at the station to Marta.[45] The ticket, however, is designated "male only." As the confrontation between Marta and the female conductor intensifies, Jerzy agrees to share the compart-ment with Marta, taking the upper berth, no. 16, since she is already in the lower bed. The comings and goings of Jerzy and the conductor draw the attention of the passengers in neighboring compartments, who tend to gather in the corridor to gossip, including a married woman who occupies the next compartment with her husband, from whom she is obviously distanced. She often tries to strike up a conversation with Jerzy, and also tries to eavesdrop across the door from the corridor. Like hers, the other compartments are occupied with traveling companions, and this chance pairing of Jerzy and Marta ignites others' speculation of erotic potential between the two—this, in addition to their speculation on the whereabouts of the murderer featured in the newspaper. The first-class passengers' favorite strands of gossip come together later, when Jerzy is arrested as the suspected murderer.

Jerzy and Marta, however, do not join in the gossip;[46] they need seclusion and quiet for their respective reasons.[47] The two main characters also gradually sense each other's distraught states of mind and need for sensitive care with which to measure space, pace, and (unspoken) attention. As Pauline Kwiatkowska points out as a recurrent somatographic image (2013, 82),[48] Marta often stands at a window, in the corridor or in the compartment, which concerns Jerzy for a reason revealed only later in the film: his last patient earlier that day had been severely injured due to a fall from a window, and Jerzy's surgical skills could not save her life.[49] Soon after Jerzy agrees to let Marta stay in the compartment, and then leaves to smoke in the corridor, she pushes down the windowpane herself[50] and feels the gust of wind as it dishevels her hair. The second time Marta goes to the compartment window occurs soon after her ex-boyfriend's first attempt to reach her by sending her a note, as mentioned earlier.[51] Upon receiving and reading his message, Marta steps toward the window. Jerzy, who is back in the compartment by this time, makes way for her a touch sooner than required (21:24), as if he had already known her intent—the viewer can sense that he is learning how to read her.

This time, Marta's approach toward the window has more consequences. First, the viewer has the first opportunity to see the bracelet on her right wrist—an important motif that recurs not only when her ex-boyfriend bangs her hand against the train's exterior wall (mentioned earlier) but also at the end of the film. After a close-up shot of Marta tearing up the note and throwing the pieces out to the wind, she turns to the camera, apparently crying (21:56). The camera then shows her face as she stands in front of the mirror. By this time, the viewer knows where the mirror is, since both Jerzy and Marta used it earlier, and the camera then moves to shoot her reflection in the mirror from behind her, confirming this. Marta produces a handkerchief and uses it to try to remove something from her right eye, which suggests that she is crying not from emotion but due to some impurity that flew into her eye while she was tossing the bits of paper out the window. Jerzy, who is later revealed to be a doctor, attends to her eye, as his profession calls for.[52] This incident in *Night Train*, of physical proximity and an impromptu doctor-patient contact, breaks the psychological barrier to the sharing of cigarettes and conversation between them. The sequence thus exploits spatial specifics that illustrate the moderated contiguity of space, such as the open window that can take away the trash and also let dust blow into a passenger's eye.

What is contiguous is not only space but time as well. Jerzy and Marta are haunted by memories of their recent past, while going about their business in the present. Thus, they occasionally erupt into impulsive actions that are difficult for others to initially comprehend. For example, when Jerzy catches sight of the white sheet tightly covering Marta's feet,[53] he loses control of himself, repeatedly yelling "Remove the cloth!" (25:46) and eventually taking deep breaths with his face buried against the mattress of the upper berth and with both his arms extended over it, revealing underarm sweat marks on his shirt. As the viewer as well as Marta learns in the course of time, his hysterical outburst is due to the recent trauma of losing his last patient (whose corpse must have been covered by a white sheet, just like Marta's feet in her berth).[54] This is why he needed quietude in the compartment in the first place. Because of his traumatic experience—and the visual similarity between two things (white sheets) in two distant spaces out of context—the space Jerzy occupies in the present can be transformed into the space where the haunting event occurred. Thus, interiority (in the psychological sense, here) can relate closely to the exteriority of a space occupied with things.

At the end of the film, passengers leave the train slowly and steadily. The viewer sees first-class passengers one more time, disappearing into the great unknown. Jerzy is met with and embraced by his wife. When the flow of passengers ends, the female conductor looks as if something bothers her. She walks past other compartments and goes straight to nos. 15/16. The viewer can surmise that she remembers that she hasn't seen Marta leave.[55] The compartment's door is open, and Marta is seen still seated on the lower berth. As the conductor urges her to leave, she says, "I've lost my bracelet." Yet the camera, representing the conductor's gaze, shows that it is on her right wrist. It is not her bracelet that she has been looking for—it is an earlier moment when, having indeed lost her bracelet, she was searching for it on the floor and, asked by Jerzy what she was looking for, uttered the same words, "I've lost my bracelet" (32:05). Jerzy found it then, noting it was damaged, and then noticed that Marta's right wrist was also hurt. (The viewer knew why.) He then concocted a story behind the bracelet, which did not quite apply to Marta and her boyfriend: she is young, he is older; he won't leave his wife or children. Marta looked perplexed, asking him why he was speculating that way. He replied that it was just a little story.

Yet the story becomes close to reality, reality about Marta and Jerzy, as if it were a foreshadowing. The screen does not show what transpires between the two after the hunt for the murderer is over and they return to their compartment, where Jerzy washes his hands and, turning from the basin to ask Marta for a towel, is embraced by her (1:20:12). The next time the viewer sees them, Marta is gaily talking about her past relationship and prospects in the seaside town that is her destination, confirming her single status and optimistic outlook.[56] Jerzy then tells Marta that his wife is waiting for him at the terminus (1:27:48). At this information, Marta remains silent and motionless. Jerzy looks at her face for a few seconds, though the camera is behind her, not showing her face. Then the camera shows her facing the bunk bed as Jerzy walks past her and exits the compartment, and moving her right hand to touch her face, which remains invisible. Thus, when the female conductor finds Marta alone in her compartment after everyone else has left, the viewer senses her state of mind, traveling quickly across time between the recent past, the present, and the future (not necessarily in that order). Her interior is reflected in the way she negotiates the exterior, whether a thing (the bracelet) or a space (the emptying train carriage). Realizing that she has been confusing the past and the present, Marta stands up and prepares to leave. The female conductor helps her, uttering, "What a night—we are not going to forget it," at which Marta kisses her cheek tightly and affectionately. With their confrontation at the beginning of the film behind, the two now share memories that unite them.[57]

Toward the end of the film, the camera mostly assumes the female conductor's perspective. First, she watches over Marta as she walks away. The exterior is a marshland on the coast, across which Marta walks, carrying her coat and bag, alone yet not quite looking forlorn. The conductor then finds the bag of apples in her compartment, tries to call out to her, and, seeing her farther away, bites into an apple. This corroborates her slippage between professional duties and intrusion upon passengers' privacy, suggested in an earlier scene of her reading Marta's ex-boyfriend's message to Marta before delivering it to her. She then inspects the rest of the first-class compartments. The camera assumes her point of view and shoots the interior of each from the corridor, toward the window, revealing in the empty-space traces of human bodies—in one compartment not only traces but bodies themselves (a glamorous couple, only seen thus far when boarding the train carrying a radio, are found still in bed). The intensity of the interior space of the compartment, with its deliberately coordinated minimal essentials, is released into the vast open space, bookending the cinematic narrative along with the opening scene.

From the camera position, another train is seen beyond, through the duplication of windowpanes—a palimpsest not dissimilar to the one seen when Iris and Gilbert are about to leave a compartment at Victoria Station toward the end of *The Lady Vanishes*, presented through layers of windows; and also similar to another palimpsest formed in the climactic scene of Brown spying on Densel from the adjacent room in *The Narrow Margin*. Unlike the Fleischer film, however, *Night Train* ends with the return of the same jazz tune heard at the beginning, at the interim station, and in the few scenes of women absorbed in solitary reflection at a train window.

In the very last scene, the camera is outside the train, showing the exterior walls of the train from the first-class carriage to the second-class carriage (deducible from the carriage numbers), looking in the windows from outside. Aurally and visually, then, the porosity of the exterior and interior spaces is demonstrated again. The emptiness of both spaces—no human figure to be seen—and the movement of the camera suggest the primacy of space-time, rather than that of the human subjects, though without them no space-time can be experienced.

3   The Intent of This Project

Through my analysis of these three mystery films set on a train, I have sought to show how the discourse (form) rather than the story (content) of the cinematic narrative is formulated in its negotiation with the space-time of long-distance train carriages as experienced by their human subjects (passengers and staff members).

We cannot separate space from time, as though either one is a measurable, tangible entity, but must recognize them always operating together, reciprocally informing and transforming each other. We also must not think of space-time as a neutral background for the story of humans. Space-time affects and informs human activities and relations just as much as they control and utilize it. Human subjects cannot be primary, autonomous of their environment, and superior to things around them, nor can they be immaterial or entitled to make judgments about inanimate objects without regard for their own corporeality. The train is a perfect space-time through which to recognize these modalities because it is structured and negotiable, spatial and temporal (as it moves across space-time), exterior and interior (both exposed to the larger system of the natural elements and enclosed under the roofs and walls of the carriages), and public yet private (especially if long-distance), with strangers sharing the same space-time with various degrees of comfort, experience, and congeniality. Preferences and requirements are also diverse, which modifies space-time according to the experiencing subjects. Human subjects also must accommodate a number of spatio-temporal-social terms and conditions during the train ride, some of which are predetermined, others incidental.

The interior space of the train is not transparent but dense, variable, and palpable. It comes with various architectural and design elements, not all of which are representable on a flat floor plan. Within compartments, there are berths (top or bottom, stable or folding) and/or seating spaces (facing either the destination or departure point), windows (openable or not, with or without shades), doors (sliding or not, lockable or not, with or without a look-out window or peephole) or shades (to draw or to pull up and down), lamps (on the ceiling, sconces, or bedside), tables (fixed or folding), shelves, closets, sinks, mirrors (in various locations), and wall decorations (posters or prints of destination spots). Outside the compartments, there are the corridor (usually beside the compartments, with windows on the exterior wall, or in the middle of the carriage, separating rows of seats into two sections), restrooms, dining cars, lounge cars, backstage areas (for railroad employees only), connecting (or dividing) doors between carriages, and the landing areas with doors to the exterior.

These sub-spaces and things are for human subjects to use, yet they are not only instrumental but also affective: practices of using or not using (avoiding, bumping into, looking at) them affect human subjects' movements. These spaces and things are also temporally invested; humans use them at specific times. These elements also contribute to forming and transforming social relations, as human subjects wait for other passengers to finish using them, ask them if they can use them, help them use them, dodge them, interfere with them, compete with them, and share them. Factors other than fixed or expected things in the space-time of the train affect the conditions of the space-time: air (smoking, smoke from the locomotives, winds); jolts, vibration, congestion; and the sounds of whistles, the shrieks of wheels, announcements, and other operational noises. These add to the passengers' corporeal experience of the train carriage as space-time, and enhance their awareness of their own physical presence there.

The train thus offers an interactive theater in which one can become a spectator at any moment, yet cannot take that privileged position for granted because one can just as easily at any moment become a spectacle oneself. One becomes conscious of the gaze that strangers cast upon one's body, and feels as if one is acquiring a new identity through their assessment. This is especially the case because the reflective or see-through surfaces of glass windows and mirrors are ubiquitous in the train. Train windows primarily allow passengers inside to look out at the passing landscape, yet they also allow people outside to peek inside when the train is paused or running very slowly. Windows, as well as the mirrors that are often fixed or hung in compartments, offer surfaces on which images appear either projected or reflected,[58] and multiply the options for the traffic of gaze. These surfaces promote voyeurism and awareness thereof, and complicate the relationships between spectators and spectacles, three-dimensional space and two-dimensional images, things and bodies themselves and their images.[59] The narrative's focalizer's authority becomes open to question, and in cinematic narratives, the presence of windows and mirrors within the screen further complicates representation, adding a metafictional layer to the visual storytelling.

These variabilities that complicate the train as experienced space-time are challenging and fulfilling at the same time, for storytellers and narratologists alike. Because space is not separable from time, and space-time is also inseparable from the human subject (narrator, focalizer, or protagonist), ambiguities complicate the essential elements of classical narratology. Still, as in my analyses of the three mystery films above, the chapters that follow employ and modify, rather than disavow, narratological terms such as "focalizers," "intradiegetic" and "extradiegetic" narrators, "analepsis" (flashback) and "prolepsis" (flash forward), "suspense" (in terms of knowledge possessed by the narrator, the focalizer, and the reader/viewer of the narrative), and others.

Repetition and variation of plot segments, especially through choreographic or cinematographic direction, create rhythms and support spiraling developments that exploit repetition and difference, manipulating expectations and coordinating surprises. The levels of discourse (form) and story (content) experienced by the viewer and the characters, respectively, are important to recognize in cinematic and textual narratives alike. In the following chapters, gestures, postures, movements, and other exteriorized elements of human subjects that help to form scenes are considered both intratextually and intertextually, as their repetitions and variations create rhythms in the narrative discourse through memories of the focalizer, narrator, and reader/viewer. Associations with similar scenes in preceding films and texts also add layers to storytelling by way of intertextual memory, thus enhancing viewers' and readers' experience of the narrative.

In the highly affective environment of the train as a space-time, the focalizer's or the narrator's mind does not control their body or its environment, but instead reacts to the state of the body and is transformed in response to the environment.[60] The mind may drift away from the space-time of the here and now. The railway route may be linear, yet each moment is invested with memories and anticipations. The train, being both mobile in its relation to the exterior space and sedentary in terms of its interior space, as noted by David Bissell (2009, 429), confuses the placement of the focalizer/narrator, which remains unstable even though illusory stability is felt. As a passenger, the focalizer/narrator is both served and inspected within a power hierarchy that is volatile. All these factors of instability/uncertainty in relations erode the focalizer/narrator's credibility, as well as the ground for narratological analysis of the narrative. Such an ambiguous and amorphous state of the narrative is an ideal challenge and opportunity for post-structuralist narrative studies, for which the train as experienced space-time provides a productive occasion.

4   THE STRUCTURE OF THIS VOLUME

The works examined in Chaps. 2, 4, and 6 are categorized according to the combination of their respective narrative discourses and the characters' usage of the train as a space-time. In each of these chapters I demonstrate the commonality in the mode of narration and train ride that warrants each grouping across languages and historical periods of publication. These three problem-based chapters are further divided into sections on critical issues that emerge in all the narratives in the chapter. In each section, I discuss all the narratives in the chapter together, comparatively. In the rest of the book—Chaps. 3, 5, and 7—I discuss one narrative at a time because the purpose of these segments is not to theorize but to exemplify the potentials of a theoretically oriented close reading that is focused on the train as experienced space-time.

In Chap. 2, "Traveling Alone on the Rails into the Future: *Sanshirō*, *My Most Secret Council*, *Night Train to Lisbon*, and *Zone*," I explore four critically acclaimed modern novels—Natsume Sōseki's *Sanshirō* (1907), Valery

Larbaud's *Mon plus secret conseil* (My Most Secret Council, 1923), Pascal Mercier's *Nachtzug nach Lissabon* (*Night Train to Lisbon*, 2004), and Mathias Énard's *Zone* (2008)—each about a solitary and voluntary male rail traveler who is seemingly in charge of his own journey and determined to leave his past behind for a new stage of life in a new territory. The principal passengers in the first two narratives are in their early twenties, while the latter two novels feature middle-aged men. Regardless of the protagonist's life stage, the train journeys they take are expected to have an irrevocable effect on their lives, changing their residence, profession, or affiliation. Their usage of the train is neither for a casual vacation nor for a daily commute. At first glance, it appears that the classic paralleling of life and journey holds.

Despite such a conventional symbolical paralleling of two processes, however, these narratives undo the forward-moving model of a *bildungsroman* of the man of use, driven by desire and purpose, equipped with a mind independent of its environs, and entitled to make and legitimize his own judgments. Instead, these narratives are loaded with a complex ensemble of things in space-time that the passengers experience corporeally and haptically, not necessarily corroborating the conventional idea of the linear progression of one's journey by the purely instrumental device of the train. Although it is a modern technological apparatus, the train is not simply a tool to move passengers across the cartographically defined space. Rather, the train offers a space-time (a temporally invested space, or spatially substantiated time) in which passengers are forced to become conscious of their physicality rather than mentality—even though in these four novels the protagonists are mentally oriented by nature, being a university student, a poet, an avid reader of literature, and a scholar and teacher of ancient languages.

In my close reading of the selected narratives, I show how the lone male subject can be affected by the space-time of the train to such an extent that his purported neutrality and authority are threatened. Each of these male characters is competent in and complacent about reading, writing, and interpreting, with a stable and capable mind. Yet the duration and relatively sedentary experience of a long-distance train ride expose him to the intrusive gaze and speech of other passengers, thus endangering his advantageous position as an observer who is not to be observed himself. Instead of commanding his surroundings at a distance, the male protagonist is susceptible to stimuli within his fluctuating environs, absorbing and grappling with sensations. A linear narrative of the evolution and/or demise of the self is therefore replaced by intermittent descriptions of his awareness of his own corporeal existence within the range of other people's visual, aural, olfactory, and tactile sensibilities, as his mind is simultaneously disturbed by remembrances of haunting experiences, consideration of parallel and alternative presents, and anticipation of future events, all of which dislocate him from the here and now. The integrity of the male train passenger is thus at risk, while the narrative focalizes on his subjectivity. Indeed, the narrative unfolds according to the formation of this multisensorial and reflexive subjectivity.

In each of the four narratives, the central passenger serves the narrative both as a protagonist and a focalizer, though not necessarily as the narrator. Two of the four texts (*My Most Secret Council* and *Zone*) are narrated in the first person by the central character, while the other two (*Sanshiro* and *Night Train to Lisbon*) are narrated in the third person by an extradiegetic and impersonal voice. Despite this diversity in the voice, however, all four narratives manifest almost exclusive ownership of the viewpoint by the central passenger, even when he feels vulnerable to the gaze or scrutiny of others. I thus have an opportunity to consider standard first-person and third-person narration that collapses due to the focalizer's dissolution as a mind outside the landscape and society as it is affected by the environment of the train journey. The four central passengers' struggle to make sense of their surroundings staggers, their observations are challenged—and this happens because of their exposure to the ambiguous and loaded space-time of the train carriage on their long-distance railway journey. This chapter thus lays a cornerstone for my project.

I insert what I call a "juncture" between Chaps. 2 and 4, and between Chaps. 4 and 6, to smoothly yet distinctly shift the direction between the two pairs of chapters. In Chap. 3: "Juncture 1: *Wendy and Lucy*," I consider Kelly Reinchardt's film *Wendy and Lucy* (2008), in which a single female traveler rides a train both to leave the past behind and to head for her dream destination. This short analysis signals a switch of the focalizer from the elite adult male protagonists traveling alone in Chap. 2 to the socially underprivileged young female or adolescent male protagonists traveling with companions in Chap. 4.

Chapter 4, "Best Friends for a While: Fugitives on the Train in "Night of the Milky Way Railway," *Night Passage*, and *The Naked Eye*," discusses narratives of conversations between traveling companions who develop special or strange bonds within the delimited space-time of a railway journey that one of the two takes out of the urgent need for an alternative life: the short story "Night Train to the Stars," by Miyazawa Kenji (1934), in which the protagonist, an adolescent male, is also the focalizer, though the narrative voice belongs to an extradiegetic impersonal narrator; *Night Passage* (2004), a film co-directed by Trinh T. Minh-ha and Jean-Paul Bourdier, a homage to Miyazawa's story, except that the two friends are young females, which does not have a voice-over, and in which the camera shifts between a third-party position and the protagonist's viewpoint; and Yoko Tawada's novel *Das Nackte Auge* (*The Naked Eye*, 2004), in which a young single woman (the protagonist-focalizer-narrator, except for the final chapter) meets an older married woman on the train.

The gender and age of the three protagonist-focalizers in Chap. 4, and the fact that they are traveling with another person, change the whole dynamic of relations surrounding them. In contrast to Chap. 2, in which a male solo traveler observes others with detachment and authority, the narratives discussed in Chap. 4 are more conversation-oriented. The protagonist-focalizers in Chap. 4 feel inferior to their incidental companions who have more wealth, social standing, emotional leverage, and knowledge than the protagonists do. Moreover, the traveling companions' lives beyond the journey may mean, or at least foreshadow, the end of their camaraderie. This uncertainty complicates the contract of alliance, solidarity, and secrecy that the train facilitates and maintains. A conversation sustained between the protagonist and their companion—whether as a soulmate, sounding board, or enemy—helps to develop the protagonist's own voice and, more importantly, their own ear (Nancy 2007). This dialogic narrative (Bakhtin 1982) prevails not only between the two traveling companions but also between them and others, thus allowing the reader/viewer to consider a narratological situation (Chambers 1984) among several diversely positioned, motivated, and skilled participants. At a parallax with those self-reflexive narratives examined in Chap. 2, the narratives here intensify the commitment of the narratee.

Another distinction of Chap. 4's assemblage of narratives from Chap. 2's is that, as passengers, the protagonist-focalizers do not know where they are going. What is most important to them is what they are leaving behind—challenging circumstances that they would rather forget. The orientation of, and the intensity invested in, the route in the three narratives featured in Chap. 4 are thus contrastive with those of the four in Chap. 2, in which the passengers have clear plans that they have devised carefully, and think they know what they are going to do at their destinations. The passenger-focalizers in Chap. 4, in contrast, suddenly find themselves on the train, and in fact their journeys may continue indefinitely, or be disrupted suddenly, without reaching any destination. The infinitude of the railway journeys seen in Chap. 4 necessitates the amorphous and elusive structure of those narratives, which challenges the classic articulate structure of beginning-middle-end.

Chapter 5 "Juncture 2: *Clouds of Sils Maria*" connects Chap. 4, on how the train enables a temporary bonding of two passengers across social barriers, and Chap. 6, in which second-person narrations exploit the train space-time. In Chap. 5, I explicate scenes from Olivier Assayas's 2014 film *Clouds of Sils Maria*, in which an increasingly ambiguous and ambivalent relationship unfolds between an established actress and her younger, multitasking assistant as they travel by train to the actress's work assignments. The process through which each woman's identity collides with and is eroded by the other's illustrates the volatility of both the space-time of the train and female–female fellowship, and also intensifies the relation of "I" and "you" in dynamic scenes that extend from the train to its exterior.

In Chap. 6, "It's Not 'I,' It's 'You': A Second-Person Protagonist on the Train in *La Modification, Blue Journey, and Suspects on the Night Train*," I explore three second-person narratives in which the deixis—as used in Mieke Bal's (1999) narratological extension of Émile Benveniste's (1973) linguistic concept, and meaning one's bearing in time-space in terms of one's relation to others and things—is formed, unformed, or transformed in the dynamism within the interior space of train carriages. Thus, I examine what it is about the specific temporal-spatial conditions of trains that contributes to the postmodern narrative structure (such as a second-person narrative), and what this reveals about the subjectivity, sovereignty, and authority of the first person that we may have taken for granted in modern times. In these three second-person narratives of a solitary passenger's long-distance railway journey—Michel Butor's *La Modification* (1957); its pastiche, Kurahashi Yumiko's *Kurai tabi* (Blue journey, 1961, 1969); and Tawada Yōko's *Yōgisha no yakō ressha* (Suspects on the night train, 2002)—we envision "you" and "I" not as discrete entities facing each other but as mutually transformative beings side by side (Levinas 1987), exchanging positions and unraveling from each other, as the train makes happen. The stable, solid, and sovereign modern subject dissolves and becomes a performative, amorphous, and porous presence. The use of second-person pronouns corroborates and facilitates this process.

In each of these three types of narrative discourse, enacted by selected narratives in Chaps. 2, 4, and 6, the long-distance rail journey offers an alternative to normative first- or third-person, retrospective, omniscient narration. Having articulated how essential the train is to this complication of the narrative norm, Chap. 7, the conclusion of the book, entitled "Stations as an Extension of the Train Space-Time," considers the railway station as an experienced space-time. First, I (re)visit scenes at stations in all the narratives discussed up to that point. Then, I consider Bae Suah's 2010 story "North Station"—in which stations are definitive of the narrative structure (form) as well as the story (content). I show how a new narrative dynamism is created via trajectories toward, inside, and out of the railway station.

The romance genre chosen for Chap. 7 is an intentional contrast to the mystery genre in Chap. 1. While space-time experienced by bodies in relation to things is obviously essential in mystery, its imperatively important contribution to the narrative discourse may not be so apparent in romance. The romance narrative examined in Chap. 7 illustrates the crucial role that the station as experienced space-time performs in terms of narrative discourse. Demonstrating this is more challenging within the genre of romance than in that of mystery, yet it became not only feasible but optimal after my own journey between Chap. 1 and the Chap. 7 of this study. By examining all these selected narratives that engage with the train in the (trans)formative terms of narratology, my goal has been to show how to read narrative discourse according to the three relations of affordances, movements, and rhythms vis-à-vis the train as experienced space-time.

NOTES

1. Peggy Guggenheim Collection 2023.
2. This corroborates Foucault's general idea of "space" in his present "epoch": "space is given to us in the form of relations between emplacements" (Foucault 2008, 15; Foucault 2004, 13). Not only is the definition of "space" historical (a topic beyond the scope of this study), but it is also act- or process-oriented (involving "emplacements," not "places").
3. This quality alone has been amply discussed by scholars of the train. See Richter 2005 for a prominent example. Not unlike the arcade characterized by Walter Benjamin as an extension of the interior space, train carriages have been recognized as interior spaces with exterior space. For

consideration of the interior space in the modern age in general, see, for example, Rice 2007.

4. In narrative theory/studies, the discourse is the form, or how events and situations are represented in words, and the story is the content, or what events and situations are said to have occurred in the "storyworld" (or the "diegesis") that characters inhabit.

5. A number of well-known mysteries set (at least partially) on a train are not selected here for analysis. For instance, in Agatha Christie's *Murder on the Orient Express* (1934, visually adapted many times), heavy snowfall stops the train between stations, disabling exploitation of the porosity of the train carriage at a station for the pretense of the murderer's escaping there and limiting the suspects to the passengers and one staff member. *Murder on the Orient Express* precedes and is alluded to by *The Lady Vanishes*, discussed below, which shares with it specifics such as the general region of Central Europe and the train stoppage due to snow. In other works, a train carriage is an essential setting for plotting the crime to be committed elsewhere. For example, Georges Simenon's novel *L'Homme qui regardait passer les trains* (1938; trans., *The Man Who Watched the Trains Go by*, 2016) has the man in the title, who is deprived of opportunities to travel by train to foreign lands, make that happen after committing a murder, and then, toward the end of the story, try unsuccessfully to kill himself by being run over by a train and instead be sent back to his homeland by train. The story thus encapsulates the three functions of the train as (1) an object of the gaze, (2) a means to travel (or to kill), and (3) an experience of a space-time. In another thriller by Simenon, *Le Train de Venise* (1965; trans., *The Venice Train*, 1974), the eponymous long-distance train (from Venice to Lausanne?) affords an opportunity for strangers to meet, one of them exploiting the other in a criminal scheme, and then to lose touch with each other despite the finite space of the train. A similar implication of an innocent passenger on the train takes place in Alfred Hitchcock's *Strangers on a Train* (1951, based on Patricia Highsmith's 1950 novel of the same title).

6. Other than the final destination of Victoria Station, London, Budapest is the only recognizable place name that offers a clue to the railway route for this train. Of the other station names, Dravska may be drawn from the Drava River that runs through southeast Europe, or be short for Dravograd station in Slovenia. If either speculation is the case, the starting point for the train may then be Maribor, Slovenia, where the Drava Valley Railway originates. The place name of Balto is heard mentioned by characters a few times and seen in an advertisement posted on a wall of the dining car, which alliterates with Balkans.

7. Iris repeats this declaration later (51:32), demonstrating in my context her conviction that the train space-time is not transparent but dense and can be probed for productive results.

8. The nail filing is one way of spending time when one cannot go any-where—literally, confined in the train carriage, or figuratively, entrapped in an impasse in life. Perhaps inspired by this scene, *The Narrow Margin*, the film I discuss next, has a female passenger who files her painted nails in a compartment, which the camera shows in a close-up. Nail filing or nail clipping effectively encapsulates a relationship between time and the human, or the biological time, conceptually and visually. I discuss this at some length in Chap. 6, in terms of *Suspects on the Night Train* by Tawada Yōko.

9. I discuss in Chap. 6 another example of a train compartment space with landscape pictures in Michel Butor's *La Modification*. The mirror figures importantly in Butor's novel as well.

10. Dr. Hartz's compartment, in which the bandaged Miss Froy and the nun are seen in the preceding sequence, and its adjacent compartment, in which Iris and Gilbert pretend to have been drugged to deceive Dr. Hartz, with the rescued Miss Froy hiding in the closet, are in a first-class car that is closer to the dining car than the second-class carriage in which Iris and the unwed couple have been traveling.

11. A significant exception to this rule (that the passenger train and the opera-tional engines should be dissociated, with the latter invisible and inaudible beyond their professional function) in cinema is *La Bête humaine* (The Human Beast, 1938) directed by Jean Renoir, which features a locomotive worker as the central character (Jacques Lantier, played by Jean Gabin).

12. The alternative mode of travel by air is thus essential in the formation of the narrative of *The Narrow Margin*. Yet flying is not considered an option for the central characters, Brown and Mrs. Neall, possibly indicating the superior affluence of the crime syndicate they are up against.

13. In *The Lady Vanishes* Iris and Gilbert first meet in the inn because of the loud music (and dance) in Gilbert's room bothering Iris, whose room is right beneath his. The loudness is an associated quality of Gilbert's, whom Iris later finds in a third-class carriage that is filled with clamorous music and dancing, an aural space distinct from the second-class carriage in which she herself is traveling.

14. As the taxi approaches the Chicago station, Brown and Mrs. Neall part ways, so that she won't be seen with him; her appearance is not known to their pursuers, whereas his is. The police want Mrs. Neall to remain incog-nito until she appears in court in Los Angeles, which (along with the mis-sion of keeping her safe) becomes a challenge throughout their train ride, and a key driving force of the narrative. The viewer is invited to stay alert

to who is where at any moment in the film. After Brown exits the taxi before it arrives at the station, leaving the fare with Mrs. Neall, she follows his instructions and is seen carrying her own luggage, declining a redcap's offer of help, and walking across the concourse (12:55). Her steps since then have not been shown on the screen. Therefore, the viewer learns of her safe arrival in her room just as Brown does. This is one of the few intentional lapses in the discourse as the screen shows only one scene at a time—and is clearly intentional because the narrative creates suspense by withholding select information from the viewer.

15. Kemp, however, does not see Brown when his vista is also clear in the straight corridor because he is reading a telegraph he has just been handed by a conductor upon leaving Brown's room and does not look up when Brown is standing ahead of him. Brown, in contrast, learns in this scene that Kemp has received a telegraph, which he searches for later in Kemp's room.

16. The same spot is featured in another scene, which enhances the viewer's visual knowledge of its spatial composition (with a fountain for drinking water and wall-mounted slats for newspapers and magazines, taking advantage of the slight width the curve allows the corridor). In that scene, Kemp passes Brown, who asks him, "Have you found your bag?," to which Kemp replies, "No, but I'm still looking" (32:28).

17. It also helps that, in this first encounter, Jennings is cooperating with Brown out of good will. Later, when they again encounter each other in this spot, Jennings is unwilling to budge (having been offended by Brown's flatly refusing his earlier request to move into Brown's purportedly empty adjacent room), insisting that "it is your turn" to make way for him (45:53). Brown finds an unlocked door to take a step backward into so as to let Jennings pass. Thus, even the physically same space can be negotiated differently to different effect depending on evolving interpersonal relations.

18. This scene, as well as the scene mentioned in note 18 above, prepares the viewer for a choreographically similar occurrence, in which Jennings finds an unlocked door through which to duck to make more room for another passenger (53:41), only to be trapped inside, as we shall see later.

19. Brown is suspicious enough to include Jennings's name in the telegraph he wires from the La Junta station to the LA District Attorney's office, so as to inquire about his background (42:25).

20. Kemp spots the two talking in the club car, in the dining car, and at Brown's compartment door. His third viewing of them together, across the window from the platform of the La Junta station, leads to his theory that Ann is Mrs. Neall, which he telegraphs the syndicate from the station.

21. Again the viewer's knowledge supersedes Brown's here. He catches up with the viewer when he arrives in Densel's room, to ask Jennings, just rescued by the conductor, who the man was that assaulted him. As Jennings replies, "He didn't leave any calling card," Brown notices the fur-trimmed coat and, pointing to it, shouts, "That's his calling card!" (1:05:22).

22. This recalls the unwed woman's act of filing her nails in *The Lady Vanishes*, discussed earlier.

23. This is how the replacement of Miss Froy is taken off guard when she returns to Dr. Hartz's compartment, never suspecting that Miss Froy has been resurrected from her bandages by Iris and Gilbert, which leads to the replacement being rebandaged and returned to her state as the ostensible patient of Dr. Hartz.

24. Other possible ways to announce a visit are aural: to knock (as Densel does for Mrs. Neall and for Tommy, in each case successfully deceiving them with his apparent decorum) or to press the buzzer beside the door (as Brown does for Ann).

25. Densel does not have much time left; he and Kemp must find the incriminating document by an appointed time at which the car that is racing alongside the train will pick them up.

26. The windows facing the outside have shades. The one in Mrs. Neall's room has been pulled down when Brown arrives to see whether she has already boarded at the Chicago station, which shows Mrs. Neall's alertness and precaution—not surprisingly, given her true identity as an internal affairs agent. However, the shade does not block the view entirely; through it, Brown sees Kemp on the platform even after he stops peeking between the fringe of the shade, creating eerie feelings about Kemp.

27. The outside-in perspective remains in effect in the ensuing scene, in which a message is dropped from the train to the highway patrol telling them to intercept the suspicious car. In that scene the camera zooms in on the officer who receives the missive as the train streams past him, rather than showing the onboard staff member who drops it. This brief sequence materializes the third relation between the human subject, the thing (= the train), and the space-time in Foucault's "Of Other Spaces" (2008)—that is, a human subject watches the train pass by. At the same time, the first relation—that is, a human subject moves across the space-time of the train—thickens inside the train.

28. William Friedkin (2005) explains that this scene was shot on the studio set, with the enhanced light that was necessary to coordinate the reflections. Light, Friedkin adds, is a key to the success of film noir.

29. A window's transparency and reflexivity allow the superimposition of the interior and exterior spaces (and things and figures in them) in more scenes: the scenes with Densel and Kemp together watching the speeding

car (1:01:35), Brown and the car (1:01:45), and Ann and the car superimposed across her window (1:04:12), followed immediately by Densel looking at the car from the window in Mrs. Neall's room are also seen in palimpsest with the automobile. The reflexivity of the windowpane becomes a very important factor in *La Modification*, as discussed in Chap. 6.

30. The viewer can see that the Los Angeles station, like the Chicago station, has an underground hallway from which slopes toward the platforms extend. This structure is unavailable in the narrative of the next film to be discussed, *Night Train*.

31. A different, fast-paced, and pulsating instrumental piece is played intermittently during the sequence at an interim station, which may enhance the passengers' alertness to their limited time to spend off the train and their elevated sense of specularity (both as spectacle and spectator, explicit in the flirtatious wife's comments on Marta and herself)—a situation similar to that at the La Junta station in *The Narrow Margin*.

32. The train and the human subject are compared with each other by Ann in *The Narrow Margin*, when she speaks to Brown on the La Junta station platform: "You are like the train. When it's moving everything is a blur. When it slows and stops you begin to notice the scenery" (44:36).

33. It is not as if passengers in *Night Train* are immune to music: a young woman stylishly dressed in white, accompanied by a man who exchanges amorous gazes with her, boards the train holding a radio (seen in a close-up). Once the couple disappear into their compartment and their door shuts to the camera that has followed them, they do not reappear until the last moment in the film, and if they listen to any music on the radio it is not audible any time in the film.

34. For more on the distinction of diegetic sound in cinematic narratives, see Verstraten 2009 and Brown 2018.

35. His action both damages the bracelet and hurts Marta's wrist, as Jerzy points out back in the first-class compartment, when he sees her searching the floor for the bracelet (32:23). He speculates that the bracelet must be a gift from her ex-lover. Her bracelet is indeed a thing in which space-time thickens, through the events of damage, loss, and recovery on and around the train, and because it is a keepsake of her past life.

36. The jacket photo used for the 2005 Polish-language DVD edition of *Pociąg* (*Night Train*) shows the gentler portion of this scene, instead of any other that might capture a more important plot segment. This may be partly attributable to the fame and popularity of Zbigniew Cybulski, on the heels of the success of the 1958 *Ashes and Diamonds* by Andrzej Witold Wajda, in which he starred to international critical acclaim, coming to be dubbed "the James Dean of the East." Another reason for the image selec-

tion for the DVD jacket may be the conventional aesthetic appeal of a woman on a train being gazed at longingly by a man on the platform (even though in *Night Train* the man is not being left behind: he gets back on board, on a whim, without a ticket). This visual configuration is also the case with the DVD edition of *Brief Encounter* (1945).

37. The two deeds are more comparable than contrastive in another way: during Gilbert's feat another train comes toward him and passes him, while the ex-boyfriend's attempt is made while the train is crossing a river, with the bridge seen in the background. In each scene, the added circumstance (consequently with more noise) makes his action look even riskier for dramatic effect.

38. The viewer's knowledge is greater than Marta's, however, in a visual/physiognomical sense, even beyond the boarding scene. Before Marta spots him, the screen shows the murderer hiding in a second-class compartment twice: when Marta's ex-boyfriend comes back on board after the interim station and enters the second-class carriage, the murderer is seen in the corner of the same compartment with his face only sticking out of a hanging overcoat (31:46); and then when a conductor arrives for ticket inspection, the murderer is seen sticking out only his right hand with a ticket to have it punched (40:30). In both cases, though his strange position is noticed by the ex-boyfriend (who looks a little mystified) and then by the conductor, they do not make much of it. For them he is just an oddly behaving passenger. Again, the viewer is given more information than the characters, even though the viewer is not yet able to identify him as the murderer but only to recognize him as a familiar face, and perhaps to wonder why the camera keeps showing him.

39. It is easier for Marta, a first-class passenger, to cross the contiguous space into the second-class carriage through the landing. The control over the flow of passengers' movements is unequally controlled, granting the higher-class passengers greater mobility—or less vigilance—because first-class passengers do not usually wish to go to the second-class carriages.

40. The conductors have a list of the first-class passengers in *Night Train*, which the police request upon their arrival. Jerzy fails to prove his identity because he has forgotten not only his ticket but also his ID.

41. Kidnapping is only a vague suspicion at the beginning of the search in the Hitchcock film, because Iris believes Miss Froy to be a governess and music teacher who did not appear to have any reason to be kidnapped. Miss Froy's political mission remains veiled until much later.

42. Before this scene in *The Lady Vanishes*, Iris pulls the emergency brake to stop the train. Though her act fails to launch a thorough search for the missing Miss Froy, as she has hoped (she faints immediately after her action and is unable to insist on the demand), with the train resuming its locomo-

tion in ten minutes, the physical act of pulling the emergency brake itself may have inspired similar actions by Kemp in *The Narrow Margin* and by the fugitive in *Night Train*.

43. The exact act of assault is not shown on screen. However, when the flirtatious woman from the next compartment arrives late, regretting that she has missed observing the critical moment, she peeks at the spot already vacated by the crowd and mutters "So much blood..." (1:12:06), which suggests the brutality of the mass of people against the captive.

44. Partly owing to this scene, *Night Train* is often compared to Fritz Lang's *M*, in which members of an underground syndicate replace law enforcement in condemning an abductor and murderer of children. The respective historical backdrops of the two films are hard to ignore—the prosecution of leftists by the mass underground organization in the late 1910s (for *M*), and the populist government's deportation, torture, and mass murder of the Jewish people in the 1940s (for *Night Train*). In *Night Train*, one first-class passenger chooses not to sleep in a berth, explaining that the bunk bed reminds him of the Buchenwald concentration camp where he spent four years.

45. A few steps in this sequence (which some plot summaries distributed to the public omit) are important in my context: Jerzy passes Marta, who is standing at a corridor window to look out, enters the compartment alone, begins to make himself comfortable, and then notices a purse on the lower bed, which he picks up and examines, sitting down on the lower bed. The camera then assumes his viewpoint when the door opens from outside, revealing legs, a skirt, and then Marta's upper body. Jerzy springs up, hitting his head against the upper bed frame, to his chagrin. Martha takes the purse and examines its contents, further humiliating Jerzy by her obvious suspicion he may have stolen something. She then produces a ticket from her purse to claim she is entitled to stay. He dashes out of the compartment to report the apparent mixup to the female conductor, with whom he returns to the compartment. When the conductor knocks and opens the door, she finds Marta already on the lower bed, reading a book, unwilling to surrender her place. Although these details may appear trivial, they confirm spatial conditions essential to the later plot development, in terms of Jerzy's height vis-à-vis the bunk bed, the placement of the door, the beds, pillows, the ladder, the sink, the closet, and other facilities in the compartment. This first encounter between Jerzy and Marta also preludes their increasing willingness to share each other's belongings, thus decreasing territoriality. These details are all tacitly and efficiently set up in this short sequence at the beginning to prepare the viewer for later, more consequential scenes.

46. Jerzy is aware of the curiosity of the other passengers, which he runs down for Marta when they are alone in the compartment (38:00). His visible amusement (this is one of the fewer occasions on which he is seen smiling), and the position he assumes of being a commentator on rather than a character in a romance, may shroud the later suggestion of their intimacy.

47. They also do not share the other passengers' voyeuristic thirst to punish the murderer; in addition to Marta's guilt-laced compassion, Jerzy offers a professional assessment of the culprit's condition as he lies unconscious after being attacked—gently, as he would for any patient (1:10:24).

48. I thank Benjamin Bandosz for translating this article (Kwiatkowska 2013) from the Polish to English.

49. There is no flashback of this incident: Jerzy tells Martha of it, after they are back from the hunt for the murderer (1:19:19). The viewer's knowledge thus remains below a character's on this matter, to enhance the mysteriousness of Jerzy's behavior (his advice that Marta should not stand at an open window may instead be interpreted as evidencing his attraction to her).

50. The singularity of this action is accentuated against the comparable action soon afterward of the wife next door, who, in the corridor, cannot (or pretends not to be able to) push open the window, prompting Jerzy, who stands next to her, to help.

51. While walking through the corridor toward Marta's compartment, the conductor opens the note to read it (the screen shows the scribble, 20:54), subtly revealing her not so professionally detached position. Her interpersonal bearing plays a part in the plot throughout the film.

52. This sequence cannot help but recall a crucial scene in *Brief Encounter* (1945), a film in which the heroine suffers the same problem and is helped in a similar manner by a doctor who happens to be there—and with whom she later falls in love. Geoffrey Macnab (Macnab 2012, 87) acknowledges that *Night Train* pays tribute to the preceding film, though without any specific pointer to this scene.

53. The camerawork here subtly leads viewers to experience the causal and temporal sequence themselves: the camera first shows a change of Jerzy's countenance as the object of attention (not for Marta but for a third party, the viewer), and then switches to a view of Marta's shrouded feet, suggesting that this is what he has seen, and that he is now the focalizer. While the camera is still focusing on the feet, on behalf of Jerzy, his yelling is heard, off the frame. Then the camera reveals a broader scope, showing both Jerzy and a surprised Marta within the frame.

54. Kwiatkowska (2013, 82) cites this scene as one of the moments making a strong "somatographic impression" that "returns to the viewer's consciousness" as the viewer later gains knowledge of the reason for Jerzy's "impulsive act of aggression" and becomes able to make more sense of it.

55. This frames the narrative discourse, through contrastive interactions between the female conductor and Marta. Marta got onto the train because she eluded the conductor's check at the door. Asked why she did so, when her ticket is inspected later, Marta replies, "You looked busy."

56. At the stop prior to the terminus, Marta does not look outside when someone knocks on the windowpane, yet Jerzy does, to spot the ex-boyfriend, who has disembarked and is trying to see Marta one last time. When Jerzy, not Marta, shows up at the window, the ex-boyfriend's face freezes (1:25:32). As the train pulls away, the camera moves outward again, showing some familiar-looking disembarked passengers walking along in the same direction as the train, yet much more slowly. A group of pilgrims previously seen in a second-class compartment, whose statue of Maria was revealed from underneath an overcoat during the search for the murderer, to comical effect, sings in a procession in this scene. Another notable passenger here is a young woman who has been seen to be pleased by the admiring gaze of a sailor in the second-class corridor a few times throughout the film, now walking alone while waving cheerfully to an invisible person on the train, whom the viewer may surmise is that sailor. This is a detail, inconsequential in the plot, that visually replaces a final parting scene between Marta and her ex. The sailor's reaction is not shown, and neither is Marta's, at this moment. In a chiasmus, the two couples' separation is confirmed, and in each case the woman is ready to move on.

57. Their camaraderie starts earlier: while Jerzy is in police custody, the female conductor says to Marta: "You are lucky ... you never know what that kind of person would do," assuming Jerzy is a wife killer who thus could have done something violent to Marta while she was in the compartment with him (54:51). At the expense of Jerzy's honor, the female conductor grows sympathetic to Marta who, as we recall, defied the conductor's ruling in order to stay in the "male only" compartment.

58. In a famous scene in Kawabata Yasunari's *Yukiguni* (1948; trans., *Snow Country*, 1956), the reflection of an eye of a passenger coincides with that of a light in the windowpane, as if the eye emanates the light, confusing the observer's sense of the depth and perspective of the space, as well as reality and fantasy.

59. Technically, however, windows are not transparent: glass is material, and, even though it is not porous, it can be fogged, smeared, cracked, or smashed, in response to the temperature of and humidity in the air, or other external and internal impacts.

60. Malabou's "plasticity" (2008) is a relevant concept to recall in this context.

CHAPTER 2

Traveling Alone on the Rails into the Future: *Sanshirō, My Most Secret Council, Night Train to Lisbon,* and *Zone*

The corpus examined in this chapter consists of four first- or third-person narratives in which the dominant focalizer (from whose perspective observations are made) is also the central character. This protagonist-focalizer (who is also the narrator in two of the four narratives) is in all cases a highly cultivated, multilingual male passenger who is fairly comfortable in a heterogeneous environment. He rides the train alone toward a life-changing relocation, whether permanent or temporary, that he has chosen himself. After the journey, his life is never the same.

In this first section, I summarize how, in these four narratives, the railway journey contributes to the formation of the discourse.

Sanshirō, by Natsume Sōseki (1907; revised 1909; trans., *Sanshiro,*[1] 1977; 1999), is a third-person narrative with an impersonal, extradiegetic, omniscient narrator. The perspective remains mostly with the protagonist, Ogawa Sanshirō (called by his given name, Sanshirō). However, the narrator exerts knowledge greater than that of Sanshirō, noting, for instance, when Sanshirō first sees Mineko, his romantic interest throughout the story, the reason that he cannot find the words to describe his initial impression of her (Natsume 2018, 40; 1977, 22–23). On the rare occasions when Sanshirō is not the focalizer, the narrator mediates other characters' gaze upon and analysis of him (e.g., Mineko watching Sanshirō unbeknownst to him—a fact that is confirmed by the narrator—at the art exhibition; Natsume 2018, 270; 1977, 144). Occasionally, the

© The Author(s), under exclusive license to Springer Nature Switzerland AG 2023
A. Sakaki, *Train Travel as Embodied Space-Time in Narrative Theory*, Geocriticism and Spatial Literary Studies, https://doi.org/10.1007/978-3-031-40548-8_2

protagonist-focalizer realizes he is being watched and judged by others and feels uncomfortable (Natsume 2018, 18; 1977, 9) or gazes back at them (Natsume 2018, 20; 1977, 10). The omniscient narrator, however, does not anticipate happenings later than the moment being narrated about: there is no prolepsis. For the most part, the story time and the discourse time progress in the same order as each other, with only a few occasions when the narrator provides events not included in the initial narration after the fact. Thus, the reader is brought up to speed later that Sanshirō has failed to disembark at the right station of an intra-city railway and had to make quite a detour both by rail and on foot (Natsume 2018, 68; 1977, 38).[2]

Sanshirō travels third class from his native town of Fukuoka to Tokyo (Shimbashi Station, the terminus between 1872 and 1914).[3] The route involves seven railway segments and a ferry ride from Moji to Shimonoseki between Kyūshū Island and Honshū Island along the way.[4] The narrative covers his journey from around Ishiyama to Nagoya, where he stays in an inn for the night, and then from Nagoya to Shimbashi on the following day. The ambiguity of the beginning is due to his slumber (more on this later). When a female passenger asks Sanshirō questions about the train, he only gives elusive answers: "He had no idea. This was his first trip to Tokyo" (Natsume 2018, 11; 1977, 6). Yet it can hardly be his first railway travel; he graduated from college in Kumamoto,[5] another city on Kyūshū Island, and thus he must have taken the train to go home several times when the school was out. The railway between Kumamoto and Moji opened in 1891 (Makimura 2020, 185); the route between Moji and Toyotsu, the closest station to the model location for Sanshirō's hometown, opened in 1895 (ibid., 15); and the story is set in shortly after the end of the Russo-Japanese War (1905).[6] Thus, railway travel in itself is familiar to Sanshirō. What is new to him is the length of the journey and the variety of travelers coming from and going to different places: for instance, he observes that the passengers' skin tones grow fairer and fairer as the train travels farther east (Natsume 2018, 6; 1977, 3). It is therefore understandable that Sanshirō is less struck by the train's technological innovativeness, its velocity, or the modernity it embodies than by the greater heterogeneity of background, social status, and purpose in life of the passengers with whom he shares the space-time as he travels beyond Kyūshū.

In addition to this main journey, which is recounted in the novel's first chapter, the narrative contains several important references to Sanshirō's

2 TRAVELING ALONE ON THE RAILS INTO THE FUTURE... 59

experience of trains of various kinds: as a pedestrian negotiating the space with streetcars around the university campus, and being baffled by the intra-city trains, both steam and electric (chapter 2); as a not-too-successful passenger on streetcars (in the aforementioned episode, in chapter 3); and as an observer of the corpse of a woman who committed suicide by throwing herself in front of a steam train on the Kōbu Line near Ōkubo, to which he had earlier traveled by an electric train on a separate track (chapter 3). Since these train rides are short-distance, I do not discuss them in earnest and only refer to them in their relation to long-distance travels in this novel or other narratives.

Mon plus secret conseil (My Most Secret Council, 1923),[7] by Valery Larbaud, is essentially a first-person narrative by the intradiegetic narrator Luca Letheil. The narrative consists most significantly of "interior monologue," or free direct discourse, in which a character's thought is ostensibly presented as it is formed, without a narrator's mediation. For this reason, this work is dedicated to Edouard Dujardin, whose *Les Lauriers sont coupés* (1925; trans., *The Bays Are Sere*, 1991) is considered the most prominent model of this narrative method. Diversions from the pattern include: tagged monologue (e.g., the first sentence, presented within quotation marks, thus clearly demarcated as representing the protagonist's inner thought through the narrator's mediation), and occasional forays into a call to "you" ("tu" or "vous") for self-questioning, and into a third-person narrative (the protagonist being referred to as "il"; e.g., at the beginning of chapter II in this work). The shift from one personal pronoun to another occurs quickly and without any notice throughout the narrative. Despite such fluctuations in the voice of narration, the focalizer remains the protagonist. The present tense is used for events and situations unfolding in the narrative present, while the past tense is employed when the protagonist recollects past events and situations. The story and discourse thus maintain a relatively straightforward and stable relationship; the narrator does not anticipate what is to come in the story ahead of its happening, but does provide the reader with information about what has transpired earlier than the narrative present (e.g., how Luca met his current lover, Isabelle, whom he is trying to get rid of in the present).

The protagonist-focalizer-(main) narrator, Luca, takes a train from Naples to Taranto, leaving Isabelle in an apartment in Naples, on August 7, 1903. Initially, he plans to go to Messina, Sicily, but at the Naples station, he learns that the train for that destination won't leave until afternoon. The urgency to disconnect himself from his lover makes him instantly change course and buy a one-way first-class ticket for Taranto instead, the destination for the next train out of Naples. This naturally alters the landscape seen from the window of his train, which leaves the coastline behind in the middle of its route.

The narrative covers Luca's journey on the train only until around Vaglio di Basilicata. The train ride begins in chapter VII of the 21 chapters, and continues until the end the narrative, when Luca apparently falls asleep during his musings before reaching his destination. The reader thus does not see whether or not the protagonist succeeds in his plans to part with his lover and begin a new affair as planned. More importantly in my context, the reader does not know whether or not the protagonist takes the return trip to Naples as planned, to make his journey into a loop rather than a one-way, linear trip.

Nachtzug nach Lissabon (2004; trans., *Night Train to Lisbon*, 2008), by Pascal Mercier, has two narrative layers: the embedding/frame narrative and the embedded narrative within it. The embedding narrative is told in the third person by an extradiegetic narrator, and with a protagonist, Raimund Gregorius (consistently referred to by his surname), monopolizing the perspective. The embedded narrative is a book of reflections told in the first person, written by a now deceased figure, Amadeu de Prado (likewise referred to by his first name), and read by Gregorius. The embedded narrative, originally written in Portuguese, is quoted in German; Gregorius is currently learning the Portuguese language, and reads and apparently then attempts to translate a small portion at a time. (In the first instance we are told he does just that [Mercier 2008, 23; 2004, 36], with little explanation of the circumstances provided thereafter.) Quotations from Amadeu's book are italicized, to make evident the narrator's mediation. The protagonist-focalizer Gregorius is also a listener for other characters (*the* listener for many) who share their reminiscences of Amadeu with him at his request, and whose voices are heard often through the omniscient narrator's mediation. It is always clear who is speaking and through what medium (e.g., by telephone, in person, or in writing), and in which time frame.

The titular train ride is the last of the three segments taken consecutively within a day: first from Bern to Paris (Gare de Lyon); then, after a taxi ride, from Paris (Gare Montparnasse) to Irún; and finally from Irún to Lisbon by sleeper. The entire trip is represented in the narrative, beginning at the end of chapter 3 of the 52 chapters as Gregorius leaves Bern, and continuing until the end of chapter 6, where he arrives in Lisbon.

Gregorius reserves a one-way ticket for the entire route by phone on the morning of his departure from Bern, as soon as the railway company's information desk opens at 6 a.m., after a sleepless night spent in preparations for the journey. Thus, his booking is without delay once he decides to travel to Lisbon. His decision itself is made within a single day, after many years of a routine life. We see the elastic nature of time that he experiences, radically shifted from slow-flowing and repetitive to fast-paced and irrevocable.

The exact reverse route is interrupted in Salamanca, where Gregorius quickly decides to visit one of the key individuals in Amadeu's life. After the resumption of the train ride from Salamanca, the narrative ends once he arrives home and prepares for a scheduled medical assessment to address the vertigo he experienced several times during his stay in Lisbon. The narrative is thus largely framed by the two train trips on the same route in opposite directions. Though Gregorius returns home, his life will never be the same, if it continues (his fate after the hospitalization is unknown); Bern appears both familiar and strange to him after his probing and extensive pilgrimage into Amadeu's life in philosophy, love, and politics, during which he has also reflected on his own life to date—with his parents, ex-wife, students, and friends, especially those newly made while in Lisbon.

Gregorius also rides other trains, notably one between Lisbon and Coimbra, where Amadeu studied medicine (Mercier 2008, 367; 2004, 420; after driving to Finisterre from Coimbra, he takes the return train ride from Porto to Lisbon). He also learns from Eça, a former anti-fascism activist and Amadeu's close friend, that Amadeu and Eça first met during the railway journey from London to Brighton in England (chapter 14). Amadeu's fascination with and extensive knowledge of the railways are significant both in his role in the underground revolutionary group and in his philosophy, which Gregorius learns from Eça; from Melody, Amadeu's youngest sister (chapter 27); from Maria João, Amadeu's long-term female confidante (chapter 39); and from further reading of Amadeu's book (chapters 24, 42).

Zone (2008; trans., *Zone*, 2010), by Mathias Énard, is a first-person narrative, whose intradiegetic narrator Francis is also its protagonist and focalizer. A distinguishing feature oft noted is that, for more than 500 page, the text is composed of a single sentence. Periods are replaced by commas, and where commas would normally be there are none. Thus, the entire narrative forms one meandering and digressive interior monologue, within which conversations of the present and the past are incorporated without quotation marks. The tense is determined by the referenced events and situations in the story; when they are happening in the narrative present, narration is in the present tense, when they happened in the past, in the past tense. Three chapters are entirely quotations from a book that the protagonist reads while on the trip, and there the tense adopts the tense of the embedded narrative. Another formal feature that has been noted is that the narrative consists of 24 chapters (from I to XXIV), the same number as James Joyce's *Ulysses*.[8] Chapters often end as the protagonist is brought back to reality by his finishing a chapter of the book he is reading or by the train's arrival at a station.

The protagonist-focalizer-narrator, Francis, begins his railway journey from Paris for Milan by TGV, and then continues on the Pendolino train to Rome, on December 8 of an unspecified year that is obviously after 1990. The narrative commences, however, halfway through the journey, in the Milan Central station, where Francis awaits the train for the second and last leg of his travel. The 24 chapters are divided into nine parts, each of which is named after a station on the route from Milan to Rome: Milan, Lodi, Parma, Reggio Emilia, Modena, Bologna, Prato, Florence, and Rome. These nine parts are listed in the table of contents, which is called "Milestones" (Énard 2010, 1) or "Bornes" (terminals, milestones; Énard 2008, 521). From Francis's intermittent recollections of the first leg, we learn that he has missed his flight from Paris to Rome because he overslept and, without even thinking of taking the next flight (he wonders in retrospect why he didn't, since it would have been easier and faster; Énard 2010, 35–36; 2008, 42), rushed by taxi to Gare de Lyon so as to travel to Rome by train. Many other routes—by rail or otherwise, on which Francis, a Croatian-French former soldier and spy, has traveled across Europe and North Africa—are remembered during the present trip. In addition, many historical transportation routes he knows about (such as several Jewish deportation routes across Europe, from Greece to Poland) are frequently and extensively described. Consequently, the present journey is geographically and historically enriched and complicated. The narrative reaches Rome Termini with the protagonist and then continues, almost without a pause, to end in the Roma-Fiumicino Airport because he does not stay in the city as planned and is anxious to get out of it.

In all four of these narratives, the male protagonist is determined to pursue his plan of changing his life by putting cartographic distance between himself and his previous life. However, the decision is not entirely without uncertainty, and its seeming irrevocability troubles them—so much so that the central passenger may try to elude responsibility by attributing his action to the train itself, an inanimate object that is often anthropomorphized, as if he is being taken away against his will by a merciless machine, with the protagonist's action construed as being fate rather than human choice. This is not a constant or ultimate state, however; in each narrative, the protagonist may fluctuate between passivity and activity, with variations and varying degrees of determination manifesting among these four narratives.

For the balance of this chapter, I examine several common themes and scenes in these four narratives in terms of the passenger's experience of the space-time of the train: (1) the act of rushing to the station to catch a train, not so much as an enslavement to absolute time as a varying experience of immanent time; (2) the passenger's obsession with and defiance of the train's timetable; (3) the location and direction of the seat in which the protagonist is seated vis-à-vis the train's movement and other passengers' seats; (4) the act of reading, and its intertextual and intersubjective merging with the main train narrative; (5) interaction with other passengers; (6) interaction with railway staff members; (7) sleeping and dreaming while on the train; (8) stations posing possible alternatives to the travel plan; and (9) the passenger's remembrances of and comparisons with other railway trips, whether in imagination or in personal or collective memory, as incited by geographical location and dislocation.

1   RUSHING TO THE STATION TO CATCH A TRAIN

A train timetable is by default rigid, determining the spatial and temporal location indisputably. Its precision in cartographic space and chronographic time facilitates modernity, as the railway system is supposed to. A passenger catching a train has to be at a designated place at a designated time, subordinated to the cartographic location of the stations and the chronological schedule of the trains. As is well known, this urgency caused immense anxiety to Sigmund Freud.[9] However, the reaction to such constraints is felt corporeally, which is manifest in the narratives under review here. These occasions reveal how passengers experience space-time and illustrate time as immanent, embodied, and elastic, rather than absolute, immaterial, and homogenous.

The protagonist-main focalizer Sanshirō recollects how he has observed another passenger, an old man, run so as not to miss the train, two stations before where the train is in the narrative present:

With a wild shout, the old fellow had come bounding onto the train at the last second. Then he had stripped to the waist, revealing a back covered with cautery scars. Sanshiro had watched him wipe the sweat from his body, straighten his kimono, and sit down beside the woman. (Natsume 2018, 6; 1977, 3)

This scene and its context are loaded with things to explore, but here I would like to focus on the way the focalizer Sanshirō experiences time, and how the sequence of events around him is presented in the discourse time.

The scene of the old man jumping onto the train is not presented as it happens, unlike most scenes in this narrative. Instead, it is recalled by the protagonist-main focalizer after the fact: Sanshiro wakes up from a nap, catches sight and sound of the man, and successfully remembers what he did earlier in the story time. This gives the focalizer Sanshirō (and the narrator) a chance to process and anatomize the scene. The narrator is in Sanshirō's mind, and presents it as an analepsis (flashback) in the narrative discourse. The way the scene is presented confirms both that the scene impressed the focalizer and that the narrator thought the scene noteworthy.

To consider the temporality of the scene from another perspective, as memorable as it is, it was deemed undeserving of opening the narrative, in comparison to the way the story does begin—with Sanshiro waking up from a nap (as I discuss further below). The narrative begins with the sedentary and shifts to the dynamic, rather than the other way round. This arrangement confirms the normativity of the seated posture in the experience of the train's space-time.

The constraints of the timetable on potential passengers' use of time compelled the old man to run to the station. He either did not consult the timetable in advance or could not fully take advantage of the preview of it. Train narratives often negotiate with the rigidity of the train schedule, to confirm a condition of modernity (i.e., chronological and absolute time) that is not always forgiving of contingencies of human lives. What is remarkable in this scene in *Sanshirō*, however, is that the narrative does not end with the man catching or missing the train, as if that is all that matters, but describes, through another passenger's eyes, how he uses time afterward. He takes time to make himself comfortable by wiping off the sweat, redresses himself, and only then takes a seat—all while the train is presumably in motion. Although his railway journey has started, he is standing on the same spot in the carriage. With no need to hurry any longer, he experiences time as though its flow is paused. This is a drastic turn in his consciousness from before to after he boards the train: before, he was enslaved to the schedule in absolute time, whereas after, he is the master of his own time, which he uses as he sees fit. The long-distance train allows the passengers to spend their time at their own pace. Time thus becomes immanent (Husserl) and is no longer absolute.

This elasticity of time—between the constraint of absolute time outside the railway journey and the relative liberty that passengers can take during the journey—is also recognized by Luca, the protagonist-focalizer-main narrator of *My Most Secret Council*. Although he comfortably boards his train initially at the Naples station, he almost fails to reboard at Salerno, where his train stops for a few minutes, and has to rush to catch it. His rush is not entirely accidental (more on this later), yet it causes the last-minute hassle just the same. To trace the process: First, he asks someone (unspecified, yet presumably the conductor; Luca speaks Italian in the scene, as he usually does when talking with a staff member) how long the train stops at Salerno. He then surmises that he has "enough time to go to the buffet to get lunch and buy the timetable" and "he jumps onto the platform" (Larbaud 1958, 681). Note that this is narrated in the third person—his action is not endorsed by his interiority but is observed from outside. The reason becomes obvious in the next chapter. "Until the minute he got off the train he was uncertain whether or not he would truly part ways with her, but now he is completely resolved" (ibid.). Thus, his action and his thinking around it are not in accordance, which results in the application of the third-person pronoun.

Yet shortly afterward, he asks himself: "And if I miss this train? Or if I let it go deliberately and return to Naples?" (ibid., 682). He considers the possibility of picking up his life as it was left off—as if nothing had happened, with excuses that seamlessly patch up the few hours of his absence. This thought does not fade in a moment but lingers in his mind. "Shall he return to Naples? He takes time in the book display at the kiosk, as if he wants to increase the chances of missing the train" (ibid.). Here the narration oscillates again to the third person, as if to shift the camera position to a short distance from which to focus on Luca.

The reason for Luca's intense self-inquiry is the crucial location of Salerno, where he is now: "Once I pass Salerno, the train returning to Naples that I can come across at other stations would not take me back to Vomero [the name of the street his apartment is on] until night falls. I must make up my mind" (ibid.). Thus Salerno is the point of no return. The first-person narration is now back, as if to suggest the intensity of his thought. "I" still hesitates—both about which book to buy, if any, and, more importantly, about whether or not to reboard the train. He talks to himself: "Pronti! I must make up my mind" (ibid., 682–83), he tells himself, repeating the same sentence as before. Luca then utters "Partenza!" (ibid., 683) at the end of chapter XI, which may be an echo of the station-master's shout that he has just heard, though it is not framed as such.[10] The removal of one layer of mediation creates a sense of immediacy and instantaneity, breaking through the barrier of his "innermost council." The call, though not unanticipated and meant for all passengers, has a decisive ring to it that sounds like an omen for the protagonist. Although it may be the conductor's utterance, Luca feels as if he owns its agency—as if it is his own inner voice that he hears.

The next chapter begins as follows: "Phew! Just in time. This is indeed my compartment? Yes. These newspapers that would have gone without me till Brindisi" (ibid.). Here Luca's sense of reunification of the self (with his belongings, and with his seat) is evident. The disintegration he experienced a moment earlier is now overcome, owing to the restoration of his affordances with things in space. His narration (in the first person now, as is evident in "mon" and "moi") anticipates what would have happened had he missed the train at the Salerno station, and how that would have affected the near future (in Brindisi). Thus, the narrative demonstrates the elasticity of time in yet another way: though Luca was bound to the train schedule, which marks a specific moment in absolute time as the departure time, and thus was obligated to make a decision during the fixed and mea-surable time, his experience of time is much more flexible; he is able to look back in time and look into an alternative future, and imagine the duration, rather than the isolated moments, of the trip that his newspapers would have made. Rushing to the train is, once again, enacted not only to confirm how enslaved human subjects are to absolute time but to show the many ways they can negotiate with time.

As mentioned earlier, Francis, the protagonist-focalizer-narrator of *Zone*, misses his flight and rushes by taxi from Charles de Gaulle to Gare de Lyon, just barely catching the train. As early as the first page, he con-firms his present location and its significance in the overall design of his travel: "I missed my plane I had 1,500 kilometres on the train ahead of me now I have six hundred still to go" (Énard 2010, 5; 2008, 11). These circumstances are elaborated on a number of times across the textual space.

To reconstruct the sequence of the protagonist's action in largely chronological order in story time: "I missed the plane and even more stupidly I rushed over to the train instead of waiting for the next flight" (Énard 2010, 35–36; 2008, 42). "I arrived at the Gare de Lyon this morning right on time, what a funny idea I hear myself saying on the phone, what a funny idea to come by train, I guess you have your reasons, I don't have any, I think, I simply missed the plane" (Énard 2010, 25–26; 2008, 32). It becomes evident that he was not thinking straight when he changed from plane to train, and that he has no viable explanation for the decision. This self-critical reflection characterizes his decision-making as instantaneous, which (though questionable in itself) helped him to catch the train "right on time."

The same sequence is then accounted for further: "I didn't know I was going to miss the plane, that I'd run to catch the nine o'clock train, just barely and without a ticket, my breath must have frightened the conductor, always these difficulties in leaving" (Énard 2010, 125; 2008, 130). This explains that the protagonist almost missed the train as well. Thus, the narrator illustrates his own state of agitation and respiration from the perspective of the conductor from whom he presumably purchased a ticket because he did not yet have one. The last word in the above quotation implies that he has experienced some last-minute confusion in the past. Instead of blessing himself for catching the train to successfully amend his travel plans, he keeps regretting missing the plane because the train's relative slowness is increasingly affecting him: "If I had caught the plane I'd have been in Rome for hours already" (Énard 2010, 127; 2008, 132), and, much later, "I could have been there at ten in the morning if I hadn't missed the plane, a trick of the gods without a doubt, a prank of Fate to punish me, with twelve hours on the train, this morning scarcely had the TGV gotten underway than I fell asleep" (Énard 2010, 317; 2008, 318–19). These repetitions remind the reader that Francis's current train ride is incidental, rather than deliberate, create a sense of fate associated with it, and thus emphasize that the journey's end is out of his hands. Moreover, it is not what time he arrives that matters to Francis; rather, it is the duration of the time he spends on the train and what he does with it ("twelve hours" "I fell asleep") versus the time he would have spent on the plane, or rather off the plane ("in Rome for hours"). Even in the obsessive attachment to the failure to oblige the timetable, Francis's sense of time is experience-oriented.

In contrast to Luca and Francis, the protagonist-focalizer of *Night Train to Lisbon*, Gregorius, makes his plan meticulously, albeit in a great hurry (within a day), yet encounters a similar hassle along the way. He nearly disrupts his own carefully coordinated plan: in Paris, where he must change trains at two stations, he asks the taxi driver to pause at the place of a strong memory with his ex-wife. He lets the taxi wait while he checks the inside of the restaurant and indeed enters another space-time. Accordingly, he almost misses his train:

> Lost in those distant events, Gregorius had forgotten the time and now the taxi driver had to drive at breakneck speed to get to Gare Montparnasse on time. When he finally sat breathless in his seat and the train for Irún started moving, a sense that had assaulted him in Geneva returned: that it was the train and not he who decided that this very awake and very real trip carrying him further out of his former life, hour after hour, station after station, would go on. (Mercier 2008, 37; 2004, 51–52)

Like the old man in *Sanshirō*, Luca in *My Most Secret Council*, and Francis in *Zone*, Gregorius is at the mercy of the unforgiving railway timetable, which is indifferent to the time set aside for remembering the past and adheres only to the absolute time that keeps ticking at a steady, relentless pace. After losing track of time at the restaurant, Gregorius must exert every effort to reclaim his membership in the society that is controlled by absolute time.

However, just like the other passengers who rush to the station to catch their train, his experience of time alters radically once he is safely within the carriage, where he experiences time differently both from his regulated life to date and from the rush he has just gone through. His time is thus elastic, accelerated at times while languid at others. In the above quotation, the passenger Gregorius resumes his reflections on his life so far, and anticipates the future into which he is being taken, without minding what time it is in the current moment. The experienced time/immanent time is thus elastic.

Just as it is the train that carries Gregorius forward into his new life, so it is his taxi that must hasten to arrive at the station. This transfer of agency is comparable to the case of Francis in *Zone*. Even though neither of the two characters has not run the course on his own feet, the rush leaves him "breathless." Yet now, as we also saw in the previous narratives, Gregorius is safely "in his seat" and sedentary, even as the train judiciously and resolutely moves forward, taking him away from where he had belonged geographically. As Gregorius reflects on the true agent of the travel (the train), he seems not as agitated as Francis, who may be trying to blame the train, but calm and content to leave his fate to the train.

Gregorius nearly misses a train once again, his last train ride in the narrative, at Salamanca. There he spends the two hours until his train's departure time in touring three properties to rent so as to come back and live in Salamanca, which would allow him to devote his life to translating Amadeu's book and learn from Estafania, his lover and professor at the university there. After verbally agreeing to rent two properties, he orders his taxi driver to drive around in the city:

> Then he rode back and forth through the city in the taxi. "Continue!" He said to the driver, "Siempre derecho, más y más!"
>
> When he was finally back at the railroad station, he made a mistake about the locker at first, and finally had to run to catch the train.
>
> In the compartment, he nodded off and woke up only when the train stopped in Valladolid. (Mercier 2008, 427; 2004, 482–83)

Gregorius yields to the temptation to stay in and explore Salamanca as long as possible, although he is aware of the time constraint. Despite his precarious heart condition, which he is returning to Bern to have checked, he runs, catches the train, and then falls asleep in the compartment, undoubtedly out of sudden relief and fatigue after physical exercise he is not accustomed to. Here, too, we see the pattern we have recognized in other narratives: time is experienced differently before and after the passenger catches the train in a great rush, biologically and existentially. The pace of time changes drastically: absolute time burdens and threatens the human subject in the name of the train schedule before the rush, while immanent time allows the passenger to experience time as he sees fit, once on the train.

2   Timetable's Tightening and Loosening Claws

The rigidity (or reliability) of the train schedule, as represented in the timetables. Cartographic space and chronological time—the two axes of modernity—inform and are informed by train timetables. In Meiji Japan, timetables were so popular, due to their practical necessity and extensive and meticulous organization, that they became sought-after books for publishing houses to release. The demand for timetables remains intense to this day. Timetables are fetishized by railway enthusiasts—whether trainspotters, or armchair travelers—as things to possess, collect, and archive. Passengers' obsession and frustration with timetables become prominent in the narratives under review in this chapter, and illustrate how passengers' experience of the space-time of the train journey contends with the paragon of modernity that the railway system epitomizes.

Scholars have studied timetables as well as other external sources from the historical moment in which *Sanshirō* is set, for facts about the railway journey in question (e.g., the presence of lunch vendors at stations) to identify trains that the eponymous character rides, and the stations at which other characters embark or disembark the train.[11] According to the scholars' research, the narrator's remark that the train to Nagoya is 40 minutes late cannot be verified; the only train with a final stop at Nagoya was supposed to arrive there at 22:39, so the train in the novel seems to be right on time. The novel may have invented the delay to agitate Sanshirō about finding a lodging quickly and calling it a day.

Scholars have successfully identified the second train that Sanshirō takes, from Nagoya to Shimbashi, on the historical timetable (departing at 8:00), as well as the train that departs Nagoya shortly after his in the direction of Yokkaichi (8:10), the destination of the woman who accompanies him to and from the inn (Makimura 2020, 17, 21). Thus, there is just enough time at the Nagoya station for the woman to offer a customary thanks for his assistance and a mental blow, "You're quite a coward, aren't you?" (Natsume 2018, 17; 1977, 9), and to see him embark at the platform, as well as for Sanshirō to look (though in vain) for the woman on the platform from the carriage window before he goes back to his seat, and realize he has been seen doing so by the man with the moustache. This first eye to eye encounter with the male passenger anticipates the vague inferiority Sanshirō will continue to feel in relation to the man for the rest of the train ride and beyond, so that the timing set by the timetable plays a crucial role in the plot. (If the woman's train was to depart sooner than Sanshirō's, then he would not have suffered the the moustachioed man's gaze upon him, as he tried to get a last glimpse of the woman who had startled him.)

The timetable affects the plot of *My Most Secret Council* significantly also, for the reasons already stated: the protagonist-focalizer-(main) narrator Luca's route is fundamentally changed due to the unavailability of a train for Messina, Sicily, the morning of his departure from Naples. Probably because Luca is less prepared for his new itinerary, he decides to buy a timetable at the Salerno station, to be on top of the course of his travel. Then he remembers an incident with his lover Isabelle over a time-table during a past trip: she insisted they had inadvertently left their time-table where they had dined before getting on the train, while he thought she had put it in her purse. They had a quarrel in the train carriage that ended with her finding the timetable in her purse and throwing it onto the seat. Although any other item in the couple's possession could have played the role of a lost article in this recollected sequence, the self-referentiality embodied by the timetable—the dispute occurred during their train ride—intensifies the narration in a centripetal force of attention toward the railway system. Although the timetable is supposed to make their railway trip more convenient and trouble-free, as a possession it creates more trouble in this case and affects their experience of the train negatively.

Something similar, yet even more evidently and hallucinatingly metafic-tional, takes place in *Zone*. The incident happened on a past trip that the protagonist Francis recollects. However, it is narrated in the present tense, effectively increasing the immediacy of the scene. On a night train from Prague to Paris via Frankfurt, Francis happens to share his compartment with another passenger, a Czech, who turns out to be a railway aficionado. Their conversation is incorporated into the narrative discourse without quotation marks, sometimes switching to a dialogue between first person and second person, as in free direct speech; at other times, as in free indi-rect speech, the other passenger is referred to in third person. The mean-dering narrative voice enhances the mesmerizing quality of the conversation:

> he looks at his watch before looking angrily out the window, it's dark out, he can't see anything, he goes back to his book, he often looks at me, ques-tioningly, he's burning to ask me a question, he asks me do you know if the train is stopping in Tetschen? Or at least that's what I understand him to say, I jabber in German that I have no idea, but it probably will, that's the last Czech city before the border, on the Elbe, the man speaks German, he agrees with me, the train must stop in Tetschen, even if it doesn't take on any passengers there, *wissen Sie*, he says, if we got out in Tetschen, we could get on the freight train that left Brno this afternoon a little before five o'clock, it would leave us in Dresden around two in the morning and we could catch this very train which isn't supposed to leave before 2:45, it's incredible, don't you agree—I agree, the man continues, his catalogue is actually a giant railroad timetable, there are *all* the trains here, do you understand, *all*, it's a little complicated to use but when you get the hang of it it's practical, it's for railroad professionals, for instance we've just passed a

train going in the other direction it's 9:23 well I can tell you where it's coming from and where it's going, if it's a passenger train or a freight train, with
such a book you never get bored when you travel in a train, he says seeming
very happy, how come he doesn't know if the train is stopping in Tetschen,
well it's very simple, very simple, see, the stop is in parentheses, which means
it's optional, but the stop is indicated, so we have the *possibility* of stopping
in Tetschen, we had another possibility for a stop a few minutes ago and you
never realized a thing, you didn't even notice that we *could* have stopped
there, *wir hatten die Gelegenheit,* you see this book is wonderful, it allows
you to know what we could have done, what we could do in a few minutes,
in the next few hours, even more, the little Czech man's eyes light up, all
eventualities are contained in this schedule, they are all here (Énard 2010,
50–51; 2008, 57–58)

With this timetable in hand, not only do you have time to kill at hand, but
also both reading about trains while on a train and observing other trains'
timing in relation to that of your own train are self-referential.[12] While
reading usually allows a passenger distance from the here and now, in this
case, the Czech passenger finds himself perpetually aware of his own bearing in space-time in relation to what he reads. This man's observation
reminds us that a passenger who appears to be sedentary is actually moving constantly and rapidly, in the eternally locomotive dynamic system of
trains. The passenger can even take advantage of the multiply mobile system of the trains to leap out of the carriage and into dislocating
possibilities.

Perhaps this much may be deemed simply peculiar. Yet the Czech passenger continues with further observations that are frighteningly self-
referential, not to Francis but to the reader:

You see everything is written here, pages twenty-six, 109 *et passim,* in either
case, whether you're there or not, the next connection will be on page
261 in the timetable, the Venice-Budapest express, where you'll get drunk
and sing "Three Drummer Book," then on page 263 you'll get into a freight
car headed for the Jasenovac extermination camp on the Sava river, then on
page 338 into a Benghazi-Tripoli train, you see, the Tangier-Casablanca
express is on page 361, all that will bring you to page 480 and the loss of a
kid you won't know, and so on, almost without your knowing it, to a final
Pendolino train *diretto* Milano-Roma that will carry you to the end of the
world, expected at the Termini station at 9:12 p.m., I listen attentively to
the little man's train litany, he is right, this catalogue is a magnificent tool,

the train professionals are lucky, I think, the man puts the book down and takes out another sandwich (Énard 2010, 52–53; 2008, 58–59)

Francis casually endorses the Czech man's general comment without realizing, either as the character in this scene or as the narrator, that there is something more: the page numbers, ostensibly of the timetable, that the Czech passenger cites, which are brought to the text through the mediation of Francis as the sole listener to his speech and also as the narrator, match exactly the page numbers of the original French edition of *Zone*, published by Actes Sud, in which these described topics are referred to. This perfect identification across levels of discourse thus blurs the boundaries between the storyworld that the characters inhabit and the world that the published book and its real readers occupy. This meta-level connection disorients the reader, who can no longer insouciantly hold the book in hand as though it is an entity independent of their own space-time, as has been presumed, and who cannot but feel threatened by the invasion of the narrative discourse into their readership.

This metafictional paradox (Hutcheon 1980) demonstrates the fact that the train is not merely a setting, or even a subject matter; rather, it controls and propels the narrative as its alter ego. Just as trains cross, meet, and miss each other, leaving behind some points and returning to others, so the narrative does so—especially this narrative, whose story (content) consists of crossing paths, meeting and leaving friends, enemies, and lovers, and whose discourse (form) contains quick changes of tracks and unexpected associations of locations and events, leaving some storylines behind as soon as they are launched and revisiting others over and again. Some departures are irrevocable, others recurrent; and memories are haunting, long forgotten yet spasmodically flashing through the mind, being connected to unrelated other memories through associations of landscapes, similar looks, references, and all the other cues that emerge out of blue.

Perhaps on the opposite pole to this all-encompassing, omniscient, and foreboding timetable is the blank one that appears in the embedded narrative of Amadeu's book in *Night Train to Lisbon*. An entry from this book on the subject of the railway that the extradiegetic narrator tells us Gregorius has already read many times is presented in the narrative discourse for the first time.[13] Gregorius chooses to read it again on his train to Coimbra, a route that Amadeu took countless times. Thus both the reading and the train ride are self-referential as well as repeated. On this interface of the two loaded actions stands the entry, which is entitled "ESTOU A VIVER EM MIM PR'OPRIO COM NUM COMBOIO A ANDAR. I LIVE IN MYSELF AS IN A MOVING TRAIN."[14] One of the many uncanny details is about the timetable: "Train schedules are available in the compartment. I want to see where we'll stop. The pages are empty. At the railroad stations where we stop, place signs are missing" (Mercier 2008, 370; 2004, 424). The blank timetable does not give any solid information to put the passenger's mind at ease. No route, no schedule is known to the passenger who is locked in the compartment and can only look out the window at other passengers similarly leaning their torsos out windows of the same train, trying in vain to see where the train is going. Here the railway clearly functions as a metaphor for life, yet not as the normally well-articulated system (as a product, vehicle, and symbol of modernity) but as its antithesis, an embodiment of uncertainty. Instead of assuring passengers of such systemic information, the timetable here offers nothingness. Rather than giving too much information to and engulfing the reader, as in *Zone*, the timetable here denies its readers knowledge and disavows their trust in it.

Human experience in and of life cannot be reduced to the place on a map and the moment in absolute time that a subject occupies who does not know their own bearing in space-time, which is itself amorphous. By visually (and philosophically) neutralizing the timetable in this small detail in *Night Train to Lisbon*, the narrative reflects on itself. Gregorius does not read Amadeu's book as a means to envision an autobiography. The manner in which he reads is fragmentary rather than linear, and the way his reading is represented in the narrative discourse is also sporadic and, as in this case, of varied frequency (i.e., many times in the story, only once in the discourse) and order (much earlier in the story, later in the discourse). The conventional autobiography's chronological and unidirectional time flow is complicated by this method of embedding Amadeu's book entries, juxtaposed with Gregorius's contact with Amadeu's former acquaintances and his musings about his own life. There is no timetable—no set course, no schedule—in life, in reading about life, and in life as reading.

3   SEAT DIRECTION/LOCATION

Whether absorbed in thought or observing/interacting with others on the train, the position and direction of the seat, the compartment, the corridor, the window, and other structural elements affect the psychological state of the passenger. Especially relevant is the trajectory of the passenger's seat vis-à-vis the train's direction; as one's body feels the train's movement and one's eye registers the moving landscape across the window, whether one is facing the train's front or its rear—and hence whether one's body is going forward or backward—has significant bearing on the emotions of the passenger. Furthermore, because the train carriage offers a public space-time, the seating arrangement creates non-negligible effects on the dynamics among passengers.

Annotators of *Sanshirō* in many editions of the novel have struggled to determine the seating arrangement in the carriage of the train to Nagoya in the novel's chapter 1. Factors to consider in their efforts are: (1) Sanshirō is able to look at the woman passenger once every few minutes; (2) when she leaves her seat and passes his side, he is able to see only her back; (3) when she comes back he is able to see her from the front; (4) she does not go back to her seat and looks out of the window on the same side as Sanshirō, one row away from him; (5) when Sanshirō throws the emptied lunchbox out of the window, it hits the woman's face; and (6) she moves to a seat diagonally opposite from Sanshirō's.

Scholars argue that (1) and (2) contradict each other: (1) indicates that they are facing in opposite directions and that the woman is seated across the center aisle from Sanshirō in an aisle seat (rather than a window seat), so that he can see her often; yet then she cannot possibly pass him by when he can only see her back. Tomatsu Izumi speculates that Sanshirō must have turned his head to take a look at the woman once every few minutes (Tomatsu 1992, 59), which seems highly unlikely because the narrator would have related such an odd behavior. According to annotations by Bando (Maruo), Matsushita, and Fujii, the standard train carriage structure of the time was divided into compartments (modeled after the UK trains), though they surmise that it seems unlikely that the train Sanshirō is on is of that type because it does not allow the range of self-positioning that the woman displays through and across the aisle in this sequence (Natsume 2018, 6; 1977, 3).

The way I read it, though tentatively, is that the woman is seated diagonally from Sanshirō, her seat facing the one next to his across the aisle. When she stands up to leave the seat, she does not exactly walk past his side, yet when she turns around to walk in the direction that Sanshirō faces, he feels the proximity of her body so much that it is described as her passing his side. Perhaps the rustle of her clothes can be heard or her scent can be breathed in when she stands in the aisle and revolves her body before she walks on, which Sanshirō describes as her passing him by. What is indeed on his side is not the woman's body per se but the aisle that she walks on, yet her body is close enough to be described as on his side. This works as a prelude to the woman positioning herself in front of him while his eyes are closed.

After the woman has returned and is standing in the row in front of his to take a look out of the open window, he throws the emptied lunchbox out his own window. The lunchbox hits her in the face, which indicates that he must be seated backward, facing the departure point rather than the destination, so that the woman's face, leaning out the window, is hit by the lunchbox he has tossed out his window a second earlier. One could read into this seating a certain nostalgia for Fukuoka, his homeland he has left behind, rather than for Tokyo, his destination.

Sanshirō's—or the narrator's—keen consciousness of the seating arrangement continues into the second leg of his railway journey. As mentioned earlier, he catches the eye of a man with a moustache, seated diagonally from his own seat, as he returns to it. Given the proximity and lack of any barrier between the two, their gazes can easily cross. After the passenger next to the man with the moustache disembarks at the Toyohashi station, Sanshirō anxiously looks out the window by his seat to verify that that passenger has not gotten off at the wrong station, since he had been sleeping until a moment before. Seeing him firmly walking on, Sanshirō takes the emptied seat. "Now he was sitting next to the man with the moustache," the narrator takes the trouble to confirm (Natsume 2018, 23; 1977, 12). The new positioning facilitates their conversation. The moustachioed man then pops his head out of the same window and buys some peaches, presumably from a vendor on the platform, and offers Sanshirō one fruit after another. Sharing of food may be easier between passengers in adjacent seats, rather than across the space between two double seats facing each other, because this carriage seems to have no tray-tables. Also, passengers feel more comfortable when seated side-by-side rather than face-to-face, because they can listen and speak without looking at each other. Later, this seating also allows them to share the same window (rather than taking turns), when they observe Westerners on the platform of the Hamamatsu station (Natsume 2018, 27; 1977, 14–15).

The positionality of the passenger vis-à-vis landscape to be seen from the window plays a significant role in *My Most Secret Council*. Coastlines along the Tyrrhenian and Ligurian seas help Luca, the protagonist-focalizer-(main) narrator, to restore his sense of direction, and his bearing in space, while seated in the moving vehicle of the train. Soon after he takes a seat in the compartment, facing in the direction of his destination, he begins to talk to himself as "vous":

> Luca, you must get used this idea: you have been expecting to leave Salerno, to follow a curve bent toward your right, and along the seashore. Yet it will be toward the left that you will be led, climbing the central ridge of the peninsula, then going down toward another sea that has a beautiful name: the Ionian. Announce the change of your sense of direction and your sense of geography, for those senses of yours deserve so much consideration, and those senses suffer for no reason, yet in a way perceptible to us, when we are in our apartment in Berthollet Street, [so that] it is impossible for us to say: Orléans is in front of me, slightly on the right, and Nancy is almost facing my left ear. Here, there is no room for doubt. If you are seated on the seat at 3/4, facing the locomotive that was just linked to the trains, then it has Taranto right in front of it, and is turning your back on Vomero, resolutely. (Larbaud 1958, 664)

The narrator-protagonist appreciates the clarity in the direction taken by the train: there is no confusion about which way the passenger is going or how the passenger's body is situated in relation to cartographic places. From the window, Luca can confirm the current location visually during the daytime, especially when the tracks run along the coastline or other recognizable geographical structures. The driving force of the locomotive is also an orientation that the train passenger can rely on and yield to. In interior space such as that of Luca's apartment in Naples, the sense of direction deteriorates and is obliterated, in exchange for the protection of the stasis and confinement. In contrast, passengers, being pulled in a certain direction toward a destination and being securely positioned as they observe outside, can verify their sense of direction in the train carriage, bestowed with the unique and definitive combination of mobility and sedentariness—two seemingly contradictory states, as theorized by Bissell (2009) and pointed out in *Zone* (Énard 2010, 83; 2008, 90).

Importantly, Luca's route is linear yet not straight: it forms a loop, and thus his way of leaving Naples will bring him closer to Naples—not cartographically, but itinerary-wise. He does not buy a return ticket, but he plans to return to Naples "within two weeks at most":

He will probably see Irene the day of his arrival—what time will the train from Sicily[15] arrive? Perhaps it may be the day after.

To depart this way means to get closer to Irene. It is true. Because this departure will remove a massive obstacle—indeed, the massive obstacle that hinders everything …

So when he embarks the train for Messina in a little while, he will mutter to himself: "I am going in Irene's direction." (Larbaud 1958, 655)

According to Luca's idea, the geographic departure from Naples means the chronological approach to the eventual arrival in Naples. Thus, the sense of direction may be bent cartographically but remains linear chronologically.

In contrast to Luca's clear vision of and confidence in his route, Amadeu, in the embedded narrative of his book in *Night Train to Lisbon*, expresses great anxiety about his lack of bearings while riding the train—not any real train he has boarded, but a fantastic train that is another form of life:

> *I didn't board voluntarily, didn't have the choice and don't know the name of the destination. […] I can't get off. I can't change the tracks or the direction. I don't determine the pace. I don't see the locomotive and can't see who's driving it and whether the engineer makes a reliable impression. I don't know if he reads the signals correctly and notices if a switch is worked wrong. […] The train makes a soft curve. The last cars are still in the tunnel and the first are going on. Maybe the train is travelling in a circle, over and over, without anybody noticing it, not even the engineer? I have no idea how long the train is. I see all the others craning their necks to see and understand something. I call a greeting, but the wind blows away my words.* (Mercier 2008, 369–70; 2004, 423)

In addition to the unreliability of the timetable, which we have already seen, Amadeu's distrust of the engineer and also of the conductor (who he believes has locked him in his compartment) becomes evident. The system of this railway lacks transparency, order, and certainty. The possibility that "the train is travelling in a circle" (rather than on a linear and finite route with a set departure point and a destination) illustrates the embedded story's radical challenge to what facilitates the railways and what they symbolize. The lack of professional accountability in the engineer and the conductor adds to the chaos of the system.

Maria João, Amadeu's first girlfriend and steadfast confidante, understands his ambivalence toward the railways: trains fascinate him yet horrify him. He thus must position her, a trusted friend, not on the same train by which he is traveling but on the platform—a platform of a peculiar kind. In her words:

> He loved trains, they were a symbol of life for him. I would like to have traveled in his compartment. But he didn't want me there. He wanted me on the platform, he wanted always to be able to open the window and ask me for advice. And he wanted the platform to go along when the train started moving. Like an angel, I was to stand on the moving platform, on the angel's platform sliding there at exactly the same speed. (Mercier 2008, 351; 2004, 403)

The ultimate companionship cannot be found within the train carriage, but instead should be on the platform. The confidante should not be affected by the uncertainty of the train ride, as Amadeu is. Yet while the train is on the move, Amadeu needs the platform, terra firma, to be moving along for him, to share his anxiety with Maria and to receive her advice. Due to the trains being "a symbol of life"—as confirmed in Amadeu's own writing as well—he cannot leave them but must be always aboard—alone, his confidante elsewhere, yet available to offer him security.

"But a train isn't circular, it goes from one point to another" (Énard 2010, 6; 2008, 12)—so says Francis in *Zone*, though he, too, has an overwhelming sense of disorientation. This remark is, rather, an effort to convince himself of the worthiness and purposiveness of the train journey that he is about to resume at Milan Central Station. He observes the gigantic station from within and notes: "You find yourself alone in an immense freezing train station obsessed by a destination that is in front of you and behind you at the same time" (Énard 2010, 6; 2008, 12). This aporia can be explained as an entanglement of the figurative and the literal: the destination is "in front of" the passenger figuratively because it is where they are going, yet it can be also "behind" the passenger literally, especially if they travel in a backward-facing seat toward their destination.

Francis takes just such a seat in the carriage, backward to the direction of the train. "I turn round once more in my seat my head facing right towards the great void outside, going backwards, I'm going backwards my back to my destination and to the meaning of history which is facing forward, history which is taking me directly to the Vatican, with a suitcase full

of names and secrets" (Énard 2010, 127; 2008, 132). The last line suggests a cynicism toward the normative history that adopts linear and unidirectional chronology, with no uncertainty about the order of events.
With his back to the future and his face to the past, Francis's positioning
literally defies "the meaning of history" or the itinerary of this journey:

> in the middle of middle-class Emilia, a train where the travellers are all sit-
> ting nicely, a car of passengers ignoring each other, pretending not to see the
> fate they share, these shared kilometres entrusted to the Great Conductor
> friend of model railways of halberds and of the end of the world, some fac-
> ing forward and others with their back to their destination, like me, their
> gaze turned to the rear, to black night, to Milan the departure station
> (Énard 2010, 156; 2008, 161–62)

As the train changes its direction at Florence, a cul-de-sac, so Francis's
physical direction shifts from backward to forward: "We're leaving in the
other direction, like Santa Lucia in Venice or Termini in Rome Santa Maria
Novella is a dead-end, we start up again, now I'm facing my destination,
Rome is in front of me" (Énard 2010, 330; 2008, 333). With this change
of direction and the fact that Florence is the last station before Rome,
Francis's fate seems to be settled as indisputable. He appears now ready to
accept his destiny as well as destination. Yet this does not stop his endless
reflection on the past, personal and collective, and his panic over the inevi-
tability of the consequences of the trip intensifies further.

4   Interaction with Other Passengers

As Komori Yōichi has discussed, tangential meeting with strangers on the
train was made possible by the modern state-building that Japan anxiously
engaged in. After the Russo-Japanese War (1904–5), the railway system
throughout Japan was largely nationalized, and citizens were able to travel
across the country with greater convenience because the war had demanded
the extension of the railways for military transportation purposes (Komori
1996, 313). It had been unimaginable until then for people from different
families, neighborhoods, and regions, and of different genders and social
classes, to share a space for a long duration of time. In *Sanshirō*, the old
man who rushes into the train and the woman who later manipulates
Sanshirō engage in a conversation in which they talk about their families,
both affected seriously by the recent war. Their willingness to share

personal details with a stranger is a by-product of the modern device of the train. This was how passengers learned to use the train's peculiar space-time for activities other than those aimed toward nationalistic goals (ibid., 314–15).

Even though Sanshirō's attention expended on the old man is divided and secondary—since the narrator reveals that he takes time to observe the woman more attentively when the old man is about to be seated (Natsume 2018, 7; 1977, 4)—it is undeniable that the old man's manners leave a strong impression on Sanshirō's mind: to expose one's skin so liberally in public, especially a scarred skin showing signs of paramedical treatment—something others may consider quite private—demonstrates either the old man's lack of awareness of his body as a spectacle to the public eye or his not minding being seen. Since he is soon to get off the train and the story, the function of his action is to demonstrate the heterogeneity of the train space-time that passengers of varying levels of decorum, discretion, and awareness of the spectacle-spectator dynamic share with each other.

Sharing the train carriage, however, does not mean equality or solidarity between passengers. Despite the initial awkwardness (discussed earlier) that Sanshirō feels about the moustachioed man, he does not lose his footing entirely but looks at the man and assesses his social standing ("if he was riding in the third-class coach, he could not be anyone of consequence"; Natsume 2018, 22; 1977, 12). After this, they finally speak to each other—about a newspaper lying between the sleeping man and the moustachioed man, and thus right in front of Sanshirō's eyes. After Sanshirō has "made a point of asking the man with the moustache" whether the newspaper is available, the man says "Go ahead" (Natsume 2018, 21; 1977, 11), that no one is reading it. This exchange questions the ownership of a thing in public space. The newspaper belongs to the sleeping man, yet because he is not in a state to grant or deny Sanshirō permission to read it, Sanshirō instead asks permission of the moustachioed man, "ma[king] a point of asking" ("wazato," or "deliberately," in the original), and receives it even though the latter does not own the newspaper.[16] What Sanshirō requests and receives, then, is not permission per se but an accomplice in using someone else's possession without their permission. Here we see social relations being formed through negotiation of affordance, in the train carriage in which strangers may share their belongings.

The protagonist-focalizer of *My Most Secret Council*, Luca, shows no hesitation in buying a first-class ticket at the Naples station, whether to Messina as originally intended or for Taranto-Brindisi as the alternative route (Larbaud 1958, 663). Obviously he can afford it but, more importantly, he can exploit privacy and solitude to listen to his innermost voice—his "most secret council," as in the title—to reflect on his life so far and deliberate on his life from then on. Invigorated by coffee he purchased at the station and pleased by the scent of the cigar he is smoking in the first-class compartment, he hopes that "this carriage will become his little room" (ibid., 664); he prays to God that no one will come into his compartment to take an empty seat (ibid., 689). His wish is granted: at least until he falls asleep at the end of the narrative, he remains secluded from other passengers, with no mention of anyone else on the train.

Francis, the protagonist-focalizer-(main) narrator in *Zone*, is very conscious of incidental "neighbors" ("viosins") around his seat, as well as those whom he finds in the bar. Around his seat, which appears to be on the narrower side of the aisle—a single column between the aisle and the window, facing the other single seat—are a few passengers who are repeatedly described:

> The long list of those I had observed for a while just as I am now observing the passengers in this oppressively hot train car, the crossword enthusiast and his wife, I could offer them my dictionary for their puzzles if they weren't Italian, my neighbour the *Pronto* reader, in front of me the heads I can glimpse, a blond girl, a bald man, further on boy scouts or something similar with scarves and whistles on a chain, I can still see them with my eyes closed, a professional habit maybe (Énard 2010, 123; 2008, 128)

The initial "neighbor" opposite Francis reads *Pronto*[17] so intently that it motivates Francis to read as well (more on this later). The woman who, at Florence, takes the seat left empty by "the *Pronto* man" at Bologna does not even glance at Francis and is absorbed in reading a book, which again motivates Francis to resume reading his. Francis affords attention to a couple across the aisle, on the wider side, where two sit across from another pair of seats facing in the opposite direction: the man, whom Francis imagines to be a professor of violin, is absorbed in a crossword puzzle, while the woman, often seen asleep with her head on his shoulder, is supposed by Francis to be the professor's former pupil (though she appears to him more like a flautist or harpist) and now his wife. These

observations show how attentive to detail Francis is, partly from his training as a spy, and also how imaginative he is; he is able to weave a narrative
about a stranger based on his keen observations.[18] Yet another and perhaps
more important reason for such descriptions is to alert the reader to the
heterogeneity of the passenger experience of the space-time of the train
carriage. Even though the train is a shared space, according to the passengers' time (or timing), inclinations, and physical and mental conditions
(e.g., sleepy, tired, bored), they are not exactly sharing the same spatial
experience. It is a smooth space into which anyone can step and across
which anyone can move, but not without variations in activities and situations, not to mention affects.[19]

Francis takes in some behaviors of other passengers in the train bar, and
despite his drunkenness his observations are clear and coherent: "a couple
enters the bar they ask for a mineral water and a beer before going back to
second class" (Énard 2010, 258; 2008, 261). Likewise, when he returns
to the bar later:

> the swaying makes me stagger in the middle of the car I almost sprawl onto
> an offended nun, she must have gotten on in Florence I hadn't noticed her
> before, there always has to be a nun in an Italian train, a nun some Boy
> Scouts some bohemian musicians a *Pronto* reader a spy a pretty blonde and
> an illegal immigrant, all the characters needed for a play or a genre film, or
> even a canvas by Caravaggio (Énard 2010, 367; 2008, 369)

He remembers the blonde woman and boy scouts (noted in the previous
quotation), though not the nun (hitherto unmentioned), which reassures
the reader as to the reliability of Francis's observation and memory, as well
as to how accustomed to and competent he is at cataloguing strangers
around him. His comparison of the scene to a play, a genre film, or a can-
vas by Caravaggio illustrates how a jumble of incidental passengers can
share the same space-time of the train, just as different characters can end
up in the deliberate composition of an artwork.

Night Train to Lisbon shows the protagonist-focalizer Gregorius's keen
sensibility toward the exact seating arrangement, distance from other passengers, and their and his own affordances (i.e., how they use things in the
shared space of the carriage). Gregorius notes any touch or sound their
clothes or belongings make (e.g., the rustle of silk stockings when a female
passenger crosses her legs; Mercier 2008, 428; 2004, 483). He remains
sensitive to the immediate environment while being absorbed most of the

time in recollections of his own past or in reading and contemplating the contents of Amadeu's book. In other words, he oscillates between elsewhere and other moments in history and the "here and now," in both cases, fully taking in the effects.

In the narrative, inconsiderate and vulgar passengers talk loudly among themselves without regard to other passengers in their proximity, and disturb the peace for Gregorius. When encountering French tourists who behave that way, he grabs his luggage and leaves for first class, even though it is out of character for him to travel in that class (Mercier 2008, 32; 2004, 46). His impatience with such passengers flickers in another moment on his way back home, at Gare de Lyon, this time when he is disturbed by Swiss tourists. "Tourists—such a sad word!" (Larbaud 1958, 690), says Luca in *My Most Secret Council*, before offering a sizeable commentary on the status of travelers in Europe. He cites a hotel manager's word that those travelers who reveal in their behavior where they are from are "of the second-rate" (ibid.). To extend this remark to the context of *Night Train to Lisbon*, Gregorius is not a tourist, as he has taken in all the space-times and has evolved consequently.

Gregorius is not unwilling to communicate with other passengers who are not imposing themselves on his space-time. On the second leg of his railway journey, from Paris to Irún, some Portuguese passengers are about to get off the train, mistaking the station for their destination. Gregorius speaks to them in Portuguese, saying, "This isn't yet Irún" (Mercier 2008, 42; 2004, 59). It is the first time he speaks in Portuguese in real life, beyond replying to the recorded tape of the language lesson. The foreign accent in his speech makes the passengers hesitate to take his word for it, but, seeing the station sign, they realize he is right and thank him in Portuguese. Although this is a simple episode, the narrator notes that "Gregorius [is] never to forget this scene" (Mercier 2008, 43; 2004, 59).[20] He has entered a new stage, in which if he speaks to another person in Portuguese, it causes an effect. That this happens with strangers whom he may never meet again is important: the space-time of the train journey across lingual boundaries (in this case, from a German-speaking area to a Francophone zone to a Spanish-speaking region to a Portuguese-speaking area) grants such opportunities, without pressuring a beginner in a language to either speak fluently or remain silent. The multilingual and forgiving environment of the long-distance transnational train journey serves as an important transition in the life of the protagonist-focalizer, which is emphasized by the narrator of *Night Train to Lisbon*.

A decisive encounter with a passenger occurs in the sleeper from Irún to Lisbon. The compartments around Gregorius's own are empty. He and the passenger in the nearest occupied compartment spot each other for the first time in the corridor as each stands outside the door to his compartment, with no distraction to the line of his sight. They then exchange a "Good night" ("Boa noite") with each other, and Gregorius sees that his foreign accent is noted and congenially received by the other. After an incident in the dining car (discussed later, in the section on interaction with the railway staff), the two passengers speak in French and introduce themselves. The other passenger, José António da Silveira (thereafter referred to as Silveira), a ceramics company executive, confesses to Gregorius that he travels on business frequently by rail because he is "afraid of flying" (Mercier 2008, 46; 2004, 62). Although the narrator does not remind the reader in this instance, we know from earlier in the narrative that Gregorius renounces traveling by airplane for its lack of authenticity in experience of space: "Getting on an airplane and arriving a few hours later in a completely different world with no time to take in individual images of the road—he didn't like it and it bothered him. *It's not right*, he had said to Florence" (italics in the original, to demarcate a quotation from Gregorius's memory archive from the narrator's discourse; Mercier 2008, 18; 2004, 30). Air travel does not grant the passenger an opportunity to appreciate the spatial continuity between the departure point and the destination through the change of scenery, and thus is "*not right*" ("*nicht richtig*"). This episode functions as a prelude to Gregorius's conviction that he must find a way to get to Lisbon by rail no matter how many hours it may take (Mercier 2008, 27; 2004, 41). Knowing this by the time of Silveira's statement, the reader may sense that Silveira has a qualification to become Gregorius's kindred spirit.

Indeed, Silveira becomes one. When Gregorius explains in Silveira's compartment how he comes "to be in this train," Silveira listens carefully and then falls silent, which makes Gregorius worry that he has said too much to this stranger whom he has just met. Yet it turns out that Silveria's silence is due to his careful consideration, rather than rejection, of what he has heard, for when he opens his mouth he asks Gregorius to repeat the quotation from Marks Aurelius's book that Gregorius has mentioned, writes it down in his notebook, and goes over the sentence with his pen in hand as the latter leaves him (Mercier 2008, 46; 2004, 63). This type of listening and asking pertinent questions about what Gregorius cares about becomes a pattern in the conversations between Silveira and Gregorius through the rest of the narrative.

A different yet also appreciable companionship with a stranger on the train is developed much later in *Night Train to Lisbon*. On his return journey, Gregorius shares a compartment from Lisbon to Irún with a woman who, after changing trains in the same way as he does, though separately, at Irún for Paris Gare Montparnasse, passes by his compartment first, then turning her head to recognize him, walks back and hesitantly comes into his compartment. She then proposes sharing a ride from Gare Montparnasse to Gare de Lyon, and finally takes the same compartment in the sleeper from Paris to Lausanne, where she gets off. They do not talk much—only when they have something simple to discuss, such as Gregorius's question (they speak in French) about the use of the word "glory" in Portuguese ("glória"), which would enhance his comprehension of a section in Amadeu's book (though he does not disclose the context to her; Mercier 2008, 429; 2004, 484). Yet obviously they feel comfortable to share the close space-time of the train compartment. Mostly silent and reading their own books, contemplating on their own, or sleeping at different times, they share togetherness in silence. They neither disturb nor ignore each other. She leaves, without exchanging names or addresses with Gregorius, with the simple words, "This was fine" ("»C'était bien, ça«"; Mercier 2008, 432; 2004, 488). Unlike the case with Silveira, there is no consequence, for better or worse: this is a one-time companionship, on a one-way train ride in three legs, and does not extend to a friendship beyond the railway journey. Yet they appreciate each other and the space-time they experience together. It is thus deemed worth recounting at length, for the considerable duration in discourse time, even though the woman remains nameless and does not have any effect on the plot.[21]

5   SOMETHING TO READ

While traveling on a fixed route and on a relatively reliable schedule, the passenger travels to yet another space-time by reading. The protagonist–(main) focalizer of each narrative examined here is an avid reader, and thus each text becomes notably intertextual when their books are mentioned. At times, the contents of their books converge with the narratives of the train journeys they are taking.

Sanshirō is about to enroll in the Faculty of Letters at the Imperial University of Tokyo, and has a book by Francis[22] Bacon and a few others in his suitcase. Not by choice, however; rather, as the narrator explains, and thus deems it important for the reader to know, he has simply thrown into the suitcase those books his checked luggage could not contain. He cannot become absorbed in a book but instead keeps thinking about the incident with the aforementioned female passenger. He is even conscious that the Bacon book is a facade. As we will see in Chap. 6, books are often used as shields for privacy from other passengers with whom one does not wish to interact. In this case, although no one is speaking to Sanshirō, the moustachioed man glances at him occasionally—glances that Sanshirō can avoid by keeping his eyes glued to Bacon, page 23. Later, he borrows a fellow passenger's newspaper, which he doesn't find particularly engaging, either.

It is notable that the moustachioed man is not reading anything, even though he is a teacher at The First College, or Ichi-kō, in Tokyo, as we learn later, so that he may well be accustomed to reading. This is not his first journey on this route, so that he is not captivated by the landscape outside the window, either. The way he uses his time—or does not use his time—is the antithesis of the idea of time as a resource to be invested in productive or entertaining activities. Instead of using time for some purpose, he is experiencing it just for the sake of itself. This is similar to the way Luca in *My Most Secret Council* spends time on the train, though Luca's valuing of time otherwise seems completely different from that of the moustachioed man in *Sanshirō*.

Luca is an aspiring poet, so it is not surprising that he frequently cites literary sources. Among them is Virgil's *Géorgics* (Larbaud 1958, 689).[23] As Luca prepares for the trip, he considers taking with him a book by Thomas de Quincey (ibid., 658), presumably *The Caesars*, which he is seen reading earlier, as he tries to stay awake so that he won't miss a morning train as planned (ibid., 652). He decides against taking the de Quincy because he thinks he won't be able to read it while on the train and will be able to find it once he gets to Sicily (his initial destination)—perhaps in paperback, in the "Tauchnitz" edition (ibid., 658) by the Leipzig publisher of Anglophone authors.[24] Instead he purchases some French fashion magazines at the Naples station, "without checking the titles" (ibid., 667),[25] and browses books at the Salerno station, but only by the names of authors, listed in quick succession and with some repetition—"D'Anunzio. D'Anunzio. Serao, Serao, Serao"—presumably glancing at their spines on a shelf without opening their pages (ibid., 682). These decisions indicate his view that one should have something to read while traveling on a train alone, and that serious books are not suitable for the purpose, even if one reads such books at home. He does not read, however, and instead recalls passages from books he has already read and stored in his memory archive. Thus, reading is not undertaken but remembered while Luca travels by rails. This expands the train's space-time yet another way.

In *Zone*, Francis reads on and off a story about a Palestinian female fighter, Intissar, by the Lebanese author Rafael Kahla.[26] He is captivated by the story while reading it, yet takes long breaks before picking it up again where he left off. He finishes the story by the time he arrives in Rome. The book is first mentioned as follows: "I have a little book in my bag, three stories by a Lebanese writer named Rafael Kahla recommended to me by the bookseller on the Places des Abbesses, a handsome book on slightly ochre laid paper, barely a hundred pages, how much time would I need to read them let's say a page a kilometre that would take up a good part of the 500 milestones left to travel" (Énard 2010, 46; 2008, 52). Francis is motivated to read the book because his neighbor is engrossed in reading a tabloid. The simulation or influence of the other passengers becomes a pattern for his reading from this point on. Francis carefully calculates the time he would need to read this book according to the distance the train will cover, rather than calculating the time it takes the train to reach Rome or the pace at which he reads. Thus, the physical distances outside the train and inside the book are matched, as if to suggest that the train and the passenger will proceed together, respectively exploring the world around him and the storyworld of the book. Yet at this first moment of temptation to read the book, he decides against it: "I put the little book on my fold-out tray, don't have the courage, I feel feverish exhausted by the drugs and the day before, I have a pain in my right temple, I'm sweating and there's a slight trembling in my hands—I close my eyes, might as well return to the Dardanelles or to Venice, to Cairo or Alexandria" (Énard 2010, 46; 2008, 53). Despite the desire to escape the here and now, Francis's physical condition is such that reading a book is not an enticing proposition. Instead he chooses to recall scenes from his past.

The book thus remains merely part of the material conditions of the passenger's surroundings. But not for long. Now that the book is no longer in Francis's bag but within his sight, it asserts its presence: "The little Lebanese book winks at me on the tray-table, why not go there after all dive into it go out of myself for a bit enter the imagination of Rafael Kahla and his stories, for lack of Dalton Trumbo and *Johnny Got His Gun*, the slightly textured paper is pleasant to the touch, let's see if the bookseller on the Place des Abbesses was mocking me or not:"[27] (Énard 2010, 54; 2008, 60–61). This marks the end of chapter III, and chapter IV consists in its entirety of a quotation from Kahla's book, out of which Francis reemerges into his present world shortly after the beginning of chapter V, saying, "what a story I wonder if it's true Intissar pretty name I imagine her beautiful and strong, I am luckier than her" (Énard 2010, 65; 2008, 73).

Francis does not immediately continue reading the rest of the book, however, instead delving back into his own recollections. The book remains not only in his sight but also in his consciousness, as an engaging story, yet it takes a while for him to choose it over recollections of friends and lovers. He considers resuming reading the book in chapter VII—"I close my eyes, where would I like to go now, to Beirut the blue to find the Palestinians again and Intissar in the little cream-coloured book, not yet, or to..." (Énard 2010, 146; 2008, 152)—and tries to convince himself that there "is nothing I desire more then than a novel, where the people are characters, a play of masks and desires, and little by little to forget myself, forget my body at rest in this chair, forget my apartment building, Paris, life itself as the paragraphs, dialogues, adventures, strange worlds flow by, that's what I should be doing now, going on with Rafael Kahla's story, finding Intissar the Palestinian again and Marwan dead on a corner in Beirut, a journey within the journey, to ward off fatigue, thoughts, the shaky train, and memories" (Énard 2010, 150; 2008, 155). Still, his self-reflection is more captivating. Although he notes that his neighbor across the aisle is reading, and tells himself "that's what I should do, go back to my book, find Intissar" (Énard 2010, 278; 2008, 281), his resolve wanes: "I'm too sleepy to go on reading" (Énard 2010, 283–84; 2008, 286). He finally returns to the book, saying: "Rafael Kahla [...] in his elegant little book, [...] what will happen to the noble Intissar, where was I, I ear-marked a page, here:"[28] (Énard 2010, 290; 2008, 292), which, in a manner similar to the first reading of the book, ends chapter XII, followed by chapter XIII, which is entirely a quotation from the book, and a remark by Francis soon after the beginning of chapter XIV: "what a story I wonder if it's true Intissar washes Marwan's body it's very sad all that so sad, I'd have liked to wash Andrija's body caress it with a sponge one last time, the stories intersect" (Énard 2010, 313; 2008, 315).

Francis's repeated query as to whether the story is based on true events may sound naïve, yet it turns out to be profound. Indeed, the book does not distract him from endless remembrances, as he has hoped it would; instead, it revitalizes memories of his best friend Andrija's death (and Francis's desertion of his friend's body to save himself from the enemy's attack), and leads him to imagine an alternative, better end to their friendship, inspired by the work of fiction. As Francis notes, "the stories intersect," thereby intensifying the impact of the past that Francis is trying to forget—not only during the train ride but *by means of* the train ride, the journey to the Vatican, and by taking on a new identity and starting a new life: "farewell Marman farewell Andrija and shit now I'm crying, this story made me cry I wasn't expecting this, it's unfair I rub my eyes turn my head to the window so no one sees me [...] that story is taking me back without me realizing it, too many details, too many things in common, better set the book down for now" (Énard 2010, 315; 2008, 317). Failing to distract himself from the past and the present, Francis is struck by the parallels between his life and the fictional character's. His remark that "I didn't cry much and now almost ten years later I'm weeping like a schoolgirl" (Énard 2010, 315; 2008, 317) suggests the power of fiction—it is not that he is or has been immune to the real events, but that he has just now been awakened to a deep shock he has been numb to while reading a comparable story.

The next time we see Francis return to the book, his eyes linger on its cover: "I pick up the book on the tray, Rafael Kahla was born in Lebanon in 1940, says the back cover, and lives today between Tangier and Beirut, strange phrase" (Énard 2010, 346–47; 2008, 349). This finding of the author's location—or locations, or in-betweenness of his bearing—ignites another chain of remembrances for Francis. After a long detour, during which he walks to the bar, leaving the book on the tray-table, and stays there for a while, he finally turns to the story's conclusion: "opposite me the lady who got on in Florence does't even glance at me absorbed in her book, I'll pick mine up again, I want to know what will happen to Intissar, maybe she can save me, she was washing Marwan's body in the hot Beirut night, and now:"[29] (Énard 2010, 436; 2008, 438). Again the seemingly intensive reading of the passenger who is facing Francis motivates him to read as well. The quotation above marks the end of a chapter once again, this time chapter XIX, and in a familiar pattern, chapter XX consists in its entirety of a quotation from Kahla's book. It begins with "And now" (the capital letter as in the original, indicating that this is a quotation and does not follow the style of the frame narrative of which Francis is the narrator), repeating the words that end Francis's free direct discourse/interior monologue just quoted, like ripples washing the shoreline between the physical world surrounding him and the storyworld of the fictional characters. The end of chapter XX coincides with the end of the story,[30] and chapter XXI begins with: "what a story poor Intissar Marwan puts his gun in her hand, his ghost saves her, there are loves, promises that withstand death, especially in books, books and plays" (Énard 2010, 444; 2008, 445). (Intissar was about to be raped when she kills the perpetrator with the gun left by her deceased lover Marwan.) Although the circumstances may not correspond to any in Francis's past so directly as in the previous instance, he immediately begins to consider it personally, wondering whether he has ever saved anyone as Marwan does:

> sometimes you come across books that resemble you, they open up your chest from chin to navel, stun you, I'd like to have Marwan's nobility, is that still possible, let's think about it Yvan what are we going to do in Rome aside from getting properly plastered taking a bath and treating ourselves to a new suit, dark and luxurious, how to become Marwan, tomorrow morning, once the money is acquired and the dead in the suitcase are buried in the Vatican archives, what am I going to do with the piece of gold of Charon the ferryman, how to set death's obol on each eye of all my corpses (Énard 2010, 445; 2008, 446)

Francis, having stolen a deceased person's identity and expecting to receive from the Vatican a considerable reward for the suitcase full of secret information, now has a model to compare himself to, which gives a clear shape to his hitherto ambiguous hesitation about his plan. He admits "I haven't saved anyone, [...] neither Andi nor Vlaho, and no one has saved me, not Marianne nor Stéphanie nor Sashka" (Énard 2010, 444; 2008, 445), considering all his friendships and relationships, including, significantly, the last one, Sashka, whom he has planned to be together with in his new life. Francis's life has not been like Marwan's, and it will never be—this is a revelation for him.

Francis is not a naïve reader, easily swayed by sentimental fiction or likely to confuse fiction with reality, as the following passage confirms: "I wonder if Rafael Kahla is like me, why does he write these terrifying stories, did he try to strangle his wife like Lowry, or did he kill her like Burroughs, did he incite people to hatred and murder like Brasillach or Pound, maybe he's a victim like Choukri the wretched, or a man three times vanquished like Cervantes" (Énard 2010, 445; 2008, 445–46). His realization that he himself falls short of "nobility" and a profound commitment to relationships is founded on his wide reading knowledge and competence in literature. His wondering "Who will wash my body once I'm dead" (Énard 2010, 445; 2008, 446) thus comes across not as sentimental longing for a caring lover but as surrender to the final verdict of what he is and what he cannot be, after long and careful deliberation over a six-hour-long, 500-kilometer-long, or 444-page-long journey, partly through a story he reads yet cannot be part of.

Structurally, the way the story of Intissar is embedded into the frame narrative in fragments—at varying intervals, and with comparable yet also distinct reactions on Francis's part—evokes the complexity of time experienced on the train. Although the train schedule is never far from the reading passenger's mind, the act of voluntary reading cannot be articulated by absolute time. Rather, the act of reading (and not reading) variates the pace of time spent, with hesitation, motivation, distraction, resignation, and other emotions variously affecting it. In *Zone*, the time the protagonist-focalizer spends on the train and the time it takes him to narrate that time go along with each other. Thus coordinated, the pace of reading and that of embedding another narrative in the discourse are synchronized with each other, enhancing the effect of the narrative rhythm with the irregular yet repetitive rhythm of the story.

For Gregorius in *Night Train to Lisbon*, a book is the whole reason he travels by rail from Bern to Lisbon—namely, Amadeu's book, *Um Ourives das Palavras* (*A Goldsmith of Words*), which he first notices when another customer, a young woman who only appears in this scene, contemplates it for so long in the Spanish bookstore that Gregorius visits to find something to read about Portugal (Mercier 2008, 16; 2004, 27). After she has left the bookstore empty-handed, the bookstore owner, noticing Gregorius's interest, translates the title for him. Gregorius asks him to pronounce the original title. Seeing that the bookstore owner enjoys its sound, Gregorius lets him recite a passage, and the bookstore owner then offers to translate it into German. He continues to talk about the book, ending his chat with another quotation from Amadeu's book, in translation—"Given that we can live only a small part of what there is in us, what happens with the rest?" ("Wenn es so ist, daß wir nur einen kleinen Teil von dem leben können, was in uns ist—was geschieht mit dem Rest?"; Mercier 2008, 17; 2004, 29)—the passage that Gregorius remembers later. With this memorable exchange with the bookstore owner, Gregorius buys the book and tries to read it slowly with his Portuguese, which is at the beginner's level.[31]

Gregorius reads bits and pieces of the book, relying on his dictionary, while on the train to Lisbon and beyond. To read the book and to find one person after another who knew its author become his main preoccupation while in Lisbon. In other words, the book becomes Gregorius's life, which is both surprising and unsurprising: surprising because the book causes a complete disruption of his life, which has to that point been regulated and without any notable incident, except perhaps for his divorce from his former student; and unsurprising because he has been learning and teaching languages all his life, and he knows the power of words. His life has been spent with texts—but no text has prompted a physical journey until this time.[32]

6   INTERACTION WITH THE RAILROAD STAFF

It is noteworthy that the railroad staff members scarcely make an appearance in *Sanshirō*. When they do, their presence is neutralized, and only the service they provide and its consequence are described. Thus, the footsteps heard overhead when technicians light the lamps from the rooftop[33] serve as a cue for Sanshirō to have supper, leading to the aforementioned meal package accident with the woman, but there is no further word on the lamplighters. The following day, the man with the moustache buys peaches from the window, yet there is no word on his transaction with a vendor presumably on the platform. The conductor's visit for ticket inspection is never mentioned in the narrative. Sanshirō registers "the conductor's whistle reverbrat[ing] from one end of the station to the other" announcing the train's departure from Nagoya, yet by that time Sanshirō has left the window and the conductor's figure is not seen (Natsume 2018, 17; 1977, 9). The staff members thus remain transparent in the train's space-time in *Sanshirō*.

The railroad staff are also obscure in *My Most Secret Council*, though to a lesser degree. Their presence is felt through the protagonist-focalizer Luca's conversation with them, which is mostly in Italian,[34] and is represented in that language in the otherwise French-language text. However, only Luca's answers or questions to them are represented in the text, with their words to him eliminated. Thus, the staff members' voices are neutralized. The previously seen conversation with the ticket vendor at the Naples station is an example. Another is as the train arrives in Salerno:

"«Senta? Quanti minuti si ferma qui? Bene. Grazie»" (Larbaud 1958, 681). That Luca asks a question and receives a satisfying answer is clear, yet the answer from the conductor is absent from the quotation. Thus the reader does not know how many minutes the stop at the Salerno station will be, only being told by the narrator (mediating Luca's thought in free indirect speech) that "he has enough time to get lunch in the dining room and buy a timetable" (ibid., 681).

Later, at the Potenza station, Luca does not need to ask the conductor how long the train stops; he is already in possession of a timetable, after consulting which he surmises he has "enough time to eat a sandwich at the buffet and have a hot coffee" (ibid., 709). This plan leads to his decision to offer a porter a boxed lunch he purchased earlier that he wants to get rid of, so that the following conversation with him in Italian ensues:

> I have no desire for what's in the lunchbox. Let's give it to a porter. (Try to speak in a casual manner.) «Facchino, senta. Prenda quel coco li; si, è Buono, tutto fresco dentro, l'ho comparato a Salerno, ma sono svogliaxto e mi farebbe male.» (My voice on the platform of the Potenza station. It must be cooler than in Naples.) (ibid., 709)

The theatricality of the speech is intentional, and so is the elimination of the porter's response. Luca's ear is keen enough to note the sonority of his own voice, but as the narrator he does not register the porter's. When Luca becomes conscious of the stationmaster's voice announcing the train's departure: "Partenza! Oh, we said at the same time, the stationmaster and I! Yet what I meant is departure for Paris!" (ibid., 709), it matters to Luca only because it enhances the effect of his own voice, as an accompaniment to his own predominant tone.

The protagonist-focalizer-narrator Francis in *Zone* has a limited number of interactions with the railway employees, yet all in friendly terms. Beyond an initial encounter with the conductor—from whom he must buy a ticket after jumping onto the train from Paris to Milan without one, and whom his agitation may have frightened—there is only one other interaction with a conductor, who wakes him out of a dream for ticket inspection on the Milan-Rome train: "I make a U-turn stumble miss the bridge and plunge into the dark canal head first, a hand grips me, I'm drowning, it's the conductor waking me up, he shakes me, asks me for my ticket I hand it to him mechanically, he smiles at me, he looks pleasant" (Énard 2010,

105–6; 2008, 112). The conductor's "hand" brings him back to life in a dream, and to reality outside it.

Yet Francis has much more intimate and phantasmal interaction with the bartender:

> The traveling bartender has a uniform too, he's alone behind the shaking bar that's crossing Italy at full tilt, what'll I get drunk on, how many mini-bottles will I have to gulp down, whisky would smack too much of a depressed tattletale, of the barracks, I'll choose something more bucolic, some gin, (Énard 2010, 246; 2008, 249)

> It's disagreeable at the time you feel its journey down your esophagus and all alone in this bar tearing through the countryside I'll have another, a gin to the health of my zealous Croatian mother, a gin *za dom*, the bartender has guessed my intentions, he smiles at me and gets out another mini-bottle, *spremni*, a gin to the health of the firemen of Venice [...] a patriotic gin, my second lukewarm gin (Énard 2010, 248; 2008, 251–52)

The words they exchange are limited in number and in kind; the bartender is so quick to guess what Francis wants at the bar that they can dispense with words. Yet Francis develops a story about him, or, rather, about his family in history: "The bartender, he looks rural, almost like a miner, thickset, rugged forehead, short dense curly very dark hair over fifty I imagine he was born in early 1946 after his father had been busy with his Mussolini adventure" (Énard 2010, 249–50; 2008, 253). Prompted by the illusion of temporary intimacy across the bar, Francis considers opening a personal conversation with the bartender:

> I'm close to asking the bartender his father's first name, Antonio maybe, he's watching me observe him as I sip the last of my gin, the train suddenly slows down, brakes to approach a curve, probably the train that brought him home in June 1945 had paused here too, a red light between the world that had just been erased and the one that still remained to be destroyed, a woman was waiting for him at the end of the journey (Énard 2010, 250–51; 2008, 254)

The "pause" not at a station, not on the timetable, in the narrative present makes Francis imagine another in the past, historical and fictional, informed by his knowledge of the war and geography, fueled by his imaginative flight. The parallel between the bartender's family history and his own begins to take shape from there.

That parallel becomes explicit when Francis recalls his grandfather's return from the war, and takes a leap to his own course of action in the present:

> My paternal grandfather comes back from deportation, in a train, all the trains are leaving in the other direction, southwards now, the soldiers the deported the conquered the conquerors are taking the same route in the opposite direction, just as Antonio the father of my busy bartender goes back to Calabria or Campania and pauses by the train tracks in the middle of a field, will I go back home, what's waiting for me in peace (Énard 2010, 258; 2008, 260–61)

Thus, the Antonio story merges with Francis's own story. We will see more of the story later.

Gregorius in *Night Train to Lisbon* plays chess with a waiter in the dining car in the night train from Irún to Lisbon:

> Shortly before midnight, Gregorius went into the dining car. The car was empty except for the man with graying hair playing chess with the waiter. In fact, the car was closed, the waiter indicated, but then he got Gregorius a mineral water and beckoned him to join them. Gregorius quickly saw that the man, who had put on a pair of gold-framed glasses, had fallen into the waiter's cunning trap. With his hand on the piece, the man looked at him before he moved. Gregorius shook his head and the man withdrew his hand. The waiter, a man with calloused hands whose coarse features didn't seem to conceal a brain for chess, looked up surprised. Now the man with the gold eyeglasses turned the board toward Gregorius and gestured to him to play. It was a long, rough struggle and it was two o'clock when the waiter gave up. (Mercier 2008, 45; 2004, 61)

This chess match on behalf of the other passenger triggers their friendship, which we have seen in another section. Here I should only note that a board game, in this case chess, often opens a door to strangers who are to expend the shared space-time, allowing them to get to know each other without regard to their lives off the board.[35] Such a mode of communication—and one that takes hours to complete, as described above—is perfect for a long-distance train ride. So much so that the other man, Silveira, tells Gregorius that he always plays chess with the waiter because he takes the same train every other week, and that he has never beaten him except once. The waiter is mentioned toward the end of the novel, again by Silveira, because another couple of losses to the waiter have dampened his mood (Mercier 2008, 358; 2004, 411). The waiter's availability once he is off duty (after the dining car is officially closed for the night) and his being a fixture on the train enable the repetition of chess matches for Silveira. The waiter is both apart from and part of the train as space-time.

7   SLEEPING IN THE CARRIAGE

Passengers inevitably fall asleep at one point or another during a long-distance railway journey, whether planned and prepared or not. Passengers sleep, in some cases on makeshift beds, when traveling on the night train. Even during the daytime, passengers may be too exhausted to stay awake. In addition, the isorhythm that the wheels and the rails creates can lull passengers to sleep, as is often mentioned in the narratives under review here.

The narrative of *Sanshirō* begins as the title character awakens from his slumber. As we have seen, this creates a little adjustment of story time against discourse time, with the narrator, through the protagonist-focalizer's consciousness that is being regained, filling the gap with things that have happened before the narration begins. Sanshirō, however, slides back to the space-time of reality relatively smoothly, easily remembering his fellow passengers and eavesdropping on their conversation, of which he is able to make sense.[36]

In a complete chiasmus, *My Most Secret Council* ends with the protagonist-focalizer Luca falling asleep, as becomes apparent from incomplete sentences and words without connectors filling textual space. He has not slept well the previous night because he tried to stay awake by reading a book so he could leave before his lover woke up. After the excitement of launching his departure and his subsequent relief that no one, including himself, can take him back to Naples past the point of no return in Salerno, he is finally yielding to sleep. In addition, the landscape outside the window has become less eye-catching once the train has left the coastline to cross the Italian peninsula, where the tracks are closely surrounded by mountains that do not allow sweeping views.

As Luca realizes that he has four more hours to spend in the train before it reaches Taranto, he muses, "if you could drowse—after a white night and council this morning" (Larbaud 1958, 711). He recollects that "in childhood I used to pray so as to sleep," yet now that he is no longer a believer, he wonders if he should count numbers on his fingers so that he can fall asleep (ibid.). After considering sending a telegram to Isabelle to reveal the news that he is separating from her, he begins to talk to himself in Italian, "Io ride, adesso, in vice di dormer. Ma voglio dormer. Andiamo a dormire. An-dia-mo a dormer... An-dia-mo a dor-mire" (I am laughing instead of sleeping, but I want to sleep, let's sleep, let's sleep, let's sleep...; ibid., 714). He regrets the empathy he felt a moment earlier, and declares the "incompatibility of volition and sleep" (ibid.). As he is falling asleep, thinking of Irene, his new love interest, he wonders if falling asleep will help him forget her as well. Without drawing any conclusion as to his plans or reflections, his narration stops.

The open-endedness of falling asleep at the end of *My Most Secret Council* matches the in-media-res opening of waking from sleep at the beginning of *Sanshirō*. Each dissolves the tangibility of the narrative structure, framed rigidly by absolute time (or its representation). Whether awakening from sleep or falling asleep, one experiences time corporeally, without its being measured or ordered as in the chronological time that controls people when they are awake and alert. The narrative structure of *Sanshirō* and *My Most Secret Council* defies the dictates of absolute time and lets itself yield to the embrace of immanent time.

Sleeping may be considered among the most private of human activities, and thus it could be awkward to let it happen while in the public space of the train. Fellow passengers can watch you fall asleep, talk in your sleep, or otherwise lose control of your consciousness. Sleepers lose track of space-time, dreaming of being elsewhere or in another time frame. Sleepers' bodies are exposed to possible embarrassment or even harassment. The ambiguous state of sleeping in a public space—and of oscillating between the here and now and another space, another time—is encapsulated in a scene in *Sanshirō*. A sleeping passenger opposite Sanshirō's seat apparently responds to his speech, saying "Ah, of course" when Sanshirō tells the moustachioed man that he is a graduate of the college in Kumamoto (Natsume 2018, 22; 1977, 11). "That he was still sleeping, there could be no doubt. He is not just sitting there talking to himself" (Natsume 2018, 22; 1977, 11–12).

The blurred boundaries between two states of being awake or being asleep, and between being in another space-time and being in the train carriage, are crossed in scenes in *Sanshirō* and *Zone*. "When the train reached Toyohashi, the sleeping man bolted up and left the car, rubbing his eyes. It was amazing how he could wake himself at the right time like that, thought Sanshirō. Concerned lest the man, still dazed with sleep, had alighted at the wrong station, Sanshirō watched him from the train window" (Natsume 2018, 22–23; 1977, 12). Yet the man seems confident and leaves the station promptly, as Sanshirō looks on anxiously. A similar sudden awakening at the right station of a passenger who is fast asleep occurs in *Zone*: "The pneumatic locks wheeze, the doors open, my neighbour a little surprised a little sleepy gets up picks up a little suitcase takes his magazine and goes out" (Énard 2010, 238; 2008, 242). The man who was previously absorbed in reading the *Pronto* tabloid magazine and was then fast asleep is thus perfectly ready to manage his bearing in the exterior space-time. A common-sense interpretation of such behavior would be that the passenger in question has simply been pretending to be asleep to avoid interaction with others on the train. However, there is a perfect phenomenological explanation for the state of mind of such a passenger, called by Husserl "passive synthesis," studied by Victor Biceaga especially in terms of sleep, which designates a state in which one can be asleep yet still retain a level of consciousness.[37]

Whereas in these episodes the passengers in question are agile in leaping the boundary between the two states, some are not so ready to cross the boundary, remaining in between for a longer time. In *Night Train to Lisbon*, Gregorius first struggles to fall asleep, even though he, like Luca, was sleepless the night before, and despite "the monotonous beat of the wheels," which should lull him to sleep (Mercier 2008, 44; 2004, 60). He is just as slow in getting up: he spends so much time thinking, after waking up in the bed on the sleeper, that he finally visits the dining car only when other passengers have all but finished their breakfast (Mercier 2008, 49; 2004, 65). Considering how regulated and punctual Gregorius has been in his life to date, this newly acquired liberty is something that he has yet to learn how to handle. His compartment, meanwhile, is rearranged while he is in the dining car, with its makeshift bed pushed up and the seats restored. The multi-purpose compartment—which has different faces for different times—is another revelation of the complexity of space-time: its space is meant not only for one time and designated function but can be experienced in multiple ways, depending on what the passengers are to do. Their corporeal experience is a priority rather than a function. Sleeping is a perhaps most corporeal experience of space-time, which is supported by and endorses immanent time.

When Gregorius shares a compartment on a sleeper with a stranger on his way back from Lisbon, they fall asleep at different times. When Gregorius falls asleep, the woman turns off the main light for him, relying on the reading light on her side; when she falls asleep, he turns off the reading light for her (Mercier 2008, 431; 2004, 487). Their respect for each other's flexible and embodied space-time is evident in these gestures. Their schedule does not have to be premeditated or punctuated according to the absolute time that applies to everyone. They have their own biological time, reading and sleeping as is natural to them. The facilities in the compartment can be controlled by the passengers, and as long as they understand each other's needs and are willing to offer any help, they do not have to agree upon when to do what. The immanent time of each is respected by the other, which is another reason that the ride is "fine" for both.

8   STATION AS INTERSECTION OF POSSIBLE ALTERNATIVES

During long-distance railway travel, the train stops and passengers can disembark or embark at multiple stations along the way. For most passengers who are traveling farther, those stops are only lapses in pace, diversions from an otherwise monotonous journey, opportunities to pick up something practical such as snacks, drinks, things to read, or the chance to run an errand (such as sending an urgent telegram, as we saw in *The Narrow Margin* in the Introduction). For those who are in doubt about the execution of their travel plans, however, stations may seduce them to get off the train and take a train either in the opposite direction or on a different line, or set off by another means of transport altogether. These options are considered, and in some cases executed, by the passenger-protagonists of the four narratives discussed in this chapter, thereby fundamentally questioning the purposiveness and linearity on which the railway system is premised.

Sanshirō exhibits keen awareness of other passengers' itineraries— where they get on, where they get off—and thus must sense the unique significance of each station for each passenger. For him, the Nagoya station, an important intersection of the San'yō Line and the Tōkaidō Line, comes to materialize a pivotal moment in his life beyond its prescribed pragmatic function because of the incident with the woman passenger whom he sleeps next to for a night in an inn there. He never considers changing his itinerary before or after Nagoya (following the woman to

Yokkaichi, for example), but continues his journey to Tokyo as scheduled. He is determined to pursue his academic study in the nation's capital, which is the sole purpose of his journey and, indeed, of his life to date. Despite the woman casting doubt on his courage, and the moustachioed man renouncing the value of the nation-state on which the university system is founded, Sanshirō is not prepared to change his career plans at this point.

Once in Tokyo, he is "startled" by many of its urban features, including streetcars that ring bells. Before Sanshirō sets foot on them, Nonomiya—a remote family acquaintance from the same region who has lived in Tokyo for several years and is now a researcher at the university—warns Sanshirō indirectly by telling him how confusing the streetcar system is to him, and that he still has to ask the conductor for the right station at which to transfer every time he rides (Natsume 2018, 46; 1977, 25). This serves as an omen in the narrative discourse: as mentioned earlier, Sanshirō fails to change streetcars at the right station, which compels him to devise an alternative route, get off at a wrong station without realizing that he has done so, and then walk even farther away from his destination (Natsume 2018, 68; 1977, 38). Although none of this is a deliberate choice Sanshirō has made in his bid for an alternative life, such incidents suggest that passengers can disappear into an adjacent yet distinct area to pursue something other than what they originally intended. The network of the railway system is complex, multiply oriented, and confusing, despite its builders' original intention to facilitate modern life with greater speed and efficiency. As Nonomiya puts: "The more 'convenient' it gets, the more confused I get" (Natsume 2018, 46; 1977, 25).

Luca in *My Most Secret Council* takes similarly decisive action by leaving his lover in Naples by train. However, his motivation appears more contested than Sanshirō's. At the Salerno station, Luca considers taking the train in the opposite direction, back to Naples, so as to resume his relationship with Isabelle by making up some excuse about his whereabouts that day. As we saw in the section on rushing to the train, he almost deliberately misses reboarding the train. Once it leaves Salerno, he knows he has passed the point of no return, and at another station, Patenza, he even considers living there sometime.

As Luca imagines returning Isabelle to her ex-husband, he is afraid that the whole plot may dissolve after reaching the station: "If she lets him take her to the station without resistance, at the last moment both of them will not have the courage to carry out the plan and will reconcile in front of the train, and they will have to have her luggage retrieved from the container" (Larbaud 1958, 654). The station stages a theatrical scene, not only for those who embark or disembark the train, but for those who cancel their train ride. The station thus becomes more than a functional space-time to facilitate a railway journey—it becomes a space-time of its own that is not serving the railway system.

Francis, the protagonist-focalizer-narrator of *Zone*, considers going back to Paris at Bologna and at Florence, while remembering an earlier crossroads where he could have taken a train to Syracuse from Venice St. Lucia Station instead of going back home to Paris, after Marianne, his then girlfriend, left him in Venice:

> The landscape of the Po plain is very dark also, little fireflies of farms and factories are disturbing ghosts, in Venice at the Santa Lucia station I had wondered for a while about going back to Paris, another night train was going south at around the same time, headed for Sicily, terminus Syracuse, a journey of almost twenty-four hours, I should have taken it, if there had been someone on the platform to guide me, a demiurge, or an oracle I would have taken the train to Syracuse to settle on the rocky island on the slopes of Etna home of Hephaestus the lame (Énard 2010, 161; 2008, 167)

Francis recollects the option he had at hand, an option of going to Sicily instead of Paris to live a new life there, mythically inspired.[38] All he needed was someone to guide him, a mythical figure. Instead, he took the train for Paris and worked as an intelligence officer for the French government for years, since then until now, when he thinks he is finally disconnecting himself from that way of life.

The multiplicity of railway directions at some hub stations is baffling and enticing at the same time. In *Zone*, this is most manifest at Bologna, a station that is exposed to the exterior and thus makes visible the spectacular cobwebs of rails extending in so many directions. The remarkable horizontal stretch at Bologna is elaborated on—in comparison with Milan, which manifests a vertical extension instead—in the following passage:

> like train tracks at night straight lines infinite networks relays and us, usually silent, strangers who don't open up to each other any more than we do to ourselves, obscure, obstinate, lost in the countless tracks that surround the inextricable railroad knot of the Bologna station, endless huntings, circuits, sidings, a station divided into two equal parts where unlike Milan the gigantic size of the building is replaced by the profusion of the tracks, the

verticality of columns by the number of crosswise, a station that has no need
of any architectural excessiveness because it is in itself excessive, the last
great crossroads in Europe before the Italian cul-de-sac, everything passes
through here, bottles of Nero d'Avola from the slopes of Aetna that Lowry
drank in Taormina, marble from the quarries of Carrara, Fiats and Lancias
meet dried vegetables here, sand, cement, oil, *peperoncini* from Apulia, tourists, workers, emigrants, Albanians who landed in Bari speed through here
on their way to Milan, Turin or Paris: they've all come through Bologna,
they've seen their train slip from one track to the other according to the
shunting, they didn't get out to visit the basilica, they didn't take advantage
of any of the charms of a pleasant bourgeois city, suave and cultivated, the
kind of city where you like to settle, [...] a city whose labyrinthine train station protects you from the uncertain world, from outside trains from the
throb of the irregular from speed and from foreign places, a station I'm
entering now the platform is sliding by in an orangey light (Énard 2010,
237–38; 2008, 241–42)

In addition to the contrast between the vertical Milan Central station and
the horizontal Bologna station, the enclosure ("building") of the former
and the opening of the latter, without any need for "architectural excessiveness," are also contrasted. Francis further contemplates the centripetal
movement (arrivals from many places) and centrifugal movement (departures for many places) that stations the size of Milan or Bologna encapsulate. As George Revill observes, "[a]s a location where heterogeneous
voices and cultures interact, commune and conflict, the railway station acts
as a simultaneously centrifugal and centripetal force in the production of
modern urban life" (Revill 2013, 55). Still, the observation of Milan and
Bologna stations in *Zone* here is less socio-cultural (as Revill's is) than
physical and graphic. Francis seems to be more fascinated with "entering"
a station than with pulling out of it, because he appreciates protection
from the disturbing rhythm and velocity of train travel and from exposure
to the uncertain international world. He also notes that this is the "last
great crossroads," and that what is left for him to expect is the "cul-de-
sac," suggesting a sense of urgency and the inescapability of fate.

Francis looks back and muses on the missed opportunities at Bologna:
"if I had gotten out in Bologna I could have gone back to Venice, to the
Paradise Lost or the Flying Dutchman to drink spitzes with Ghassan, his
crucifix tattooed on his Lebanese biceps, or take a boat to Burano and
look at the little fishing houses slant their blues and ochers over the canals,
observe the incongruous angle of the bell-tower and spin round in circles

the way I'm spinning round in this train" (Énard 2010, 248; 2008, 252). He can appreciate the "profusion" of options the Bologna station can offer, so much that his imagination of alternatives bursts into his personal memories of Venice, literature, opera, and geography that he is familiar with, before he is brought back to the train through the spinning move-ment caused by its tremors and his own unstable condition. From this enumeration of the options at the crossroads (Bologna in this case), missed opportunities for diversion from the plan are felt even more sorely than usual by the swaying man, a figure of both uncertainty and the paradig-matic expansion of the supposedly syntagmatic progress of the train, just like Duchamp's sad young man in a train discussed in the Introduction.

Having considered and renounced the idea of getting off the train at Bologna, Francis contemplates the alternative change in the course of his life by leaving the train between stations. He weaves a storyline, ostensibly not involving himself but featuring Antonio, the imaginary father of the bartender,[39] in 1945, on his way home from the battlefield by rail:

> I hope he got out of the train I hope that he ran across the mountains until he ran out of breath, sneezing in the blossoming wheat fields, that he let the coolness of the moon caress his shoulder the better to enjoy his unsettling solitude slumped beneath an olive tree I hope he dared to run away during this unhoped-for stop, the train immobilized in the middle of the tracks sometimes you sense you have a chance, there are doors to escape through—Antonio back from the Eastern Front runs through the countryside to escape the fate of Ulysses, the village, his sewing wife, the good hunting dog who will sniff between his legs, he flees the future that he guessed at, sweat-ing blood to support a large family in poverty, [...] where the dog will die first without ever running down a single hare: Antonio back from the war lying near a Tuscan fig tree at night listens to the train start up again, he did well to get out, he thinks, he did well, it's such a beautiful spring night, the first one that smells of hay after years of grease and cordite and stretched out thus between two lives, between two worlds (Énard 2010, 251; 2008, 254–55)

In this imagined scene, cinematic but with added olfactory and tactile senses, Francis imagines an alternative life through a fictive character, which indicates vicariously his own desire to deviate from his plan. The passage conveys the corporeality of absorbing the sensuality of the natural environment, the fear of an anticipated future, satisfaction with exploring the in-between space-time (neither the departure point nor the destination that is his family home; neither his past as a soldier at war nor his future as the hard-working head of a poor family). His mention of the myth of Ulysses enhances this deviation from the master narrative of a soldier's homecoming, its modern version set in motion by the rails of the deportation trains. The space beyond or irrelevant to the railways beckons the passenger who dreams of a life away from the predetermined route, literary, historical, or current/real. Francis continues his musings about "Antonio," whose circumstances are further elaborated in the following:

> He speaks to the stars I doubt it, he's not a shepherd out of Pirandello, he's a man coming home from the war, lying there in a field because the train has just stopped, an incident on the tracks, maybe there are many of these soldiers wondering if they want to go back home, trembling still from the German defeat under the caress of green wheat, a little afraid, disarmed, in ragged outfits or in civilian clothes, [...] he has never seen Tuscany before, has always gone through it in a train or in a truck he's never really taken advantage of these landscapes so civil, so tame, so noble, so human ... (Énard 2010, 252; 2008, 255)

The purposiveness and determinacy of the railway journey burdens the passenger so much that the space beyond the tracks becomes enticing. The unexpected stop between stations can thus be taken advantage of by "Antonio" or by Francis himself.

Indeed, he continues to consider the option of leaving the train, just as he has made Antonio do in his imagination, between Bologna and Florence:

> between Bologna and Florence, which must not be far now, are we already in Tuscany, what time is it, 7:15,[40] another half-hour before Florence then 300 kilometres till Rome and the new life, if I don't get out on the way, if I don't take advantage of an unexpected stop to try to escape Fate, but the choices were already made a long time ago, I'll hand over the suitcase, I'll follow it through to the end (Énard 2010, 273; 2008, 275–76)

An alternative life, following deviation from the plan, is considered again here, in the same wording, "take/n advantage of" ("profit/é"), to emphasize the repetitiveness of the consideration. The idea is, however, only to be refuted here. Instead of getting out of the train during an unexpected stop between stations, Francis arrives in Roma Termini and takes another measure to renounce his plan—a flight out of Roma Fiumicino.

Francis's oscillation between a fantasized exit from the railway system and judicious adherence to his premeditated itinerary is obviously inseparable from the way he lives his life. His desire for escape from fate and entry into greater self-fulfillment remains unsatisfied until after his arrival in Rome. Instead of meeting with representatives of the Vatican for the transfer of his suitcase full of secret information, or visiting Sashka, with whom he has dreamt of spending the rest of his life, Francis heads for the airport. There he meets a mysterious person who offers him "the last smoke before the end of the world" (Énard 2010, 517; 2008, 517)—just as a stranger at the Milan Central station offered him "the last handshake before the end of the world." Evidently the two strangers' approaches to Francis frame the narrative, marking the beginning and end of his journey, even though we are not told what awaits Francis in his life.

Similar hesitation crosses the mind of Gregorius, the protagonist-focalizer of *Night Train to Lisbon*. It is evident that his decision to leave for Lisbon will change his life, yet how it will do so remains unclear, unlike the plan of Francis in *Zone*. The initial fluctuation in Gregorius's mind has less to do with what the future owes him than with what he has left behind, namely, his teaching responsibilities at the school to which he has devoted himself, earning a reputation as a teacher with an impeccable work ethic. He considers returning to Bern from Lausanne, before the first of the three legs of his railway journey takes him as far as Paris, in a way not dissimilar to Luca's thinking of making a U-turn at Salerno:

> The stop in Lausanne was a temptation. Across the same platform was the train to Bern. Gregorius imagined getting off in the Bern railroad station. He looked at the clock. If he took a taxi to Kirchenfeld, he could still make the fourth period. [...] Now his look fell on the notebook on the compartment table. Without opening it, he saw the list of student names. And all of a sudden, he understood: what had started as the temptation to hold on to something familiar after the last Bern houses slipped away, had become more a farewell as the hours passed. To be able to part from something, he thought as the train started moving, you had to confront it in a way that created internal distance. You had to turn the unspoken, diffuse self-understanding it had wrapped around you into a clarity that showed what it meant to you. And that meant it had to congeal into something with distant contours. Something as distinct as the list of the many students who had meant more to his life than anything else. Gregorius felt as if the train now rolling out of the railroad station also left a piece of him behind. He seemed

driven onto an ice floe that had come loose in a mild earthquake, onto an open cold sea. (Mercier 2008, 31–32; 2004, 45–46)

Gregorius thus anatomizes the cause of his hesitating to pursue his impulsively made plan and the temptation to change his plan and return to the status quo. As the train pulls out of the Lausanne station, he realizes that there is no return, not only in terms of the practical patchwork he could have made, but in terms of his way of life, value, and vision.

However, on his way back Gregorius does yield to temptation to deviate from his plan of returning to Bern; he gets off the train he took at Lisbon for Irún, just as he acknowledges the station sign that says SALAMANCA, without giving it much thought at this time. In fact, earlier in the narrative, the station catches his attention on his way to Lisbon:

> When he woke up at six o'clock and saw the name SALAMANCA before his compartment window, out of the blue, a sluice gate of memory opened that had remained closed for four decades. The first thing it released was the name of another city: *Isfahan*. Suddenly it was there, the name of the Persian city where he had wanted to go after he finished school. The name bearing so much mysterious strangeness touched Gregorius at this moment, like the code of another possible life he hadn't dared live. And as the train now left the Salamanca station, once again after so long, he lived through the feelings back then when that other life had both opened and closed. (Mercier 2008, 47; 2004, 63)

At this time, Gregorius is more motivated to visit Lisbon, and thus he does not leave the train or the plan. Still, this brief recognition of the station name is remembered because the name of Salamanca acquires new significance in Amadeu's life story, related to his femme fatale, of whom Gregorius has learned from Joao Eça: "slowly, the details of the story about Estefânia Espinhosa came back into his mind. Salamanca, she had become a lecturer in Salamanca. The railroad station sign with the dark medieval name emerged before him. Then the sign disappeared" (Mercier 2008, 287–88; 2004, 333–34).[41] In Gregorius's second encounter with the station, Salamanca's impact is sufficient for him to get off the train. This time, when he is hurrying to Bern, where his medical assessment awaits him, he disembarks the train on the spot and visits Estefânia Espinoza, who now teaches at the university there.

Passengers already on the train experience stations in two ways: either as markers of their progress toward their destination—to assure them that they are on the right track, from which they must not digress—or as an exit from the preordained route for an alternative possibility in life. Stations can remind passengers of absolute time, which is homogenous, monotonous, and unidirectional, and can also remind them of the expansion of space beyond and irrelevant to the linear railway. Passengers such as Francis and Gregorius realize that the space between the departure point and the destination is not only to be passed by but to be explored. And the stations, initially built to serve the railways, invite passengers to such experience of greater space, off the schedule, beyond the constraint of the rails.[42]

9   Different Trains

Though Sanshirō's first trip to Tokyo is one-way at that point, he does return home when school is out, as is customary.[43] The narrative ends as we learn, in retrospect, that Sanshirō traveled home by train during the university's holidays around New Year's Day and is already back in Tokyo. This train journey is anticipated in Sanshirō's mother's telegram, asking for the date of his departure home (Natsume 2018, 392; 1977, 209). The telegram consists only of the two words "itsu tatsu" ("when leave?") at the end of chapter 12, which is spent on the separation of Sanshirō and Mineko, his love interest. The train journey itself can be surmised to have taken place only because his "return to Tokyo" is mentioned in passing (Natsume 2018, 396; 1977, 212).[44] It merely proffers a setting for an anticlimactic ending: Mineko marries during Sanshirō's absence from Tokyo; he finds the invitation to her wedding reception on his desk in the boarding house the day of his return there (Natsume 2018, 396; 1977, 212). This is also a case of analepsis, or narrating what had happened after the story unfolded further than the event in question, and thus a deliberate manifestation of rupture between the story time and the discourse time. The drastic difference between the duration of the event in the discourse time devoted to Sanshirō's initial one-way train trip to Tokyo and the deliberately insouciant way his later round trip is mentioned is noteworthy. There is nothing more to say in the narrative because Sanshirō's experience of the train for the second time contains nothing of significance.

Luca, the protagonist-focalizer-main narrator of *My Most Secret Council*, often muses about train trips in Italy and elsewhere, whether taken or imagined. He recollects past unpleasant incidents traveling with Isabelle on the train, either to convince himself that his decision to leave her is right, or to design the best way to accomplish his plan to split up with her. The former includes the aforementioned dispute over the whereabouts of the train timetable. The latter consists of the idea of taking Isabelle back to her ex-husband by train, an idea that begins the narrative:

> One can imagine the trip, at Naples Station, getting onto the Paris-Rome train; arriving in Paris, at Gare de Lyon. The iron gate of Jardin des Plantes. You will pass by Boulevard Saint-Michel and you will stop before the tobacco shop of Medici Square. Finally, our home, no, my home, Rue Berthollet. We need to go to bed there. The last night spent together! Yes, but supported by this idea: I return her to her husband; I do not abandon her, and I do something surprising, romantic, and moral. The next morning: a car loaded with her luggage; Gare de l'Est; the cluster of the brown-red wagons, better yet: color of chocolate (these are the third class; why did someone choose this color? Who had this idea? Here's one of those things we will never know.) We are arriving; in a city of the East rail network. (Larbaud 1958, 649)

Luca exploits his familiarity with stations and their surroundings to weave together this story of an alternative travel by rail.

The omnipresence of railways in his recollections may also reflect his present location in the train. His body is feeling the movement of the train, confirmed by names of stations on the platform, which divide chapters into sections without regard to the articulation of his interior monologue. That is to say, his thought process is complicated by the present corporeal experience of the railway, which encourages him to think of railways.

The way Francis, the protagonist-focalizer-narrator of *Zone*, juxtaposes his current train journey and others from his memory archive, either personally experienced or historically known, is not dissimilar to Luca's, though much more extensive. On one occasion, Francis enumerates memorable places he has been to, and muses succinctly: "life can seem like a bad travel agency brochure, Paris Zagreb Venice Alexandria Trieste Cairo Beirut Barcelona Algiers Rome" (Énard 2010, 25; 2008, 32). During his train ride from Milan to Rome, he recollects events in these cities named here, many of which he has visited by train. Francis remembers all these cities to remarkable and diverse effect. For instance, an episode in

Alexandria holds special significance within the context of alternative railway journeys:

> I remember in Venice I had asked in a travel agency if there were any boats to Alexandria and the employee ... had looked at me stunned, to Alexandria but there's a train, and in that immediate confidence one has in professionals I had pictured, for a second, a train that would go from Venice to Alexandria in Egypt, direct via Trieste Zagreb Belgrade Thessalonica Istanbul Antioch Aleppo Beirut Acre and Port Said, a challenge to geopolitics and to the mind, and even, once I had understood her confusion, Alessandria in Piedmont, I began to dream of a train that would unite all the Alexandrias, a network connecting Alessandria in Piedmont Alexandria Troas in Turkey Alexandria in Egypt Alexandria in Arachosia, possibly the most mysterious of them all, lost in Afghanistan far from railroads, the train would be called the Alexander Express and would go from Alexandria Eschate in Tajikistan to Piedmont through the lips of Africa in thirteen days and as many nights (Énard 2010, 17–18; 2008, 24)

This anecdote of a funny miscommunication about the two cities of the same name immediately builds two imaginary railway routes in Francis's mind—one from Venice to Alexandria, Egypt, and the other across the Euro-Asian continent connecting all the cities that bear the name Alexandria. The two routes defy "geopolitics" and "the mind" because the railway system cannot be extended in either of these ways, however splendid they may be; railways are built for reasons of politics and economics, as is demonstrated over and again throughout *Zone*, and not for reasons of myth or fantasy. Railways that would connect places and people in them are in fact a product of divisive and contesting territoriality, driven by desires to attack, possess, confine, or preserve—not to associate, correspond, or unite. There is a reason for the absence of a Venice-Alexandria Line or an Alexander Express. Thus these fantastic railway routes evaporate as soon as Francis and the railway employee realize their miscommunication.

Francis as the narrator takes the reader farther into his past, to his first meeting with Marianne, on a train: "I met her by chance in the train that goes from Cairo to Alexandria, in a luxurious first-class an extraordinarily slow car, a real cliché of Oriental laziness, and along the Nile delta" (Énard 2010, 88–89; 2008, 96). This sentence renders ambiguous not only the most important attribute of the train (speed) but also the geopolitical characterization ("cliché") of the Orient, which is imagined to appreciate a slower pace. Thus, space and time are doubly, if not triply, entangled with each other. On this train, a public space in which strangers meet, and talk, Francis and Marianne realized that they were practically neighbors in Paris but "had never seen each other there this coincidence seemed, in an Egyptian train jolting along 4,000 kilometres away from the Rue de la Convention, like a divine sign" (Énard 2010, 90; 2008, 97). The distance between two persons is not cartographically measured but fluctuates in accordance with their movement and timing—informed by space-time. And this distance can be nullified in the unexpected space-time of the train in a distant land. In this case, what makes Francis and Marianne meet is their shared touristy interest in the historical city of Alexandria and the purposive construction of the railway route to the city from the modern city of Cairo, serving and fueling the desires of modern Western consumers and the business of tourism. Yet something other than this initial purpose or intended service occurs—the two tourist passengers not only visit places of interest and eat, drink, and shop, but also fall in love with each other, which could have happened anywhere, especially in Paris, but which didn't happen anywhere but in the space-time of the passenger train.

Francis's memories of a Marianne are further illustrated by train journeys, which both enrich and confuse his sense of space-time so that he loses his bearings in the here and now: "rocked by memories as well as by the rails, I left Venice as Marianne left me and I fell asleep, I fell asleep in an Intercity train that was going to Milan to bring me to Paris, everything's mixed up everything's muddled I get younger in my sleep disturbed by the memory of Marianne" (Énard 2010, 89; 2008, 96). While Francis is on the Milan-Rome train in the present, he therefore remembers the Venice-Milan train that used to connect him to the Milan-Paris train. The superimposition of the two routes, one present and the other past—and the extension of another couple of routes, both in the past and adjacent to each other—expand the space-time in more directions than one. He feels "rocked" both by the present train and by memories, both physically and psychically, that is. He remembers his sleep in the past train, and while doing so, his consciousness in the present train is "muddled"—so much so that he feels as though he is back in his younger days.

Even though Francis's present railway journey is motivated by a personal purpose, he cannot but contemplate wars and conflicts for which trains were used. Indeed, just before he sets in motion remembrances of Marianne, he was thinking: "immediately I thought of Croatia of course but especially of the end of Salo, the Italian Social Republic, worn away little by little by the partisans who themselves were exterminated en masse from Bolzano to Mauthausen, sent by train beyond the Brenner Pass to die in Teutonic land, [...] trains carry soldiers and the deported, murderers and victims, weapons and ammunition" (Énard 2010, 88–89; 2008, 95–96). Just being in a train carriage and on rails in Europe is enough for Francis to commemorate those who were forced to travel by rail toward concentration camps, battlefields, and other excruciating fates. Superimposed with the collective memory of atrocity, trans-European railways are multilayered space-times by which some passengers are haunted. He muses: "a new map another network of traces of roads of railroads of rivers continuing to carry along corpses remains scraps shouts bones forgotten honoured anonymous or decried in the great roll-call of history" (Énard 2010, 26; 2008, 32).

Amadeu, the narrator of the embedded narrative in *Night Train to Lisbon*, reflects on the significance of visiting foreign places by rail for the second time in the section entitled "INTERNAL EXPANSE" in his book, which Gregorius opens during his short visit home in Bern:

> And not only in time are we expanded. In space, too, we stretch out far over what is visible. We leave something of ourselves behind when we leave a place, we stay there, even though we go away. And there are things in us that we can find again only by going back there. We go to ourselves, travel to ourselves, when the monotonous beat of the wheels brings us to a place where we have covered a stretch of our life, no matter how brief it may have been. When we set foot for the second time on the platform of the foreign railroad station, hear the voices over the loud-speaker, smell the unique odors, we have come not only to the distant place, but also to the distance of our own inside, to a perhaps thoroughly remote corner of our self which, when we are somewhere else, is completely in the dark and invisible. Otherwise, why should we be so excited, so outside ourselves when the conductor calls the names of the places, when we hear the screech of the brakes and are swallowed up in the suddenly appearing shadow of the railroad station? Otherwise, why should it be a magical moment, a moment of silent drama when the train comes to a complete halt with a final jolt? It is because, from the first steps we take on the strange and not strange platform, we resume a life we had interrupted and left, when we felt the first jolts of the moving train. What could be more exciting than resuming an interrupted life with all its promises? (Mercier 2008, 243; 2004, 285–86)

As in *My Most Secret Council*, the resonance between the exterior space and the interior space is recognized here. The "internal landscape" has been "temporally and spatially expanded" (Mercier 2008, 243; 2004, 286) by the first trip to a foreign land, which has been obliterated until one goes back to the place. The distance one has traveled internally can be recognized only if the external travel is taken yet again.

Not only visiting the same place again, but also feeling as if they were traveling on a different route, complicates the relationship between the internal and external landscapes. Like Gregorius, Amadeu, too, was fascinated with the Trans-Siberian Railway[45] (Mercier 2008, 32 and 264; 2004, 46 and 309), by which he hoped to visit Vladiostock someday. Although that dream of his had not been fulfilled—just as Gregorius's dream of visiting Isfahan has not been—the habit of thinking of other places while traveling by rail enriches and confuses Amadeu's (and Gregorius's) experience of the train. As with Francis's superimposition of different trains while traveling on one route, so Gregorius and Amadeu are able to intensify and ambiguate their experience of the train. The sensations they feel as passengers—the shrieks of the wheels and rails, sway of the carriage, whistle of the conductor, fluctuating temperature and airflow resulting from the confinement and porosity of the compartment, and slowing down, stopping, starting, and accelerating of the train—remind them of traveling on the same routes, other routes, and imagined routes. Their personal experience becomes collective, associated with transhistorical and translocational affects. By representing such complicated space-time entanglements, these four narratives of a solo male passenger make the most of a variety of rhetorical alternatives, in terms of voices, perspectives, and temporalities.

Notes

1. The translator Jay Rubin omits the macron for the long vowel on the "o" in the English title *Sanshiro* and throughout his translation itself; here, however, the "ō" is retained when referring both to the book and to its eponymous protagonist.
2. In Japanese, the account of the incident begins with "Jitsu o iu to" (To tell you the truth), which is omitted in the translation. The phrase not only suggests the narrator's gesture of communicating to the (unspecified) audience, but also Sanshirō's silence over the mishap for others. One can surmise that the incident in question occurred while Sanshirō was alone.

The narrator says that Sanshirō took the train because he had a plan to visit "Commercial College," without imparting the reason for the planned visit. This omission also suggests that the narrator selects only what they deem relevant to the story out of a wider range of activities the protagonist is engaged in.

3. See Alisa Freedman's chapter "Boy Who Feared Trains: University Students, Railway Trauma, and the Health of the Nation" (Freedman 2011, 68–115) for both the railway trip to Tokyo and the intra-city train rides in the city as described in *Sanshirō* against their historical background and ideological implications.

4. Sanshirō's itinerary is analyzed by many, including Fujii Hidetada and Bandō Maruo Jitsuko, the annotators of Natsume 2018.

5. The Fifth College, or Dai-Go Kōtō gakkō, "Go-kō" for short.

6. For a comprehensive historical overview of the development of the railway system in Japan in the late nineteenth century to the early twentieth century, see Grunow 2012.

7. All English translations of extracts from Larbaud's *Mon plus secret conseil* are mine. I appreciate assistance given by Kornelia Drianovski for the preparation of the translation.

8. Although Joyce's novel remains unmentioned, Homer's *Ulysses* is explicitly referenced.

9. Laura Marks cites Ernest Jones and Hanns Sachs for episodes of Freud's anxiety about the possibility of missing the train and his consequential proclivity to arrive at the station much in advance to the train's departure time (Marks 2007, 160; Jones 1953, 305–7; and Sachs 1945, 81).

10. In chapter XIX, Luca and the stationmaster pronounce the same word, "Partenza!," in sync (Larbaud 1958, 709).

11. See, for example, Takeda 1999 and Makimura 2020.

12. Here we see the combination of the first and third relations between a human subject and a thing (the train) in Foucault's definition (see the Introduction): one can experience the train as a space-time ("with such a book you never get bored when you travel in a train") while observing another train pass by ("we've just passed a train going in the other direction").

13. This reveals a rupture in Genettean frequency between the story time and the discourse time.

14. When an entire section from Amadeu's book is quoted, it usually starts with the section title in Portuguese (and thus in the original, given by the author Amadeu) followed by a German title (which must have been given by Gregorius), both in block letters. This one is no exception. The English translator Harshav keeps the Portuguese portion in Portuguese, while translating the German portion into English.

15. This passage is from an earlier part of the novella, where Luca still plans to travel to Messina, Sicily, instead of Taranto.

16. In the original, the man says "Aite irudeshō" (The newspaper is not occupied, as you can see, can't you?), somewhat qualifying his authority and making the decision more communal.

17. Unlike Gregorius in *Night Train to Lisbon*, who decisively leaves a compartment once a popular newspaper is spread by a new passenger, Francis does not mind sharing the space with a man who reads a tabloid. In addition to the fact that he is not in a compartment and thus does not feel as bound to other passengers in nearby seats, Francis's interiority is less penetrable than Gregorius's, so passengers of tastes or lifestyles different from his own do not matter because he would not talk to them, again unlike Gregorius.

18. This is not dissimilar to the inclination of "you" in *La Modification* by Michel Butor, *Blue Journey* by Yumiko Kurahashi, or *Suspects on the Night Train* by Yoko Tawada, three narratives that I discuss in Chap. 6.

19. In Chap. 6 I discuss this recognition of the heterogeneity of the space-time of the train compartment in the final chapter of *Suspects on the Night Train*.

20. This is one of the few occasions when the extradiegetic narrator offers a prolepsis, or a flash forward, to refer to a future occurrence that the protagonist-(main) focalizer Gregorius does not know about yet.

21. We might recall the incidental companionship in a sleeper compartment of Jerzy and Marta in *Night Train*—two passengers who both prefer quietude (discussed in the Introduction to this volume).

22. *Bacon's Essays* (1892), according to the annotation in Natsume 2018, 18.

23. For this text's narratological affinity with Michel Butor's *La Modification*, a narrative discussed in Chap. 6, in terms of the use of second-person narration, see Cowan 2018.

24. The volume selection is indeterminate because Luca has the "*Complete Works*" (cited in English, in the French original) by de Quincey (1863–67) at home (Larbaud 1958, 658). This must have been in hard cover published in England, given his somewhat pejorative tone when he refers to Tauchnitz, a Leipzig publisher of paperbound books. See more at "Tauchnitz Edition" n.d..

25. This insouciance toward the purchase of reading material at the station is shared by the protagonist of *La Modification*, which I examine in Chap. 6 below.

26. Although this book of three stories is fictive, Stephen Mitchelmore (2015, 134) points out the story's distinct similarities to John Berger's *From A to X*.

27. The colon after "not" is placed at the end of the chapter, followed by the entire following chapter, which constitutes a long excerpt from the book

Francis is reading—and which is therefore formally a clause after a colon, rather than after the comma that usually ends a chapter in *Zone*.

28. Here, too, a colon ends the chapter.

29. As in the two previous cases, a colon closes a chapter before another chapter.

30. It turns out that the book has two more stories: "I still have two stories left to read by this Rafael Kahla, other war stories" (Énard 2010, 445; 2008, 446).

31. Although Gregorius's life-changing day begins with an encounter with a woman on the bridge who he thinks was about to throw herself into the river, she disappears without a trace, and he does not try to find her or solve the mystery of the phone number she wrote on his forehead. Only the word she utters—"Portuguese"—remains ringing in his ears, triggering a chain reaction of acts, all to do with Portugal.

32. Gregorius also notices that the female passenger in his compartment on his way back from Lisbon reads a book called *Silence before Language*. The title undoubtedly resonates with Gregorius's taste and proclivities, possibly contributing to their quiet companionship during their train ride.

33. The ceiling lamps were to be inserted from the rooftop, so the technicians did not enter the interior of the carriages. See Natsume 2018, 9; 1977, 4–5.

34. An exception to this rule, at the Naples station, occurs when Luca speaks in French to purchase a ticket to Taranto. The ticket-booth operator's words are, however, neither quoted nor summarized (Larbaud 1958, 663).

35. The protagonist of *The Man Who Watched the Train Go By*, by Georges Simenon—a title cited in *Night Train to Lisbon* (though not as a novel but as a film adaptation)—also loves to play chess.

36. Katō Norihiro, relying on Kurata Akihito's graduation thesis, attributes the composition of the opening scene to Shimazaki Tōson's *Haru* (Spring), which ends with a scene on the train. See Katō 2008, 170–72.

37. See Biceaga 2010, especially chapter 3, "Secondary Passivity." I thank Carlos Arceo for finding the term and references to it.

38. Luca, in contrast, does not evoke ancient myths associated with Sicily—instead he associates the Ionian Sea, surrounding his new destination, with myths.

39. Francis even imagines Antonio's training as relevant to the railway: "He learns how to blow up railroad tracks around Marseille" (Énard 2010, 253; 2008, 256).

40. It is unclear how Francis is able to check the exact time while in the washroom; we have been told he does not wear a watch, and his cellphone is in his bag because he does not want to be tempted to check messages. From photographs of washrooms in comparable trains that I have been able to see, they do not seem to be equipped with clocks.

41. Isfahan, on the other hand, becomes a recurrent place name in the narrative. Maria João points out that Gregorius is making up for his unfulfilled juvenile desire to visit Isfahan by visiting Lisbon, when she notes the pictures of Isfahan on the wall of the principal's room in the boarding school that Gregorius has camped in during his stay (Mercier 2008, 351; 2004, 403).

42. The station as a space-time is a topic that is revisited as the theme of the Conclusion.

43. The section title "Different Trains" is inspired by the title of Steve Reich's composition (1988), which accompanies Beatriz Caravaggio's (2016) cinematic images in which two storylines are juxtaposed: one is Reich's childhood recurrent railway journey between the East and West Coasts of the United States, traveling between his parents, who were divorced; the other is of railway journeys Jewish people were forced to take across Europe in early 1940s.

44. The information pops up in the middle of a paragraph that mostly describes Nonomiya's search for a pencil in his pocket (he instead finds the invitation to Mineko's wedding reception, which he tears up and throws away in public).

45. The Trans-Siberian Railway is hidden deeply in *Zone*, through its reference to Guillaume Apollinaire's poem "Zone" (Énard 2010, 244; Énard 2008, 247), which in turn alludes to Blaise Cendrars's "La Prose du Transsibérien et de la petite Jehanne de France" (1913; translated by Ron Padgett as "The Prose of the Trans-Siberian and of Little Jeanne of France"). See Cendrars 1991. I appreciate Kornelia Drianovski's intertextual research on this.

CHAPTER 3

Juncture 1: *Wendy and Lucy*

The male characters examined in Chap. 2 dream of a better future when they board their trains: university education and (probably) a good professional career (*Sanshirō*); life with a newfound love and (likely) a celebrated career as a poet (*My Most Secret Council*); life with a newfound love and much wealth (*Zone*); and life with newfound friends, utilizing a newly acquired language (*Night Train to Lisbon*). Each man envisions a future that is rosy in its own way, and each has resources to count on—education, social connections, money, linguistic competence—during his railway journey and beyond. Passengers' experience of the space-time of the train can be affected by factors other than the corporeal: the purposiveness of their travels, the extent of their readiness and deliberations for the journey, and the prospect of its success. However, these conditions cannot be taken for granted as universal. When long-distance train passengers are not so well-to-do, their hope is dismal and the liberties they can take are limited, compared to those of male elite class members.[1]

The film *Wendy and Lucy* (2008), directed by Kelly Reichardt, proffers the story of a single woman, Wendy Carrol (Michelle Williams), who is in need of a well-paying job and who has no resources other than her able mind and body. She has no fixed abode, no supportive family (a sister indicates over the phone that no help can be expected from her), no mobile phone, little money to spare, few connections to rely on (a security guard at a supermarket offers local information and, at parting, a few

© The Author(s), under exclusive license to Springer Nature
Switzerland AG 2023
A. Sakaki, *Train Travel as Embodied Space-Time in Narrative
Theory*, Geocriticism and Spatial Literary Studies,
https://doi.org/10.1007/978-3-031-40548-8_3

dollars [1:04:12]), and no apparent professional training. Given the strin-
gency of her life, Wendy maintains remarkable composure, which she is
seldom seen to lose throughout this film full of misfortune. The lives of
such working-class women are precarious, so they must play their cards
prudently and in a timely way; danger may loom around the corner at any
moment, and their options are limited. Even romantic relationships are
not always desirable or fulfilling, but should be carefully screened because
they may threaten their well-being.[2] Wendy keeps her distance from men,
speaking to them only when necessary, as little as possible, and in a courte-
ous manner. She trembles with fear when a male thief sneaks up on her
while she is sleeping in a park (because her car has broken down and is at
the auto mechanic's). In the story "Train Choir" (Raymond 2009), on
which the film is based,[3] the worst consequence is avoided, and so it
appears in the film; as the man walks away, Wendy hurries into the public
bathroom, and nearly breaks down before she pulls herself together
(1:00:00). These single women without resources do not have much margin for error.

Wendy and Lucy may appear to be primarily an automobile travel narrative, or what Elena Gorfinkel calls "a road film, a genre of mythic, mascu-
linist American mobility and individualist adventure" (Gorfinkel 2012,
334); Wendy, with a dependent (her dog Lucy to feed), has driven hun-
dreds of miles from Indiana to Oregon. Though the film does not include
the circumstances that led her to this action, its source story, in which her
name is Verna, recounts that her apartment in Indiana was flooded and
that, consequently, she has fallen into credit card debt. From the screen,
too, it is obvious that she does not have much she can call her own: her
backpack and large plastic bags in the back seat and the trunk contain
nothing but clothes, underwear (she uses public bathrooms for washing
and grooming), a jewelry box (which holds nothing of value, the story
tells us, so that even a thief leaves it untouched), and Lucy's bowls and
dog food, which is running low (12:34). Still, those possessions require
storage space and transportation, which her car offers. Wendy intends to
drive as far as Bellingham, Washington, and take a ferry to Alaska so that
she can work at a cannery there to pay off her debts. She keeps a book of
her finances, which shows she will barely be able to reach her final destination. However, a series of misfortunes happen to her while street-parking
in Oregon —the most devastating being the car's mechanical failure (a
Honda Accord in the film, Toyota Camry in the story), which the local
garage declares unrepairable within her budget. This requires a major

change of plan, and she is eventually forced to leave town, without Lucy, by rail.

This last surrender of what Wendy must have deemed the essentials of her life—after her home, job, family, car, finally her beloved pet and companion—illustrates both the limits of happiness in the American lifestyle and the limitations of train/public transportation culture as anthropocentric and unforgiving toward animals. Lucy has been reported to the local pound while Wendy was in jail for shoplifting dogfood for her, and is living with a foster family. When Wendy assesses their home from outside, she quickly decides to leave Lucy there because she will obviously be cared for by the dog-loving family, who have a yard and a stable if not affluent life, whereas Wendy no longer has a car in which Lucy could have traveled with her.

In the story "Train Choir," the foster family's house is located next to the rail yard, which the heroine Verna walks into, catching a freight train that has begun to move. The adjacency of the spaces enables—and illustrates as smooth and compelling—her transition from one lifestyle to another. In the film *Wendy and Lucy*, Wendy is seen walking along the rails (1:13:28) for what appears to be some distance. This setup affords the camera opportunities to contemplate her procession from various angles. Though at the beginning of the walk her sobbing is audible (without her face seen), her footsteps are brisk and steady when the camera closes up on her feet treading gravel and weeds between the rails (1:13:41). Through this take, the camera establishes her as a determined traveler and prepares the viewer for her final departure on rails.

The train, however, is not a deus ex machina in *Wendy and Lucy*: images of rails recur, on the fringe of the town, usually empty, though seemingly irrelevant to the plot until the last sequence; and trains are present, too, either as immobile carriages or just passing through, often invisible yet audible. Gorfinkel situates such images of immobility in the context of "Wendy's performative stillness" which is:

> framed by a compositional arrest and an attention to emblematic shots and framings that often highlight emptied-out spaces and stripped-down, evacuated, or flattened opaque surfaces. Shots of freight train cars held in station, birds resting on electrical lines, bus stop intersections, and graffitied walls suggest an eerie motionless world wound down in a timeless anachronism. This is the visualization of the dead time of postindustrial arrest, of the hypostasis of manufacturing. (Gorfinkel 2012, 335)

As J. J. Murphy, too, confirms, images of cargo trains begin and end *Wendy and Lucy* (Murphy 2010, 166). So does their sound, drawing a slightly larger frame over the cinematic narrative. Gorfinkel observes that "we find Wendy returning to and reuniting with the freight train—a motif that has subtly and aurally leavened the entire film from its opening moments" (Gorfinkel 2012, 341).

To follow the "motif" of the train sound: Before the screen lights up for an image, the sound of trains is heard (0:12). Then it is heard again at the closing of the film. In the interim, the sound of trains is heard off-screen recurrently throughout the film, while characters are doing other things— that is, when the train has nothing to do with the matter at hand (3:00, 7:29, 8:26, 15:37, 34:03, 34:39, 55:21, 57:06, 1:13:00). The audience is aurally reminded of the functional railway's presence,[4] which is elusive yet ubiquitous.[5] When images of rails or carriages are shown on the screen (0:27, 8:26, 8:32, 52.18, 52:58, 1:13:28), they are usually inactive: rails empty, carriages immobile.

After Wendy fails to get to the Alaska ferry by car, she does not renounce her goal but instead changes her mode of transportation: she hops a freight train. She is on the route along the Pacific Northwest coast with no visible human aboard. The train serves forestry and fishery, both core industries of the Pacific Northwest that capitalize on the area's natural wealth and fuel passengers' dreams of a better life. This life differs, however, from the kind of life entertained by urbanite bourgeois, highly educated, literary-minded males such as Sanshirō, Luca, Francis, and even Gregorius in the narratives discussed in Chap. 2.

Unlike inter-city routes—such as the one from Chicago to LA in *The Narrow Margin* considered in Chap. 1, or the one from Milan to Rome in *Zone* in Chap. 2—the Pacific Northwest Coaster connects cities and sub-urbs to access points to the wilderness, for another world order and another lifestyle. Urban residents who travel on inter-city railways often either objectify the vast extension of land traversed by trains as a moving landscape or dismiss it as a neutral zone of no intrinsic value. Thus, as discussed in Chap. 1, the two Englishmen on the train in *The Lady Vanishes* are concerned only with arriving in London in time for the cricket match. Yet instead of traveling across such space between one city and another, Wendy's train is venturing into a space that is significant and resourceful in ways that are unimaginable to urban residents (perhaps with the exception of Francis, who can appreciate the plain in Tuscany).

Wendy pulls herself up into the open side of a freight car while its pace is slow. The point of view then shifts presumably to Wendy's own (1:14:25), from the interior of the train looking out, the screen showing tall trees passing outside the opening. Gorfinkel situates this aesthetic transition as follows: "Wendy resigns and disappears from the frame, her point of view inscribed from the position of the moving freight train, a mobile shot that indicates a release from stillness and waiting as well as an evanescence into the trope of itinerancy itself" (Gorfinkel 2012, 341). Then the sound of Wendy humming a familiar tune, heard earlier in the film while she was walking with Lucy (1:10, 14:22) or on her way to the foster home (1:08:46), comes from off-screen (1:14:45). This suggests that some sort of normalcy has been restored to her mental (and physical) state. Despite the loss of her beloved dog and old car, through arrest and potential assault, she remains the same person and is on her way, on the train. The train liberates her, whereas the car bound her.

That this sound of Wendy's humming is heard from off frame suggests that she has become a part of the space around her. Her agency in the sound-making is unimportant; what matters is that the sound is being heard. It is not the human subject who creates the environment; rather, it is the human biological system that is affected by and becomes immersed in the environment, which acquires "sonic spatiality" (Revill 2016) or "acoustic spatiality" (LaBelle 2010). Space is never passive and given for effects such as sound. Neither is it a human subject who creates (inanimate) sound that is heard across (empty) space. Rather, the sound forms space and the human subject. The viewer of *Wendy and Lucy* is ushered into a post-human, non-anthropocentric realm, which the train lets the passenger experience.

Even though Wendy's story ends before the train reaches her destination, her journey is consummated in terms of affordances, or how she negotiates with things in the space she navigates. She has been expelled by automobile culture and has in a way disavowed it, for she is now leaving it behind, on board a train. It is not even a passenger train, intended for human travel, yet it offers a space-time in the most physical sense. As long as humans like Wendy do not mind sharing space with inanimate things, they can be moved by such trains. In due course, the film and its original story imply, she will be at her destination. The dream that her car could not help her realize, but instead inhibited her from realizing by constantly

causing logistic and financial troubles, may come true thanks to the train
on the railway. A conclusion is yet to be drawn, but the prospect is provided, visually and aurally.

NOTES

1. The social inequality across long-distance train passengers is highlighted in
   Tickets (2006), a three-part film directed by Ermanno Olmi, Abbas
   Kiarostami, and Ken Loach. The three short narratives are threaded together
   by the Albanian migrant family that appears in all of them, in varied relevance to the plot, in the course of taking one train after another across
   southeastern Europe. The first segment traces the travel of a first-class passenger whose plan to fly home to Rome, Italy, from Innsbruck, Austria, has
   been changed due to a terrorist alert. This passenger witnesses migrant family members spilling the milk intended for their baby in the connecting area
   around the bathroom when an anti-terrorism soldier jostles them (saying
   they shouldn't be loitering there in the first place), and then orders warm
   milk and offers it to the baby's mother. The second part (in which the
   Albanian family is seen only in the background) features a wealthy woman
   traveling with a young male assistant whom she bosses around to the extent
   that he quits his job; and the third is about Celtic football fans traveling to
   Rome to watch a match, one of whose train tickets is stolen by a member of
   the migrant family because the family is attempting to ride the train even
   though they are one ticket short.
2. Thus, in *Dancer in the Dark* (discussed in Chap. 4), Selma keeps rejecting
   Jeff when he approaches her with romantic interest, yet she is nevertheless
   wrongly accused of trying to seduce another man whom she has befriended
   without any such intention.
3. "Train Choir," by one of the film's two screenwriters, Jon Raymond, was
   published in 2009, the year after the film's 2008 release.
4. The aurality of the train is also a significant feature in the three narratives
   discussed in Chap. 4.
5. Some scenes have background sound other than the train's, such as the traffic of individual cars.

CHAPTER 4

Best Friends for a While: Fugitives on the Train in "Night of the Milky Way Railway," *Night Passage*, and *The Naked Eye*

> *Mr. Bennett has never once looked at Mrs. Brown in her corner. There she sits in the corner of the carriage—that carriage which is travelling, not from Richmond to Waterloo, but from one age of English literature to the next, for Mrs. Brown is eternal, Mrs. Brown is human nature.*
> —Woolf 1924, 16

Shari Benstock explicates Virginia Woolf's point in "Mr. Bennett and Mrs. Brown," from which the excerpt above is made, as follows: in the case of "Mrs. Brown in the train carriage traveling from Richmond to Waterloo" "with Bennett, Wells, and Galsworthy," "[t]hese men ignore Mrs. Brown's presence, pointedly look in other directions, as though there were something inherently embarrassing about Mrs. Brown's presence in their midst." Among these three authors, "[o]nly Bennett has the courage to 'sidle' sedately towards Mrs. Brown, not to inquire of her health or comforts but to comment on the copyhold lease in mortgage to her solicitor" because "Bennett has no real interest in the woman in the train carriage" (Benstock 1985, 10). Benstock goes on to recognize a merit of Woolf's participation in the history of prose fiction, saying that Mrs. Brown

> has been found in her corner of the train carriage by a woman writer who bothered first to look carefully at her and next to set aside traditional claims

© The Author(s), under exclusive license to Springer Nature Switzerland AG 2023
A. Sakaki, *Train Travel as Embodied Space-Time in Narrative Theory*, Geocriticism and Spatial Literary Studies, https://doi.org/10.1007/978-3-031-40548-8_4

to "character" as a method of fictionally representing her. She has been found by a woman critic who drew a tentative (and silent) connection between the situation of women in patriarchal society and the place of "character" in turn-of-the-century fiction written by men. (Benstock 1985, 12)

Benstock summarizes Woolf's contribution as follows: "The discovery of Mrs. Brown in the train carriage itself constituted a first effort at dismantling the patriarchal literary tradition—a dismantling of the social and political institutions that support the production of literary texts themselves" (Benstock 1985, 13).

How, then, would our authors in Chap. 2—Natsume, Larbaud, Énard, and Mercier—treat Mrs. Brown, an old, plain, and financially pinched woman in a train carriage—in their works of fiction? Indeed, equivalents of Mrs. Brown have little business in the narratives examined in Chap. 2, with the exception of a nun in the carriage in *Zone*. (Gregorius befriends some older women, but while in Lisbon rather than on the train. The female he develops some temporary friendship on his return trip is young and rich.) These narratives' protagonists and focalizers, and sometimes even narrators, are solitary male passengers, and what they deem worthy of registering in their minds does not include a woman like Mrs. Brown. They may deliberately or subconsciously eliminate her presence in the train carriage as irrelevant to the stories they wish to tell.

In this chapter, we will look at passengers who may not matter to the authors of such accounts of male travelers who are preoccupied with themselves, their professional, personal, or aesthetic pursuits, and who have little time or inclination to consider a character such as Mrs. Brown who does not have a role to play in their lives. We will see how just such characters can claim a space in a narrative, and how their trajectories (how they have gotten on the train), perspectives, and/or voices may prevail in a railway journey. Characters deemed irrelevant by the elite male passengers begin to demonstrate their presence on the train through their communication with another passenger—not only with their voice but, perhaps more significantly, in their ability to listen, respond, and change accordingly. In this chapter, the central character of each narrative is not simply the focalizer or the narrator, projecting their gaze or voice onto others, but an absorbing subject who is open and receptive to a dialogic narrative—and even to an affective environment and things that occupy it.

Having sufficiently delinked the train from its idiomatic association with modern industrial social value, I will now examine how those who are marginalized by or even excluded from the development of the nation-state engage with the train. Ever since Woolf's call to novelists for attention to Mrs. Brown, we have seen those who used to be deemed negligible by the (narrative) authority because of their social class or gender come to occupy not only a "corner" of a train carriage but the center of narratives that are set on a train. These people take trains not to command a world that is at their disposal but due to necessity, the urge to make ends meet, or the need to escape a crisis. Their predicament may be momentarily assuaged in the transitory and alternative space-time of the train. Or they may be comforted by strangers on the train, precisely because of those strangers' distance from or irrelevance to the space-time outside the train.

In this chapter, I examine the special bonds that are developed or enhanced during a train journey between two significant characters in each of three narratives: (1) the children's story "Ginga tetsudō no yoru" (1934; translated by Sarah Strong as "Night of the Milky Way Railway" in 1991; translated by John Bester as "Night Train to the Stars" in 1992; hereafter simply "Night"), by Miyazawa Kenji (1896–1933); (2) the film *Night Passage* (2004), by Trinh T. Minh-ha and Jean-Paul Bourdier, which is a homage to Miyazawa's story; and (3) the novel *Das nackte Auge* (2004; trans. Susan Bernofsky *The Naked Eye*, 2009), by Yoko Tawada. As diverse as these works may be in terms of the historical moments they represent, their languages (Japanese, English, German), and their genres, they share the way the train becomes essential in the formation of narrative discourse, and also the way the train functions in the storyworld.

Miyazawa's "Night" is told by an extradiegetic narrator. The style is in a polite (*teinei*) form that is more common in formal speech, or in children's stories that are to be read aloud by adults (or that simulate such a format of transmission), than in modern Japanese texts, especially those meant for grownups to read silently (the practice of "mokudoku" [Maeda 1993, 2004]). This formal style enhances a dialogic atmosphere in which the narrator appreciates the audience's presence and engagement.

"Night" is probably the best-known and most discussed work by Miyazawa, who was also a poet, agricultural scientist, and educator. He revised it several times, without publishing it during his lifetime, and scholars have strived to establish the most definitive version from remaining fragments of manuscripts. The two of several English translations indicated above—Sarah Strong's "Night of the Milky Way Railway" (hereafter

Miyazawa 1991) and "Night Train to the Stars" by John Bester (hereafter Miyazawa 1992)—are based on different versions. Strong uses what is considered the author's final version, though with some missing pages (*kōki-kei*), whereas Bester's translation is based on an earlier, complete one.[1] In this chapter, I quote from either Strong's or Bester's translation as appropriate for the given context. When I discuss "Night" in relation to *Night Passage* by Trinh T. Minh-ha, for example, I quote from Bester's translation because Trinh explicitly cites it as a source.

This distinction aside, the core of the story remains the same in both versions/translations. Giovanni, the protagonist and focalizer, is a young boy alienated from his best friend and his father's best friend's son, Campanella, due to social inequality: Campanella is a son of a rich family, while Giovanni has to work before and after school because his father has gone missing and his mother is sick in bed at home. Giovanni is often ridiculed by classmates because of his social standing.[2] On the night of the Festival of the Centaur (an imaginary event the author seems to have invented by mixing Greek mythology and Japanese ethnic tradition [Yonechi and Richter 2009]), Giovanni suddenly finds himself aboard a train that is running along the galaxy, from one constellation to another, along with Campanella and a number of other passengers they meet for the first time, who board and disembark at various stations. Finally, Campanella disappears from the train without a trace, and Giovanni wakes up from a dream to learn Campanella is missing in the river after rescuing a friend from drowning. Though a fantasy, the story conveys an extensive knowledge of science, especially astronomy, geology, and zoology, as well as literature, history, and religion, to substantiate the space-time of the train and the course it takes.

Night Passage is a film co-directed by Jean-Paul Bourdier and Trinh T. Minh-ha; the latter also wrote the screenplay. Trinh cites Bester's translation "Night Train to the Stars" as a source of inspiration for the film, as well as Antoine de Saint-Exupéry's *Le Petit Prince* (1943; trans., *The Little Prince*), in which the Little Prince travels across the universe from one planet to another, seeking a true friend (Trinh 2013a). In the film by Trinh and Bourdier, the genders of most of the main characters are switched from those in Miyazawa's story (and in de Saint-Exupéry's). The central character is Kyra, a young woman who travels across the universe on the train with her estranged best female friend Nabi and a little boy called Shin. On the train, they meet many people, including some whom they thought were deceased. This is quite a departure from Kyra's everyday life, which she spends working as an apprentice carpenter and caring for her bedridden father, the two having been left by her mother. The camera position does not usually coincide with Kyra's perspective, as her figure is most often in the frame of the screen. She is more seen than seeing.

In both "Night" and *Night Passage*, the railway journey is framed by more realistic accounts of the protagonist's life at the beginning and the end of the narrative. Life in reality is difficult for the central character, so taking the train into the universe, and with their best friend as a traveling companion, is a liberation. Yet the bonds of friendship that are restored through the train are suddenly broken by the other person's (Campanella or Nabi's) disappearance from the train, followed by the revelation of the friend's death by drowning in reality—a devastating blow to the protagonist, who must endure it and keep living. The story closes with a spot of hope, however, as the deceased friend's father informs the protagonist that their missing parent is about to return home. With this news, the protagonist heads home at the end of the story.

There is no initial clear marker of the transition from the terrestrial portion of the story to the celestial railway journey. It is all of a sudden that Giovanni realizes he is riding a train:

> Giovanni heard a strange voice calling out, "Milky Way Station! Milky Way Station!"
>
> At the moment everything before his eyes became suddenly bright [...]. Giovanni rubbed his eyes over and over again.
>
> Looking around him, Giovanni found that the noisy little train he had been riding on for some time now was continuing on its way. Giovanni was seated, looking out the window of a narrow-gauge railway car. (Miyazawa 1991, 25–26; 2016a, 102–3)

The end of the journey, however, is more discernible. The narrative resumes after a line break with Giovanni waking up:

> Giovanni opened his eyes. Tired out, he had been sleeping on the grassy slope. His chest was strangely hot and cold tears ran down his cheeks.
>
> Like a coiled spring suddenly released, Giovanni leaped to his feet. [...] And the Milky Way, beside which he had just been strolling in his dream, now stretched as before, filmy white across the sky. Above the inky-black southern horizon it was particularly hazy, with the red star of Scorpio

twinkling prettily to the right. The position of the stars in the sky had not shifted very much, it seemed. (Miyazawa 1991, 76; 2016a, 146)

In *Night Passage*, the transition between reality and dream is visually presented. Kyra lies down on her back on a wooden bridge (though the script does not mention Kyra taking the action). The screen goes black, perhaps suggesting Kyra's loss of consciousness. The next thing we see is the interior space of the train, in which Kyra is seated on a dark green leather-like seat, alone. The carriage is dimly lit, with a few lamps on the ceiling. The isorhythmic sound of the wheels and the arrhythmic sound of whistles resound, off the frame of the screen. Then, as if startled, Kyra stands up, walks across the aisle, and moves to the other side, seating herself facing Nabi. The lack of explanation of the transition from one place (over the river) to another (the train carriage) also suggests that this is not happening in what we know as reality.

When Kyra and Nabi get off the train at another station, to explore the exterior space, they leave Shin behind because he is fast asleep. Storyteller 2 (a passenger who sings) says to them: "Don't wake him. He's having his own trip. You two should complete yours" (Trinh 2013b, scene 22, p. 47). The suggested confluence of "trip" and sleep (or a dream while sleeping) may anticipate Kyra's own later realization that she dreamed of her railway journey during her sleep. The word "trip" is mentioned again by Storyteller 1 (another passenger, a philosophical one) toward the end of the train ride, speaking to Kyra: "The whole of your friendship/ is condensed in this one passage/ A new dimension has come to you/ You'll have to go on all by yourself" (ibid., scene 36, p. 60). This remark concludes scene 36 of *Night Passage*. Scene 37 begins with the following direction: "Kyra wakes up from her sleep with tears in her eyes, lying in exactly the same position as when we last saw her lying down in scene 6. She slowly gets up, looking around strangely, and heads back home. WIDE shot of Kyra bicycling away in loneliness" (ibid., scene 37, p. 60). The film viewer can surmise that what they have seen since the time when Kyra was seen in the same place, was in a dream she has had.

Whereas the framing structure between reality and dream is shared in common by "Night" and *Night Passage*, there are also several significant discrepancies between the two narratives. To highlight only what matters in my present context: (1) people whom the central characters encounter in "Night" are strangers who embark and disembark at various stations, whereas in *Night Passage*, the central characters are accompanied by the boy Shin, whom they know, and visit deceased family members or friends off the train; (2) the stations are named after constellations in "Night," but in *Night Passage* stations are called "Words and Signs" and "Lights and Dancing," with Scorpio the only constellation mentioned; (3) things the two young female passengers come across in Trinh's film are more notably artificial—industrial tools, scientific experimental apparatuses, or artistic objects—rather than the natural flora, fauna, and geological materials that are conspicuous in Miyazawa's narrative; and (4) *Night Passage* lacks any equivalent of the forgotten home delivery of bottled milk that, in Miyazawa's narrative, triggers a string of events—Giovanni's leaving home, being ridiculed by nasty classmates he encounters, falling asleep on the grassy hill for a moment of respite afterward, and dreaming of a railway journey across the stars.[3]

Das nackte Auge (2004a; trans. *The Naked Eye*, 2009)[4] consists of 13 chapters, the first 12 of which have a first-person intradiegetic narrator "ich" ("I") who is also the protagonist and the focalizer. The last chapter is narrated in the third person, by an extradiegetic narrator, with a perspective stably set in a character who cannot be identified with and yet is connected to "I" in the preceding 12 chapters, as will be looked into later. In these 12 chapters, the narrator-"I" paraphrases scenes from films as she watches or recollects them. The narration is in the past tense, yet it does not appear as if much time has passed since the events and situations narrated, without any retrospective perspective, analepsis, or prolepsis (e.g., no anticipation of events to take place that are known to the narrator, no reflection on any event with the advantage of time).

As the novel begins, "I" is a high school student in Saigon, Vietnam, who visits East Berlin to give a speech at a communist youth convention and is kidnapped by a young capitalist male who takes her to Bochum, West Germany. Later, "I" moves to Paris inadvertently because she takes a wrong train when she is trying to board one for Moscow, and ends up staying in the French capital for ten years as an unregistered foreigner. Unable to enroll in school or be employed on a regular basis, she in chapters 2–12 frequents the cinema and begins to cross borders between the life she lives and the lives of film characters. As she admits and others attests to, "I" sees the same films many times, and frequency (Genette) is drastically different between the story time (how many times the protagonist sees a given film) and the discourse time (how many times the narrator talks about her viewing experience). Her recollection of any film must be informed by her perpetual processing of her multiple viewings, and thus multilayered, for her memory may wane or grow on its own.

The title of each of the 13 chapters is that of a film in which the actress Catherine Deneuve appears. Although the films are not arranged in the order of their release dates, the chapters appear to tell a story in chronological order. Indeed, in the Japanese edition of *The Naked Eye*, each chapter title includes the year in which its content is presumably set, ranging from 1988 to 2000, with no leap, repetition, or reversal in order. The table of contents in the Japanese edition (2004b) also supplies the dates of the film releases, and in chapters 5 (1992), 9 (1996), 11 (1998), 12 (1999), and 13 (2000), the film release year and the historical setting of the protagonist's story match. In no chapter does the film release postdate the year in which the chapter is set. It is thus historically plausible that in the first 12 chapters, the protagonist-focalizer-narrator sees or hears of the titular film.[5] Chapter 13, though, is related to the film in the title in a more complicated manner. The chapter tells a story that appears to be a prequel to the title film (*Dancer in the Dark*) and to indicate, in a certain way, what may happen to the protagonist-focalizer, whose name, Selma, and partial circumstances (she is to immigrate to the United States and to be executed there) coincide with those of the heroine of the film.

The novel's relevance to my study lies mainly in "Chapter 1: *Repulsion*," in which the railway and train are of critical importance. However, there are also other, subtler connections to the ways the train as a space-time is experienced and represented. For the time being, suffice it to say that there are some parallels between the train as space-time and the cinema as space-time, and that the companionship (mostly with other females) of fellow film viewers is comparable to the companionship between passengers who share a train journey with each other.

As may be evident by now, these narratives are significantly different from those I have already examined in Chap. 2—the four narratives explicated there are about railway journeys for passengers who have goals to achieve and things to look forward to in the future, whether or not their aspirations materialize. In contrast, the narratives discussed in this chapter are about characters who are leaving behind what is undesirable. The point of their travels by rail is to flee rough situations—as we saw in *Wendy and Lucy* in Chap. 3. They might hope for something better, but they haven't really thought it through. Their journeys are oriented more toward departure than toward an end goal. These narratives generously set up their situations for the reader/viewer at their departure point, and then these characters grow increasingly fascinated with the train itself, which becomes an embodiment of the protagonists' hope, and of the alterity that they long for in the face of adversity. Furthermore, whereas the four narratives studied in Chap. 2, as well as *Wendy and Lucy* in Chap. 3, feature solitary passengers who stick to or mull over their plans, the three discussed below have their protagonists meet friends, allies, and enemies with whom the space-time of the train becomes significant and transformative in itself. Conversation with companions, rather than silent reflections, becomes critical in the narratives discussed in this chapter.

The rest of this chapter is divided thematically into the following sections: (1) with *no place to belong to*, the protagonists head for the train as a heterotopia or an other space (Foucault 2004, 2008), a transitory space, yet not a non-place (Augé 2009) but a special place; (2) *death by rail or a second life by rail* are the options trains can offer those who are up against walls of the harsh life off rails; (3) *rushing to the train*, not due to enslavement to and release from the timetable, as we saw in Chap. 2, but due to the narrative demands of an encounter that will change the protagonist's life and also mitigate and reset the power of the protagonist; (4) *sudden beginning and end* to friendship—not love but empathy at first sight, instantaneous recognition of sameness—illuminating the irrevocable nature of meeting a stranger on the train—whether or not it is desired; (5) *different trains*, again, as we saw in Chap. 2, as hypertexts for the current one, which, in the narratives chosen for this chapter, feature the collective memory of suppressed people and the violated land evoked on personal journeys; (6) *all things that flow*—cosmic time, celestial terrains, currents, *chemins de fer*, films, milk—which unearth an even larger context than geopolitics, archeological, geological, and astronomical knowledge, between earth and heaven and between nature and artifices, and provide perspective for characters, with the train emerging as a more ambiguous and potent existence than a modern utilitarian instrument; and (7) a constellation of *alternative lives in adjacent spaces*, rather than binary or triangular relationships of contrasts, desires, and competition.

1   No Place to Belong to: Fugitives Ride Trains

Giovanni, the protagonist-focalizer of Miyazawa's "Night," transitions from an observer of the train that passes by to a passenger who experiences the interior space of the moving vehicle of the train. As verified in Chap. 1, these are two of the three positions in relation to the train configured by Foucault (2004, 2008). Like the protagonist of Georges Simenon's *The Man Who Watched the Trains Go By* (mentioned in Chap. 2), Giovanni is initially outside the train, looking at the passing train with both his eyes and mind:

> From the direction of the fields he could hear the sound of a train. The windows of the little train were a tiny row of red. When Giovanni considered that inside there were people on a journey laughing, peeling apples, doing all sorts of things, he felt unbearably lonely and shifted his gaze once again to the sky.
>
> They say that white band across the sky is all made of stars. (Miyazawa 1991, 24; 2016a, 101)

Giovanni cannot afford to travel for fun, as he imagines those invisible train passengers do; he is poor and responsible for looking after his ailing mother and earning a living for the two of them[6] during his father's extended absence from home. The remoteness of the sound and the elusiveness of the image of the train accentuate a sense of exclusion Giovanni experiences on earth. He looks up to the sky, presumably to fight tears in the first place, but also to the effect of observing the nocturnal sky full of stars.

The sky does not seem too far away or unfamiliar to Giovanni; instead, he thinks that the sky is "a great stretch of countryside with little woods and pastures and the like" (Miyazawa 1992, 27; 2016a, 102). Two things are to be noted here: first, a sense that the sky and earth are not separate but adjacent to each other; second, that the sky is not empty but filled with things, as the earth is. The former realization prepares for an easy transition between the earth and the universe that Giovanni is about to experience, as well as a fundamental challenge to Euclidian space in which the horizontal and the vertical lines cross as distinct axes rather than being parallel or merging with each other. The latter point, about the sky's state as dense rather than vacuous, is verified by the description of things, solid, liquid, and gaseous, that fill the universe as observed, breathed in, smelled, touched, and tasted by Giovanni during his visit there. In sum, the distinction and connectivity of the earth and the sky are confirmed in this transitional segment in the narrative, between Giovanni's unfortunate interaction with his classmates and his fantastic railway journey with Campanella: although the earth and the sky are places of contrastive character, one of exclusion and the other of inclusion, they are neither far nor detached from each other, but close to and contiguous with each other.

Yet even on board the Milky Way Railway, he still struggles with the stigma of his sense of exclusion: when the conductor visits their carriage for ticket inspection, he immediately feels insecure, thinking he does not have a ticket[7]—not only because he does not remember purchasing one, but also because he knows he could not have afforded one. Eventually, however, he finds a piece of green paper in his pocket, which, unlike Campanella's ordinary gray ticket, turns out to be a free pass valid forever and for as far as he goes.[8] The conductor treats him with increased respect, and so does the Bird Catcher, another passenger who has recognized Giovanni's ticket as a rare possession. Thus, Giovanni's status on the train is confirmed as privileged, completely different from his status on earth.

Kyra's circumstances in *Night Passage* evidently parallel Giovanni's: she works in a carpentry firm (while Giovanni works at a printer) and cares for her sick father (while Giovanni cares for his sick mother); she is also ridiculed by her classmates for her missing mother (as Giovanni is for his missing father). She is also troubled by the conductor's visit for ticket inspection, and yet finds a green ticket just as miraculously as Giovanni does, with which she can travel anywhere in the universe and forever, much to the exaltation of Storytellers 1 and 2 (Trinh 2013b, scene 22, pp. 43–44). In the transitional scene in which Kyra lies down on her back, the sound of the train is heard in the background—just as it is audible to Giovanni's ears in his transitional scene. The distant sound of the trains—which is heard throughout *Wendy and Lucy*, as discussed in Chap. 3—materializes a liminal space from where one can transition to the other world.

These appearances—and disappearances—that cannot realistically be accounted for indicate the proximity and adjacency of heaven and earth, which are to be translated as the land of the dead and that of the living. After Nabi and Shin walk out of the carriage, never to return, Kyra is shown a train car full of people, each with a candle in hand, who, like specters, fade out just as suddenly as they have appeared. The closeness and constant emergence of the deceased in the train carriage is a shared predilection in Miyazawa's story and Trinh's film, enhancing the liminality of the train. Just as Kyra feels alienated from the community on earth but finds her place in the train, so the deceased who are unwelcome on earth are freer to come and mingle with others on the night train across the universe. Trinh remarks: "Since the journey is visualized primarily as a passage, great attention is given to 'the time of the between' and the 'crossroads'—that is, to transformation and transition as time-spaces of their own. Thus, rather than at the cut, it was the *dissolve* (and the *cross-dissolve*) that I chose as an aesthetic principle for the transitions" (Trinh 2013a, 14).

"I" in *The Naked Eye* is driven from East Berlin to Bochum in West Germany while she is drunk and unconscious, where she is loosely held captive by a man called Jörg who sexually abuses her. She dreams of fleeing by train from Bochum to Moscow, since she has heard of this railway (discussed further below, in the section on "Different Trains")—so much so that at night she hears the sound of the trains: "From a distance I could hear the faint grating sound of the drive axle, the clatter of the couplings, and a long, howling reverberation from the train tracks. Somewhere not far from my pillow a train was passing. Only insomniacs were aware of its existence" (Tawada 2009, 27; 2004a, 28).[9] This ambiguity of the presence, or the elusiveness, of the train—what Nancy A. Adelson calls "convergence of real and imagined dimensions" (Adelson 2016, 287)—seems comparable to the case in "Night" and *Night Passage*: the train is a phantasmagoria, an object that desire allows to emerge in the sensible world, and that seems unattainable for those whose lives are difficult, surrounded by predators. The unlikelihood of the train passing Bochum is confirmed later in *The Naked Eye*:

> At first I couldn't see the grass-covered railway tracks on the far side of the cross. The rails were rusty, perhaps many years had passed since they'd last been used, perhaps no one had ever looked at them in all this time. The tracks disappeared to the left in the shade of trees, to the right in the sunny no-man's land. [...]
> I wanted to wait for a train to board, but there was no train station. I returned several times on other days and walked along the tracks in both directions. I found no trace of any station present or past. Nor did I ever see a train pass by. Only on sleepless nights when I lay in bed, my eyelashes on fire, could I hear the sound of a train far off in the distance. (Tawada 2009, 34–35; 2004a, 34–35)

The liminal being connects aurally, not visually, to obsolete things neglected in the society. Sound remains prominent in the narratives we examine in this chapter, perhaps because sound is antithetical to the modern norm that has verified truth visually: aurality is a resource left to those who are ostracized from the normative society. And those socially under-privileged people demonstrate superb abilities to listen to others' voices, to music, and to the sounds of things[10]—to the sound of a distant train, in this case.

2 Death by Rail or a Second Life by Rail

Suicide by rail has long been a narrative device for dramatic effect. Leo Tolstoy's *Anna Karenina* (1877), in which the eponymous character ends her turbulent life by throwing herself in front of a running train, is, of course, the example that first springs to mind for many. *Karenina and I* (2017) is a documentary film by Tommaso Mottola about a Norwegian actress, Gørild Mauseth (also the co-screenwriter of this film with the director), who plays the role of Anna Karenina in a theatrical adaptation of the Tolstoy novel. The cinematic narrative tells how the actress's horizon expands as she travels across Russia by train for research in preparation for the performance. Whereas the train is a medium of suicide for Anna Karenina, and a device to end the novel thereby, the actress who is to play Anna finds a second self, or a second life, as she travels by train. One persona stands outside the train, waiting for its arrival, while the other sits inside it after its departure from where she was. As the title of the film suggests, the two personas come to exist and evolve through each other, as a model and embodiment, as a way of coming to life and becoming a character, and as a way of dying and living.

While suicide by rail has been discussed as an encapsulation of symptoms of modernity, the focal characters considered in this chapter instead give themselves a second life through fleeing by train from the current state of their existence. Suicide by rail is allowed to happen in one narrative discussed in this book—*Sanshirō*, examined in Chap. 2—and is prevented in another in *The Naked Eye*, one of the focal narratives in this chapter. Comparing the two scenes illuminate not only the plot distinction between the two novels, or different functions that the train plays in them, but also the relationality of two characters—one suicidal, and the other observer-like.

In *Sanshirō*, the protagonist is house-sitting close to a railroad for Nonomiya, and overhears the utterance of a woman who, moments later, is found dead on the rails:[11]

> Suddenly a voice cried in the distance.
> "Oh, oh, just a little longer."

It seemed to come from the rear of the house, but he could not be certain. It was too far away and had ended too quickly. But this single cry had sounded to Sanshiro like a true soliloquy, the solitary utterance of one who had been *abandoned by all, who sought an answer from none*. An eerie feeling came over him. Another train echoed in the distance. He heard it drawing nearer, and when it passed below the bamboo grove, its roar was fully twice the volume of the earlier train's. Sanshiro went on sitting there vacantly while the room continued to tremble, but in a sudden flash, he brought together the cry he had heard and the roar of the train. A shock ran through him when he saw what a frightening connection he had made. (Natsume 2018, 75–76; 1999, 1977, 42; emphasis added)

As he hears some staff members of the railway station come running, Sanshirō joins them:

Sanshiro went back through the study to the garden and stepped into his wooden clogs. He scrambled down the six-foot embankment and started after the lanterns.

He had gone only a few yards when someone else jumped down from the embankment. The man spoke to him.

"What is it? Someone hit by a train?"

Sanshiro tried to say something, but his voice would not come. The man's black shadow went on ahead. This must be Nonomiya's next door neighbour, he decided, and followed after. Walking another fifty yards down the track, he came to where the lanterns and the men had stopped. The men stood mute, holding the lanterns high. Sanshiro looked down without a word. In the circle of light lay part of a corpse. The train had made a clean tear from the right shoulder, beneath the breast, to the left hip, and it had gone on, leaving this diagonal torso in its path. The face was untouched. It was a young woman. (Natsume 2018, 77–78; 1977, 42–43)

As Freedman (2011, 107) highlights, Sanshirō is so deeply affected by this experience that he cannot forget the suicidal woman's face and voice, and even dreams of her that night. The narrator even resorts to rarely used prolepsis to emphasize the lasting impact of the incident on his mind: "Sanshiro would always remember the way he felt at that moment" (Natsume 2018, 77; 1977, 43).[12] Even so, Sanshirō lacks the ability to save the woman from suicide by rail. The sensations he experiences due to the immediacy of the sound and sight of the incident (the woman's voice, the extraordinary roar of the train presumably as it goes over the woman's body, the sight of the corpse) are authentic, yet he cannot act upon them.

Indeed, unlike Nonomiya, whose voyeuristic reaction to the media reports the next day shocks Sanshirō, he does not reduce the woman to an object of curiosity. With no name, no story behind her suicide known to Sanshirō, however, she remains a stranger to him.

The only sign of empathy Sanshirō may have felt for the woman is his sense that she has been "abandoned by all" and that she seeks "an answer from none." Like Giovanni in "Night," Kyra in *Night Passage*, and "I" in *The Naked Eye*, the woman is supposedly excluded from the world and desperate to find a way out of it. Whereas these characters in the narratives examined here get on the train to escape their circumstances, the woman in *Sanshirō* seeks refuge in death—death by train, that is. The train can take away those who wish to depart quickly and far from where they are at its tremendous speed, and it can also destroy those who wish to end their lives quickly by its weighty hardware.

In stark contrast to Sanshirō, the narrator-protagonist "I" in *The Naked Eye* impulsively does all she can to save the suicidal woman she runs into at the rails near *Sieben Planeten* in Bochum, a point of contact with the railway tracks that she has formed the habit of visiting in the hope of catching a train to Moscow, as mentioned earlier:

> Another woman was already standing in my favourite spot by the rusty tracks. Her long coat had a high collar that resembled the gills of a tropical fish. On her head she wore ornaments that looked somehow extraterrestrial. Perhaps she was a singer who'd fled from the stage of an opera with futuristic sets. What could be the reason for her having hurried here without removing her makeup and changing clothes? She was older than I was, and had something extraordinary about her. Her presence even seemed to be changing the consistency of the air around her. (Tawada 2009, 37; 2004a, 36)

The other woman is a perfect stranger whom "I" has never seen. No word is exchanged between the two women, yet there is an instantaneous camaraderie, which is a pretext for the action taken in the next moment:

> Suddenly the woman lay down on the tracks and pressed her face to one of the ties. I ran to her, took her by the shoulder and tried to roll her over, but she was as immovable as the spire of a temple whose root is buried in the earth. I thought I heard the sound of a train approaching from a distance— this was impossible though. These tracks had known nothing but rust and weeds for years, certainly no wheels. Then I heard it once more, the sound of an approaching train. Or was it just a streetcar heading into the city

centre? Or was it the drone of a refrigerator that had been implanted in the depths of the eardrums during my days of loneliness? I wanted to tell the woman to get up, but I couldn't think of any words. The old words had left my skull, I needed new words to be able to speak to her. But what were new words? The heavy iron wheels continued to turn, coming closer and closer. I glanced about helplessly. Somewhere there had to be an alarm system. In a bush I saw something red—a box with a painted lightning bolt. A lever was growing crookedly out of the box like the tail of a dragon. It wouldn't budge. I pressed the lever down with the whole weight of my body, my legs dangling in the air, and then crashed down with the lever. The frozen silence gave way to a siren. Innumerable tiny red blinking lights set in a line at regular intervals into the distance began flashing on and off. (Tawada 2009, 37–38; 2004a, 36–38)

"I's" efforts to save the woman on the rails pay off: the train stops at the alarm signal she has sent, and the staff members attend to the woman. Even though "I" subsequently takes advantage of the incident to board the train unnoticed, initially she had no motive besides saving the other woman, whose only connection with her consisted of appearing at the same spot and nodding to her. The incident gives "I," as well as the suicidal woman, a second life—a life after the life from which they wanted to flee. Whether or not it turns out to be a good life is another question.

The story of "I" moves past the other woman behind and forward as she steps into the train carriage without knowing what might happen to the other woman. Yet "I" re-encounters her in the cinema, as a character in a film she is watching. Indeed, each of the two, "I" and the other woman, has earned a life aside from the "real" world, that is, a life in cinema—either as a spectator in the auditorium or a character on the screen. These two incidental encounters frame "I's" life. She reflects on the railway track incident as a turning point. By saving the life of someone who wanted to die, "I" begins to live a life as she did not intend to, in two ways: as an illegal and officially non-existent alien, and as a cinephile lurking in the dark space of the cinema interior. In a way, "I" dies instead of the other woman, and lives a second life as a dead person, a specter.

Although the act of railway suicide does not materialize either in "Night" or in *Night Passage*, the theme of death abounds in both. Just as "I" in *The Naked Eye* tries to save the suicidal woman from the railway tracks, so Campanella in "Night" tries to save Zanelli, a classmate who has fallen into the river from a boat while floating a light on the surface of the water, as is a custom on Centaur Festival Night. Campanella succeeds in saving Zanelli, yet is swept away by the rapid current and presumed dead himself. This sequence of events is revealed retrospectively, in the last section of the story, after Giovanni awakens from a dream of the railway journey. Yet during the train ride there are hints of something having gone terribly wrong with Campanella, such as his looking wet and pale, which readers will appreciate in retrospect at the end of the story.[13]

In *Night Passage*, Nabi and Shin say something that Kyra cannot quite comprehend, which is related to her attempt to save Shin, who has fallen from their boat in a manner similar to Zanelli's fall in "Night." In their case, however, Nabi can save neither Shin nor herself, and they both appear on the train, to Kyra's surprise:

Nabi
The water was too strong, Shin couldn't help it. I couldn't help it. By the time I got a hold of him, I couldn't find my way up.
(Trinh 2013b, scene 7, p. 28)

Shin
It was so dark, so dark. . . . My light got carried away. I couldn't run fast enough to catch it.
(ibid., scene 7, p. 29)

Although Kyra hears their words, notices that both Nabi and Shin have wet hair, and knows that they appear suddenly, out of nowhere, she cannot thread those mysterious events together. In an earlier scene that comes close to a foreshadowing, she saw them together on the river shore, preparing for the Festival of Lights.[14] In retrospect, this is the last time Kyra sees them alive, and it occurs close to the place of their deaths.

During their railway journey, Kyra and Nabi step out of the train at a station and watch a performance of dancers with lights from a boat, the significance of which is explained in the script: "Later in a dance, Nabi's death by drowning is enacted, which Nabi watches herself" (ibid., scene 35, p. 57).[15] In the last scene Kyra, now awakened from her dream, arrives at the scene of the incident and is told by an unidentified acquaintance there (by voice only) of the accident. Eventually, she hears Nabi's father declare his daughter's presumed death.

In both narratives, death by water is the reason for characters who have died to suddenly emerge on the train in the living protagonist's dream. I will consider the general connection between water and the railways later in this chapter. For the time being, I would simply like to argue that it is not entirely arbitrary that the protagonist's best friend is killed by water, an alternative to the train as a wielder of a fatal blow, and joins the railway journey of the protagonist. Whereas water separates the living and dead, the train reunites them, for the duration of the ride. The train in each narrative is a space-time in which the living and the deceased mingle. The train does not serve as a killing machine, as it often does elsewhere, yet it does serve as a space-time of mourning and reuniting with the dead.

It is widely known that Miyazawa was deeply affected by his younger sister Toshiko's death (from illness) and responded to the event by repeatedly writing with her loss in mind. One such text, the poem "Aomori banka" ("Aomori Elegy"), is loosely set in the train from Hanamaki to Aomori, the first leg of a trip Miyazawa took to Sakaehama, Karafuto (Sakhalin), while he was still in mourning for his late sister. This may account for the parallels that the poem often draws between the present-day railway journey and the journey of the dead to the underworld. When his train passes a station, the poet muses:

Did she pass, all by herself, such a desolate station?
In a direction not knowing where to
Through a path not knowing into what
Did she keep walking on, all by herself?
(Miyazawa 1973, ll. 55–59, pp. 156–57; my translation)

In Miyazawa's imagination, the train is both fascinating and moribund; it cannot but remind him of his sister's passing, and thus becomes a space-time for mourning. "Aomori Elegy" and "Night" evidently share the blurring of the boundary between life and death and the concurrence of mourning and traveling by train. The reader can identify several motifs present in both texts: for example, "The scent of apples" in the poem, which "permeates even the smooth and cold vitrine of the window" (ibid., ll. 219–21, p. 165), is present in the narrative (Miyazawa 1991, 54; 2016a, 123) as well.

The other passengers who disembark midway in "Night" are inspired by those who perished in the shipwreck of the *Titanic* and who are taking the train to their final resting place among the stars.[16] Though not in the train carriages, Kyra and Nabi in *Night Passage* see people known to be deceased acting as though they are alive in places they visit temporarily off the train. The contiguity of the terrains for the dead and the living is evident in both stories, and it is the train that makes it possible to meet the deceased, either in its own interior space or in places that the train enables passengers to access.

3 RUSHING TO THE TRAIN AGAIN, AND ITS VARIATIONS

Let us return to Virginia Woolf and Mrs. Brown for a moment. Having set up the premise of her essay in terms of what characters male writers neglect to observe in their writings, Woolf submits hypothetical material for narration in "Mr. Bennett and Mrs. Brown": "One night some weeks ago, then, I was late for the train and jumped into the first carriage I came to" (Woolf 1924, 6). "I" is behind schedule and has to dash for the train. As with the late arrivees observed in Chap. 2, time is critical before such a departure and then expands once boarding is accomplished. In this case, no reservation has been made, no preference honored; the carriage is just grabbed as needed, then an empty seat found, and taken promptly.

So far, this is an ordinary occurrence, yet the encounter that follows is a one-time-only event, as stressed in the text—"I watched her disappear, carrying her bag, into the vast blazing station. [...] And I have never seen her again, and I shall never know what became of her" (Woolf 1924, 9)— not the repeated act of sharing a commuter train or bus day in and day out, to increase reciprocal visual familiarity in the absence of conversation, as observed by Georg Simmel (2002). The one-time encounter leaves an indelible impression on the female passenger's mind, an impression marked by undeniable empathy sufficient to consider the writing of a story (if not sufficient to actually write one).

The singular, irreplaceable, and unforgettable encounter is also present in the three narratives under discussion here. In Miyazawa's "Night," it is not the protagonist-focalizer but his best friend who has run to catch the train. Campanella speaks to Giovanni, who is surprised to find him unexpectedly:

> "Everyone ran as fast as they could, but they were too late. Even Zanelli ran as fast as he could but he couldn't catch up."
> "Do you want to wait for the others somewhere?" he asked.
> "Zanelli's already gone home," Campanella replied, "His father came for him." ... "Darn, I left without my water bottle, and I forgot my sketchbook, too. It doesn't matter, though. We'll be at Cygnus Station soon." (Miyazawa 1991, 26; 2016a, 103–4)

As will be revealed much later in the narrative, Zanelli, who initially falls into the water, is saved by Campanella, who is then swept away by the rapid current and disappears. The saved one is taken home by his father, whereas the savior's father will wait 45 minutes after the accident to pronounce his son dead. In this earlier sequence, however, Zanelli is described as having missed the train and been taken home by his father, whereas Campanella has made it onto the train. The train is indeed a special space-time, which only those who are deceased (like Campanella) or marginalized (like Giovanni) can enter.

Later in "Night," Giovanni and Campanella run for their lives as they try to catch the train at a station where it had paused for a fixed time: "The two boys raced off over the white rock at top speed in order not to be late for the train. They found that they could truly run like the wind. They did not grow short of breath and their knees did not get hot and sore. Giovanni thought that if they could run like this, they could gallop all over the world" (Miyazawa 1991, 40; 2016a, 113). The act of running for the train may accentuate its being a privilege, a precious opportunity granted only to chosen ones. Those privileged passengers are entitled to travel by the special train across the universe and access the truth of the universe, which is not open to ordinary living humans.

The "I" in *The Naked Eye* does not run, yet also has only a moment to spare in boarding the train that she has stopped by sending a signal to save the suicidal woman's life: "I crept through the bushes that ran alongside the train and reached its centre. One side of a double folding door was still open from where a conductor had leaped out. I slipped into the train and walked down the deserted corridor" (Tawada 2009, 39; 2004a, 38). When "I" executes this feat of sneaking through the narrow gate of space-time into the carriage, she feels as if her dream has half come true: in time, she will arrive in Moscow. For her, a communist youth, this would have been a privilege, the rarity of which is especially noteworthy because there is no station in Bochum at which the Moscow-bound train would stop. Though the train she boards turns out to be Paris-bound and her plan fundamentally thwarted, at this point, her action of quickly entering the train is a version of dashing for the train and jumping onto it—an alternative version, certainly, yet using equally limited time, a rare accomplishment.

4   SUDDEN BEGINNING AND END

The duration of a train journey is finite, and so is that of the narrative. The narrative thus needs to be structured efficiently in order to cover the necessary content of what transpires on the train. The way the short story "A Dream of Armageddon" (1901) by H. G. Wells (1999) is configured is a good example: the narrative begins at the moment the narrator of the frame narrative, who is already seated in the carriage, catches sight of the other passenger, the narrator of the embedded narrative, boarding the train. The long account of the embedded narrator has not arrived at its conclusion when the frame narrator becomes aware that the train is slowing down and entering the London-Euston station where he is about to get off the train. The frame narrator urges the embedded narrator to tell him what happened at the end of his dream which he has been telling him about, just as the noise of the station fills the carriage through the opened door and a porter inquires about his luggage. The end of the embedded narrative is the end of the whole narrative, too, precisely because the frame narrator disembarks and runs out of time to properly frame it in the story-world—to the great effect of the sudden finitude in the narrative discourse. The abruptness of the beginning and the end of the space-time that two passengers spend together corresponds to the suddenness of the opening and closing of the narrative.

The test narrative of the railway journey that Woolf inserts into the essay "Mr. Bennett and Mrs. Brown" also begins and ends in a rush. As seen earlier, the narrator-"I" jumps into the train carriage and takes an empty seat, then realizes that her fellow passengers seated near her are taken aback:

> As I sat down I had the strange and uncomfortable feeling that I was interrupting a conversation between two people who were already sitting there. [...] They were both elderly, the woman over sixty, the man well over forty. They were sitting opposite each other, and the man, who had been leaning over and talking emphatically to judge by his attitude and the flush on his face, sat back and became silent. I had disturbed him, and he was annoyed. The elderly lady, however, whom I will call Mrs. Brown, seemed rather relieved. [...] There was something pinched about her—a look of suffering, of apprehension, and, in addition, she was extremely small. Her feet, in their clean little boots, scarcely touched the floor. (Woolf 1924, 6)

Then, the end of the story of Mrs. Brown, the train passenger, is related as follows:

> I had no time to explain why I felt it somewhat tragic, heroic, yet with a dash of the flighty, and fantastic, before the train stopped, and I watched her disappear, carrying her bag, into the vast blazing station. She looked very small, very tenacious; at once very frail and very heroic. And I have never seen her again, and I shall never know what became of her. (ibid., 9)

The apparently inconsequential encounter with and losing sight of Mrs. Brown is, however, deceiving. As "I," who is no longer the narrator, but the author of the story, explains:

> The story ends without any point to it. But I have not told you this anecdote to illustrate either my own ingenuity or the pleasure of travelling from Richmond to Waterloo. What I want you to see in it is this. Here is a character imposing itself upon another person. Here is Mrs. Brown making someone begin almost automatically to write a novel about her. I believe that all novels begin with an old lady in the corner opposite. (ibid.)

Woolf here obviously champions stories of characters who tend to be deemed insignificant and negligible by male authors in the tradition of English literature. In the present context, however, I would like to take the abruptness of the beginning and end of "I's" acquaintance with Mrs. Brown as a mandate of railway journey narratives. In other words, the issue at stake here is also about the genre set in a specific space-time, in which strangers may develop a certain kind of intimacy that is to last only for the duration of their train ride together.

As mentioned earlier, the railway journey in "Night" begins suddenly and ends as the protagonist wakes up from a dream:

> In the seat directly in front of his was a tall boy in a black, wet-looking jacket, with his head thrust out of the window watching outside. Something about the set of the boy's shoulders was so familiar that Giovanni felt a strong urge to find out who it was. He was just about to stick his own head out of the window to see, when the boy drew his in and looked at Giovanni.
> It was Campanella. Giovanni was going to ask him whether he'd been there all along, when Campanella said:
> "The others—they ran like mad but they got left behind. Zanelli was the same. He ran as hard as he could, but he couldn't catch up."

Of course, thought Giovanni, we decided to leave together. (Miyazawa
1992, 28–29; 2016a, 103)

Then Campanella disappears just as seamlessly and tracelessly as he appears:

Feeling an indefinable sadness, he [Giovanni] was still gazing absently in the
same direction when, on the opposite bank of the river, he saw two telegraph poles standing with their red crossarms lined up as though they were
linking arms.
"Campanella," said Giovanni, turning around as he spoke, "we'll go on
together, eh?"
But there was no Campanella in the seat where Campanella had been
sitting until just now. There was nothing but the dark velvet of the seat,
shining at him there.
Giovanni shot up like a bullet. Leaning out of the window so as not to be
heard in the train, he beat his breast and shouted wildly, then burst
out crying.
Everything round about seemed suddenly to have turned dark. (Miyazawa
1992, 87–88; 2016a, 146)

In the original, Giovanni's remark intended for Campanella has a stronger
tone, indicated by "doko made mo" ("as far as we go," "until the end of
the road"), indicating Giovanni's wish to continue traveling with his best
friend infinitely, endlessly. Yet, just as he voices the resolve and requests his
friend's agreement, he realizes that their journey has ended abruptly. This
realization is instantaneous; he does not look for Campanella or call out
for him. Instead, he worries that his emotional reaction may draw attention from other passengers and leans out of the window to avoid embarrassment. Then he reacts with chest beating, shouting, and crying—rather
than by way of words. The spontaneity and immediacy of Giovanni's outburst of emotion are unmistakable there, though his sense of propriety in
a public space—as well as his recognition of the train as a public space—is
also evident.
Unlike Giovanni in "Night," Kyra in *Night Passage* is more expressive
of her confusion at the sudden appearance and disappearance of Nabi and
Shin. With respect to Nabi's appearance, the script relates:

Kyra is sitting inside a train all by herself. She looks around at the empty
seats and looks out from her window to the dark sky. When she turns back
she is startled to suddenly see someone sitting against the window on the

other side. The person's head is turned toward the window, and it is not until this person turns around that she recognizes her friend Nabi. Kyra goes over to sit in front of Nabi, whose hair looks wet.

KYRA

"Nabi! You were here all along!"

(Trinh 2013b, scene 7, p. 28)

Slightly later, Kyra is similarly surprised by the sudden appearance in the train carriage of Shin, the little boy Nabi has befriended, and remarks: "Shin! Where did you come from?" (ibid., p. 29). The script notes that footsteps are to be heard off the camera, which enhances the contiguity of the space-time he originates from, if the audience is paying attention. But Kyra is probably too engrossed in Nabi's mysterious words about the current (discussed in the section on death) to notice Shin's footsteps.[17]

The film spectator is granted greater knowledge than Kyra the protagonist, in contrast to the reader of Miyazawa's narrative, whom its extradiegetic narrator does not offer such a privilege but lets be surprised together with Giovanni by Campanella's disappearance. Toward the end of their train journey in *Night Passage*, the camera captures Nabi and Shin from behind, leaving the carriage through the corridor, just as innocuously as any passenger may move across the train's interior space, while Kyra is distracted by the Storytellers. In the screenplay, however, "Kyra and Nabi return to the train. Kyra walks ahead of Nabi. Nabi goes to fetch Shin, who gets up from the seat where he was sleeping and joins Nabi in the aisle. They leave the train in the background while the camera focuses on Kyra" (ibid., scene 36, p. 57). The camera eye can have a different and perhaps greater perspective than a character does (as is the case in this scene), no matter how central that character is to the story (as Kyra is to this one). Thus, the viewer may perhaps anticipate Kyra's separation from Nabi—and, on a second viewing, will already know why Nabi's exit is within the frame of the screen.

When Kyra finally realizes her two companions are gone, she looks for them first, as one might in reality, unlike in "Night":

She turns toward Nabi. But Nabi and Shin are nowhere to be seen.

KYRA (Crying out in shock and looking all around)

Nabi!

(Going up and down the aisle yelling desperately)

Nabiii! Where are you?

[...]

Kyra sits down and cries.
(ibid., scene 36, p. 57)

Though the acting in the film is arguably more restrained than the script
suggests, still Kyra's reaction is more predictable and less fantastic (choreographed) than Giovanni's almost instantaneous realization that
Campanella has gone, not to return, and immediate visceral reaction of
weeping and wailing in mourning for his best friend. The way Kyra acts
upon Nabi's disappearance here, in contrast, corroborates how she has
been asking logical questions about passengers' comings and goings (even
though they have not been answered in an equally logical manner).
Although Giovanni in "Night" also harbors some realistic questions about
fantastic events, he is ready to accept the events at face value and attribute
his own wonder to his forgetfulness or ignorance of the ways of life and
the universe.

In *The Naked Eye*, "I's" sudden encounter with a compatriot on the
train she has snuck onto opens the floodgates for conversation in
Vietnamese:

All the compartment doors were locked except for one at the end. White
light seeped through a crack in the door. I opened the door carefully and
saw a woman my age who looked like me. She *immediately* spoke a language
that *ambushed* me and *swallowed* me *up*. The meaning of her sentences
reached my brain cells *at once*: The woman had reserved a woman-only
compartment for two persons and had been horrified when no one else
joined her. She hated to be alone in a closed-off little space—her relatives
had already experienced more than enough of this. I *immediately* replied
that I was in the exact same situation. With clots of tears in my throat I asked
if I might spend the night in her compartment. She *immediately* gave an
energetic nod as the siren of an ambulance wailed in the distance.

My countrywoman was named Ai Van, but unfortunately I couldn't refer
to her as a comrade, for she had emigrated to France with her family when
she was still a little girl. [...] and was now pursuing a degree in film studies.
As we spoke, the train began to move again. [...]

I told her I'd married a German tourist I'd met in Saigon and now was
living in Germany. "At the moment, though," I added, "I'm travelling
through Europe alone to figure out what I want to study." (Tawada 2009,
39–40; emphasis added; 2004a, 38–39)

The repeated use of "Immediately" ("sofort" in the original German) and its synonym "at once" ("umgehend"), as well as verbs for actions of speed and force ("ambushed," "swallowed up," in German "überfiel," "verschluckte"), indicate the unexpected and fast-paced unfolding of the sequence of action, which all happens because the woman in the open compartment is of similar age and appearance. The recognition is first visual and then aural, in a language that "I" does not need to struggle with, unlike German, which she refuses to learn, and Russian, which she has studied at school. Perhaps driven by the speed of speech, "I" even improvises her identity, and pretends to be a rightful ticket-holder on the train they are in—unlike Giovanni or Kyra, "I" did not have to show a ticket to a conductor/ticket inspector.

During their conversation, "I" learns something devastating from Ai Van's inadvertent words: the train is not bound for Moscow, as "I" thought it was, but for Paris:

> "Where are you planning to stay in Paris?" Ai Van asked. It took me a little while to grasp the meaning of her question. I almost started screaming, "Isn't this train going to Moscow?!" In the faint hope of having misunderstood, I asked her when we were arriving in Paris. "Early tomorrow morning, I think," she replied gaily.
>
> Everything went black before my eyes. The train grated to a higher speed to aggrieve me. Moscow was drawing farther and farther away behind the invisible horizon. Ai Van's lips effervesced with the luxuriantly ornate names of Parisian buildings that didn't reach my ear. (Tawada 2009, 40–41; 2004a, 39)

It is one of the most common mistakes any train passenger could make, to take a train going into the opposite direction; the railways are not a static infrastructure but invested with two vectors, either of which can inform them distinctly.

As is notable here, however, "I" is careful not to share her surprise and disappointment with Ai Van; instead, she is remarkably quick in stopping herself from blurting out her intention to go to Moscow. Her conversational agility is matched by Ai Van's effervescence, from which one can sense her excitement at meeting a compatriot whom she immediately and unquestionably embraces as a friend. Yet "I" does not rejoice in this chance encounter just because they share the same language. Part of her caution may originate in the fact that Ai Van is a defector, but more importantly, "I" does not believe in the natural bonding of those who share a mother tongue.[18] In Paris, "I's" mother tongue becomes the cinema, rather than Vietnamese or any other national language. She does not seek other compatriots, and even loses touch with Ai Van, who turns out to be overbearing, if well-meaning. Although "I" runs into her by chance on the street, just as unexpectedly as in their first encounter, "I" then drifts out of Ai Van's reach again, intentionally.

These immediate reckonings and renunciations of the two women belonging to each other are most effectively presented in the delimited space-time of the train. Theirs is an intense exchange between two passengers who have only each other while then and there, yet their journey together is framed and separated from the space-times of before and after. Their bond does not translate into lasting friendship. Still, the immediate pact and special feeling for each other are significant in that spot in time and space, and are memorable in their lives afterward.

5   DIFFERENT TRAINS, AGAIN

In Chap. 2, I discussed how memories of different trains haunt passengers. Whether they are on the same route or on different yet somehow comparable routes, routes taken by themselves or known through historical or literary sources, these railway travelers cannot help but associate their current journeys with others, through incidents, scenes, and impressions of some commonalities (geographical, choreographic, lingual). The corporeal experience of being seated in the moving train carriage of a standard structure and more or less uniform mode of operation may evoke memories of a similar experienced space-time. The narratives examined in this chapter are notably more fantastic than the four discussed in Chap. 2, but they are still informed by real and historical railways.

One of the different trains is distant not geographically but temporally, and not historically but biographically. In "Night," Giovanni and Campanella used to play with a toy railway system in the latter's home. As Giovanni tells his sick mother in retrospect: "He [Campanella] had a toy train that ran on alcohol. There were seven pieces of track and we would fit them together to make a circle. It had electricity poles and a signal post, and the signal light would only turn green when the train passed. Once when the alcohol was all gone we used kerosene, but the boiler got all sooty" (Miyazawa 1991, 12–13; 2016a, 95). This childhood memory may have informed Giovanni's dream of the Milky Way Railway, for Campanella first speculates that the train he and Giovanni ride may be running on "alcohol" (Miyazawa 1991, 30; 2016a, 106). There is also the mention of a signal post with a green light (Miyazawa 1991, 33; 2016a, 109). The euphoric memory of playing with the toy train is what prepares the two boys' railway journey along the Milky Way in the narrative present. Giovanni and Campanella are juveniles, in the process of growing into young adults—much younger than Francis, the protagonist-focalizer-narrator of *Zone*, who recalls how fascinated he was with the toy railway his father set up for him in his early childhood (Énard 2010, 144–45; 2008, 163–64). For them, memories of toy trains are assumed to be still vivid, and, more importantly, merged with other memories, so much so that the boundaries between artificial and real trains can be crossed easily.

"Night" is informed by a couple of local railway systems that the author Miyazawa rode: the Iwate Keibin tetsudō (Iwate Light Railway) and the Karafuto tetsudō (Sakhalin Railway). The former was established in 1911 between Hanamaki, Miyazawa's hometown, and Kamaishi, a famous mining town, and the Miyazawa family was a stockholder of the company. It recycled old rails originally installed in Northeast China to transport soldiers and equipment during the Russo-Japanese War. After the war they were replaced with wider rails for the South Manchuria Railway, another imperialist railroad instrumental to Japan's ambitions to tighten its grip on the region. The original rails were shipped to Iwate, along with the carriages designed for them. The scientific journalist Terakado Kazuo proffers that the train in "Night" is inspired by those on this route.[19] The Sakhalin Railway operated while the southern half of the island of Sakhalin was a territory of Japan as part of the Portsmouth Treaty signed by Russia and Japan after the Russo-Japanese War.

Miyazawa's itinerary, on the aforementioned trip that inspired "Aomori Elegy," originated in Hanamaki, and its destination was Sakaehama, Karafuto (Sakhalin). It combined three railroads across northern Tōhoku, Hokkaidō, and a part of Sakhalin Island, and two ferries (over the Tsugaru Strait between Aomori on Honshū Island and Hakodate on Hokkaidō Island, and over the Sōya Strait between Wakkanai on Hokkaidō and Ōdomari on Karafuto [Sakhalin]).[20] Terakado examines timetables and features of stations on the Sakhalin Railway to identify Toyohara with the Hakuchō (Cygne) station, Kotani with the manless little station, and Sakaehama with the Southern Cross Station in "Night." Thus, these stations associated with constellations also have models on earth. Celestial terrains and land on earth are merged in the description of stations along the Milky Way Railway.[21]

4 BEST FRIENDS FOR A WHILE: FUGITIVES ON THE TRAIN IN "NIGHT...   153

The five segments of the trip on land and water are horizontally adjacent to each other. The horizontal extension of the route is experienced by the passenger, who may have felt more viscerally the contiguity of the land (and the sea) rather than territorial demarcation that would be made visible on maps. Trinh resonates with this spatial consciousness as follows:

> With the light writing on the night sky, I see, near and far and in between, Miyazawa's blue illumination. For him, death is a passing from one state to another. To come to terms with his sister's death, he followed her in her passage. He crossed land-water borders and took a ship to Sakhalin a year after she had left. Viewers paddle up the river of *Night Passage*, not knowing where exactly it may lead, and find the lit energy of bodies in performance. (Trinh 2013a, 15)

The "blue illumination" Trinh refers to is from another story by Miyazawa, "Nametoko yama no kuma" (1934; trans., "Bears of [Mt.] Nametoko," 1968, 1997, and 2018) in which a hunter sees a blue illumination a moment before he loses his life to a bear and communicates with him. It is thus a phenomenon between life and death, and between humans and animals. Such "boundary production"[22] is a state that is ubiquitous in Miyazawa's literature, including yet not limited to his works inspired by the passing of his sister. The trip in question further ambiguates the boundary between land and water, suggests Trinh. She here further highlights the inspiration she has received from Miyazawa for the scenes of light performance in her *Night Passage*.

The Trans-Siberian Railway is the most significant route for Tawada's *The Naked Eye*. Its construction by the Russian Empire extended that empire's territory in Northeast China and Korea, prompting Japan to build its own railway system on the continent. These geopolitical circumstances are the backdrop of *Sanshirō*, examined in Chap. 2. The Russo-Japanese War both accelerated and impeded the railway systems in Japan; railways were constructed due to the need to transport soldiers and military resources, but their military use was prioritized over other needs.

The geopolitical conditions surrounding the Trans-Siberian Railway become a serious and constant concern for the narrator-protagonist of Tawada's story "Wo Europa anfängt" (1989; trans., "Where Europe Begins," 2002).[23] The history of the Russian Empire's colonization of Siberia, its conflict with the Qing Empire of China, and its war with the Japanese Empire are the basis for the narrator-protagonists's discomfort with her fellow passengers who treat the vast land the train runs through merely as space to be traversed. For many passengers, the Trans-Siberian Railway was nothing but a way to travel as far as Moscow (or Paris), with the expanse of the land between Vladivostok or Nakhodka and Moscow perceived as empty and neutral. For the narrator-"I" in Tawada's story, however, the land covered by the rails is of interest; she keeps thinking of the indigenous peoples who live there, the creatures and spirits in their myths, the colonial invasion of the Russian Empire into the area, and its historical implication on Japan's diplomatic and military relations with its neighbors.

Although "Where Europe Begins" is not part of the corpus for this chapter, the historical and geopolitical consciousness seen in this story is latent in *The Naked Eye*. The novel's protagonist-focalizer-narrator has grown up after the second Vietnamese War, been educated in communism, and is well aware of the adjacency of the land enhanced by the railroad connectivity across the Eurasian continent. Furthermore, "Where Europe Begins" encapsulates the fundamental idea of the train as corporeally experienced space-time (Foucault's first definition), rather than as a transparent instrument of travel (his second definition). Passengers on a long-distance train in Tawada's stories (and readers of her stories) are reminded of how to spend time and experience space.

The Naked Eye is set from 1988 to 2000, the end of the Cold War era and somewhat beyond. At its outset, the contrast between the Eastern bloc and the Western bloc is sorely felt. The contrast between Moscow, which "I" plans to pass through en route to Beijing, Hanoi, and Saigon, and Paris, where the train she boards happens to take her, is made obvious in this novel. Although Paris was the ultimate destination for many Japanese artists and writers of earlier generations, with Moscow being a mere stop on the route, for Tawada's heroine, hailing from communist Vietnam, it is Moscow that is invested with geopolitical value.

The railway's significance becomes manifest through its absence in *The Naked Eye*. "I" has the impression that a Moscow-bound train passes Bochum, West Germany, where she is being held hostage. Her captor, Jörg, asks a Russian resident in Bochum, Anna, "if she knew about the Trans-Siberian Railroad extension passing through Bochum. This railway line once provided a direct link between Moscow and Paris. Anna's face brightened: 'Yes, I know. Don't the tracks run beside *Sieben Platenen*?'" (Tawada 2009, 26; 2004a, 27). Though the train on this route seems to operate infrequently and no longer stops at Bochum, the narrator awaits the train as her only hope of escaping from her kidnapper, or, perhaps more importantly, from the capitalist nation of West Germany.

As she is allowed to walk around Bochum, "I" extends her walk to Sieben Planeten, a street that leads to the rails:

> These train tracks summoned up a secret link tying together the past months and days that hadn't vanished and gone astray. It excited me to think that the tracks I saw before me continued all the way to Moscow. A cousin of mine was studying in Moscow. I didn't know his address, but I would surely be able to find him right away since people there would be able to understand me. My cousin would put me on a direct train to Peking.[24] In Peking I would buy a ticket to Hanoi. [...] From Hanoi it would take only another two days to reach Saigon, and surely nothing else bad could happen to me on this stretch of the journey. If only I could get to Moscow! (Tawada 2009, 35; 2004a, 34–35)

"I" is keenly aware of the contiguity of space even though she lives in 1988, in the Cold War era, when the Berlin Wall was still standing. Train tracks extend across the Eastern bloc, and one can physically move as long as a train appears and lets one enter the railway system through a station. With no sign of a station along the railway tracks, however, the narrator-protagonist is unable to do so, even though rails are right there "before" her.

Tawada's spatial consciousness, evident in her work in general, posits lines as connections, rather than divisions: thus roads, railroads, rivers, canals, inland seas, and other routes for surface travel are highlighted in general, rather than walls, borders, and partitions. It is not territoriality but adjacency that prevails in her fiction. Lines are there not to delineate and circumscribe territories, but to connect points across space. "I" in *The Naked Eye* states: "I tried to get away from the idea that there were separate places called 'here' and 'there.' Despite the distance between them, 'here' and 'there' had to be connected" (Tawada 2009, 30; 2004a, 30). This consciousness is manifest in many of Tawada's works, through the figures of rivers, ferry routes, and railways. Her *Amerika: Hidō no tairiku* (America: A Continent of No Roads) is a part-travelogue, part-fictional exploration of the United States; to classify its land as having "no roads" suggests how essential connecting paths by boat, foot, or trains are in her spatial consciousness.[25] (The idiomatic meaning of *hidō* is "unjust/injustice," which contributes to Tawada's renunciation of the land with no roads.) Abhorrence of the automobile is evident in this book.[26] The train, in contrast, navigates smooth space without boundaries, enabling its passengers to remove boundaries imposed upon them by identificatory markers such as nationality, gender, and class.

The renunciation of dividing lines and endorsement of connecting lines are manifest in Trinh T. Minh-ha's aesthetics as well. Her resistance to identity as "a clear dividing line" "made between I and not-I" seems uncannily relevant to Tawada's positioning of characters in adjacent and proximate (or approximate) spaces, rather than contrasting them with each other or excluding one or the other from a given group. The "real" world is territorial, and divisions are constantly made and verified. Thus, Giovanni (or Kyra) is poor, and Campanella (or Nabi) is well-to-do; they miss their deceased loved ones, yet cannot be reunited with them; they are humans who may discover, conduct research on, claim to know, and use things around them (such as stars, earth, water, plants, animals), objectifying these non-humans and inanimate objects. Yet the space-time of the train is unlike such a divisive and hierarchical order. On the train they can sit next to each other, and they can see deceased people come and go fluidly, as if there is no boundary between this world and that, or between the exterior space and the interior space of the train carriage. Indeed, Campanella (or Nabi), too, is dead, yet they can appear to and interact with Giovanni (or Kyra) with ease on the train. And they can touch, listen to, breathe in, absorb, taste, and be affected by things around them, such as water, fire, air, light, and food, as well as birds (in Miyazawa) and art and industrial products and scientific tools (in Trinh). Their bodies change temperature, color, and texture through such exposure to their environs, and thus the subject-object binary dissolves. Identity, based on nationality, gender, race, and other modalities—as encapsulated in the concern with the passport in Tawada's narrative—is anthropocentric, and would have had no bearing in the pre-anthropocene age. Miyazawa wrote many stories and poems of animals, plants, and minerals; Trinh visualizes elements and things in material and spiritual interaction with humans; and Tawada considers non-anthropocentric and post-human conditions in her fiction (especially of late). All three envision spaces inhabited by many beings, including humans—spaces that are not geometric or striated but organic and smooth. Trinh suggests: "Traveling is the very place of dwelling (and vice versa)" (Trinh 2013a, 10), just as Tawada is not crossing borders between two places (Germany and Japan) but considering "the violence of boundary production" (de Bary 2012, 6).

6 ALL THINGS THAT FLOW

In all three narratives featured in this chapter, boundaries are also blurred between things and words—between things, between words, and also between a thing and a word. The interdisciplinary music critic Umezu Tokihiko suggests that the neologism "die Milchbahn" coined by poet Arno Holz—a play on "die Milchstraße" (Milk Street, equivalent to the Milky Way in English) and "Bahn" (which can mean either "road" or "railway")—may have given Miyazawa (who had a copy of Holz's book in his personal library) the idea of merging the Milky Way and the train in his story. Umezu further attributes the skipped milk delivery at Giovanni's home—which prompts him to leave to get a bottle from the milk supplier—to the association of the railway and milk delivery evoked by the word of "die Milchbahn" (Umezu 2005, 134–41). Mundane though it may seem, the milk delivery is important enough in Giovanni's (and his mother's) life to recur in the story: as soon as he awakens from the dream, Giovanni looks into the sky and then remembers the milk bottle he must pick up and bring home for his sick mother (Miyazawa 1991, 76–77; 2016a, 146–67). The contiguity of the words "Milky Way" in English and "die Milchstraße" and "die Milchbahn" in German (two languages that Miyazawa was proficient in) prompts the contiguity of the two referents in the plot.

And just as milk and the galaxy, and the everyday life on earth and the celestial adventure, can be contiguous, so are the river and the galaxy. In Japanese, the Milky Way is called "Ama no gawa" (Heavenly River) or "Ginga" (Silver River). Terakado has discovered via astronomical software that, on the night that Miyazawa's poem "Kairosei" (Blue is the dew on the allium leaves)—a poem that shares some scenes and words with "Night"—is dated, the Milky Way was reflected on the Kitakami River, which flows southward (Terakado 2013, 62). This suggests that Miyazawa may have seen the reflection and perhaps conceived the palimpsest of the river and the Milky Way in the scene near the end of the story, after Giovanni learns that Campanella has gone missing in the river: "Downstream the breadth of the river reflected the whole vast Milky Way so that it did not seem to be water so much as the sky itself. Giovanni could not help thinking that the Campanella they were looking for only existed now at the end of that Milky Way" (Miyazawa 1991, 79; 2016a, 149). The striking reflection of the Milky Way in the river makes the river look as if it is "the sky itself," so that Campanella is now in the sky because it is the river "itself."

A step forward, and the Milky Way that is associated with the river runs along with the railway. As soon as Giovanni finds Campanella in the train carriage, "Campanella began examining a disk-shaped map, turning it around and around. Sure enough, the river of the Milky Way showed white down the centre of the map and along its left bank ran a line of railway track heading further and further south" (Miyazawa 1991, 27; 2016a, 104). The southbound railway is obviously evocative of the Kitakami River, which, as already mentioned, flows southward. In Miyazawa's aforementioned poem "Aomori Elegy," the poet wonders: "My train is supposed to be running northbound, yet/ here, it is running to the south, farther to the south" (Miyazawa 1973, ll. 21–22, p. 155). Later in the poem, this aporia intensifies: "the reversal of the trains is the earnest spiritual quest's nature of simultaneous contradiction/ From such a desolate fantasy/ I must resurface quickly" (ibid., ll. 30–32, p. 155). This seeming contradiction can be geographically accounted for: the train the poet rides is both the real northbound train from Hanamaki to Aomori and an imaginary one that runs south along the Kitakami River (more on this later), the flow of which reflects the Milky Way.

In "Night," the railway and the river run along with each other: "Then the river of heaven was flowing there beside the train, glittering from time to time as though it were moving with more force than before. Here and there along the river bed, soft red wild carnations were blooming. The train ran more slowly, as though it had finally settled down" (Miyazawa 1991, 66; 2016a, 137). The "river of heaven" is, again, the Japanese name for the Milky Way, and thus the Milky Way, an imaginary river, and the train are running alongside each other. The light of stars, the galaxy compared to milk, the water of the river down below, and the railways made of iron are interchangeable with each other, less metaphors than metonymies of each other, precisely because they are drawn together less by resemblances among their substances than by the transposability of their "movement."

Yet another sequential thing—film—is to join the triad of the galaxy, river, and train. Let us enter it through the opening lines of Miyazawa's poem "Aomori Elegy," which share a great deal of imagery with his "Night Train to the Stars" (the version translated by Bester), a source for *Night Passage*:

> When the passenger train traverses the field in such a pitch-dark night
> Every window becomes a glass display in the aquarium.
> (Miyazawa 1973, ll. 1–2, p. 154)

The connection made here between train windows and aquarium displays evokes not only the connection of the train and water, but also Trinh's vision of the correspondence between the train and film, which she describes in her essay on *Night Passage*, "Lotus Eye" (Trinh 2013a). In the film's initial scene, before the opening credits, a carriage appears with almost square windows,[27] lit orange. Seated passengers can be seen, and a man wearing a hat (later identified as Storyteller 1) walking through the aisle, apparently (though inaudibly) talking to other passengers. Shot from the outside, from the side, the scene corresponds to Miyazawa's description of the passing train that saddens Giovanni, the outsider. (It should be noted, however, that passengers are not imagined but visible in the film, and that the train is much closer to the camera position than it is to Giovanni's eye in the story.) Trinh explicates the significance of the sequence as follows:

> *Night Passage* begins with what may first appear to the viewer as a shot of a passing train, in which passengers appear, disappear, and reappear with no apparent continuity, except for the continuity of the movement of the images themselves. [...] what they [viewers] see are not "natural" images of a passing train but the collage of a repeated series of window images taken from outside a train and reanimated to reproduce the movement of a train passing across the screen. [...] The opening sequence not only encapsulates the spirit and rhythm of the digital journey; it also plays on the movement *both* of the train outside and inside and *between* train rider and video viewer. Thereby a reflexive and performative relation is maintained between the images of the train within the story space and the train of images that moves linearly in finite sequences across the screen. (Trinh 2013a, 13)

Trinh's commentary here about the use of the square windows of the train carriage resonates with the opening of "Aomori Elegy": the transparency of the vitrine goes both ways, from inside out and from outside in, and in both the train carriage and the aquarium. The train passengers not only view outside landscape from the window, but also are seen from the outside, just as images on the screen are seen by viewers of the opening scene of the film *Night Passage*, and just as fish are seen by aquarium patrons, as suggested in the opening lines of "Aomori Elegy." As mentioned earlier, this poem was inspired by the poet's railway journey from his native Hanamaki to Aomori, where he took a ferry to Hokkaido, then crossed the island by rail to take another ferry to Sakhalin, and finally rode another train to Sakaehama, Sakhalin. Just as the contiguity of land and water is repeatedly verifiable on this itinerary, so is the contiguity of the train windows and the videographic scene-making.

In *Death 24x a Second: Stillness and the Moving Image*, Laura Mulvey proposes the connectivity between the train, water, and film, extending Gilles Deleuze's theory in *Cinema 1: The Movement-Image*. Explicating the film *Wavelength*, Mulvey notes:

> A still photograph of waves, the insubstantial combination of wind and water into perpetual motion, stops the movement of the zoom, the drive that had carried the camera forward from its point of departure, in its tracks. This image gives a twist to Deleuze's comments on the relation between the machine (motor car, train), water and cinema in his discussion of early French cinema:
>
>> This was in no sense a renunciation of the mechanical: on the contrary, it was the transition from a mechanics of solids to a mechanics of fluids which, from a concrete point of view, was to find a new extension of the quantity of the movement as a whole. It provided better conditions to pass from the concrete to the abstract, a greater possibility of communicating an irreversible duration to movements, independently of their figurative characters, a more certain power of extracting movement from the thing that moved. (Mulvey 2006, 83)[28]

A mirroring of stars on the surface of the river, on the train windowpanes, and on the glittering surfaces of metal, glass, and other reflective surfaces invites chiasmic parallels across surfaces that may seem contradictory but that are a most earnest, if "desolate," fantasy. Film, the surface for projection of light, joins the ranks and, furthermore, enhances the reflection of movement that the train embodies par excellence.

Not only images but also sounds and touches can be transferred. Umezu points out that how the word "*reirō* 玲瓏," often dubbed "*toransurūsento*" (translucent), can be used interchangeably for aural, visual, or tactile sensations. An example is the "glassy whistle" (*garasu no fue*) that appears twice in the narrative: "A transparent, glassy whistle sounded and the train began quietly to move. Campanella whistled a lonely-sounding version of the star song" (Miyazawa 1991, 64; 2016a, 135). Here, the conductor's figure is not present in the frame of the scene, so we can assume that the "glassy whistle" also remains out of sight for the boys. Yet the narrator describes the instrument as "transparent, glassy." In the original Japanese, "*sukitootta garasu no yōna fue*," or "a whistle like translucent glass," suggests that the instrument is invisible, yet the narrator imagines its visual appearance from its sound. In this case of synesthesia, the aural effect evokes a visual image, since both the sight and sound can be described as "transparent glass-like," highlighting their lucidity, physically or metaphysically.

The amalgam of sight and sound materializes in the other mention of the whistle:

> They looked and saw all the people kneeling devoutly in rows on the shore of the Milky Way river in front of the cross. Both boys saw a god-like figure robed in white approaching with outstretched arms across the invisible water of the heavenly river. But at that moment a glassy whistle blew and, just as the train was beginning to move, a silvery mist rolled smoothly in from further downstream and blocked their view. (Miyazawa 1991, 74; 2016a, 144)

"The heavenly river," once again, is a literal translation of "Ama no gawa," the Japanese term for the Milky Way. Its water is "invisible" because it is transparent, yet when it changes form through evaporation, it becomes "a silvery mist," recalling "Ginga" (Silver River), another Japanese name for the Milky Way, and this mist is opaque enough to "block their view." All that reaches the boys is the sound of the "glassy whistle," again evoking its visual appearance while remaining invisible, piercing the mist. The sound is felt visually, while the sight is imagined in the presence of a sound. Sensations are transferrable and translatable across senses, which the reader is reminded of through the interaction of the river, the Milky Way, and the train.[29]

7   ALTERNATIVE LIVES, ADJACENT SPACES

Senses function along with each other. The Milky Way, the river, and the train run along with each other. Contiguity seems a formative principle of Miyazawa's poetics. Indeed, Hirasawa Shin'ichi has stated that Miyazawa "could not but face the impossibility of 'similarity/metaphor'-based representation, and move toward 'translation' by way of 'contiguity/metonymy'" (Hirasawa 2008, 14). He names the principle of sensibility across the space-time "*sen'i*" (lit., "transfer/shift"), a term that gained currency through Amazawa Taijirō, a poet, scholar of French literature, and another devoted literary critic of Miyazawa's work. Referring originally to the natural environment, *sen'i* means translation or transformation into another aspect (*sō*). It is not as if one thing is identified with another, but as if one state shifts to another.

Trinh T. Minh-ha's standpoint in terms of experience and knowledge-formation, and the subject-object relation, seems comparable to Miyazawa's. As the scholar Khadidiatou Guèye explicates Trinh's way of thinking: "The counter hegemonic feature of 'speaking nearby'" rather than "the hegemonic and binary rhetoric of the 'speaking about' method" "in the conservation of systems of binary opposition (subject/object, I/it; We/They) on which territorialized knowledge depends" "(e)xudes the fragmented, heterogeneous, and heterotypic nature of images, sounds, and ethnic voices" (Guèye 2008, 15). Though Guèye is specifically discussing Trinh's position evident in her works other than *Night Passage*, this focus on proximity or adjacency, rather than distancing, objectification, and representation, seems relevant to our understanding of the physics of the film in question. Thus, Kyra does not speak *about* Nabi, but speaks *nearby* Nabi. Their conversation is not for the sake of pinning each other down and claiming to know each other, but in order to listen to and absorb what the other says and transform oneself accordingly.

This is happening not only to two human beings but between humans and "images" and "sounds" as well. In Trinh's film, the human subject is not to dominate and utilize inanimate things, but to absorb and process them—often literally, as Kyra, Nabi, and Shin play with things, which causes their own countenances to change (Trinh 2013b, scene 9, p. 32). Kyra is a rhythmic gymnast, maneuvering the ribbon and ball occasionally, an activity that does not serve any immediate pragmatic purpose yet enhances one's sense of being with things in a space as a body. As Nabi tells her, they are "just going" (Trinh 2013b, scene 23, p. 48), rather than going to any destination. Purposive travel is renounced, and travel for the sake of traveling is pronounced. As they move from one place to another, seeing alternative persons or things in each scene, they feel their own presences not as autonomous or primary but in relation to others and their environments.

Such relation-oriented or adjacency-oriented being is conspicuous in *The Naked Eye*. "I" has one after another encounter with a female other, a being of alterity: Anna, the Russian woman in Bochum who first informs

"I" of the Trans-Siberian Railway passing Bochum, and who only speaks in German and thus is renamed "Anne" in "I's" mind; Ai Van, the Vietnamese woman whom "I" bumps into on the train, and who, after a period of separation, lets her stay in the apartment she and her French husband live in; Marie, the street worker who mistakes "I's" intent ("I" is looking for lodging but is taken to be a customer) and sleeps with her, then offers her refuge in her basement apartment and, importantly, a cinema magazine in which "I" finds Catherine Deneuve's interview (more on this later); Megumi Yamada, who never appears in person, yet whose passport, stolen and sold, is used by the narrator-protagonist, who, even after it is confiscated, claims on one occasion to be the person of that name; and the librarian Mrs. Finder, who used to live in Essen, near Bochum (the location itself suggesting adjacency), and who bonds with "I" when "I" tells her she is from Bochum. Through her varied relationships with these women, "I" manages to navigate her turbulent life. It is always through a twosome that her story unfolds. "I" never becomes permanently associated with any of them, as a family member or a lover, but moves through them, like a train traversing the space from station to station. This is another manifestation of contiguity or adjacency—the type of relationality and spatiality endorsed by both Miyazawa and Trinh, as seen earlier.

There are also characters that Catherine Deneuve plays in the movies that "I" watches in cinemas, characters whom "I" thinks intensely about. "You" ("Sie" in the original German; "anata" in the Japanese version) is consistently used to address the on-screen presence of Catherine Deneuve, as if "I" is talking to her directly through the characters that Deneuve plays. "I" comes to address "you" after she reads the actress's interview in the magazine Marie brings her, in which the interviewer always addresses Deneuve as "you" (it would have been "vous" in the French magazine, *Écran*, which "I" reads with her French dictionary in hand), while the actress, in response to her questions, naturally speaks in the first person and mostly about herself, hence using "I" ("ich," likewise "je") repeatedly. "I" becomes keen not only about Deneuve as a film actress but also about the format of the conversation between "you" and "I," and comes to enjoy the position of being the one who always says "you"—the one who only exists to ask the other questions and listen to her answers.

The roles Deneuve plays in the 13 films after which the chapters of *The Naked Eye* are titled are: Carol (*Repulsion*, 1965), Marie (*Zig-Zag*, 1974), Tristana (*Tristana*, 1970), Miriam (*The Hunger*, 1983), Éliane (*Indochine*, 1992), France (*Drôle d'endroit pour one rencontre* [*Strange Place for an*

Encounter], 1988), Séverine (*Belle de jour*, 1966), Catherine (*Si c'était à refaire* [*Second Chance*], 1976), Marie (*Les voleurs* [*Thieves*], 1996), Marion Steiner (*Le dernier de métro* [*The Last Metro*], 1980), Marianne (*Place Vendôme*, 1998), Gabrielle (*Est-Ouest* [*East/West*], 1999), and Kathy (*Dancer in the Dark*, 2000). These names get stuck to Deneuve in "I's" mind—so much so that she cannot call another character "Marie" in *Est-Ouest* because for her that name now belongs to Deneuve through her character in *Les voleurs*. Significantly, these characters that Catherine Deneuve plays—out of a broader repertoire of hers—tend to be associated with another important female role in each of these films, whether that of a family member, friend, lover, rival, predator, or enemy. For instance, "I" describes a scene from *Indochine* in which Éliane and her adopted Vietnamese daughter practice the tango:

> Is the tango a contract between a man and a woman? [...]³⁰
> Eliane and the Vietnamese girl, who is now approximately seventeen years old, dance the tango together in their living room. The sweetly undulating melody binds them together like lovers. ["however" in the Japanese, not in the German] With the movements of their chins, they challenge one another to a duel. [...] Another misstep. Who kicked whom? (Tawada 2009, 99–100; 2004a, 85–86)³¹

It takes two to tango, and in its intense though voluntary commitment to the act between the dancing partners, tango is a "contract." The two who tango do not have to be "a man and a woman," however—the dance partners can be two women, as is the case here, and as is perhaps implied in a sentence missing in German and English.³² And the two are not separate from each other. With the close entanglement of two bodies, they lose track of who is who, and whose foot is kicking (or stepping on) the other's. This scene anticipates the ever-intensifying and complicating relationship between the two women in *Indochine*. In the other films, too, the ties between two women are a driving force of the plot, regardless of the nature of their relationship, just as "I's" relationships with other women are in *The Naked Eye*. Thus, the penchant for female-female contiguity operates on several levels in the novel.

It is mesmerizing that sometimes in *The Naked Eye* there is a relationship across planes, that is, between a character on the screen and the viewer of the film. Again in *Indochine*: "Eliane and the girl cannot be blood relatives. The girl bears a strong resemblance to someone. I can hardly believe my eyes, but the girl resembles me as I appear in a specific childhood photograph" (Tawada 2009, 98; 2004a, 85). Here and in many other places in the narrative, "I" experiences the convergence of her life story and the stories in the films she views, and feels disoriented by the contiguity of the two worlds. Where is "I," really—in the film or outside, watching it?

Of the Catherine Deneuve characters listed above, that of Kathy in *Dancer in the Dark* (dir. Lars von Trier, 2000) occupies a special place in Tawada's novel *The Naked Eye*. In that film, Kathy is a friend of the heroine Selma (who is played by Björk), yet in chapter 13 of *The Naked Eye*, titled "Dancer in the Dark," Kathy is not a friend of Selma, even though the chapter does have a character called Selma, who is its protagonist and focalizer, obviously named after the heroine of the film. Chapter 13—in which Selma's perspective, though not her voice, dominates—is the novel's only chapter that is narrated by an extradiegetic narrator.[33] Another exception to the rule is that there is no citation, paraphrasing, or review of the film from which it takes its title.

From the circumstances, the woman referred to as "the lady with the lapdog" in chapter 13 appears to be the person whom the reader knows from the preceding 12 chapters as "I"; she tells Selma that she had been born in Saigon, into a family of all Asians, lived in Paris for ten years for reasons beyond her control, then moved to Bochum, and now lives in Berlin, a city that she calls her "point of departure"—"Ausgangspunkt" in the original German (Tawada 2009, 226; 2004a, 184). There is a strangely unreconcilable aporia to her more recent turn of events; the extradiegetic narrator tells us that she has lost her eyesight due to a rampage in Alexanderplatz, Berlin, in which she tried to help a victim of assault and was injured herself. Yet the woman tells Selma that she had an eye surgery in Bochum, which did not go well, before she moved to Berlin. The latter seems to corroborate the last words of "I" to Jörg, in the chapter 12 of *The Naked Eye*. After an argument about the East–West trans-border experience enacted in the film *Est-Ouest* and in her own life, when Jörg suggests that she should strip away the traces of her life in the Eastern bloc and start living as is appropriate in the Western bloc, "I" remarks: "the images of the past. Yes, I will forget them, but to do that, I'll have to poke my eyes out with the second hand of the clock" (Tawada 2009, 222; 2004a, 181). In the film *Dancer in the Dark*, it is Selma who is losing her eyesight, whereas in chapter 13 of *The Naked Eye* the character called Selma is sighted and is asked to help the "lady with the lapdog" by reading a letter for her. Yet the Selma in the chapter does share some biographical details with the Selma in the film: she is from Czechoslovakia, works in a factory, and dreams of becoming a stage actress.[34] The first sentence explains that Selma lived in Berlin for three years before she moved to the US, where she was executed (as in the film).[35]

The most significant discrepancy in my present context is that it is not Selma but the "lady with the lapdog" who mentions, as a friend of hers, Kathy—the name of the friend of Selma in *Dancer in the Dark*, played by Catherine Deneuve. The Selma in the chapter, who more or less represents rationality, attests to the fact that she has never seen Kathy, or anyone for that matter, with the "lady with the lapdog." Yet the lady says that Kathy accompanies her to the cinema, to provide the story that is unfolding or that should be unfolding on the screen (she is said to often revise the plot on her own), which is exactly what Kathy in the von Trier film does for her best friend Selma, who is losing her eyesight.[36] These constant flips between the world of the cinema and that of people who may or may not see films, as well as switches between "I" and "you" in the conversation between Selma and the "lady with the lapdog," contribute to the weaving of alternative lives into the story—lives that are essential in *The Naked Eye*.[37] The lady with the lapdog insists to the confounded Selma that "Kathy" has become her companion sitting next to her in the cinema—thereby sitting in adjacent space in the cinematic theater rather than appearing within the storyworld presented on the screen. In this way, not only does Kathy the character in the film become Kathy an invisible (perhaps nonexistent) character in the chapter, but also Selma and the lady with the lapdog switch positions.[38]

Back to the train. One of the best examples from *Dancer in the Dark* happens to involve trains: when Selma, joined by Jeff, her wannabe-boyfriend, sings the film's theme song "I've Seen All," the two characters are supposed to be on the wooden path beside the rails on which a long freight train is passing. The train is carrying timber and many men who look like lumberjacks. Without any transition, while the song is being performed, Selma and Jeff are seen on the train, off the train, with lumberjacks dancing to the tune, camera positions changing several times to offer diverse views of the train, and many scenes from elsewhere being inserted abruptly, with the train seen passing various locales. The sequence is longer than it should take the train, however long it may be, to pass the two characters in the place where they are located. At times it appears that they are on board and leaving with the train. This fantastic sequence, feasible only in cinema—and also the way that the song is performed both in voice and dance, even though the lyrics relate to some extent to the everyday life of the heroine—encapsulates how porous the boundary between imagination and reality is, and how compelling it is to live on the border between the two. As Selma and Jeff enact this improvisational scene that could be right out of musical theater, the mundane setting of the local railroad with a freight train going by becomes a stage. The bordering of the two spheres of imagination and reality is demonstrated through the ambiguity of the train—equipped with both exterior and interior spaces, accessible to those who wish to board it but dispensable to those who are not determined to continue their trip on the train, and both slow enough for people to board and fast enough to take people away from their everyday lives.

An equally fantastic merging of the viewed world and the viewer's physical world takes place in *The Naked Eye*, also involving the railroad and the train. In chapter 12, "I" watches the film *Est-Ouest* with the newly reunited Jörg, who in the first chapter kidnapped her, in a cinema in Bochum, to which he has just brought her back. Catherine Deneuve's character in the film, a French stage actress touring in Kyiv, who is to help a French expat woman return home, appears on screen after a long wait:

> "No," I said aloud. "What?" Jörg asks in bewilderment. "She's the actress who stopped the train to Paris for me that night." Finally you've appeared on the screen—a stage actress arriving from France to perform a play by Victor Hugo. [...] Your costume is a fusion reptiles and flesh-eating plants. Gemstones glitter in your labia. Like a ...
> ... an angel from *Sieben Planeten* you stand onstage, exactly as on that day beside the train tracks in Bochum. What freedom did you mean to promise me that day? (Tawada 2009, 214–25; ellipses with no [ ] are original; 2004a, 174–75)

Let us recall the first appearance of the suicidal woman near Bochum, this time in full:

> Another woman was already standing in my favourite spot by the rusty tracks. Her long coat had a high collar that resembled the gills of a tropical fish. On her head she wore ornaments that looked somehow extraterrestrial. Perhaps she was a singer who'd fled from the stage of an opera with futuristic sets. What could be the reason for her having hurried here without removing her makeup and changing clothes? She was older than I was, and

had something extraordinary about her. Her presence even seemed to be changing the consistency of the air around her. (Tawada 2009, 37; 2004a, 36)

The suicidal woman at the rails near Bochum at the beginning of the story, with a wig-like hairstyle and ostentatious gown, who looked like a stage actress in a costume, appears much later in the film "I" is watching as a non-suicidal actress named Gabrielle performed by Catherine Deneuve. To confirm, the actual film *Est-Ouest* was released in 1999, eleven years after "I" is kidnapped from East Berlin by Jörg at the beginning of Tawada's novel *The Naked Eye*, though *Est-Ouest*'s story is clearly set in the Cold War era (the story time of the film begins in 1946 and lasts for ten years), before the breakdown of the Berlin Wall, which is the pretext for "I"'s presence in Berlin (to speak at a communist convention) and for her kidnapping into the capitalist West Germany. The distinction between fiction and reality, narrative (form) and history (content), and the presumed order of the representation (newer) and the represented (older) are multiply complicated here. "I's" life, or any devoted cinephile's life, is submerged in cinema, influenced not only by films they have seen but by the extent to which they can anticipate films they are yet to see. Their vision is always already cinematic—just as the train passenger's corporeal experience is always already informed by the train as space-time.

Film and the train have long been compared in terms of their mobility: moving camera, moving vehicle, moving image (either seen on the screen or from the train window). However, quite a different comparison is being made here because the focus is shifted from the view from outside to the corporeal experience from inside. It is not mobility but sedentariness that connects the two. The experience of the space-time by those who are inside the cinema and those who are inside the train is similar because film viewers and train passengers are generally seated and largely still. Their spaces are public yet interior. They spend a considerable amount of time together with strangers—with those who are seated nearby (as Kathy is to Selma in the cinema in the film *Dancer in the Dark*, or as Kathy is to the "lady with the lapdog" in the cinema in the novel *The Naked Eye*), and also with those who are on the screen, in the storyworld of the film they watch. In the novel, the arrival and unexpected stopping of the train for Paris is a turning point in the protagonist's life; and much later it is the cinema, which has been her life ever since, that finally reveals to her who the suicidal woman was—not in a sense that appears on a passport but in an existential way, in the way that matters to the formation of one's life. The woman who rescues another woman from the communist bloc and transports her to Paris in the film *Est-Ouest* has also enabled that transition for "I"—except that it was not a happy ending for her, as indicated in the section above on "Different Trains." The railways and film, two of the inventions of modern times, launch and conclude a woman's life—through her other, "you."

NOTES

1. Bester's 1992 translation includes another character, Dr. Vulcanello, who suggests to the bereft Giovanni, after Campanella's disappearance, that Giovanni place his loss in perspective and move on in search of happiness for all mankind. In contrast, Strong's 1991 translation uses the edition in which Dr. Vulcanello has been eliminated and the conversation between Campanella's father and Giovanni concludes the narrative. Many scholars have compared these two and other editions, including Irisawa and Amazawa 1973 and Sugiura 2016.
2. Sarah Strong cites *Kuore*, Maeda Akira's 1920 Japanese translation of *Cuore* by Edmondo de Amicis, as a source that informs many of these circumstances surrounding Giovanni. See Strong, "Reader's Guide to Night of the Milky Way Railway" (Strong 1991, 83). The cited translation was published by Katei Yomimono Kankōkai as volume 12 of the series *Sekai shōnen bungaku meisakushū*.
3. As we will see, the motif of milk is not to be taken lightly.
4. The Japanese edition of the novel, *Tabi o suru hadaka no me* (Tawada 2004b), is neither a translation of nor a source for *Das nackte Auge*, but what Miho Matsunaga (Matsunaga 2002) has termed "Partnertext" (though in terms of a pair of short stories also written both in German and in Japanese by the author, "Im Bauch des Gotthards" and "Gottoharudo tetsudō"). See also Adelson 2016, Knott 2007.
5. The first chapter relates "I's" story before she learns of Deneuve, and the film in the chapter title, *Revulsion*, is mentioned only in chapter 2. *Zig Zag*, the film in the title of chapter 2, is cited as a film yet to be seen in the present of the story time, hinting at the retrospective mode of the narrative discourse.
6. Giovanni's sister lives elsewhere and visits occasionally. The story does not describe her circumstances, nor does she make any appearance.
7. In *Through the Looking-Glass* by Lewis Carroll, the heroine, Alice, is subjected to similar questioning from the conductor ("the Guard"). See Terakado 2013, 50–53, and Carroll 1893, 57–61.

8. An eternally valid train pass features in *Suspects on the Night Train* by Tawada, discussed in Chap. 6.
9. Petra Fachinger (2010, 305) highlights a similar episode in "Where Europe Begins," in which a Russian woman who fell from a train carriage in the middle of Siberia, suffered a head injury, and lost her memory would wake up at night when she heard the sound of the train and go out to the rails. This episode reincarnates in another narrative by Tawada, *Suspects on the Night Train*, discussed in Chap. 6.
10. A character in *Night Passage*, Storyteller 2, quotes from Birago Diop's "Souffles" in English: "Listen more often/ To things than to beings" (Trinh 2013b, scene 7, p. 30). Meanwhile, the author of "Night," Miyazawa Kenji, was an aficionado of Western classical music. See, for example, Umezu 2005. In *The Naked Eye*, the last chapter alludes to the keen aural sensibility of Selma, the heroine of the film *Dancer in the Dark*, to noises that everyday tools (e.g., pipes) make.
11. For an informative and elucidating analysis of this incident in *Sanshirō* and its socio-historical context, see Freedman 2011, 106–15.
12. A more literal translation of the original would be: "Sanshiro still remembers how he felt then."
13. Another foreshadowing of the death by water is Giovanni's mother's earlier admonition when he mentions his plan to stop by the river to watch the festivities of the night during his outing to get a bottle of milk: "Mind you don't go in the river, though" (Miyazawa 1992, 16; 2016a, 95). This parental alert is repeated in *Night Passage*: Kyra's father tells his daughter to "[o]nly stay out of the water," and, when she assures him that she will he adds the reason that "[t]he current can be quite strong there" (Trinh 2013b, scene 3, p. 27).
14. This is what the event, parallel to the Centaur Festival or the Festival of the Milky Way in "Night," is called in *Night Passage*.
15. This scene precedes the revelation of Nabi's (and Shin's) death to Kyra— and to the viewer of the film—so the implied author's knowledge surpasses that of the protagonist Kyra and of viewers of the film.
16. The sinking of the *Titanic* was reported by the media accessible to Miyazawa, in whose text there are traces of the historical incident. See Terakado 2013, 53–55.
17. Kyra asks the same question of the Storytellers 1 and 2 when they appear with no warning and out of nowhere. Nabi and Kyra are wondering what the train runs on, steam or electricity, just as Giovanni and Campanella do in "Night" (and as acknowledged as a source in the following excerpt):

> (They jump in surprise and turn as they hear a booming voice from the back say)

STORYTELLER 1
This train doesn't run on stream [sic.] or electricity. It just runs, because that's what it is supposed to do. You may think you hear its clatter, but that's only because you're used to trains that make noise.— (Miyazawa)
STORYTELLER 2 (Making train sounds)
[...]
KYRA (Puzzled)
You appeared from nowhere. I didn't hear you coming in. Who are you?
STORYTELLER 1 (Matter-of-factly)
We are Men of the Night and Masters of Words.

We come in with the night train. We exist in transfinite numbers and words, and you *may* rely on us to tell you stories that emerge when you are silent.

(Trinh 2013b, scene 7, pp. 29–30)

18. Tawada's aversion from the mythicization of a mother tongue ("*bogo*" in Japanese) is made obvious in her essay *Ekusofonii: Bogo no soto e deru tabi* (2012), and her novel *Chikyū ni chiribamerarete* (2008; trans. *Scattered All Over the Earth*, 2022).
19. See Makimura 2020, 205–6, and Terakado 2013, 83–85.
20. Terakado 2013, 85–94.
21. See Terakado 2013, 94–101.
22. See de Bary 2012, 6, 12.
23. As we will see in Chap. 6, three chapters of *Suspects on the Night Train* are set on the route of the Trans-Siberian Railway.
24. She would have needed to change the trains at Karymskoye for the route to Beijing via Harbin.
25. For more on this book, see Mitsutani 2010.
26. Crossing of the national borders (or the border between the Eastern and Western blocs) tends to happen while one is sleeping. "I" is served vodka in East Berlin, loses consciousness, and is apparently transported in Jörg's automobile to Bochum, West Germany. In one of the films she watches, *Est-Ouest* (*East/West*), the heroine, a Frenchwoman who moved with her Russian husband to the USSR in 1946, crosses the border from Bulgaria (the East) to Greece (the West) in a car with her son many years later. The character's own voice confirms that she was asleep at the very moment of border-crossing: "I don't remember—I was asleep." In both cases the vehicle of transportation is an automobile, which makes passengers less conscious of their bearings in space-time.

27. The sequence of windows creates the motif of square/rectangular objects that recur throughout the film, such as the boxes that contain nascent artificial intelligence (Trinh 2013b, scene 31, pp. 51–53).
28. The quotation within the quotation is from Deleuze 1986, 43.
29. For more on invisibility in Miyazawa's imagination, see Hirasawa 2008, 112–21.
30. A sentence present here in the Japanese is absent in the German and in the English: "There is a tango of another kind." Or "There is a tango that which is not" (Tawada 2004b, 118).
31. In the German: "getreten" can mean either "kicked" or "stepped." In the Japanese, "funda" means "stepped on" (Tawada 2004b, 118).
32. See note 31 above.
33. Hansjörg Bay (Bay 2010, 565) points out the disappearance of the first-person narrator in chapter 13 of *The Naked Eye*.
34. This convergence of the world within the performing arts and a spectator's everyday life is in fact a feature shared by *The Naked Eye* and *Dancer in the Dark*: cinema in the former, and musical theater in the latter, goes beyond being an entertainment or a diversion to become an essential way of living and apprehending life for the heroines "I" and Selma, respectively. As a result, they live on the borderline between art and the everyday, often slipping into and out of one or the other realm without announcing the switch.
35. The chapter does not mention Selma's son, who, in the film, is the reason for her to work and save money. Such similarities and slippages seem to fit the principle of contiguity/metonymy rather than resemblance/metaphor seen above by Hirasawa in Miyazawa's work.
36. Selma in *Dancer in the Dark* is going blind from a hereditary ophthalmic disease and comes to the US to work and save enough money for her 12-year-son to have surgery to spare him the same fate. From the timeline (only up to three years prior to her departure for the US), her fine eyesight and the aforementioned absence of her son in the chapter are critical departures from the film.
37. Chapter 5 examines a prominent case of the volatile relationship between "I" and "you" in *Clouds of Sils Maria*.
38. On the exhilaratingly ambiguous relations of blindness, invisibility, the act of seeing, and non-seeing, the eye, and the body in this novel, see Nakagawa 2008.

Juncture 2: *Clouds of Sils Maria*

Two train passengers traveling together while their identity is formed and dissolved—that configuration shared in common by the three narratives discussed in Chap. 4—is similarly evident in Olivier Assayas's 2014 film *Clouds of Sils Maria*. Though only the first 11 minutes of this film of 124 minutes take place on a train, this opening sequence eloquently and decisively captures the dynamic of the two main characters. I will first closely read the train sequence, then highlight how the established dialogic relationship evolves in other key scenes, and finally return to the train to conclude my analysis of the cinematic narrative as it replicates the topic at its end.

Like the film *Wendy and Lucy* discussed in Chap. 3, *Clouds of Sils Maria* begins with the sound of running trains as the opening credits appear against a black ground. This sound thus contributes to the proper introduction to the film in its entirety, as well as to the backdrop of the first scene. In other words, the frame of the narrative smoothly extends into the storyworld, in which the sound of the train is heard and felt by the characters. They are passengers on the train itself (Foucault's first relation, as outlined in Chap. 1), rather than hearing the train pass at a distance (Foucault's third relation).

The first scene features a woman (Kristen Stewart) standing in a train corridor, with the windows on the left of the screen, closed compartments on the right—the typical asymmetrical structure of a first- or second-class

© The Author(s), under exclusive license to Springer Nature   173
Switzerland AG 2023
A. Sakaki, *Train Travel as Embodied Space-Time in Narrative
Theory*, Geocriticism and Spatial Literary Studies,
https://doi.org/10.1007/978-3-031-40548-8_5

European long-distance sleeper carriage.[1] The camera faces her, showing her with her smartphone in her hand, speaking into it. She is negotiating with the person on the line on behalf of her employer, arranging her appointments: she won't attend a proposed event in Jakarta or Lima, but she will do an interview in New York, on a tight schedule. The woman closes the conversation with a reminder that the caller should confirm the schedule the following week because another call is coming in that she has to take. Then, to this new caller, she identifies herself as Valentine, slightly mumbling and giggling at herself for doing so, the personal assistant of Maria Elders (Juliette Binoche). This call, too, is essentially for her employer Maria—in fact, about her divorce hearing—yet Valentine responds in a calm and collected manner that suggests she is used to this type of dealing, and speaks on Maria's behalf, and in her defense, to her benefit. Another call comes in on a smaller phone, but she can barely hear it and loses the call.

In the next scene, Valentine is in the train bar, picking up two bottles of water and some food, obviously for her employer and herself.[2] The second phone rings again, but she cannot hear what the caller is saying, which she communicates to them: "We are in the Alps, tons of mountains and tunnels" (2:08). It is clear from this sequence that Valentine, often abbreviated as Val, is a factotum who handles both professional and personal matters for Maria, verbally as her representative and physically as her personal assistant, with confidence and knowledge of what her employer can or will do.

These first two scenes quickly establish the nature of the space-time of the train in question: it is connected to others all over the world and to moments in the future. Within the contemporary setting of *Clouds of Sils Maria*, main characters are in frequent contact with their friends and associates through their mobile devices. Whereas the seclusion of the train from the world its passengers have left behind is a major condition for the structure of the narratives discussed so far, constant reminders of the circumstances outside the train carriage are an important element in this film. Despite the physical confinement—no stepping out at an interim station or transacting across the window (which wouldn't open anyway) throughout the 11 minutes sequence—the space-time of the train carriage proves to be porous.

The film is keenly concerned with circumstantial factors that are not only details of the story's settings, provided for realistic effects, but are themselves essential parts of the story. Thus, noise from the moving train wheels prevents Val from comprehending the speech of the caller. The noise is not a neutral sound effect in the background of the film: it matters to the characters because it affects their conversations. So does another circumstantial factor: incessant interruptions of the telephone connection, due to the fact that (as Val also explains to the callers) the train is passing through the Alps.[3]

This film is replete with conversation. Conversations as speech acts matter not only because of the contents discussed but, perhaps more importantly, because of the conditions in which they take place and unfold. The conditions that hamper the quality of Val's conversation on the phone illustrate the mobility of her existence—and perhaps even the volatility of her everyday life that she has been dealing with as best she can. The itinerancy of her life demands that she excel in affordance, or dealing with things in space and in communication with those who are elsewhere, about things to do elsewhere and at different times. She has to explain her physical circumstances to those who are not in the same space-time with her, and understand their own physical and material conditions, so as to successfully maintain communication with varied parties in their distinct space-times.

Returning from the bar, Val enters a compartment that has an upholstered bench on each of its two side walls, each long enough to seat two or three passengers, though no passengers are there besides Val and Maria. Val is seated diagonally opposite Maria, who is positioned near the window, facing their destination (in the direction of the train's movement), which should make her more comfortable than otherwise. It appears that Maria has granted herself the best seat in the compartment.

Val communicates to Maria another business matter (about removing a movie clip from IMDb) that has not been represented on the screen. The film viewer thus catches up with Val's knowledge as Maria does. Maria asks about the arrangements in Zurich, their destination, where she is to accept an award on behalf of the honoree, the theater and film director Wilhelm Melchoir. In response, Val outlines Maria's schedule and her hotel accommodations, asking Maria to confirm that the Dolober is indeed her preferred hotel. Ignoring Val's question (and making Val look vaguely slighted), Maria asks Val if she wants to hear her speech, to which Val says "Sure," almost imperceptibly suggesting that she has no choice but to agree.

Maria slides to the corridor side of her sofa and, surely so as not to be overheard, closes the sliding glass door that has been left open by Val, whose arms had been full of refreshments from the bar when she entered the compartment. Maria reads from a handwritten script (notepad with horizontal lines), rather than from any electronic device. As soon as Val hears a mention of the place name Sils Maria, where the awardee-director lives and where Maria will be visiting him after the ceremony, she opens her tablet and, as the screen shows, thanks to the switched camera position, locates the map for the route from Zurich to Sils Maria, while (the camera in front of her again) raising her eyes occasionally to assure Maria that she is paying attention to the dry run of her speech (3:49).

Maria closes the rehearsal without finishing the script, saying that from that point on "it's all downhill, fragments." Hearing this, Val asks if she wants her to finish the draft. Maria declines, claiming that she has to find her own words—but ends her reply with, "If I'm stuck, I will ask you, OK?" (4:24). Maria's tone of voice is resolute yet gentle, further softened by her smile. Val's prompt offer to ghostwrite Maria's speech suggests that she may have done so before, and that Maria trusts her assistant's judgment, style, and capability. This is the start of Maria's sharing her mind with Val, suggesting how their minds cross each other, and how Maria, while claiming independence from and superiority to Val, also opens up to and relies on her as a listener, a confidante, a sounding board, and even a potential collaborator.

Val then informs Maria that it takes 2 hours and 30 minutes from Zurich to Sils Maria, and that a driver has been booked. The film viewer now knows that this is what Val was working at on her tablet while listening to Maria rehearse her speech, because the viewer, unlike Maria, has had a view of Val's tablet's screen, showing a map of the area with the directions in question, in the earlier scene shot from Val's point of view. Thus, the viewer's visual knowledge supersedes Maria's, and the import of the image seen (unseen by Maria) becomes obvious to the viewer as Maria hears Val's report. This imparting of visual information to be aurally complemented later shows that the film takes advantage of the multimediality of the register of film.

Val's timely judgment, efficiency, and multitasking skills are thus amply documented in this short scene. She also tells Maria that she has texted Wilhelm's wife Rosa (again, off the screen time) but has not heard back from her. Maria seems slightly concerned, saying it is atypical of Rosa, which not only suggests her close acquaintance with Rosa but also anticipates the extraordinary circumstances that turn out to have prohibited Rosa from returning Val's call. At that moment, a call comes into Maria's own phone in her bag. It is from her husband's lawyer, and she walks out of the compartment with her phone, presumably for privacy, even though her personal matters are so well known to and well handled by Val. This suggests a degree of opacity in terms of where the two women draw the line between them. Though it appears they are quite open to each other, the space they share is not entirely transparent or smooth. Like a sliding door or a shade to be pulled down or up in the train compartment, barriers for privacy may emerge at any moment.

In Maria's absence, Val quickly checks her own smartphone, then walks out of the compartment and looks for Maria. It appears to the film viewer, who is not privy to the screen of Val's device this time, that Val has learned something she must tell Maria right away. Maria is found seated in a landing area outside the second-class compartments, engrossed in talking about her divorce procedure. When Val tries to interrupt her, she waves her off. Then another call comes in to Val's phone, which she takes, walking back into the corridor so as not to disturb Maria. Val's reaction to the new call suggests that it is another source informing her of the same development, and that they want Val to inform Maria as soon as possible. Val promises to do, and once off the phone, scribbles something with a felt pen on a loose sheet of paper, walks back to Maria, and shows it so that she can read it since she won't let Val speak to her: "WILHELM HAS DIED" (6:13). The viewer sees the message from Maria's point of view, learning the news at the same time she does, which enhances the shock of the news. The camera then switches back to a third-person position, from which the viewer can see Maria's expression freeze. The scene turns to a cut. This sequence confirms that the crucial information arrives in Maria's hands through Val, even though Maria might think she is in control of her own affairs, as indicated by her gestures trying to fend off Val's approach during the phone call. Val holds the key, and she knows how to get to Maria's mind even when it is closed against her voice.

In the next scene, the two are in the dining car, facing each other across a table covered with a linen tablecloth. Maria still is seated facing their destination, Val, in the opposite direction. The window is now on Maria's left, Val's right. The dining car has an aisle in the middle rather than on the side, separating two rows of tables, not unlike the ones seen in *The Lady Vanishes* and *The Narrow Margin*. The camera closes up on them from the aisle side. Val tells Maria that the organizer of the award ceremony has contacted her (off screen time) about modifications to the procedure in light of the awardee's passing. As Maria expresses her discomfort with proceeding with the ceremony and speech, Val encourages her to go ahead, assuring Maria that she is the best person for the task and that she should carry it out for Wilhelm. The exchange comes across almost as if Val is mothering or mentoring Maria while trying not to sound overbearing—Val cares for Maria and knows what would work best for her.

Then Val's smartphone, on the table, rings. While closing her encouraging remarks, Val stands up and takes the call in the aisle between tables, perhaps to give Maria a moment to think through what she should do. The call is from "French Inter," apparently requesting a comment from Maria about Wilhelm. Having informed the caller that the connection is unreliable and may be cut off (perhaps as a last resort in case Maria should refuse to take the call), Val passes the phone to Maria, saying, "You kind of have to, sorry" (8:31)—again showing that she knows best and, albeit politely, imposing her decision on Maria. Maria takes Val's phone and again walks away while speaking French. Val takes Maria's seat, without hesitation or any display of special deliberation, which suggests the permeability of the border between the two women: Maria is on Val's phone, Val is on Maria' seat. In addition, now Val is seated facing the future, which is appropriate as she thinks ahead and plans matters for Maria, while Maria may be dwelling on her past with Wilhelm that the interviewer on the phone asks her to recall.

As soon as Val moves to Maria's seat, Maria's phone, left on the table, rings. At first, Val hesitates to answer it—which suggests that Maria's phone is her own territory, whereas Val takes incoming calls to her own smartphone on behalf of Maria. But she sees on the phone's screen who the caller is—it is hard to make out on the screen itself, but it becomes obvious that the call is from Rosa, Wilhelm's widow. Val takes it in Maria's absence. We do not hear her conversation with Rosa because the camera cuts to Maria standing in the corridor beyond the dining car, answering the interviewer's questions about Wilhelm. When she returns to their table (and to Val's old seat, facing the past), Val tells her that Rosa just called. When Maria says she must call Rosa back right away, Val informs her that Rosa won't be available because she is "really busy" and "she still has to go to the morgue" (9:40). As if to corroborate Val's report, the screen cuts to a long shot at a chalet from which Rosa (Angela Winkler) emerges, being escorted by someone and getting into a police car (10:42). In a later insert, she emerges from a building, seen off by a man in a white lab coat, and is driven back to the same chalet (15:24). Exploiting multiple viewpoints, the film completes the story unfolding on multiple locations around the same time.

The screen is back to showing the train interior. As the two women leave the dining car for their compartment, Maria asks Val, in the corridor, if she has found out anything. Here again, the film viewer is informed together with Maria of what has transpired off screen as Val fills her in on what she has heard from Rosa: Rosa had left Wilhelm in Sils Maria to go to Basel for a checkup, and when she tried to call she could not reach him; this worried her so much that she called their neighbor and asked them to check on Wilhelm; they couldn't find him at home, and then the search resulted in finding his body "out of nowhere"—"they think it was a heart attack," Val concludes (10:16). The scene ends with a shot of Maria, silent and expressionless. From this sequence, we learn that Val is trusted by Rosa as well, who has disclosed so much to her (except for a crucial detail that Rosa herself doesn't know at this moment, and later confides only in Maria, also by phone—that the cause of Wilhelm's death was suicide by lethal substance). Rosa must know that Maria trusts Val, and thus that Val can be trusted. Rosa thus imparts what she would have told Maria, with Val functioning as a surrogate for Maria.

The matter-of-fact manner in which Val performs as a contact person for her employer assigns her not only responsibility but also power. She knows Maria's business relations better than Maria herself does. It's Val whom people call when they want to enlist Maria in any public event or for a work project. Val drives a car for her (36:08), carries Maria's bags (37:36), and totes her lunch when they are hiking (1:18:24), wakes up Maria after napping in the mountains (1:20:39); Val has a better sense of hiking trails (Maria insists she knows a path better than the one Val suggests, proves to be wrong, and ends up riding a bus with Val in silence (1:22:31), who has apprehensively followed her); and Val finds a cigarette case for Maria (47:17), provides information from the internet, and coaxes her to do her job. Undoubtedly Maria feels very close to Val, even though—unlike Helena and Sigrid in the play *Maloja Snake* within the film (explicated below)—the two women do not become romantically or sexually involved. There are, however, hints at this possibility, in the swimming scene (1:00:28) and in the scene in which Maria briefly observes—with the camera apparently assuming her point of view—Val looking crushed, in her bed in her underwear (1:05:55), exhausted after a date with a cameraman[4] and a two-hour drive each way through dusk and morning fog between Sils Maria and Lake Como. The latter sequence closes with the camera focusing on Maria's face so that the viewer can witness her eyeballs moving—and realize that Maria is assessing Val's body. This subtle instance is, however, the extent of their intimacy, without reciprocation from Val.

An important developing storyline within *Clouds of Sils Maria* is Maria's acceptance of an offer to play a part in *Maloja Snake*,[5] the deceased director Wilhelm Melchior's play in which, 20 years prior to the narrative present, her portrayal of the young female character Sigrid had been critically acclaimed to such an extent that she reprised the role when the play was adapted as a film by Wilhelm himself. The director and screenwriter of *Clouds of Sils Maria*, Olivier Assayas, cites as a source for the fictional play/film *Maloja Snake* the play (and later also the film) *Die bitterer Tränen der Petra von Kant* (1971; trans., *The Bitter Tears of Petra von Kant*, 1984), by Rainer Werner Fassbinder. Despite the parallels between *Maloja Snake* and Fassbinder's play, which are both about the dynamics between a female employer and her female employee, a more significant comparison may well be drawn between the Fassbinder play and the frame narrative of *Clouds of Sils Maria* itself.

In the source play, the eponymous character Petra has a "factotum," Marlene, who attends her in many capacities—serves drinks (juice, coffee, cognac, champagne), clears her bedside table and other surfaces of used glasses, cups, and plates, answers the door and ushers in visitors, brings in the mail, types a letter and posts it. In addition to these predictable practical duties of a servant, Marlene assumes one remarkable task: she has been told to draw Petra's portrait. This mission, which suggests Marlene's creative gift, should entail her close observation and representation of Petra. Although Marlene does not take on the responsibility of public relations for Petra, as Val does for Maria, Marlene's interpretation of her mistress will be shown to Petra's friends, and thus will have a public place to occupy. Petra must know and appreciate Marlene's understanding of her to entrust Marlene with this assignment, despite her vocal underestimation of Marlene's general qualifications (Petra's daughter, for one, reproaches Petra for her unjust mistreatment of Marlene). Indeed, Petra is happy with the portrait in progress.

Qualities of the serving woman that Assayas appears to have inherited from Fassbinder include her versatility, devotion to her responsibilities, and tolerance of a constant flow of diverse and often difficult demands. However, although Marlene's resourcefulness and insight may be comparable to Val's in Assayas's film, Marlene is remarkably different from Val on one account: she does not speak at all throughout the five-act play. The only response Marlene makes is to shrug her shoulders when Petra gives her an opinion, usually a negative one, about someone who is not present. Marlene shows she is listening to Petra but withholds her own reaction. Marlene is a trusted confidante—and Petra even characterizes her to her friends as "part of the furniture" (Fassbinder 1984, 20), thus indicating that her presence is harmless when they are gossiping about their common acquaintances. Whether in need of a listener or taking Marlene for granted for her near-inanimate status, Petra is comfortable with Marlene's presence. Marlene's complete silence and emotional placidity are in stark contrast to Petra's verbosity and volatility, as well as to Val's vivacity.

The utter contrast in self-expression between employer and employee depicted in Fassbinder's play is replaced in *Clouds of Sils Maria* by a series of vibrant exchanges between the employer Maria and her employee Val— exchanges that hint at the interchangeability of their positions first seen in the film's opening train sequence. Val speaks clearly and liberally, though she knows when to do so and where to stop, being a listener and assessor par excellence. Occasionally Val offers her opinion and gently nudges Maria to reconsider a decision or interpretation that she has made and is adamant about, and often Maria acts exactly as Val has suggested she should or predicted she would (e.g., fully engaging the packed audience when delivering a speech to accept the award on behalf of Wilhelm, despite her initial expressed hesitation to do so on the heels of his death). However, Val's frustration with Maria's depreciation of her more intelligent and directive capabilities, beyond mere factual management, grows and reaches a point where Val suggests she will quit her job, to which Maria responds with "Stay. Please stay. I need you" and a hug (1:26:39). Yet eventually Val vanishes, without any announcement, while on a hike to Maloja with Maria (1:39:15). Here, too, a contrast with Fassbinder's *The Bitter Tears of Petra von Kant* is obvious: as Petra admits, at the end of the play, Marlene's importance to her, and declares that they will be partners on equal rather than hierarchical terms, Marlene quietly kisses Petra's hand, suggesting her agreement to continue their working relationship.

If Val's vanishing feels slightly anticlimactic, it may be because a climax arrives in an earlier scene. In advance of the first official rehearsal of the new production of *Maloja Snake*, Maria practices her part of Helena at Rosa's home, where she and Val are housesitting, enlisting Val to stand in for the part of Sigrid, Helena's young assistant and love interest. The few scenes represented on screen reveal the volatility of the relationship between Maria and Val. It becomes apparent first through how they participate in the practice—Val has the script in hand and knows the correct line for Helena that Maria misspeaks, and, as Maria realizes her mistake, gently utters the line (53:28); Val also offers a perspective on Helena's character that Maria says repels her (56:43). But then, and more seriously, the maelstrom materializes because the relationship between Helena and Sigrid in *Maloja Snake* to a great degree reflects Maria and Val's. "You've become too dependent on me. It's unhealthy" (1:24:07) is a sentence that is not Val's own but Sigrid's in the script, yet it is so illustrative of the relationship between Val and Maria that when Val utters those words the boundary between the quoted text and the frame narrative dissolves. Their practice scenes after this first instance are not framed with the explanation of what they are doing, and sessions happen not in a theater or studio but in an everyday life setting, which creates an impression that the film viewer is witnessing an actual confrontation between Maria and Val, rather than their enactment of one between Helena and Sigrid.

Tension is visible not only between Maria and Val, or between Helena and Sigrid (who manipulates Helena and drives her to self-destruction),[6] but also between other binary configurations: between Maria who played Sigrid 20 years earlier and Maria who is about to play Helena; between Maria's past performance of Sigrid and the young Hollywood starlet Jo-Ann Ellis's (Chloë Grace Moretz) performance of the same character; and between Wilhelm Melchior, the playwright and the original director of *Maloja Snake*, and the theater director Klaus Diesterweg (Lars Eidinger), who requests Maria's participation as Helena in his direction of the play. During a quick private meeting in Zurich, tactfully engineered by Val, at Klaus's request, in between Maria's aforementioned speech and her attendance at the official dinner, the younger director mentions the plan that Wilhelm had for a sequel to the play, a plan that did not materialize because of his death. As Maria tells Klaus that she thought she would play Sigrid 20 years later in the envisioned sequel, Klaus submits his own view that Helena is Sigrid 20 years later—the two "are one and the same person. One and the same person" (27:56)—and thus the role of Helena can only be played by Maria because she originally played Sigrid. This conversation confirms the complexity of the Helena-Sigrid dyad; the passage of time in Maria's 20-year career as an actress between two moments playing the age-appropriate characters, Sigrid then and Helena now; and the succession of directorship from Wilhelm to Klaus, who is taking over the older director's incomplete project with Maria.[7] Are Maria and Val "one and the same," then? Perhaps, except that in their case, it is Val, not Maria (who is the equivalent of Helena in the dyad) who disappears into the mountains. Thus, their roles are not only superimposed upon but also exchanged with each other.[8]

These identity palimpsests and switches are multilayered and are anticipated from the opening train scene in *Clouds of Sils Maria*. The swapping of mobile phones (and of seats) between Maria and Val is a physical materialization of the entanglement and interchangeability of their roles—they live as they play roles for each other. And while there are many layers (Maria-Val, Helena-Sigrid, Petra-Marlene), on each layer it is a twosome relationship—between "you" and "I"—complete with intense exchange between the two, and with the volatile hierarchy between employer and employee. Although it may appear that the employer is more powerful than the employee, the employer becomes reliant on and in need of the employee—to repeat what Sigrid says (in the voice of Val): "You have become too reliant on me—that's unhealthy." This relationship has already materialized at the outset of the film, in which Val is protective of Maria and manages her affairs, professional and private. Val is the ultimate, definite, irreplaceable "you" to Maria, and Maria is "you" to Val when they are alone. The complex yet outstanding binary is established in the way they travel together on the long-distance train, by affording the space-time in ways that are not possible on other modes of transportation. Two, if by train, travel into the intricacy like no other.

NOTES

1. The train Val and Maria are riding is headed for Zürich, though it is not stated where they boarded it. It appears they spend a considerable amount of time on the train, judging from the change of light in the carriage from semi-dark to bright. Maria appears to live in Paris; her husband's legal representative says to Val that they should meet with Maria there. (Paris to Zürich by rail takes slightly less than 5 hours, according to Google Maps.)
2. That Val buys two bottles of water instead of one is significant, in comparison with a later scene of the two characters hiking, in which Maria offers the bottle from which she has been drinking, saying, "You want some?" (58:22). Val declines the offer without hesitation. It seems that the line between the two is thicker for Val than for Maria.
3. The Alps are an area through which a train carries many literary characters, such as Cecilia, northbound from Milan, in *To the North* (1932) by Elizabeth Bowen (2006); Justin, from Venice en route to Paris, in *Le Train de Venise*

(1965; trans. *The Venice Train*, 1974) by Georges Simenon (1965, 1974); and the "I" (*watashi*), through Gotthard Pass, the setting and the topic of "Gotthard Railway" ("Im Bauch des Gotthards," 1996; "Gottoharuto Tetsudō," 1995; English translation, 1998), a short story by Yoko Tawada. All these pieces describe character-passengers' experience of frequent long tunnels along their routes. The mountains were successfully overcome owing to the risks taken by laborers and the technological advancement of tunnel construction, yet the tunnels still fascinate and frustrate passengers with their frequent disruption of the area's scenic views. For the history of the construction of the tunnel and railroad through it, see Institut für Bauplanung und Baubetrieb ETH Zürich and Institut für Geotechnik ETH Zürich 1996. For the knowledge formation and literary representation of the tunnel and the railroad through it, see Previšić 2016.

4. He is acquainted with Val through Maria's photoshoot in Zurich, where the screen shows Val flirting with him during an intermission as Maria talks with Rosa on the phone and is informed of Wilhelm's cause of death as suicide (17:31). The photographer's split interest (professionally in Maria, personally in Val), the simultaneity of two women's activities of distinct natures (one somber, the other jovial), and the duality of Val's life (she also has a personal life) are all suggested in this brief sequence, perhaps foreshadowing the two women's eventual separation from each other. Though Val's date with the cameraman appears to have gone awry, he thus functions effectively in the discourse.

5. Maloja is the name of a place that is within hiking distance of Sils Maria. In *Clouds of Sils Maria*, first Maria and Rosa, who wants to show Maria the location where Wilhelm's body was found and the cloud that inspired him to entitle his play *Maloja Snake*, take a walk there. Then Maria and Val hike there, except that Val disappears just steps short of the place. Maloja Snake is a nickname of the compound of clouds in the area that sometimes emerges in anticipation of bad weather. Thus, "Maloja Snake" is a more figurative way of referring to "Clouds of Sils Maria," further indicating the intertextuality and nested structure of the cinematic narrative. The embedded play is not at a safe distance from the frame narrative of the film, but mirrors and illuminates it. To add another layer, Arnold Fanck's 1924 film *Das Wolkenphenomen von Maloja* (The Clouds Phenomenon from Maloja), a documentary of the clouds, is watched by Rosa and Maria in Rosa's living room (while Val stands in the hallway, also watching) in *Clouds of Sils Maria* (the film insert starts at 39:40, the viewing scene at 40:28).

6. Helena's downfall may possibly result in her suicide: she goes into the mountains never to return in the play, which leaves her fate an open question—a question on which Val and Maria disagree. Maria thinks it is obvious that Helena commits suicide, perhaps influenced by the playwright Wilhelm's

recent suicide in the mountains, which in itself might have been inspired by Helena's possible end. Val's interpretation that Helena leaves to seek a new life elsewhere anticipates Val's own action later in *Clouds of Sils Maria*.

7. The meeting between Maria and Klaus is replicated toward the end of the film by a similar meeting, that is also squeezed into a tight schedule (though not set up by Val): Maria is five minutes to curtain for the opening of *Maloja Snake* when a director visits her in the green room to request her participation in his new film (1:57:23), before leaving London (where they are) for a film location that night (just as Klaus leaves right after meeting with Maria in Zurich, without staying for the dinner). Formally speaking, this is an extension of the Wilhelm-Klaus sequence and also a replication of the Maria-Klaus binary.

8. Maria's new assistant (credited as "Maria's London assistant," played by Claire Tran), who appears in a scene close to the end of the film, seems to be just as capable a multitasker as Val was: like Val, she takes care of Maria's divorce procedure as well as her professional engagements. The only difference is that the new assistant buys a single ticket for Maria to travel alone, while offering she could travel with her if she would prefer (1:51:30). Maria declines the offer, perhaps because she is not as attached to her new assistant as she was to Val, or because she is reassessing the way she acts toward her assistant. Still, the booking of a seat on a Eurostar frames the narrative with the train theme at the beginning and the end, as seen in *Wendy and Lucy* discussed in Chap. 3.

CHAPTER 6

It's Not "I," It's "You": A Second-Person Protagonist on the Train in *La Modification*, *Blue Journey*, and *Suspects on the Night Train*

How is second-person narration—in which the central character is referred to neither as "I" nor as "she/he/they" but as "you"—different from first-person or third-person narration? Seminal narratologists such as Gerald Prince, James Phelan, Robin Warhol, Monika Fludernik, and Evgenia Iliopoulou have theorized second-person narration based on a substantial corpus. They usually associate, and occasionally dissociate, the character referred to by the second-person pronoun with the narratee—or the audience of the narrative within the narrative discourse, whether intradiegetic (within the story) or extradiegetic (outside the story)—and the implied reader, because either of the two may be addressed as "you" by the narrator or the implied author. I would like to take a cue from Mieke Bal (1999), who, in *Quoting Caravaggio*, illuminates the interchangeability between "you" and "I" and considers the second-person character to be in liaison with a narrator who is invisible in the story yet obviously audible in the discourse, and who thus is presumed to be physically present in such a way that the character "you" can register and potentially address that character. I would like to first consider why the character whose experience constitutes the center of the story is referred to in the second person (rather than in the third person) when there is no "I" and no personal contact between the second-person character and the narrator in the storyworld. Under what circumstances—other than in dialogues, taking place in person, in writing, or in imagination—would one address someone in

© The Author(s), under exclusive license to Springer Nature Switzerland AG 2023

A. Sakaki, *Train Travel as Embodied Space-Time in Narrative Theory*, Geocriticism and Spatial Literary Studies, https://doi.org/10.1007/978-3-031-40548-8_6

the second person? In other words, how does one emerge as the narrator when one addresses in the second person someone who does not share the same plane of existence?

As Monika Fludernik has shown, there are more second-person narratives than have been studied in literary criticism, yet the one most frequently discussed—and even considered inevitable to refer to in any study of the form—is Michel Butor's *La Modification*. More recently, Evgenia Iliopoulou has selected *La Modification* as one of the three featured narratives in her study of second-person narrative, *Because of You*, in which she discusses "associations and memories" that are "constantly interrupting the narration of the current trip" (Iliopoulou 2019, 125). Iliopoulou's study reveals parallels between the form and the content, the narrative structure (mode of telling, tense, etc.) and the interiority of the protagonist (his decisions, assessment of two significant others in his life, memories, reconsideration of plans). Here I focus instead on material aspects of the story, which, as she points out, are "obsessively" depicted as typical of nouveau roman. While Iliopoulou rightly suggests that "the modification" of the title occurs not only in the protagonist's life but also in the formation of the book of fiction itself, I would add the modification of physical and material details—in the train compartment and in the carriage, and the exterior space beyond the structure of the train—as a significant aspect in *La Modification* and the other second-person narratives discussed in this chapter.

Before analyzing the second-person narrative, I would like to quickly illustrate what it is not. In so-called third-person narratives (such as *Sanshirō*, *The Night Train to Lisbon*, and "Night"), the unnamed, disembodied, and impersonal narrator accounts for others' acts, speech, and thought with the authority of putatively objective, neutral, or scientific truth-making. In comparison, the first-person narrator, especially the intradiegetic one who appears as a character in the story being told (as in *My Most Secret Council*, *Zone*, and *The Naked Eye*), claims the authenticity of their account of the event or situation that they have gone through themselves, witnessed at first hand, or otherwise been granted privileged access to in a way their audience wasn't (Benjamin 2006). In contrast to both, the narrator of second-person narratives is both proximate yet removed, emotionally invested yet tentative in their narration of the person called "you." Without claiming omniscience or absolute truthfulness, the narrator does not recount the past situations or events but traces with renewed suspense ongoing events or unfolding situations with the second-person character. The effect is the thrill of immediacy without personal consequences.

Though the narrator naturally casts a gaze upon "you," this gaze turns out to be not objectifying or judging but "uncoercive," to borrow Gerhard Richter's terminology, elaborated in his *Thinking with Adorno: The Uncoercive Gaze* (2019). Drawing upon Theodor Adorno, Richter proposes that "the uncoercive gaze (der gewaltlose Blick)" "embodies the specific comportment of thinking (through) the primacy of the object because it enables the one who thinks to snuggle up to the object by tarrying with it, by lingering with its singularities, its idiomaticities and differences" and "does not seek to superimpose upon the object a variety of standards and assumptions that are alien to it." "The lingering, intent, and focused gaze," Richter elaborates, "seeks and invites the other into an intimate critical communion because it sees in the very otherness of the object upon which it fastens its ownmost conditions of possibility" (Richter 2019, 38). Likewise, the narrator's gaze in second-person narratives is the gaze of a friend—concerned rather than indifferent, affectionate rather than critical, offering moral support rather than imposing judgment. The care, empathy, respect, frustration, and curiosity of the narrator are invested in the use of the second-person pronoun. Unlike the she/he/they who is/are objectified, silenced, and anatomized in third-person narratives, or even in some first-person narratives in which "I" is a peripheral character mainly observing the protagonist, the "you" is afforded reciprocity because the narrator is aware of the possibility (not real, but theoretical) that "you" might react to the way "you" is represented. The person called "you" is no longer estranged but special, even for a passing moment, under some specific circumstances, or in an incidental encounter. "You" is someone whom the "I" could talk to, and someone who could potentially talk back to "I." "You" is no longer the objectified other but an intense presence whom "I" is engaged with, committed to, concerned with, and whom "I" cares for and respects. The narrator is, however, restrained from acting for the "you." Instead of stepping into the scene and directing "you," the narrator lurks in the corner and remains an onlooker—a concerned yet helpless observer.

The next legitimate question for us to ask in our current context is: How do the account of the railway journey and the second-person narrative come together? What special effects does the second-person narration create in the train as space-time narrative, and vice versa? Indeed, the use of second-person narration is an established practice in qualitative ethnography and non-representational tourism studies, two of the fields of space-oriented social sciences in which the train is a frequent focus. Informed by Henri Lefebvre's *Rhythmanalysis* (2013) and many later studies of rhythmscapes, Jensen, Scarles, and Cohen's essay "Multisensory Phenomenology of Interrail Mobility" (2015) addresses a train passenger's experience in a way that does not aim to define and describe the essence of places visited. Instead, they highlight singular qualities of the space-time of the train ride that affect passengers: the coexistence of the mobility and the institutional fixity of travel by train, during which passengers are mainly sedentary while their vehicle is almost constantly moving; and the coexistence of isorhythm (repetitive) and arrhythm (irregular), which is to say that events during the train ride (such as stops at stations) may be repetitive and yet irregular (Jensen et al. 2015, 64).

In search of an effectively revealing and ethically conscious mode of writing about the passenger experience of train rides with those elements of mobility and rhythmscape in mind, non-representational tourism and qualitative ethnography have established a method of second-person narration of the process of the journey (rather than its purpose, medium, itinerary, and other infrastructural facts) as it unfolds. This "impressionistic" practice is an act of writing "toward disappearance rather than preservation" (ibid., 65–66). Such narrations are true to the coming and passing of moments through the passenger's body and mind, rather than to the researcher's choosing and confirming what to remember of those moments in retrospect for the formation of universal and timeless knowledge.

Instead of claiming and exhibiting the narrative authority—as in third-person "scientific" or "transparent" narration from outside the space-time of an experience (of the railway journey in this case) by means of relying on indisputable measures such as timetables and maps—second-person travel writing relives the course of the travel, thus productively complicating a sense of time that becomes not insubstantial, linear, and syntagmatic but loaded, layered, and paradigmatic. In this way, traveling appears as though it is concurrent with reading, and involves the reader not as a passive recipient of the established knowledge but as a co-producer of experience as it is evoked: "Allowing the actual travel experiences of the lead author to be animated through the second person, 'you,' seeks to induce in the reader a suspended reading that stimulates memories from the past, inducing the multiplicities of personal origins to the tales told (Bachelard, 1958)" (ibid., 65). Each moment is informed not only by the present but also by the past remembered and the future anticipated, and not only by the present traveler's agency but also by the collective memory of all those who have traveled, including the current traveler's past self. Time is thus multilayered, and agency is multiplied. We shall see this happening in the literary discourse of the three second-person narratives examined in this chapter.

Jensen, Scarles, and Cohen also suggests that second-person narration provides "post-hoc reflections on the sensory traits (such as warm compartments, smells, or the feeling of fatigue)" (ibid., 66). This method thus has the potential for the emergence of "the non-representational and affective spaces of interrail" (ibid.). Instead of the indisputable, firm, solid, autonomous mind from which the narrative is woven, there is the skin that is exposed to the environs shared with others and that absorbs multiple, ubiquitous, incidental, and variable sensations. As demonstrated below, second-person narratives such as those discussed here are particularly well suited to highlighting those sensations experienced by train passengers. The use of second-person pronouns ("vous," "anata") corroborates and facilitates this process because the subject referred to in the second person is not established a priori but evolves in relation to and in accordance with the environment they share with others and with various things. The second-person character's openness and yielding to the space (rather than autonomy from and control of it) are ideal for the study of sensations that are fluid, smooth, and mutually immersive. As Steven Crowell (2015) has overviewed, phenomenologists from Husserl and Heidegger to Levinas and Lyotard have considered second-person narration and the dynamics between "I" and "you." This is no arbitrary connection.

The train is a lived/experienced space (Lefebvre 1991) of elaborate and malleable structure in which choreographed and incidental movements occur. Indeed, the train is imagined here as a stage for bordering in which linear temporality—the very notion on which the train schedule is predicated—is complicated by multiple trajectories, variable pace, and fluctuating frequencies. Geometrical space (as confirmed by maps and floor plans) warps as rhizomatic space spreads in both the train's interior and its exterior, sometimes even literally (as we will see in *La Modification*). In the process, the stable, solid, and sovereign modern subject dissolves, sometimes even literally (as we will see in *Suspects on the Night Train*), and becomes a performative, amorphous, and porous presence.

In what follows, I trace some of the many threads that three second-person narratives throw into motion: (1) Michel Butor's *La Modification* (1957; translated into English as *Second Thoughts* in 1958, *A Change of*

Heart in 1959, and *Changing Track* in 2017; and into Japanese as *Kokoro-gawari* in 1959 and 2005);[1] (2) Kurahashi Yumiko's *Kurai tabi* (Blue Journey, 1961; revised edition, 1969; paperback edition 2008);[2] and (3) Tawada Yōko's *Yōgisha no yakō ressha* (Suspects on the Night Train, 2002; translated into French as *Train de nuit avec suspects* in 2005).[3] This allows us to consider the complication of one's sense of bearing during each protagonist's train journey. Instead of imagining the central character as a stable, cohesive, and autonomous Cartesian subject, and the train as a modern, mechanical, and utilitarian vehicle for transfer across cartographically representable space in measurable time (as in Foucault's second relation, outlined in Chap. 1), I will reveal disjuncture in subjectivity in multiple factors—disjuncture that fragments, twists, and ambiguates the passenger's register of space-time during the train ride. The passenger's memory and anticipation expand the narrative present space-time paradigmatically, and disturb the sense of a measurable space-time by challenging the geometrical or linear composition of discrete units thereof.

La Modification by Michel Butor places the male protagonist, referred to as "vous" ("you"), on a train from Paris to Rome, in the guise of a business trip (for his wife) and a vacation (for his company), to inform his extramarital lover Cécile that he has finalized the plan to relocate her from the ancient city she feels trapped in to Paris, to which she has longed to return, in order for him to live with her, separated from his wife.[4] However, "you" changes his mind during the 25-hour train ride, realizing that living with his lover in Paris would ruin their relationship, rather than fulfill its potential, because their memories of each other are intrinsically tied to the processes of arrivals in, explorations of, and departures from Rome, where she knows how to let him spend time with her. The narrative ends as the narrator anticipates that "you" will return to Paris without even seeing his lover in Rome this time, let alone mentioning his erstwhile plan—and can be expected to resume his usual visits until the relationship with Cécile runs its course.

La Modification has been compared to Valery Larbaud's *My Most Secret Council* considered in Chap. 2. Its similarity in terms of setting—a solitary man traveling by rail, while reconsidering his relationship with a woman—is so conspicuous (Simon 1962, 162) that Butor was asked whether he had consulted Larbaud's novella, to which he replied that he had not. Butor's novel has also been explicitly compared with Mathias Énard's *Zone* (also examined in Chap. 2) in the introduction by Brian Evenson to its English translation (Evenson 2010, ix). *Zone* and *La Modification* are comparable on two accounts. First, they are both about a man's solitary one-way long-distance railway journey, during which he changes his plan with his girlfriend. Second, the male protagonists ("je" in Énard's narrative, "vous" in Butor's) are both traveling in a peculiar way, of necessity: in *Zone*, he travels by train because of missing his flight from Milan to Rome, and in *La Modification*, he travels in third rather than first class so as to avoid being recognized on the train he frequents as an executive on business trips. In each case the change affects the traveler's experience significantly in terms of the passage of time, the comfort of his body, and exposure to a space he shares with people he wouldn't otherwise encounter.[5]

In Kurahashi's *Blue Journey*,[6] the female protagonist ("anata," or "you") rides an express train for six and a half hours from Tokyo to Kyoto, not so much to hunt for her lover, who has suddenly disappeared, as to seek her own position and direction in space-time. Her destination, the ancient capital of Kyoto, is imbued with the past, both cultural and personal ("you" was once a resident there, and a "guide" [Kurahashi 1969, 172] for her lover, "kare" or "he," in the city), and is thus a perfect setting for probing the complicated sense of temporality. Though the first and the last parts of Kurahashi's narrative unfold on the ground in Tokyo and Kyoto, respectively, much of her self-inquiry takes place on the train between the two cities, in the second part of the three-part novel.

The protagonist in *Blue Journey*, a solitary female traveler with a missing man in mind, is not tracing his corporeal presence so much as verifying the *disappearance* of the person of interest. The impossibility of finding him is almost the premise of her journey. She does not expect to find him anywhere in Kyoto, except in her memory as it is sparked by revisiting the places she went to with him ("voluntary memory," Benjamin 2005) or by falling into situations similar to those they had shared ("involuntary memory," ibid.). As foundational to the narrative as the absence of "he" is, the *existence* of the missing "he"—or, rather, the relationship between "you" and "he"—is irreplaceable for Kurahashi's "you." Indeed, the fact that the protagonist is "you" (significant other) to that "he" requires that the second-person pronoun be employed as the referent to her.

The easily recognizable resemblances between Butor's *La Modification* and Kurahashi's *Blue Journey* in narrative voice (the second person) and setting (a train journey from a modern capital to an ancient capital, as the protagonist stands at a crossroads vis-à-vis their significant other) led to accusations of plagiarism by the newer author, Kurahashi, voiced by the then-influential Japanese literary critic Etō Jun.[7] As I have discussed in an earlier essay, Etō's claim and Kurahashi's response, as well as others' comments on this matter—including that of Shimizu Tōru, who published his first Japanese translation of Butor's novel in 1959, two years prior to Kurahashi's *Blue Journey*—centered on parody's position in modern literature, as well as on the higher expectations placed on female writers to represent the perceived national, native, and natural identity (Sakaki 1999). In this chapter, my focus is instead on the space-time of railway journeys during which the principal subject's existential transformation as bodies takes place in reaction to the space-time.

Unlike *La Modification* or *Blue Journey*, the driving force of the plot of *Suspects on the Night Train* is not romance but suspense—or suspicion of criminality, as suggested in the title. In this narrative by Tawada, the author also of *The Naked Eye* examined in Chap. 4, the subject "you" is a solitary Japanese female passenger on a night train in an area (which varies chapter to chapter). In each chapter, she comes to play one of the following roles: a suspect in criminal investigation; an unwilling accomplice in a crime (or a suspicious activity); a potential victim of crime; and a witness to what may be a criminal activity. The "criminal activity" may involve forged identity, theft, smuggling, abuse, exploitation, kidnapping, rape, or murder. It could be real or imagined in the fearful mind of "you" ("anata"). "You" is implicated in such intense situations due to her vulnerability; as a foreigner with limited proficiency in the local language and a woman without any guard, she can be taken advantage of by fugitives who exploit her as a shield from the authorities, or by authorities who suspect her of wrongdoing due to her lack of belonging.

The balance of this chapter is divided thematically as follows. (1) I first anatomize *the structure of these three narratives*, in terms of both the itinerary in each story and the discourse time in which events and situations are recounted. (2) Then I deal with the issue made central by Mieke Bal to the narratological study of second-person narration—namely, *"deixis"*—delving further into the causes and effects of the you–I relationship. (3) Next, I consider the use of the *present tense* in these three narratives and how the selection of tense contributes to the special form of *second-person narration*. (4) From there, I examine *immanent time* (Husserl)—the time experienced, embodied, and embodying—with special attention to the complication of chronological and absolute time by *rhythms*. (5) Following that is an examination of *experienced space* (Lefebvre)—the manner in which the three narratives exploit specifics of the train carriage/compartment to their advantage. (6) Then I extend the consideration of space into the *mediated space* of images, which is two-dimensional and visually oriented, and how the spectatorship assumed by the "you" characters negotiates with their corporeal presence in three-dimensional space. (7) From there we move to the consideration of how *speech and silence* can affect the space and the *social relations* in it. (8) After examining the practice of speaking (or not speaking) to each other, I look at the practice of *reading* (or not reading) during the train trip, as the three narratives in question reveal their *metanarrative* qualities in their consideration of *books*—books as things, books to be read, and books to be written. (9) Lastly, I bring back the experienced time in terms of *biological time*, specifically through time spent smoking, urinating, sleeping, and letting nails grow.

1   STRUCTURE OF THE NARRATIVE

La Modification's narrative present is set on the 25-hour rail journey taken from Paris to Rome by "you" ("vous"), a male passenger on the third-class carriage. This route is a familiar one for "you," who is now an executive in the Paris office of a typewriter company whose main branch is in Rome. Many recollections of past trips are inserted unannounced and in fragments into the story time. "You" remembers at least five trips from Paris to Rome on separate occasions. Arranged in chronological order of the story time, they are:

The first trip, on his honeymoon with Henriette (his wife) many years ago (Butor 1958, 99–100, 196–99, 231–34, 247–48; 1957, 100–101, 190–92, 220–23, 235)

The second trip with Henriette, three years prior to the narrative present (Butor 1958, 121–25; 1957, 121–24)

One of the many business trips taken alone, during which "you" meets Cécile (his girlfriend in the narrative present) for the first time (Butor 1958, 53–56, 91–93; 1957, 56–58)

Another business trip taken alone, with the anticipation of spending some time with Cécile, who is now his lover (Butor 1958, 214–17, 221–23, 241; 1957, 206–8, 211–14, 229–30)

And the trip with Cécile after her pivotal visit to and stay in Paris, during which she meets Henriette at a dinner party (Butor 1958, 119–21, 180–83, 190–92, 194–96, 223–26; 1957, 119–21, 175–78, 184–86, 187–89, 214–16)

Three trips in the opposite direction, from Rome to Paris, are also recalled during the current trip: with his wife Henriette (Butor 1958, 153–56; 1957, 149–52); alone (Butor 1958, 88–90, 93–95; 1957, 90–3, 95–97); and with Cécile (Butor 1958, 110, 125–28, 138–41; 1957, 110–11, 124–26, 135–38).

None of these trips is recounted in its entirety—fragments of each appear either without apparent reason or because something specific triggers a scene or an incident from the particular past trip. As accidental as they may seem, these recollections contribute to the thickening of the itinerary, as if in lines drawn repeatedly, which is in turn not as linear or transparent as it may seem. Rather, it expands paradigmatically, offering comparisons, variations, and changes that have occurred between a past moment and the narrative present, as well as changes that will occur between the narrative present and an indefinite future. We will see this happen in terms of selective motifs later in this chapter.

"You" in *Blue Journey* is a female passenger who has reserved a seat on the express for the six- or seven-hour journey from Tokyo to Kyoto. For her, too, the route is a familiar one, and during the journey, she recalls at least five earlier trips (complete, partial, or extending beyond her present route) in the narrative present:

The first is when "you" has failed the entrance examination to Q University (while her boyfriend "he" is admitted to it) and moves to Kyoto to enroll in L Women's College there (Kurahashi 1969, 98–99);

The second is after "you" has attempted suicide and returned to her family home in Kamakura, and is going back to Kyoto, accompanied part of the way by her mother, and is met at the Kyoto station by "he" and Makiko, a concerned friend (ibid., 104–7; 120–21);

The third is to attend the funeral of Makiko, who committed suicide after "you" left Kyoto to live in Tokyo, enrolled at Q University, and joined "he" (ibid., 162–3);

And the fourth and fifth trips are both quasi-honeymoon trips with "he" (ibid., 96–97).

In addition, "you" recalls a trip in the opposite direction, from Kyoto to Tokyo, a surprise visit to "he" while "you" was still living in Kyoto (ibid., 70–71). As in *La Modification*, the earlier trips are recalled out of their chronological sequence, thus complicating the temporality of the current trip with recollections, present experience, and anticipation of future occurrences based on experiences of the past.

Suspects on the Night Train by Tawada has a structure distinct from both *La Modification* and *Blue Journey*; it consists of 13 chapters that are read as stories independent of each other. Whereas *La Modification* and *Blue Journey* privilege particular routes—between Paris and Rome and between Tokyo and Kyoto, in both cases between modern and ancient capitals—*Suspects on the Night Train* does not, for each of the 13 trips by rail has a unique itinerary. Furthermore, most of the trips are taken for the first time, and there may or may not be return trips. Rather than layers of memories, anxiety springing from unfamiliarity imbues each trip account. The non-repetition of itineraries and singularity of each route in Tawada's narrative radically sets it apart from the two others discussed in this chapter in terms of the narrative structure and the principle of space-time formation.

The chapters are called "-*rin*," which in Japanese is a counter for either flowers or wheels. Given the consistent theme of the train ride throughout the book, the connection to wheels seems appropriate, so I will call the chapters "wheels." These "wheels" take different directions, as mentioned, and each is subtitled with the journey's destination. Below I provide in parentheses each trip's departure point, where deducible. Each route is finite, and there is no continuity, geographically or chronologically, between chapters, except perhaps for the Trans-Siberian Railway chapters, which extend from Moscow to Irkutsk and thence to Khabarovsk:

The First Wheel: To Paris	(From Hamburg)
The Second Wheel: To Graz	(From Donaueschingen)
The Third Wheel: To Zagreb	(From Trieste)
The Fourth Wheel: To Belgrade	(From Zagreb)
The Fifth Wheel: To Beijing	(From Xi'an)
The Sixth Wheel: To Irkutsk	(From Moscow)
The Seventh Wheel: To Khabarovsk	(From Irkutsk)
The Eighth Wheel: To Vienna	(From Hamburg)

(*continued*)

(continued)

The Ninth Wheel: To Basel	(From ?)
The Tenth Wheel: To Hamburg	(From Linz)
The Eleventh Wheel: To Amsterdam	(From Berlin)
The Twelfth Wheel: To Bombay	(From Patna)
The Thirteenth Wheel: To a City That Does Not Exist Anywhere	(From ?)

As Doug Slaymaker thoughtfully points out, "arriving at the city named in each chapter is not the point" and instead what matters is "the body, the space in which the body travels," and "the space of the narrative" (Slaymaker 2010, 325–26). The train in these "wheels" of Tawada is "something through which one passes" in Foucault's first relations first visited in Chap. 1 of the present book. Then, as with the other narratives that have been explored, the corporeally experienced space-time of traveling becomes associated with the space-time of the narrative discourse.

Whereas each "wheel" contains flashbacks and flashforwards to complicate its own chronological order, it does not refer to anything that happens in another wheel. Therefore, no temporal order is established between any of the chapters, except in the twelfth chapter (examined below). Each wheel between the first and the twelfth uses "you" ("anata"). Tawada concisely explains her preference of "you" for its ambiguity and fluidity, over "I" that tends to be gender specific in Japanese, or "she," or "he" (Tawada et al. 2007, 128, quoted in Slaymaker 2010, 326, in his translation). There is no "I" beyond the speech of characters on the diegetic level (i.e., outside the storyworld)—except in "The Twelfth Wheel: To Bombay," in which "I" ("watashi") provides a prehistory of "you" (how the protagonist has become "you"). "The Thirteenth Wheel: To a City That Does Not Exist Anywhere," is distinct from any other, being in the format of a theatrical play/script, and polyphonic. Each utterance is made by one of the four passengers who, all strangers to one another, happen to share a compartment on the night train. Each utterance is not in quotation marks but presented in a new paragraph to delineate the shift in voice each time.

2   Deixis

In each of the three narratives examined here, the protagonist ("you") is traveling alone. In *La Modification* and *Blue Journey*, due to the absence of the protagonist's significant other—Cécile and "kare" ("he," whose name, Michio, is rarely mentioned), respectively—from the space of the present train journey in the narrative present, the address "I" or "you" is not spoken or heard between these couples. Even though both protagonists are preoccupied with their significant others, both Cécile and "he" remain in the third person in the thoughts of each "you," except when some conversations in the past are quoted as direct speech in the text. Thus, the protagonists' human contact during the train ride, if rendered in their voices, would be between "I" and "they"—namely, "I's" fellow passengers, who do not become "you" because no conversation is launched. (This is different in *Suspects on the Night Train*, in which "you" interacts with other passengers who are strangers in consequential, potentially even criminal manners.) When this "I" is presented as "you" in the discourse of these two narratives, what happens to the protagonist's relationship with others? Or what does not happen?

In her *Quoting Caravaggio: Contemporary Art, Preposterous History* (2000), the narratologist-turned-art-critic/installation-artist Mieke Bal takes on *La Modification* within the context of second-person narration in contemporary installation art, suggesting that Butor's narrative does not fulfill the potentials of the second-person narrative. She argues that it could quite well be presented in first-person narration: the "vous" in Butor's narrative can easily be exchanged for "je" without any consequence in content or form:

> What is lacking in *La modification* is that very essential feature of deixis:[8] the reversibility, the exchange, of the first and second person. Not only is the *you* a clearly distinct, even semantically dense, individual doing certain things, but the other people in his life, hence, in the fabula, are consistently described in the third person. The *you* is cut off from the others, or cuts them off, so that rather than mutually confirming one another's subjectivity, the figure of his *you* lapses into an autistic monologism. The pronoun *you* becomes a reminder of the alienation, that recession of subjectivity rather than fulfillment of it. As a consequence, the *you* can never be identified with the reader, nor is the reader the *you*'s symmetrical counterpart, the *I*. There is simply no *you* whose turn-taking will make the written *you* into an *I*. I contend, therefore, that Butor has based his novel on a misconception of deixis. (Bal 1999, 179)

In order to have a conversation with himself in which that self is referred to as "you," the protagonist in Butor's narrative secludes himself from others, any of whom could have become "you" to his "I" by being engaged in a dialogue with him. However, the only person who can be called "you" or "I" is the protagonist himself.[9] "You" remains distant from the rest of the passengers, who are addressed in the narrative only as "they," "he," or "she." As Bal concludes, Butor is unsuccessful in the distinct and productive use of the second person; "you" can easily be replaced with an autistic "I," while "he," "she," and "they" remain objects of his distant observation, without affecting the position of "I" or "you."

Butor's narrator, who remains an elusive physical presence, readily accesses the protagonist's interiority as well as his visible action, behavior, and situation because the viewpoint—though not the voice—stays with the protagonist "you." All the observations are made from "you's" perspective. Even when he imagines how others assess him when they look at him—whether passengers in the present space-time or Cécile in the past—it does not affect him or prompt him to react. Rather, such imaginings about the others' gaze and analysis of "you" are presented to demonstrate his own insight into others' interiority. It is obvious in Butor that the gaze and assessment begin and end with "you."

Kurahashi's use of "you" ("anata") is slightly less arbitrary. The central character's awareness of her alterity has been consistent since puberty, as well as her resolve to become or perform the role of the other to indefinite male observers. While this is the dialogic nature manifest in the story (content), in discourse as well the dialogic becomes evident. Kurahashi's "you" cannot be imagined without how she becomes "you." To take the prime example, she defines the novel she is about to write as one that her significant other "he" was to write—about her. Assuming that the narrative of *Blue Journey* itself is the one she intends to write in the story, the use of "you" hypothesizes the presence of "I," who is her "he" as the narrator. It is his sight and insight as imagined by "you," as well as "you's" own sight and insight, that prevail in the narrative as those of a hidden and imagined "I" who casts his gaze upon and unleashes his understanding of "you." While "I" may not address "you," "I's" eye operates, which "you" mediates in his voice as she writes "to the 'he' within 'I'"—to echo the title of her book of essays (*Watashi no naka no kare e*). However, this "I" wouldn't have existed without "you's" rereading of his thought in her own narrative voice. She just cannot speak as "I" because her existence is only conceivable as "you" for her significant other, "I." By writing a novel about her in the way that he would have written it, she can finally become "I" rather than "you" for him.

There is no such participation of "I" who pays attention to "you" in Butor's second-person narration. Here "you" cannot be addressed by any character such as Cécile, the woman he is to visit in Rome, or his wife Henriette, even though both women address him as "vous" in real life.[10] No matter how significant their relationship may be to each other, and no matter how often their past conversations and interactions are recalled by "you" and quoted in the narrative, both women are denied the narrative voice with which to address him in the second person, much less the viewpoint from which to cast an "uncoercive" or coercive gaze upon him in the narrative discourse.

In contrast, "you" in *Blue Journey* develops a secondary dialogic relationship with a "he," Saeki by name—her former uncle-in-law and French-language professor at the university, whom she runs into in the train bar to Kyoto. In the few conversations with Saeki in the narrative present, placed in quotation marks as direct speech, "I" and "you" are used. Thus, the first exchange of words between "you" and Saeki: "Comment allez-vous?" "Je vais très bien, merci" (Kurahashi 1969, 113; French in the original). The question and answer not only establish the dialogic relationship in the present instance, but also re-establish the past relationship between the two speakers of the French language as teacher and student at the university. The quoted exchange may have been practiced in a drill of basic conversational French—the student repeats words after the teacher, becoming "I" addressing "you," and then swapping the positions. In this highly self-reflexive and repetitive linguistic exercise, the proper identification by personal pronouns wears out. One acquires new identities as a general "I" and a general "you" in the role-playing.

Kurahashi's "you" is sensitive about which of the few person-pronoun options in modern Japanese to choose, because unlike in English (and as in French), there are alternatives. First, the choice of the first-person pronoun troubles her: When she asks Saeki, "Where are you off to?" and responds to his "To Kyoto" with "So am I," using the decorous and mature-sounding "watakushi" for "I" instead of the casual and adolescent-sounding "atashi" that she intended to use, she then blushes (Kurahashi 1969, 114). The source of her embarrassment may lie in having revealed her subconscious desire to establish herself as equal rather than subordinate to Saeki. Then comes the question of how to address the person with whom "you" is conversing:

"You" cannot call him "Uncle." It is also out of the question to call him "Professor." That's why the address was "you"—[the question being] approximately equivalent to "*et vous-même?*" However, your "you" sounded almost like "*toi*." "You" have thus gained the kind of equality that a young woman can establish with a man almost twenty years her senior only by way of being his mistress. (Kurahashi 1969, 116–17; French in the original)

By addressing Saeki as "you" ("anata")—the same second-person pronoun (gender-free in Japanese) consistently used to refer to the female protagonist—this second-person narrative, unlike Butor's, achieves the "exchangeability" or "reversibility" between "I" and "you" that Bal holds to be essential, thus extending Emile Benveniste's linguistic theory.

"You" employs these first- and second-person pronouns with Saeki deliberately: "you" wonders if the "you" by which she addressed Saeki was "vous" or "tu," having dismissed other options of addressing him ("Uncle" because he used to be married to her aunt, and "Professor" because she was a student of his in college). The exclusive reciprocity between "he" and "you"—in her conversations with the absent boyfriend "he" in the past, frequently recalled and represented in direct speech, she fluctuated between "I" and "you," as in deixis—is intruded upon and replaced by the constant use of "I" and "you" between Saeki and "you." Within the second-person narrative in which others are "they," "you" finds someone whom she can call "you."[11]

This, however, does not mean that Saeki holds a special, privileged position in "you's" mind. Ever since puberty, "you" has been "you" to an indefinite number of anonymous or named men—in love letters from her classmates; in her encounters with molesters and visual and imaginary rapists; in her self-examinations in the mirror, from her search for her vagina after the visual rape by boys to looking into the mirror in the ladies' room on the train to making up her face in the mirror in the hotel room after the night with Saeki; and in his letter to her, left in the hotel room while she was asleep, requesting another night together.[12] The protagonist of *Blue Journey* has always been "you" to a given man, and she cannot be otherwise.

The deixis is most effectively highlighted in terms of violence in "The Eleventh Wheel: To Amsterdam" in *Suspects on the Night Train*, a chapter that occupies a special position in the publication history of the book. All chapters other than this one were serialized in the monthly journal *Yuriika* (Eureka), from January through December 2001. "To Amsterdam" alone was newly written for the book that was published the following year. Thus, we could surmise that there was a chasm to be filled by this chapter, or an extension to be materialized by it.

The story begins with "you" suddenly leaving Berlin for Amsterdam, having all but run out of patience with a theater director who tries to communicate not with words but with physical touch, even by slapping her cheeks. Remembering that last incident while on the platform waiting for the doors of the night train to open, "you" slaps her cheeks with her own hands, to realize that her "reaction" to the slapping "emerges out of flesh" "as if it were someone else's emotion" (Tawada 2002a, 130). "Driven by curiosity" she continues to slap herself, resuming the action even after she is settled in her bed in the compartment. She then reaches a philosophical conclusion about self and other through the act of violence:

> If your right cheek was slapped, offer your left cheek as well... you felt as if you had understood the point of the saying. When one's right cheek was slapped, one is enraged and, without thinking what one is doing, might knock the other back. If not lucky, the other might suffer a serious injury. Before that would happen, however, one could let the other slap one's left cheek as well, as an experiment; then one would understand how anger would be generated, and be afforded an opportunity to calmly observe one's own body as if it belonged to another. That was the reason for the suggestion that one should let one's left check slapped, too. (ibid., 131–32)

"I" and "you" do not exchange violence to change their positions between themselves, but instead one remains to receive violence and become able to reflect on how "I" becomes "you" in the face of violence. One learns how to see one's self ("I") from "you's" perspective, without remaining blind to it, simply driven by one's ("I's") own emotion. This complicates our understanding of the relationship between "I" and "you," and lets emerge Mieke Bal's deixis based in their interchangeability.

The theme of violence and its insight into the deixis continues in the main storyline of "To Amsterdam," which is about child abuse, and recalls a stage in "you's" past working in a refugee camp where she witnessed traumatized children biting their own limbs until they bled just to confirm that they were still alive. This practice of self-harming is radically relevant to the deixis, in which "I" and "you" are exchangeable. "I" does harm to "you," who in the pain caused is revealed to be "I." Violence and pain are among the most immediate, inescapable, and demonstrative aspects of the two-way street of the deixis.

"To Amsterdam" plays a pivotal role in terms of the deixis in yet another way; it is also the chapter in which "you" is mistakenly accused of wrong-doing (of abusing a child who fled an institution and hid himself in her compartment on the night train) and thus becomes a "suspect." The tables are turned between "you" and her others, because in the preceding ten chapters she is a potential victim, a witness, or an accomplice of criminal activities, rather than a suspected criminal herself. This chapter shows how "you" can be judged by others instead of always assessing others with suspicion, as though they are criminals. Her having witnessed self-harming at the refugee camp helps her understand the boy when he bites his arm, and also solve the mystery in the novel she is reading on the night train (about a mute child who kills her abuser), yet it does not exonerate her from the accusation. The chapter is open-ended as far as "you's" fate is concerned, which makes evident the seriousness of the conundrum in which she is trapped.

It is noteworthy that Tawada places this new chapter right after the first ten chapters in which "you's" situation is less serious (or in which she is saved from trouble) and before the crucial twelfth chapter, "To Bombay," which reveals why "you" ceased to be "I" and became "you." "To Amsterdam" is, in terms of the discourse time, a prelude to the point of no return, a cliff-hanger for a reason, rather than simply an entertaining suspense.

In one extreme instance in *Suspects on the Night Train*, the protagonist's body becomes indistinguishable not only from others but also from its environment. In "The Seventh Wheel: To Khabarovsk," "you" is accidentally dropped from the train (details below) and is offered a bath at a house where she has asked for help; while in the bathtub, her existence is transformed radically:

> you undress, and not at all surprised, gaze down at your body, which has suddenly taken on hermaphroditic features. As strange as that was, you knew that it's always been that way—moreover, even though you knew about it beforehand, you'd only been feigning ignorance of the matter. [...] From the space between your plump, buoyant breasts, you can see your male parts swaying. You truly are both man and woman, crouching there in the water. (Tawada 2002a, 92–93; 2011, 96)

Interchangeability of gender identity is in part made possible by the choice of the gender-neutral second-person pronoun "you" ("anata"). Tawada, however, does not stop at the unmaking of the male-female anatomical binary, but proceeds with interspecies metamorphoses of "you's" body into a tailed animal and then a fish with scales. Furthermore, the protagonist's body dissolves in the bath, merging the hot water of the bath with bodily fluids that may have flowed out of her body. Though this sequence turns out to be a dream, the episode compellingly neutralizes the boundaries of an autonomous self, blurring the distinction between interior and exterior, human and animal, and male and female. Thus, we may infer that Tawada takes the interchangeability of "you" to the limit.

3   PRESENT TENSE AND SECOND-PERSON NARRATIVE

The three second-person narratives I examine in this chapter split the voice and viewpoint: while the viewpoint stays with the protagonist, the voice is exfoliated from them and addresses the protagonist as "you." *La Modification* and *Blue Journey* also share the use of the present tense, which destabilizes the narrative convention of employing past tense. The sense of immediacy, the illusion that the story is unfolding right at the moment the reader accesses the text, is created by this choice.

Present-tense narration is also a property shared with *My Most Secret Council*, examined in Chap. 2. Let us recall that because Larbaud's narrative is one continuous interior monologue (though not without occasional disruptions)—that is to say, extended free direct discourse—its temporality is always in accordance with that of the story time: the main character's present experience is presented in the present tense, his recollections in the past tense, his anticipations in the future tense. Butor's narrative, too, is narrated in a manner concurrent with the events and situations that it narrates, predominantly in the present tense when representing what is happening in the narrative present. Kurahashi's follows suit.

The use of the present tense, which was and still is in vogue among postmodern fiction,[13] hallucinates the reader into the illusion that the time of the actants has been converted into the time of the reader, creating the impression that the reader is following the events of the story in real time. This is, of course, slippage from one plane of discourse to another,[14] yet as is well known, many readers, including Roland Barthes (1975, 4), have subjected themselves to this reading. Not only the address "you" but also the temporality of the present tense contribute to the impression of readers' ongoing engagement.

The convention in English is to describe events and situations represented in a fictional narrative in the present tense, claiming authority over them as a reader and suggesting that they come into being only as we read their story, whereas narration is usually in the past tense because the normative narrative represents things that have already happened. This deception—the duality of time between a reader's experience of a text and the representation of its characters' experience within the text being read—is resolved in present-tense narration, yet it may create another deception as well: that of the identification of the reader with the character.

Unlike Butor's and Kurahashi's narratives, Tawada's does not firmly persist in using the present tense. Indeed, it seems fair to anchor its predominant temporality in the past, whether recent or remote. Even when the present tense seems to prevail, its prominence is within the range attributable to the well-known grammatical feature of the Japanese language in which the sentence ending suggests not that an event takes place or took place at a specific moment in chronological time, but that the event is either completed or in progress. Linguists have argued that the Japanese language has aspects, not tense: the sentence ending with the auxiliary verb "ta" means the action that the preceding verb represents is completed, while the ending with the conclusive form (*shūshikei*) of the verb means that the action is in progress. The moment in question, then, can be either earlier than or concurrent with the narrative present. (French has its own elaborate tense system, distinct from that of English, which should also be taken into consideration.) In view of this, it appears to me that the occasional use of "present tense" (in truth, incomplete) within "past tense" (complete) in Tawada's narrative is not deliberate manipulation of the temporality of the narrative. Instead, it seems to erect a scaffold from which the subject of experience (the "you," most likely) can view the process of the action or situation—namely, her absorption in the ongoing event, rather than in an effort to document it as a fait accompli. In other words, Tawada bases her narrative in the past tense, and its temporality does not seem as experimental or deliberate as Kurahashi's or Butor's temporality does, as far as my impression of its English and Japanese translations goes.[15]

However, Tawada did not "settle" for the past tense as foundational just because it is normative in narration. Indeed, there is a specific reason for the choice. "The Twelfth Wheel: To Bombay" explains how "I" became "you" irrevocably, 20 years prior to the narrative present. Thus, I concur that "The Twelfth Wheel" relates the earliest event in "you's" life, after which she switched from using "I" to using "you" when referring to herself, as recounted in the first 11 wheels/chapters, in which events and situations of a more recent past are presented in the past tense, or explicitly recalled from "later."

Even with past-tense second-person narratives such as *Suspects on the Night Train*, which clearly retells events and situations in the past, there is a sense of immediacy, urgency, and precarity in the act of storytelling on the part of the narrator, whose special relation to the second-person character is, as we shall see, revealed only toward the end of the book. It is therefore as though the narrator in second-person narratives is holding their breath and biting their nails while waiting to witness what's next for the "you." Uncertainty about the outcome and intense attention to the subconscious actions of the "you" who is unraveling accompany the unfolding story. This is different from the experience of a first-time reader who is unfamiliar with a narrative's plot; it is not only the body of knowledge that the second-person narrator lacks but the certainty (or arrogance) of storytelling, unlike in first-person or third-person narratives.

4   IMMANENT TIME / TIME FOR BODIES TO EXPERIENCE

In third-person narratives, due to the putative objectivity of narration presented by the omniscient narrator who stands outside the story and the story time, time is like Edmund Husserl's "absolute time"—time outside bodies that is transparent, linear, homogenous, and measurable. (Of course this premise has been effectively challenged by some of the narratives examined here, such as *Sanshirō* and *Night Train to Lisbon*, through their effective engagement with passenger experience on the train.)

In second-person narratives, in contrast, the narrator-"I," though absent from the story and unidentifiable as a character, stands on the same plane as the potential narratee "you," breathing the same air and witnessing the same events and situations "side-by-side" (Levinas 1987). The narrator's time is thus "immanent time" (Husserl 1964), experienced by bodies living in time, such as the narrator's own body or "you's" body that shares the same space-time as the narrator's. It does not flow irrevocably, at an even pace, indifferent to sensations that bodies feel and emotions that arise, nor can it be measured by a unit of indisputably equal size. Instead, the time of the second-person narrative is experienced through incidents that trigger memories, and that thus generate analepses (flash-backs) and prolepses (flashforwards) less predictably and accountably than in third-person narratives. In second-person narratives, the pace of the story time (time taken by events and situations that are recounted) and the pace of the discourse time (time spent in the act of recounting) thus fluctuate more radically than in third-person narratives in terms of varying from yet entangling with each other.

In second-person narratives, recollections and anticipations that brecciate time unevenly and multilayeredly do so more visibly and consequentially than in third-person narratives. Recollections of the past (from simple facts to more experience-based wisdom)[16] take place not to confirm the self-history of the character that informs their present state of being but to inform the present anticipation of the future; the "you" in Butor's *La Modification* can predict what will transpire because he has taken many journeys on the same route and is thus informed about the routine. Even some variations do not deter him from making suppositions, with slight adjustments to experienced facts:

> the clamor of streetcars and buses will already have begun, suburban stations will file past you: Roma Trastevere (and you'll catch a glimpse of its reflection in the black water of the river), Roma Ostiense (you'll guess at the ramparts and the pale tip of the pyramid), Roma Tuscolana (then, from the Porta Maggiora, you'll make straight for the centre).
>
> And at last it will be Roma Termini, the transparent station at which it's wonderful to arrive at sunrise, as you can by this train at another time of year, but tomorrow it will still be pitch-dark. (Butor 1958, 23; 1957, 29)

Knowledge based on memories of the past enables "you" to better anticipate future events. The future is to come because of the past. The past becomes meaningful because of the future. This recollection-based anticipation becomes recurrent and constitutes a non-negligible portion of the narrative, complicating the discourse time. To add to this, the protagonist's experience-based knowledge may also allow him to surmise what must have transpired yet was missed due to a lapse in his attention (caused by distraction or sleepiness), as he deduces the past event (such as the last station) from the present state (the current station).

Let us recall that Henri Lefebvre's *Rhythmanalysis* and its descendant studies have taught us that experienced time is invested with various patterns and intensities. Unique rhythms that are made up of isorhythm (of monotonous repetition) and arrhythm (of irregular repetition) are not only effects but essences themselves, unlike in third-person narratives. In *La Modification*, one of the rhythm-creating motifs consists of moving vehicles caught sight of across the train windows (either a window in the compartment, or one across the corridor)—bicycles (Butor 1958, 114; 1957, 114); motorcycles (Butor 1958, 34; 1957, 39); a bus (Butor 1958, 34; 1957, 39); trucks (Butor 1958, 23, 31, 80, 83; 1957, 29, 36, 83, 86), especially milk trucks (Butor 1958, 78, 226; 1957, 81, 216);[17] cars or the headlights of cars at night (Butor 1958, 85, 95, 149, 153, 175, 196; 1957, 88, 97, 145, 149, 171, 189); carts (Butor 1958, 95; 1957, 97); freight trains (Butor 1958, 71; 1957, 72); and passenger trains going in the opposite direction (Butor 1958, 108, 200; 1957, 109, 193). The repeated observation of other mobile vehicles while the train is not stopped at a station creates dynamism and, more importantly, undoes the binary between the states of motion and stillness. The train is not a representation of speed but one of the numerous things in space that are invested with movement (and thus invested with space-time)—things whose speed is not absolute but relative. To recognize other vehicles at their own paces, whether slower or faster than the train being ridden, the passenger-"you" corporeally apprehends his bearing in space-time as tangible, variable, and relative, rather than abstract, stable, and absolute.

Another motif in *La Modification*—the blue light (Butor 1958, 23, 93, 94, 143, 205, 206, 207, 220, 223; 1957, 29, 95, 96, 140, 198, 199, 199, 211, 214) that is lit when the main lighting is turned off for the night—indicates more than the linear transition between evening and night. Rather than demarcating time irrevocably and indisputably, the change in lighting takes place according to the will of one of the passengers in each compartment, as conveyed to whichever passenger is closest to the switch: thus, "Who asked that the light be put out? Who wanted this night light?" (Butor 1958, 206; 1957, 199).[18] The moment of turning on the blue light is therefore not marked in "absolute time" but emerges out of "immanent time" or experienced time. The experience depends on who happens to want to sleep sooner than others (in other words, on the biological time of some passenger who cannot be so identified until the moment comes), and also on who is positioned closest to the switch—a physical, spatial condition.

On the basis of his earlier rail journeys, the "you" in *La Modification* can anticipate this way of lighting change happening on this train ride as well: "Then someone will ask that the light be put out"; "Someone will have asked that the lights be put out" (Butor 1958, 85, 172; 1957, 88, 168). As a result, the blue light that is supposed to demarcate evening and night from each other as a marker in the irrevocable flow of time is but a motif in the narrative discourse, as well as a habit/routine in the life story of "you," a recurrent incident and a reminder of the cyclical nature of time. Time can even be reversible around the blue light; one could turn on the main light that had been turned off, as the customs officer does at one point (Butor 1958, 216; 1957, 207), to disrupt the nighttime and to let the evening return momentarily.

Other motifs in *La Modification* that elaborate on the complexity of time include, from most frequent to least, visits from the ticket inspector (Butor 1958, 41, 117, 186; 1957, 41, 117, 183), customs officer (Butor 1958, 134, 194; 1957, 132, 187), and dining car attendant (Butor 1958, 77, 102, 145; 1957, 80, 103, 142) for two purposes, to take reservations and to announce the meal is ready, and for each purpose making a U-turn, passing the compartment twice.[19] Their visits to the compartment of the "you" are noted not only by their function but, more prominently, by their affect: the dining car attendant, for example, makes a stronger impression on "you" by way of his white attire or the sound of the bell he rings to announce that the meal is ready, whereas the ticket inspector's visit attracts "you's" attention to his own and other passengers' passports, their covers and purses, and other belongings that are exposed as they prepare for the inspection. In short, these visits are remembered by way of material details, rather than immaterial temporal points in the story time.

Although *Blue Journey* lacks such repeated leitmotifs, because it recounts a much shorter journey, it is filled with involuntary memories of jazz music. An avid fan of the genre, "you" has a vast memory archive, and without trying to remember anything in particular, as in Benjamin's "involuntary memory" (2005), her mental ear hears one after another jazz piece. Jazz is known for repetition of and variation on patterns, and thus functions both as content and as a rhetorical figure. Another important point about music is that "you" experiences it as recorded and mass-distributed—in other words, as a "thing" that is experienced multisensorily. As "you" involuntarily remembers a tune from a jazz piece, she then voluntarily remembers composition, performance, and recordings. When jazz pieces are recalled while "you" is on the train, a mental image of the jacket designs of each record, especially the hands of the featured musicians, such as John Coltrane and Philly Joe Jones (Kurahashi 1969,

100–101, 169), accompanies the mental sound, and grabs "you." Memories of image and sound thus interrupt the chronological time.

Tangible figures of time are also remarkable in a couple of passages in *Suspects on the Night Train*, one of which illustrates slowness (not stillness) of a movement, the other the transference of an image across the boundary between dream and reality, as well as time and space:

> What a sickening idiom, "to squash time" (*jikan o tsubusu*). As if time were a fly. There are flies named "time flies." "Time Flies Like an Arrow" (*Kōin ya no gotoshi*). You read only the day before that a computer translated the idiom from the English to Japanese as a species of flies called "time flies" that are fond of an arrow. However, time does not fly like an arrow while waiting for a night train to arrive. It wouldn't fly like a fly. In fact it's just the opposite—as if time were a snail. The passage of a snail leaves a glittering strand. Is it sticky to the touch? It's not unlike the rail behind a train. Is a snail a kind of a train? Indeed, with two antennas extended from its head, it does look as if it is exchanging signals with someone remote. (Tawada 2002a, 118–19)

In this passage from "The Tenth Wheel: To Hamburg," homogenous time is renounced; time does not flow at an even pace, but it can "fly like an arrow" or can be as slow as "a snail." Even the slowness of "a snail" is relative, as "you" realizes in the botanical garden of Linz, because it is "like an express" compared to the movement of plants, such as that of a sunflower flower changing the direction it faces according to the position of the sun (ibid., 119). Then, Husserl's absolute time is denied. Time is measured not outside the body, but processed in terms of the experience of the body. This is why time "flies like an arrow" at times but flows like "a snail" "while waiting for a night train." Immanent time is experienced and felt by bodies.

These recognitions are also confirmed in "The Fourth Wheel: To Belgrade":

> In your dream, numerous empty transparent bottles were arranged along the rails. Has the passage of a train made bottles appear? Or are they to be crushed to pieces by a train to come?
>
> When you awoke, it was bright outside the window. You must have slept well. The man on the opposite berth was still asleep. Some ten tiny bottles of vodka were scattered around on the floor. The compartment was filled with odor. (ibid., 57)

"You" does not check her wristwatch or ask anyone for the time.[20] The passage of time is assumed by way of the brightness outside the window and the number of vodka bottles that must have been consumed by her fellow passenger in the compartment (and not by "you") during the night. Time is not absolute but immanent, not homogenous but diversely experienced. Even the order of events is questionable: bottles that appear in "you's" dream may have grown after a train passed, or be awaiting a train to come and crush them. The sense of "before" and "after" is confused, as if to propose that linear and unidirectional chronology is only a hypothesis.

An attempt to restore chronological time instead reveals immanent time when "you" in *Blue Journey* decides to sort out the contents of her purse (Kurahashi 1969, 94–95). A purse—or a pocket, which "you" searches in *La Modification* (Butor 1958, 41; 1957, 41)—is a space within a space in which to keep things that have served their purpose or that must be kept until the moment they are needed, in functional or purposive terms, in the outside space.[21] Such a receptacle holds many traces of the past and anticipations of the future. To inventory and sort out its contents is loaded with temporalities; the objects it contains have been accumulated in chronological time, yet are now outside it because they do not bear any time stamp, and because they do not have any present function; the activity of sorting them itself takes time, and is often done when one has time at hand—idle or otherwise useless time, such as when riding a long-distance train without anything to read—time to kill (or "squash"), in other words.

The sorting takes place in the time within the time of travel, which is not quotidian time but carnivalesque time. This act places extra space side by side with extra time, with each serving for the other. Just as extra space is both adjacent to and yet protrudes from the space of everyday life, so extra time in which to inventory the contents of a pocket or purse is adjacent to, yet special, vis-à-vis the banality and repetition of chronological time. Extra time and space are like navigating an archive, experiencing time outside time while in a space outside normative space. "You's" inventorying exposes traces of visits to places where she thought she might find "he," and thus creates further niches for other spaces, and for memories of those places.

5   EXPERIENCED SPACE / EMBODIED SPACE / SPATIAL PRACTICES

Butor's train is the third-class carriage, without beds. Kurahashi's has two rows of seats (no beds), two seats in a row, window and aisle, all seats facing one direction unless you turn some seats to make a temporary four-seat semi-compartment. Such a structure is potent for intimacy between two passengers tucked away from the others—a kind of intimacy that Kurahashi's "you" in the window seat and "Mr. G," a nickname she assigns to the passenger seated next to her in the aisle seat, deny each other. They do not speak to each other, except when "you" needs to leave her seat for the restroom, the dining car, or at the Kyoto station, her destination. Their show of courtesy to and curiosity about each other on these occasions is almost ritualistic, choreographed, and staged.

Tawada's train space manifests three-dimensionality (or multi-dimensionality) face to face, side by side, and occasionally top to bottom when "you" is traveling in a bunk-bed sleeper. The infrastructure of the train in *Suspects on the Night Train* varies from route to route. The structure of the sleeper compartment, with two bunk-beds for four passengers, for example, complicates the binary of self-other, or subject-object, because it accentuates both the adjacency and the oppositionality of fellow passengers' bodies as they become spectator and spectacle—or pretend not to watch (or to notice being watched by) their temporary roommates—as in "The Fifth Wheel: To Beijing." "You" is first annoyed by a merchant who stands and talks to her while she is lying on one of the lower beds. Then she hears voices and creaking from the bed above her and sees a man leap from there to the upper bunk opposite her. The two women are in the two separate upper beds. It is assumed that the man sleeps with one, and then jumps across the space between the two bunks and goes to the other woman in the other upper bunk. The man then drops to the floor between the two lower beds, immobile. The ambiguous distance/proximity makes it difficult for "you" to decide whether or not to interfere. "You" blames the train's movement for her indecision, thinking, "because the train sways so much, you could not decide on anything" (Tawada 2002a, 70). Eventually, "you" decides to fall asleep while the presumably dead body of the man lies in the space between her bed and the other lower bed, after the two women on the upper beds have left the compartment (ibid.), accepting distance rather than proximity as the guiding principle of her activity.

The aporia of proximity and distance materializes in yet another way in "The Seventh Wheel: To Khabarovsk," in which Tawada's "you" wakes in the middle of the night and struggles with the desire to go to the restroom to relieve herself. She eventually gets up and walks to the restroom alone. After using the facilities, she prepares to return to her compartment. Then something unexpected—yet not unimaginable—happens:

> You put your hand on the handle to the bathroom door and push with a forceful thrust. The unresisting hinges swing the door open, and you fall forward, your feet leaving the floor behind. Swallowed up by the vast darkness swooping in, your ears are assaulted by the sound of the wheels grinding against the track, like a wave crashing down on you. The undertow pulls you in, grabs you by the arms, and washes you back to the physical world outside. Then, with a thud, you fall into a frozen field. (Tawada 2002a, 87; 2011, 92–93)

"You" has opened a wrong door, taking it as the one to the corridor, and has fallen out of the train. Doors open, not necessarily in a welcoming manner, but often threateningly, exposing one on either side to potential danger. Doors do not necessarily confirm the boundary between two discrete territories but let one realize, corporeally, the adjacency of the interior and exterior. The space is smooth, not striated. No matter how distinctly a section of it is characterized by its designated function, such as the restroom, that section of space is topologically next to the "frozen field" of Siberia. Unfortunately for "you," said adjacency is contingent upon the temporary placement of the train in relation to the field. Invested with speed, the train leaves "you" behind, with no chance for her to return to its interior space, let alone to her bed.[22] The proximity, instantaneously and irrevocably neutralized by the speed of the train, encapsulates the contingency of space-time. The here and now are not given but conditional, and with a missing link to the exact locale in the space-time, one is lost in the middle of nowhere.

As seen in Chap. 2, stations not only mark stable points on the fixed route and timetable but present scenes of the boarding and descending of various passengers, who may or may not have shared destinations or departure points with others who use the same stations. Stations are only a part of the experience of each passenger that is variable, indicating that time is not made up of discrete moments in line but is layered with the multiple diverse itineraries of passengers. *La Modification* notes changes to passengers in the same compartment at some stations: some leave (e.g., the man who took "you's" seat at one point), and then others take their seats (e.g., a young soldier, a woman in black with children, Italian laborers), while "you" and the couple presumably on their honeymoon ("Agnès" and "Pierre") remain; the latter, "you" finds out, will continue their ride to Syracuse, Sicily, the last station for their particular carriage, which will be delinked from the rest (Butor 1958, 103; 1957, 104).

In *Blue Journey*, the duration of "you's" train ride is much shorter, and passengers may get off and back on during the one-minute stops at stations such as Yokohama or Numazu in order to buy *bentō* (lunch boxes) of local cuisine in lieu of the dining-car lunch service. "You" observes the rushed movements of such passengers' bodies through doors and on the platforms, and other passengers who are newly boarding the train. The comings and goings of passengers illustrate specific material conditions of the train, whereas the train as space-time dictates the passengers' movements. In *Suspects on the Night Train*, "suspects" may get off to flee the crime scene ("The Fifth Wheel: To Beijing"), or stay in the locked compartment to avoid a predator who is suspected to have just gotten on the train ("The Eighth Wheel: To Vienna"). In all cases, stations are not only an immaterial/abstract point on the route or timetable, but a space informed by and informing passengers' and staff members' "spatial practices" (de Certeau 1984).

Another motif in *La Modification* that spotlights the prominence of experienced space through sensation is the floor heater. Its contact, or near contact, with passengers' shoes/feet (Butor 1958, 56, 93, 97, 128, 179, 228; 1957, 58, 95, 99, 127, 174, 218), old newspapers (Butor 1958, 99, 100, 128, 162; 1957, 100, 101, 127, 156), cracker crumbs (Butor 1958, 93, 97, 162; 1957, 95, 99, 156), apple cores/seeds (Butor 1958, 102, 109, 110; 1957, 103, 110, 111), chads from the conductor's ticket punch (Butor 1958, 119, 128; 1957, 119, 127), and the footprints that passengers have left behind (Butor 1958, 119; 1957, 119) are mentioned throughout the narrative. As "you" visually registers the location of a particular object, often vis-à-vis the location of the heater, which is immobile, time is both in progress (as things have changed their positions) and in stagnation (because the rubbish stays there on the compartment floor).

In addition, the warmth from the heater that transfers to the soles of "you's" feet (ibid., 17) reminds him that he exists as a sensible body. Thermoscape, as identified as a phenomenological concept by Jensen et al. (2015), citing Derek P. McCormack (2008) as a source, has long been a property of studies of railway travel. The temperature of the seat—and of the air of the compartment, in the corridor, near the window and the door, or in the depths of the carriage—affects the experience of the passenger. This is prominent in *La Modification* in many ways, such as sweating due to a rise in temperature (Butor 1958, 15; 1957, 22), fresh cold air felt at the opening of the doors at stations (Butor 1958, 36; 1957, 40), and passengers removing a layer of clothes (Butor 1958, 20; 1957, 26).

The floor heater deserves attention because of its persistent appearance in the narrative discourse despite its almost hidden location. Set beneath the floor precisely to be physically out of the way, the device reveals its presence by its distribution of heat, an invisible property, and also by way of its visual singularity. The topology of its diamond-shaped ironwork shows variations ("seems to ripple like the scaly skin of a great serpent" (Butor 1958, 153; 1957, 149), and as "you" becomes sleepy, the heater's "diamond shapes seem to waver and come apart, with the grooves between them looking like cracks gaping over an acrid furnace; they curve and writhe and taper; then it all turns black again" (Butor 1958, 162; 1957, 156). The heater is transformed in his sensibility, eventually looking like a railway route map: "the iron floor heater with its diamond pattern like an idealized graph of railroad traffic" (Butor 1958, 244; 1957, 232). From a gauge to locate other things to a thermoscapical agent to a topological figure, the floor heater functions in multiple and multi-sensorial ways in *La Modification*.

"You" of *Suspects on the Night Train* keenly observes multiple sensations. In "The Sixth Wheel: To Irkutsk," she is invited into other compartments by passengers she comes across in the corridor and offered dried fish and vodka, in a manner somewhat reminiscent of the wild bird catcher in Miyazawa's "Night," and becomes intoxicated by the smell of the distant sea, as well as by the spirits: "Gradually the surroundings of the eyeballs grew heated from inside. Accordingly, the tremor of the train grew larger. Yet, it was not as if you would be shaken out of the carriage— rather, it was as if you were entrapped within a rubber ball" (Tawada 2002a, 80). The interior of the body corresponds to the train's movement, yet it is not centrifugal but centripetal. The sense of space is further complicated, constantly oscillating between two poles: the interior of the body and its exterior space of the train carriage; and the space exterior to the train and the space inside the figurative "rubber ball."

In "The Tenth Wheel: To Hamburg," after visiting the botanical garden and the museum in Linz, "you" decides to spend the rest of her time in the city until the train's departure at a cinema. The cinematic space shown on the screen is that of a train. The film, which remains uncited in Tawada's narrative, must be *The Lady Vanishes* (discussed in Chap. 1). While "you" watches the film, both the theme of the train and the awareness of embodied and embodying space emerge prominently:

> Stepping into the cinema, you found it was sparse. Perhaps it was because you had chosen an old black-and-white film. It was not a spacious room— only five pairs of dark heads were to be seen. You were a little drowsy. The beautiful monochromatic images enwrapped your eyes tenderly. Incidentally, the film narrative was about a train. An aging woman and a young woman befriend each other as they sit face to face in the same compartment, and have tea in the dining car. However, the aging woman disappears at one point. The young one is worried and searches for her from the first carriage to the last, yet she is nowhere to be found. Even more strangely, the other passengers in the same compartment and the waiter in the dining car insist that there has not been such a woman to begin with. The young woman is troubled and tries as hard as she can to convince the conductor and other passengers of her claim, yet they look at her suspiciously. A psychiatrist who happens to be on the train declares she is neurotic. However, there is one young man who trusts her, and the two launch a resolution of the mystery. You had watched thus far when you dozed off. You wanted to know what would happen then, no matter what, yet watching the dreamlike moving monochromatic images after a sleepless night, enwrapped in the cool, still air in the cinema, you fell asleep before you knew it. (Tawada 2002a, 124–25)

What is worth noting here is that "you" pays attention to spatial details (compartment, dining car, carriages) in her summary of an earlier part of the film, instead of focusing on characters' personalities, professions, and other details that might be considered more important to the plot.

Indeed, "you's" summary is embedded in scenes in which her awareness of spatial and material conditions is manifest. Before the film starts, "you" notes the sparsity of the movie house, the number of other spectators in the space, the film's color scheme, and the size of the theater. Even the visual quality of monochrome is not optically registered but tactilely felt, turning the film from two-dimensional to three-dimensional. After the plot summary, we are told about the air quality, another condition of the space "you" is in. Her falling asleep completes her lack of grip over the plot of the film, as well as her corporeal experience of space, whether mediated on the screen or surrounding her body in the movie house. This sequence erodes the division between the interior space and the exterior space—whether between the film's storyworld and the theater, or between the body of the spectator and the theater. In addition, the purpose (to watch a movie) is overwritten by the affect (to feel the effect of the black-and-white color scheme and the cool air quality, and become drowsy). This is an environment that is not utilitarian but phenomenological, and not optical but haptic.

The memory of the film—or, rather, the incomplete viewing thereof—haunts her later, when she is in the night train. Witnessing flowers instead of humans sleeping in three of the four beds in the compartment, "you" wonders whether she should call the conductor. Recalling how the heroine in the film is treated by others on the train, "you" hesitates. She regrets that she did not find out the conclusion of the film, which could have offered her a helpful hint. The way the two spaces are conjoined—the cinema and the compartment, as well as the train in the film and the train "you" rides—shows Tawada's topological space consciousness. Sleepy as "you" might be, she remains alert to parallels drawn between distant spaces. Feeling vulnerable in the three-dimensional space in whose ambiguous atmosphere she is absorbed, she tries to resort to knowledge of the mediated space of the film, and wishes she had possessed it in its entirety.

6   Space to Be Seen: Mediated Space: Mirror and Window

Two-dimensional space (surfaces for images) and three-dimensional space (to be occupied by bodies and things), whose emersion we just saw in Tawada's scene in the cinema, coexist in the interior of the train just as they do in any other interior space. We may recall a landscape picture and a mirror in train compartments in *The Lady Vanishes*, though their roles are minor in characters' consciousness. The compartment of Butor's "you" is replete with spatial images, as Mary Beth Pringle has meticulously elaborated, in terms of their placement and effects (Pringle 1985). Butor's "you" often observes the four landscape photographs mounted in glass and hung above passengers' heads on the two side walls of the compartment, and when he does so they transport him to other interior spaces, such as to his own apartment in Paris with Piranesi's *Prison* etching, a birthday gift from Cécile, or to Cécile's flat in Rome, where landscape photographs arc mounted on the walls.[23] Mediated spaces travel across physical space to appear and reappear on different flat surfaces, exhibiting their own presence in space-times they share with their viewers, rather than the places they represent within the frame. There are also mirrors in the restrooms—and windowpanes between the interior and exterior of the train, or between the compartment and corridor, that reflect one's body or let one see through it—complicating sight yet reinforcing the visual regime. Visual representation entitles the viewer to claim the power of the gaze upon an object from which one is detached. While this visual regime corroborates the alienation of the subject from the rest in Bal's aforementioned critique of Butor, Butor also adds a few layers to make "you's" position more vulnerable and potentially erosive.

In the carriage in *La Modification*, reflexive surfaces are prominent:[24] they include four windows, two toward the exterior, the other two toward the corridor, and the glass covering the photographs on the walls. These reflexive surfaces become most functional when the moon appears in the sky outside. It can be seen through the transparent exterior windowpane, or it can be seen reflected on the corridor windowpane or on the glass protecting the photographic prints. To complicate the distinction between the sight and reflection (Butor 1958, 217, 223, 226, 227, 231; 1957, 208, 214, 216, 217, 220), the moon can be seen in one way fairly soon after it is seen in another, owing to the way the train's position vis-à-vis the moon constantly changes.

When "you" observes the moon for the second time in the narrative, the scene captures a passage of time during which the moon appears in various different forms:

> Once more above Agnès' hair, in the glass of the invisible photograph of boats alongside the quay in a little port, the distorted reflection of the moon looks like the footprint of some nocturnal creature, not merely its footprint but its very claws, stretching and slackening as though impatient to clutch their prey; it shifts toward the edge of the frame, toward the window, and disappears, but then through the window the moon itself appears before you, fastening tremulously to the middle of the pane, and all at once its light flows directly into the compartment, flooding it so that you can see, between your feet, the renewed glitter for the diamond-shaped scales on the floor heater. (Butor 1958, 223; 1957, 214)

This is an apex of the complication of the binary between the interior and exterior, as well as one between transparency and reflexivity, and another between reality and illusion. It even merges the window and the floor heater—two significant props repeatedly observed—toppling the sense of vertical space.

The first of these contested binaries reconfirms that the train is exposed to the exterior while it has a guarded interior, and that the two spaces are next to each other. The flooding of the moonshine into the compartment is the final evidence of the adjacency of the two spaces. Yet this does not mean the connection between the two spaces is seamless; the windowpane divides as well as connects the two spaces, and other objects and passengers' bodies complicate the division as they are reflected on surfaces. Angles at which "you" observes the moon and its reflection vary according to the train's relative location and his own posture.

The second contested binary, between transparency and reflexivity, does not only illustrate the functions of the glass surface but, more importantly, stand for the mode of literary representation. An analysis of *The Lady Vanishes* in Chap. 1 verified that glass is not as transparent as it seems and exists as a thing in itself. It is therefore conditioned by its own qualities, as well as by tangential factors such as vapor (Butor 1958, 131; 1957, 129), snowflakes (Butor 1958, 191; 1957, 185), the presence or absence of falling or dried raindrops (Butor 1958, 78, 80, 82, 90, 93, 95, 108, 114; 1957, 81, 83, 86, 93, 95, 97, 109, 114), tremors (Butor 1958, 156; 1957, 152), and light (Butor 1958, 162; 1957, 156–57). In addition, the line of light from an object can be straight or refracted, or can itself be a refraction of a straight light (if, for example, moonshine comes through the corridor window and is then reflected on the exterior windowpane; Butor 1958, 223; 1957, 214). Similarly, even though language may seem an immaterial and neutral tool for mimetic representation, it can never be neutral, and its material conditions (sound, script, etc.) affect the way stories are told. The multiplicity of the trajectory of sight further complicates how anything is represented in language, as well as in vision.

In *Blue Journey*, the two qualities of transparency and reflexivity are highlighted and attributed not to a mirror or a glass surface but to "you's" facial skin: "Until a few years ago you have been proud of the transparency of your face, yet now, you treat it as a well-polished metal mask" (Kurahashi 1969, 110). Later, upon her second visit to the "room for solitude" (her naming for the restroom on the train), she extends this metaphor: "others' gazes slide over the surface without capturing you. Like a *noh* mask, it is a mask that changes infinitely" (ibid., 136–37).

The third contested binary, between reality and illusion, is one most conspicuous in Butor's *La Modification*, especially in terms of the dream, imagination, and memory, all three of which can enable one to depart from the present chain of events. The transition between actual scenes and dreamed, imagined, or remembered scenes is frequent, rapid, and unaccounted for. Their frequency and abruptness intensify the confusion with reality. This confusion between image and reality, or between the two-dimensional space of visuality and the three-dimensional space of corporeality, occurs in *Suspects on the Night Train* as well. In "The Tenth Wheel: To Hamburg," "you" spends several hours in Linz until her night train's scheduled departure time. One of the place she visits is a museum, where she sees a strange picture:

> It was like an out-of-focus monochrome photograph, like a photograph of a station taken out of the train window without flash, perhaps taken as the train enters the station. That was why lines were duplicated, blurred, and unintelligible, [making it] unclear what the picture had been taken of. An uncanny photograph. Such a photograph was simulated in the picture, painted in something like ink. It was just the size of a window of the night train. Was the association because you were about to ride a night train? Or would it appear that way to everyone? (Tawada 2002a, 122)

Perhaps a piece by Hiroshi Sugimoto or Gerhard Richter, this photo-like painting not only looks blurry within the frame but also blurs the boundary between photography and paintings. It may also be life-sized, taken out the window and kept the size of the window. The frame of the picture is the same as the frame that informed the scene. The distinction between reality and representation is thus blurred as well.

In *Suspects on the Night Train*, the scenery outside the window of the train complicates the passenger's sense of space. Thus, in "The Sixth Wheel: To Irkutsk," "you" remarks: "Even though the vast plain of Siberia extended outside the window, the corridor was hardly wide enough to pass each other" (ibid., 79), illustrating the fluctuation of a sense of space, by way of contrasting the exterior and interior, and also between the visual measuring of distant space and the physical handling of the space in which one moves (we may recall scenes from *The Narrow Margin*, discussed in Chap. 1). The latter dichotomy is a spatial equivalent of the dichotomy between third-person and second-person narratives, or between the omniscient narrator and the intradiegetic narrator (the narrator who is also a character in the story being told). "You" further observes: "Outside the window lay Siberia. Vast as it may be, as a landscape framed by the window, it was no more than a picture" (ibid., 80). Here boundless three-dimensional space is limited to a two-dimensional image of the manageable size of the window. This, too, contrasts experiencing space with one's body and viewing space with one's eyes. These comparisons of the relationships between space and the human subject evidences that in Tawada's narrative—and in all the second-person train narratives discussed here—it is essential to seek embodying and embodied three-dimensional space. When the central character is "you" (rather than "she/he/they," who are objectified and fixed by the narrator-I, in stable positions in a geometrical space at a given moment), their position is defined in relation to other human subjects, things, and space-time.

The body and the eye meet most crucially when one looks in the mirror. In *Blue Journey*, when "you" looks in the mirror in the "cabinet de solitude," she smiles at her reflection, which smiles back at her—an exchange that "you" says "all women are accustomed to" (Kurahashi 1969, 110). The mirror thus serves as a confirmation of the deixis—the interchangeable relationship between "I" and "you." Although there are similar scenes in *La Modification*, when "you" visits the restroom with a pouch of grooming tools in hand to shave, the significance of the exchange of gaze across the mirror does not seem to extend beyond the specific space or occasion in Butor's narrative as it does in *Blue Journey*.

In Butor's narrative, there is a degree of interchangeability between "you" ("vous") and "he" ("il"), but not between "you" and "I" (unlike in Larbaud's *My Most Secret Council* in Chap. 2).[25] Occasional slippages into the third person that occur toward the end of the journey may be understood as the merging of "you" and "you's" imaginings about a central character in the unidentified pulp novel that he carries with him but does not read. While reviewing its imagined plot and picturing the footsteps of its protagonist, "you" becomes sleepy, loses track of the boundary between the storyworld of the book he has and the world he occupies (the storyworld of *La Modification*), and becomes "he" in the narrative he is envisioning. Returning to clearer consciousness, he resumes the status of "you." Such slippages from "you" to "he" signal the loss of control over the mind due to fatigue and drowsiness toward the end of the railway trip.

The interchangeability between "you" and "he" has been indicated in other ways as well throughout the novel. Thus "you" keeps comparing other male passengers with himself, assessing them in terms of relative

height, build, age, material possessions (constant comparison of the quality of their luggage, clothing, cigarettes, and so forth, and comments on
their financial and social status and career stage), and behavior. "You" also
compares himself and others in terms of the act of mistakenly opening the
door to the wrong compartment, carried out repeatedly by presumably
different male passengers during the present train ride (Butor 1958, 100,
121, 125, 156; 1957, 101, 121, 124, 152), and by himself in the past
while traveling with his wife Henriette (Butor 1958, 99; 1957, 100–1).
Although such errors are inconsequential in terms of the plot of *La
Modification* (unlike in *The Narrow Margin*, as seen in Chap. 1), the
repetitiveness of this opening of a compartment door, and of hesitating on
the threshold, as well as other lapses in returning to one's seat expedi-
tiously due to intoxication and sleepiness, requires particular attention on
the discourse level.

In *La Modification*, "you" confuses his own reflection in the external
windowpane with what seems to be a stranger transfixed on the threshold
of the compartment, and thus elicits his fellow passengers' probing gaze.
Butor is also very specific about the placement of the streaming landscape
outside vis-à-vis the body—that is, whether the landscape is on the left or
the right from the perspective of the passenger in question. These instances
of corporeal consciousness qualify the power of "you" that seems otherwise uncontestable.

There are two scenes in *La Modification* that look not dissimilar to
Duchamp's painting of the sad young man described in Chap. 1—and that
evoke an image in an episode of Sigmund Freud's *The Uncanny*.[26] In tan-
dem, these two scenes in Butor's narrative demonstrate their topological
similitude to each other and articulate the transformation that the protagonist "you" goes through in the narrative:

> The man who took your seat earlier comes back into the compartment and
> slips on his black raincoat, swaying between the two seats as if he were tipsy;
> he loses his balance and just manages to save himself by clutching at your
> shoulder. (Butor 1958, 86; 1957, 89)

> But why are you still standing in the doorway, swaying about with the con-
> tinuous motion of the train, your shoulder bumping against the doorpost
> almost without your being conscious of it? Why are you standing transfixed
> like a sleepwalker interrupted in his wanderings, why do you shrink from
> entering that compartment as if all the same old thoughts were going to

pounce on you again the moment you sat down in that seat which you chose at the beginning as your rightful place?

Everybody stares at you, and in the window opposite you see your own reflection swaying like that of a drunken man about to fall, until the moon appears through a rift in the clouds and obliterates you. (Butor 1958, 168; 1957, 164–65)

In the second scene above, which unfolds much later than the first, "you," as he tries to reenter his compartment, simulates the man who *took his place* in the train earlier, but is unable to return to *his own place* at this time, both literally and figuratively. Literally, he can scarcely handle the sidelong movement of the train (like Duchamp's sad young man), and figuratively, he hesitates to resume the thinking about his life that will ensue by his taking the same seat. This instability and indecision are translated visually into his suspension within the oscillating motion of the train that halts any forward motion, physically or mentally, spatially or temporally.

Although these incidents are irrelevant to each other in terms of plot, one involving a minor character and the other the protagonist, the two swaying men are clearly connected graphically and kinetically, and thus contribute to the cohesiveness of the narrative structure on its rhetorical level. The repetition of the motif produces a rhythm and threads the narrative together. The interchangeability of these two scenes, despite the disparity of the characters and the roles the protagonist performs in them, is predicated on and hints at the anonymity of individuals, who tend to simulate each other's behaviors in the public space of the mass transportation system. Each passenger is everyone; "you" (the eye) can become "he" (the body), and vice versa. Despite the commonality of experience between "he" and "you," however, the two figures do not exchange notes with each other. They never develop a deixis—they do not become "you" and "I." They remain distant from each other, as the observer and the spectacle. Their positions may be exchanged, but they do not establish a dialogue. Thus, as Bal maintains, Butor's second-person narrative does not achieve any special effect different from that of a first-person narrative.

The primacy of the existence of "you" persists in Kurahashi's narrative as well. The body of "you" does not cease to occupy a space in the train, and it continues to exist throughout the time spent on the train:

You open your eyes. You are in the train. This is your place. As long as you are a lump of substance, weighing 47 kilograms, you must hold your place and stick to it. It would make no difference how far you might flee. However far a location you might take flight to, you cannot lose your own body as if it were a fooled pursuer, or desert your place, flying into a place of lightness, nothingness. And your sorrow, too, in the shape of a body, shall follow you in your escapade. (Kurahashi 1969, 166)

Unlike Butor's protagonist, however, Kurahashi's shows more acute and constant awareness that she (and everyone) exists as a spectacle for another, creating effects on another's mind. In the scene last excerpted above from *La Modification*, "you" is conscious of the stares of other passengers but does not think about how they are affected by the sight of him. Their gaze establishes them as observers, but not as people who are involved in "you's" existence. In *Blue Journey*, "you" ceases to be "she" and becomes "you" to another individual—as is evident in the scene in which "you" smokes in front of Saeki.

7   Silence and Speech and Sound: Communal Space

Further complicating the interior–exterior distinction is "you's" wish for silence in *La Modification*—that is, for lack of communication with his fellow passengers in the compartment. At no point during the 25-hour train ride does he initiate or invite conversation. Neither does he appreciate listening to others converse among themselves: "Oh, don't say they're going to start talking," "you" thinks when seemingly chatty new passengers arrive (Butor 1958, 165; 1957, 159). His preference for privacy or predilection for territoriality is constant, showing no signs of erosion. He is willing only to recognize those he has seen earlier in the dining room (Agnès and Pierre, in the nicknames he assigns to them) and to see Agnès smile at him (Butor 1958, 162; 1957, 157) Passengers and "you" may watch and assess each other frequently, yet the gaze does not develop into any vocal engagement. All of them are strangers to "you," meeting by chance on this train for the first time.[27] This insistence on silence stands in stark contrast with his earlier urge to keep talking with Cécile when they first meet on the train. Having shared a table in the dining car, he follows her to her compartment in third class because of the strength of his desire to talk with her about himself. He stays so long that he even falls asleep there, and wakes up to find Cécile surprised to see him when she, too, awakens (Butor 1958, 91; 1957, 93–94).

"You's" preference for non-communication with his fellow passengers, while wanting to and continuing to speak with a special other, is shared by his equivalent in *Blue Journey*. She recalls how she and her boyfriend "he" kept chatting and munching snacks "as if you were a couple of birds" (Kurahashi 1969, 96) when they traveled together on the same route. Yet in the narrative present, in her solitary trip surrounded by strangers, she prefers silence. When she sees that the passenger in the next seat is not keen on reading the newspapers and magazines he has brought, she tells herself: "You'd better be careful; this way, he may start talking to you; he may not be as talkative as enwrapping you in a cocoon of saliva, yet he might resume chatting every half an hour, so that he won't really leave you alone" (ibid., 94). With this premonition, she produces and puts on a pair of glasses for protection from any potential intrusion from him, which seems to have the desired effect; though he occasionally looks at her, they don't speak until she disembarks at the Kyoto station, when he offers a customary word of farewell, to which she only smiles in return (ibid., 180).

"You" in *Blue Journey* also generates silence among a group of three male business travelers with whom she is seated for the reserved lunch in the dining car:

> They are properly relaxed, and exchanging properly formal words at a slow pace—feeling completely safe, with apathy, like tamed birds in a cage. There comes you, an intruder into the "Intimité" [Sartre] moment in the homo-social circle, who does not appear to be a businesswoman or a student, cannot be discerned either as a "miss" or "madam," young yet not a girl. They steal glances at this unidentifiable woman, eyes glittering with curiosity. Because of that, their conversation stagnates and sediments over the table. (ibid., 158)

The barrier between speech and silence erodes in the ambiguous space time of the train—public space, yet not entirely borderless, with those traveling in groups building invisible walls within which they can talk as insiders, in a homogenous circle. The walls are not secure or impenetrable, however, and can be infiltrated at any moment, since passengers are free to move across the carriages and may walk into their space unexpectedly.

In both Butor's narrative and Kurahashi's, "you" wants to be secluded from others who share the interior space of the train in physical proximity for many hours, despite the potential for developing communication. Kurahashi's "you" likes to keep her aural environment as pristine as possible, perhaps so as to listen to sounds from her memory archive (such as jazz tunes), and anticipates irritation with a baby's cry and noise from another passenger's transistor radio. Aural effects can intrude upon one's own small territory within the shared space of the train carriage.

In contrast to Butor's and Kurahashi's central characters, who rarely engage in conversation or interaction with other passengers, "you" in Tawada's narrative is noticeably communicative. She is always becoming involved in conversation and action with strangers with whom she won't associate beyond the current trip, despite her caution, appropriate for a single female traveler in an unfamiliar land. Her space is unmistakably porous, which is the essential premise of the story. Rather than dwelling on someone who is absent from the present train trip, as Butor's and Kurahashi's protagonists do, Tawada's "you" does not have any significant other on her mind, and instead listens to and talks to strangers on the train. She makes efforts to converse even when she does not feel like it, when strangers approach her. She is aware of the benefit of incidental encounters: "You decided not to fly but to take a night train to go to Vienna for a performance. ... These days you had not gotten in touch with interesting people. Wasn't that because you had been taking the shortest cut because you no longer needed to be economical? If you take a night train as you used to do in younger days, then you might encounter something thrilling" ("The Eighth Wheel: To Vienna," Tawada 2002a, 95).

In "The Ninth Wheel: To Basel," "you" is feeling weak, as if all her blood has left her brain. She sits up when another passenger appears in the compartment, and stays upright out of courtesy as the woman talks on, yet becomes unable to hold her position any longer: "'I am going to lie down; I am getting tired. But please keep talking if you like,' said you. You didn't know why you said such a thing. Did you want to hear more of Mimi's stories, or did you not want to disappoint her since she seemed to want to talk on?" (ibid., 114). The concerted attention to the posture here is important in choreographing the dynamics between the two women, to which, as a professional dancer/choreographer, "you" may be especially sensitive. Posture dictates the way the voice is heard and the level of its affect, especially when the listener cannot see the face of the speaker: unlike the patient speaking from the couch to their psychoanalyst without seeing the listener, the listener who is not watching the speaker is thus doubly deprived of control over the other. "You" remains a listener, that is to say, "you" is "I" only as a listener. It is in this situation that the use of the second-person pronoun becomes even more relevant.

"You's" keen awareness of the choreographic position of the speaker versus the listener is apparently not shared by Mimi: "It didn't seem to matter to Mimi whether you were sitting up or lying down" (ibid., 115). As Mimi keeps talking, "you" falls asleep "in the horizontal and immobile posture, closed, dark, speechless, selfless, diminishing, fading, quietly, into the night" (ibid., 116), being granted silence she needed. Unlike "you" in *La Modification* falling asleep in the company of Cécile in her compartment, and waking to observe Cécile asleep and then waking up, sharing togetherness in the same space during their mutual silence, Tawada's "you" and her one-night compartment-partner Mimi are a world apart from each other during "you's" slumber.

One may not always have control over silence or speech with others on the train. In "The Eighth Wheel: To Vienna," Tawada's "you" feels clueless and isolated by others who talk the way only they understand:

> The female conductor, seeing the face of the passenger who had just got on, said "Oh!" in surprise. The two stopped and looked at each other in the corridor. Something thrilling must begin, finally. You held your breath. … In suspense, you eavesdropped their conversation. …
>
> Just before departure, [the conductor] hurried back and said, "I remembered." The woman in the black dress nodded and remarked, "Me, too, just now." Then they giggled jointly. You felt as if you were excluded from the pact and felt displeased, yet you did not have the courage to ask them to impart their secret. Tormented by curiosity, aroused yet neglected, you covered yourself with the blanket yet could not sleep. (ibid., 97–98)

The communication between them and their silence toward "you" intrigue her, yet exclude her from a chance for conversation on the night train. She is so upset that their "secret" is not shared with her that she even tells herself, "You shouldn't have taken a night train. The window is shielded by a thick curtain, and even if you had forced open the curtain, it is pitch dark outside and you could not get any information" (ibid., 98). Here, the voice and sight are paralleled in terms of the failure to share information.

This sound-sight coordination corresponds to "you's" observation—from the window in the corridor—of a glass-walled restaurant behind the station before the train departs Hamburg Station:

Well lit, the inside was clearly visible. ... Their motion seen alone made you feel as if you were observing a bees' dance. You realized it was because their speech was inaudible. In front of you was the glass of the train; behind it was the hotel's glass. [Such was] the time you were spending watching far across several layers of glass. (ibid., 96)

Sight without sound is a matter of course when observing through several layers of glass. Yet when one considers it (as "you" does while waiting for the train to leave the station), it alerts one to the material conditions of the given space-time (glass is a substance that does not shroud sight yet shuts off sound from either side) and makes one aware of the contingencies that equip a conversation with both sound and sight. The illusory transparency of glass windows that we have seen in several narratives is on display in this passage.

What Tawada's "you" likens to "a bees' dance" is encapsulated in another metaphor by the "you" in Kurahashi's *Blue Journey*:

Outside the window, a young businessman-like man is tapping the glass and saying something. Not to you or to the gentleman next to you. Whomever he may be speaking to, his voice is hardly audible. It is like watching a fish bumping against the glass of a water tank and struggling. How sad is it to open and close the mouth so vigorously yet to fail to make his voice heard. (Kurahashi 1969, 92)

The metaphor of "a fish" "struggling" may be better suited than that of "a bees' dance" to the "you" in *Blue Journey*, who is less humorous and more despondent at the moment than the "you" in *Suspects on the Night Train*. In both cases, however, a non-human actant assumes the voiceless action, as if to indicate that speech is fundamental to human communication only. These two scenes, in two different second-person narratives, verify more than the "you's" autonomy from "him/her/them": they verify the train's seclusion from the outside aural space, while simultaneously confirming the visual adjacency of the two spaces—adjacent yet separated, framed and thus somewhat staged.

The unstable boundary between speech and silence materializes in yet another trip in "The Sixth Wheel: To Irkutsk" in *Suspects on the Night Train*. Here "you" happens to come across a man who previously made her scribble a letter, ostensibly from a man called Mike, obviously to counterfeit the handwriting, and who is now in the company of the addressee of the letter, a woman named Marie, on the train:

> You sat next to Marie and said to her, "Your name is Marie, isn't it?" Looking pleased yet surprised, Marie said, "How did you know?" Ken uncrossed and crossed his legs, looking awfully nervous, and coughed, so you laughed and placidly said, "I happened to hear you speak to each other in the corridor yesterday." Ken hurriedly introduced himself, "My name is Ken." He must have wanted to prevent you from blurting, "I believe you are Mike." (Tawada 2002a, 77)

Ken is startled and worried that "you" might disclose to Marie the details of their previous dealing. After the courtesy exchange of introducing themselves, "you" struggles with the invisible line between sitting in silence and overhearing the couple's conversation, or trying to listen and not to listen:

> Marie and Ken exchanged words in a whisper from time to time. Their voices emerged as if a product of the shrieking friction of the rail and wheel, and disappeared engulfed by their noise. You were troubled because your ears were pricked and extended toward the two against your will. ... You became wearied with trying to listen and left the compartment. (ibid., 78)

The distinction between speech and silence, between the private and the public, and between interest and indifference is drawn and withdrawn against the train's noise in the background, which is presented in Tawada's narration in purely physical rather than metaphysical terms. The acoustic (or sonic) spatiality—of space formed by sound—exhibited in some of the narratives examined earlier materializes in *Suspects on the Night Train* as well.

"You" is coaxed into silence by Ken while Marie is out of the compartment yet becomes talkative when inebriated, declaring to Marie while Ken is absent that she is an "omniscient Siberian Shaman," telling her what she knows about her circumstances, and advising her to act differently from the way Ken wants her to—all without disclosing his plotting (ibid., 81). These examples demonstrate the slipperiness of communication (or lack thereof) between passengers who are incidental companions, as well as the erosion between speech and silence. On the one hand, conversation can take place, develop into a long chat, and take unpredictable turns; on the other hand, silence can prevail and create some effects, too.

8   BOOK AS A THING: BOOK (NOT) TO BE READ; BOOK TO BE WRITTEN

It is common practice, in fiction and in real life, for a long-distance train passenger to carry something to read into the carriage with them. The reason is potentially to read during the extended time of the travel, which appears blank and void if traveling is considered a mere means to move from the departure point to the destination (as in Foucault's second relation), and also if time is considered to be a transparent, homogenous, and measurable property (absolute time) that should not be wasted. Reading a book on the train is also designed for the sedentary body that nulls the actual distance traveled by the moving vehicle (as seen theorized by Bissell in Chap. 2), translating the carriage into an interior space rather than an exterior space. Thus considered, reading a book is one practice radically involved in space-time on train journey. Indeed, Butor himself has written an essay, "Travel and Writing," about reading while traveling and then writing about the trip completed (Butor 1974).

As we saw in Chap. 2, the book that Francis, the narrator-protagonist of *Zone*, brings onto the train is read in earnest. Indeed, a story in it is quoted in its entirety, extending over three whole chapters of Énard's novel, and is emotionally responded to by the reader-passenger. For Gregorius, the protagonist-focalizer of Mercier's *Night Train to Lisbon*, the book by Amadeu is the reason for the trip. In contrast to these two characters (and not unlike Sanshirō in *Sanshirō* and Luca in *My Most Secret Council*, discussed in Chap. 2), the central characters in the three second-person narratives considered here do not seem to read in depth while on the train; rather, their books serves purposes other than reading. On the present trip in *La Modification*, for instance, "you" uses his book, which he purchased at the kiosk at Gare de Lyon without checking its title, almost exclusively as a seat marker when he leaves for the dining car, restroom, or for a smoke break in the corridor or on the platform. As Iliopoulou has pointed out, each of the nine chapters in *La Modification* ends with "you" leaving the compartment, and from the second through eighth chapters—regretting not having done so the first time and thus having lost his original seat—"you" places the book on his seat to mark it as taken (Iliopoulou 2019, 131–32). Interestingly, the narrative insists that even the book's title remains unknown to "you" (unlike on a train journey in the past, where he is seen reading *Letters of Julian the Apostate*; Butor 1958, 176, 188, 221; 1957, 172, 182, 211). Although "you" does not read the book, he notices other passengers' practice of reading—not only what they are reading but in what posture and with what degree of absorption. "You" knows that their reading is not too intense: "The train stops and all eyes look up at once, all books are forgotten in the sudden silence and motionlessness" (Butor 1958, 35; 1957, 40). Reading, for them, is only a pastime, or a facade to create a cocoon of privacy within the public space of the train compartment.

During "you's" dreams, it appears he becomes a character in stories and thus loses his second-person status and is addressed in the third person, as discussed earlier. Here we lose touch with the physical and sensible presence of "you" in real time, and instead encounter "he" in a novelistic discourse. His storytelling after slipping into a dream state suggests that his mind is not immune to formation of the novelistic discourse. "You" is inherently a reader who happens not to be reading intently on this specific train trip. This perplexes him:

> Why haven't you read that book, since you bought it? It might perhaps have protected you against all this. Why, now that you're sitting down and holding it in your hands, can't you open it, don't you even want to read the title? Why, ... do you merely stare at the back of the book, the cover of which seems to grow transparent and the white pages underneath to turn over automatically, with lines of letters on them forming words which you can't recognize? (Butor 1958, 168; 1957, 165)

Butor's "you" may be too preoccupied with the current state of his private life to delve into another life recounted in a book. However, as the plot of his plan to separate from his wife and set up housekeeping with his lover begins to dissolve amid an excess of thought, memory, and anticipation, "you" wonders whether he could have rather benefitted from setting aside his musings and being distracted by another plot.

Butor's "you" nevertheless reaches a conclusive answer to the question, even though his approach to the book is more analytical and imagined than is Francis's emotional and direct reaction to the book he reads in *Zone*, as we examined in Chap. 2:

> in this book which you bought so that it might distract you and which you haven't read precisely because during this journey you wanted, just for once, to be wholly involved in your action, and if under these circumstances it had been able to interest you sufficiently this would have meant that it bore so close a resemblance to your own situation that it would have set out your

own problem before you, and consequently, far from distracting you, far from protecting you against this disintegration of your scheme, of your precious hopes, it would only have precipitated things, (Butor 1958, 169; 1957, 166)

These reflections "you" immerses himself in, on what he could have found in the book that he hasn't read, reveal in earnest his literary sensibility and aptitude for experiencing literature beyond entertainment. Without reading the book in hand, he begins to suspect it holds relevance to his own life that is unfolding at the moment. The book "you" hasn't read, he becomes convinced, would offer too similar a story to his own to let him avoid facing his own life problems (just as we saw Francis experience in *Zone*) and would even drive him to reverse his decision:

in this book there must be somewhere, however lightly sketched, however unconvincing, however badly written, a man in difficulties who wants to save himself, who is making a journey and realizes that the path he has taken doesn't lead where he expected (Butor 1958, 169; 1957, 166)[28]

The parallel that "you" imagines between the unread book's content and his own life cements the path to his resolve to write a novel about the turning point he is experiencing: "Then in that hotel room, alone, you'll begin writing a book, to fill the emptiness of those days in Rome deprived of Cécile, debarred from going near her" (Butor 1958, 239; 1957, 228).

The end of the novel presents almost a supernatural integration of the book he didn't read and the book he is to write:

You stand up, put on your coat, take your bag and pick up your book.
    The best thing surely, would be to preserve the actual geographical relationship between these two cities and to try to bring to life, in the form of literature, this crucial episode in your experience, the movement that went on in your mind while your body was being transferred from one station to another through all the intermediate landscapes, toward this book, this future necessary book of which you're holding in your hand the outward form. (Butor 1958, 249; 1957, 236)

Iliopoulou reads "this future necessary book" whose "outward form" "you" holds in his hand as being Butor's book *La Modification* itself; thus she reads "you" as being one and the same as the reader here. This leap out of the storyworld and even out of the narrative discourse, thereby concluding the narrative with a metafictional paradox (Hutcheon 1980), is what Irene Kacandes has called the "narrative apostrophe" or "anomalous communicative circuits in second-person narrative fiction at the levels of the story and of the reception of the story" (Kacandes 1994, 329), using Butor's *La Modification* as her precise model.

A perhaps less captivating hypothesis would be to read "this book" as the book that the character-"you," the protagonist, is literally holding in his hand—the book he did not read, the book whose pages went white, and the book he is convinced is telling his story. He only needs to fill the pages with his own writing. However similar the content of the provisional book may be to *La Modification*, it is imagined on a different plane, in the material form clutched in the character's hand, rather than in any reader's hand. The transformation between the unread book and the book to be written is indeed mysterious, but it is a different mystery from the transformation of the book "you" is to write into the book Butor has written. It is, however, the turning point for "you," not only in terms of his romantic relationships but in terms of his position: he ceases to be "you"-the-passenger when his train journey is over, and becomes "I" the author.

In Kurahashi's *Blue Journey*, "you" is an avid reader, as can be expected of a graduate student in modern French literature. Yet she deliberately decides not to bring any book with her on the long railway journey. While waiting for her train at the station, "You pop your head in the bookstand, you take in hand a few weekly magazines, yet you stop. As you do not have any appetite, so you do not have any desire to read. You do not read anything. If you must to read a detective fiction or a sci-fi ..." (Kurahashi 1969, 91; ellipses in the original). It is noteworthy that "you" draws a parallel between desire for food and desire for books, thus positing the body and the mind as relatable to each other. Reading is as natural to "you" as eating, yet she renounces the habit of either one. In the first and second parts of the novel (the latter of which is dedicated to the railway journey), we are repeatedly told of her lack of appetite. She forces herself to eat out of rational considerations during the train ride, yet does not read. The only exception she considers making before the departure is for "detective fiction" and "sci-fi," two genres that are structure-oriented, with content distinct from the everyday life of most readers—no relevance to her present personal issues.

One of the many similarities—or tributes—to *La Modification* found in *Blue Journey* is "you's" resolve to write a novel. The decision is not unpredictable, given that "you" is a highly literary person and has planned to "«establish my own *style*»" (ibid., 234), as quoted from her personal notebook.[29] Still, it is a radical turning point in her life for "you" to write a novel at this point because it means release from "he's" "binding" of her that has persisted for many years. After the railway journey, however, "you" seems to realize that his disappearance is her liberation. "He's" discovery of the aforementioned declaration in "you's" notebook "baffled you thoroughly" (ibid., 234), yet "now you could engross yourself in this endeavor [to write in your own style] in your atelier that he wouldn't invade" (ibid.). "You's" existential position of being always "you" will be reconsidered, and "you" will become "I," replacing "he."

This transformation is made possible because "you" begins to suspect that "he" must have been writing a novel that she can find in his apartment upon her return to Tokyo and complete on his behalf—"To compose his fragments and organize the entirety of 'he'—to write his «novel that was unwritten». That is to discover 'he' and the novel he may have written" (ibid., 242). The novel she is to write has a theme of "in search of the novel that is yet to be discovered," and "for the time being, what you will deal with is he, his love, and your love that will be re-deciphered through his love once again" (ibid., 243). "He" who disappeared from "you's" life will not disappear from her mind or her work. Yet "he" will be reconstructed through "you," as "you" will be reconstructed through the "he" that "you" reconstructs. The binary is not canceled but reconfigured into a form in which "you" is more in charge.

"You" in *Suspects on the Night Train* reads to protect herself from the intrusion of other passengers. When her fellow passenger in the compartment seems to have a criminal record in "The Fourth Wheel: To Belgrade," "you" decides to "pretend to be engrossed in a book" (Tawada 2002a, 56). Reading also rescues "you" from the awkwardness of lying in bed when another passenger steps into the sleeper in "The Fifth Wheel: To Beijing": "You ... began to read a paperback. Not as if you wanted to read a book—it was like a little shield to cover your face. It was somewhat embarrassing if a stranger stepped into the space where you were horizontal. It would make you feel less improper if you were reading" (ibid., 65).[30] As a space-management tactic, reading—or holding a book in hands—is quite effective.

Reading also offers a strategy to deal with space-time that "you" doesn't otherwise know how to negotiate. In "The Sixth Wheel: To Irkutsk," "you" muses:

> You yielded to the immensity of the time that was dumped in front of you, and stopped counting and calculating it. There is nothing else you could do other than soak yourself in it. For the time being, you produced a paperback book out of the backpack, and began to read it as if to confirm word by word; if you read it as if to slide across the text, you would finish reading soon. Then, you would not know what to do with your own gaze [in the compartment]. (ibid., 77–78)

Reading a book is choreographically convenient because one can drop one's gaze onto the pages without accounting for its placement. Reading is also a good engagement when one has too much time at hand—if one knows how to pace one's own reading, as "you" does.[31]

However, reading can exceed the role of being a handy way to manage space-time while on the train. In "The Eleventh Wheel: To Amsterdam," as we have seen, the plot of the detective novel that "you" is reading and the unfolding mystery about the child who sneaks into her compartment and bites his own arm reflect each other, and resolve both conundrums as a consequence. Let us take a closer look at the entanglement of the two mysteries: "You produced a book of detective fiction out of the bag, lay down on one of the lower beds and began to read. You did not usually like detective fiction, yet thought it would do best in distracting your mind from [the obnoxious theatre director]" (ibid., 132). Her rationale for the choice of detective fiction is similar to that of her counterpart in *Blue Journey*, as seen earlier. "You" then summarizes the plot of the detective novel at length. A man was murdered, apparently hit by a hammer from behind while angling at a lake, and fell into it. The only witness is a seven-year-old girl who suffers from a speech hindrance and will not answer any questions from the police. The case remains unresolved. When "you" has read thus far, she becomes involved in the mystery with the child who appears and disappears from the compartment, and is accused of abusing him by the conductor. Then "you" reflects on her responsibilities:

> What had you done? ... Certainly you could not save the child. That was you to blame. You did not notice that the child had been biting his own flesh. That was because you had been absorbed in the stupid detective fiction. Then, all of a sudden, you realized the conclusion of the detective fiction that you had not finished reading. The girl who could not speak was always physically abused by the man. Thus, that morning, she assaulted him from behind and murdered him. (ibid., 137)

While "you" here is not killed, she is accused of wrongdoing, and her fate is undisclosed at the end of the chapter. Since, according to my aforementioned estimate, this is the most recent chapter in terms of story time, the reader surmises that it is possible that "you's" life will never be the same. Just as "you" has begun her journey twenty-some years earlier because of a life-changing incident in India (to be seen shortly), so her journey may end here, because "you" is no longer a carefree bystander but an accused person in a precarious position. The meaning of being addressed in the second person has changed, and "you" is now the other in a criminal investigation, to be addressed by the police in the second person—and the perpetrator, who has been, to the victim, the only one who could be referred to in the second person. The second-person address may not always be made out of love or friendship: it may be made out of condemnation.

9   BIOLOGICAL TIME

The three second-person train narratives examined here contain many more references to physical urges and demands, such as thirst, hunger, fatigue, pain, desire for fresh air, desire to urinate, and desire to sleep, than the other long-distance railway journey narratives we have seen so far. Some narratives discussed earlier do not even tell us what passengers ate or drank. When they do, it may be to fill a gap in realism, or because of some development of the plot (e.g., the eating of game birds and apples in Miyazawa's "Night"). The remarkable wealth of physical-urge descriptions in the three narratives examined in this chapter may be attributed to how second-person narration enhances the processing of sensations, as noted by phenomenologists and scholars of qualitative ethnography at the beginning of this chapter. Because second-person narratives are more concerned with the multi-sensorial experience of the protagonist, we are presented with much more detail than usual about food, drink, and other things to be consumed or processed by the subject's body.

In *La Modification*, "you" does go to the restroom, yet his urge to urinate is hardly described. As his trip is for more than 24 hours, he must have been to the restroom more often than mentioned in the narrative. If so, the discrepancy of frequency between the story and the discourse indicates the author's deliberate downgrading of the importance of the visits to the restroom. The scenes are an opportunity for him to look at himself in the mirror, and thus provide visual effects rather than corporeal effects.

This can be accounted for by the essentially first-person subjectivity in Butor's narrative formation, as pointed out by Mieke Bal.

For "you" in *La Modification*, which is set in the 1950s, the biological urge is more acutely felt for smoking. His breaks from the compartment to smoke on a station platform (Butor 1958, 36, 133; 1957, 41, 131) or in the corridor (Butor 1958, 133; 1957, 131) are meticulously noted. "You" even tries to keep track of the passing of time by counting the number of remaining cigarettes (Butor 1958, 184; 1957, 178), and tries to remember restocking his case with Nationale, the Italian brand, when his reservoir of Gauloise, the French one, becomes meager. This is a merging of biological time (a version of immanent time) and chronological time (absolute time); "you" still relies on, or is controlled by, the linear and measurable time, yet the way he articulates its flow is by way of his desire to smoke.

Smoke erodes boundaries between passengers, reminding them of sharing of the space. As is the case with Jerzy and Marta in *Night Train* seen in Chap. 1, sharing a light for cigarettes brings strangers together—a common practice between smokers in public spaces that can trigger social relations. Not all the smoking-related acts remove barriers. Smoke may be inhaled by another in the same space-time, thus invading others' internal systems. At one point, "you" remembers refraining from asking Cécile for a cigarette because she was engrossed in reading (Butor 1958, 182; 1957, 177). "You" also burns his fingers while smoking, before he is visited by the ticket inspector (Butor 1958, 41; 1957, 45). While these incidents do not change the course of his journey, let alone his life, they affect experienced space as spatial practices.

In *Blue Journey*, "you" goes to the restroom twice during the six or seven hours of the train ride. In scenes elsewhere, the narrative mentions "you's" visits to restrooms (e.g., in a jazz cafe in Tokyo, seated near the restroom and noticing many boys entering and leaving the space, handling their zippers; and in another jazz cafe, in Kyoto, hastily, before the record she has requested will start playing). So Kurahashi is aware of the strategic use of the motif to present time, as well as space, as embodied and embodying. "You" in *Blue Journey* (set in the early 1960s), smokes in her seat and in the train bar, stating that it is not so much for the sake of inhaling the nicotine as of watching the smoke (Kurahashi 1969, 157). Thus, she smokes to confirm her status as the producer of spectacle and as the spectator thereof, by way of offering her own body interior to the stimulus.

Although smoking is scarcely featured in *Suspects on the Night Train* (probably due to the socio-historical condition of the early 2000s, when the narrative was written), the motif of restroom visits is prominent in the narrative. Thus in "The Seventh Wheel: To Khabarovsk," "you" wakes up in the middle of the night and reluctantly goes to the restroom, or so she thinks:

> Right after waking up in the wee hours of the second night, you feel an almost apologetic pressure in your bladder. You have to go to the bathroom, you think as if it were somebody else's problem. You really don't have any inclination to wake up right now. Oh, if only this were a dream. You take into account the person who needs to use the w/c, the person who woke up in the middle of the night and the person who hates getting up, but when you add them all together it's still only one person. *There's no moment that would make you feel you were merely one person more sorely than this one.* Well, even if you were traveling with other people, you couldn't very well wake them up so you could all take a dump together. When people need to relieve themselves, they always do so alone. It's a fate you simply can't escape. You'll just have to peel your body out of bed and cut through the chilly night car all alone. (Tawada 2002a, 86–87; 2011, 92)

The biological time pressure asserts itself with more urgency when the child cannot wait to go to the restroom at the end of the corridor[32] in "The Twelfth Wheel: To Bombay":

> After a while you woke up again. Your hip was gradually growing warm and wet. The smell of ammonia stung your nostrils. It appeared the child next to you had peed. You wanted to stand up, yet your feet were immobile; several people lay curled up on the floor around your feet. You didn't feel like changing either. You didn't mind being wet. All of a sudden the child began crying, ... You remembered you had candies, called coconut something, groped in your pocket, found some, took the child's hand and let her grab one. The cry stopped immediately. You and she were united in being wet with the same urine. You threw a candy into your mouth. (Tawada 2002a, 151)

The carriage is absorbed in multi-sensorial effects, by way of traces of other passengers' bodies, as studied by Jensen et al. (2015), seen earlier. In this extreme case, the spatial boundary between self and other is multiply violated by moisture, smell, and taste. This instance also dissolves the organization of homogenous time. The child cannot act according to schedule, holding her urine until she has a chance to go to the restroom. Nor can her cry be scheduled. It starts unexpectedly, and ends as her mouth gets busy with something else to do. Time is experienced within the body, rather than administered from outside.

Another reminder of biological time emerges in "The Twelfth Wheel: To Bombay." Another passenger approaches, this time not horizontally but vertically:

> Then a voice was heard from the bed above, followed by a face dangling upside down. The eyes in it looked pinched into the shape of inverted triangles.
>   "Do you have a nail clipper?" (Tawada 2002a, 151)

Typical of Tawada, the passage is full of topological elements, to precisely set up the scene. The bunk-bed's vertical structure is most effectively exploited as a prop for a dramatic event. "You" indeed has a nail clipper, which she lends the passenger on the bed above hers. He likes it so much that he asks her to sell it to him.

Why should a nail clipper matter—such a mundane thing, hardly allegorical? To tackle this question, we might begin by defining nails in terms of practices they facilitate: (1) to scratch the surface of something to cause some (lasting or temporary) damage (a crease, scar, or cut); (2) to pluck strings to make (musical) sound; (3) to paint or have someone paint, to enjoy/endure the process of designing, painting, and letting dry, possibly talking with the nail artist, and to admire or to have others admire for the duration of the completed art;[33] (4) to bite while watching/listening to some ongoing event that is tantalizingly suspenseful, and potentially to lose, attesting to one's spectatorial absorption in the other's action; and (5) to clip, as they grow and become potentially dangerous to others and to the self.

A weapon, a tool, a stage, an exit of frustration, or a thing that has its own vitality: nails are loaded with temporality. The nail clipper is thus an instrument to curtail the variously potent time, to control the time of nails that grow—a brand of biological time—and to manage that time. Nails grow of their own accord, thus not only being embodied by but also embodying immanent time. Unclipped nails are a testament to a digression from normativity. "The Eighth Wheel: To Vienna" includes a story of a female passenger whose madness is revealed in her nails "grown 3, 4 centimeters," "bent, twisted, soiled, with a trace of manicure" "like a bird" (ibid., 102–3). This particular episode is mediated by Mr. Beck, "you's" friend who greets her at the Vienna station. His comment that the woman with the spectacular nails was mad concludes the wheel and meets with no response from "you." Although that "wheel" suspends judgment on the divide between mental normalcy and deviation therefrom, the image of the nails growing out of control paints the divide between the absolute time whose rule is maintained by periodically clipping one's nails and keeping them to a socially acceptable and functional length, and the immanent time—specifically, biological time in the current context—that lets nails grow.

Let us return to the conversation between "you" and the other passenger in "The Twelfth Wheel: To Bombay," a stranger who happens to be on the upper bed above "you's." That seemingly innocuous beginning of a conversation leads to a fatal bargain between the two passengers, of a nail clipper for a pass that allows its owner to travel infinitely (Tawada 2002a, 153). This may be an allusion to the eternal railway pass in Miyazawa's "Night" discussed in Chap. 4: its protagonist, Giovanni, while traveling on the train amongst stars in the universe with his estranged best friend Campanella, miraculously finds an eternal railway pass in his pocket when a conductor asks for a ticket that he thought he didn't have.[34] Then, at the end of the Milky Way Railway journey, upon the disappearance of Campanella, Giovanni is consoled by a man who tells him, in a voice like a cello, to hold onto the ticket as he keeps living strongly in the world outside the Milky Way. Since the story ends as Giovanni wakes up from a dream that same night, we cannot fathom the importance of the eternal ticket or even confirm that the ticket remains in Giovanni's possession after his dream is over. Yet in Tawada's narrative, the eternally and universally valid train ticket that "you" is offered has strings attached and causes grave consequences:

> On that day, I purchased the insolence of calling myself "I" and became "I." You, on the other hand, ceased to call yourself "I" and have since always been "you." Since that day, there has been nothing you can do other than continually traveling on a night train, as an object to be depicted in the second person. (ibid., 153)

The passenger who gave the eternal ticket and gained the nail clipper becomes "I"—"I" who can terminate the trip at any moment they like and clip the nail to punctuate the passage of biological time. "I" is the existence of "insolence," a human subject that claims to control its environment and life as an autonomous being outside space and time. Meanwhile, for the passenger who is given the eternal ticket, though it seems a privilege, it turns out to be an obligation. She stays on the night train and cannot but always be called "you" because she is someone for other passengers to encounter and interact with in the space-time of the train. "You" stays in a deixis, never to be able to transcend relationality and dialogism as the sole origin of authority.

At the beginning "The Twelfth Wheel: To Bombay," the "I"—undefined at this point—speaks to "you" twenty years later, as they claim it to be, and the story begins to unfold in retrospect:

> Do you remember, or do you not, the day you sold off your nail clipper while on a train? You must have realized even before that trip was over that it was not an ordinary nail clipper. You may have tried to console yourself, telling yourself that you could clip your nails with scissors or file them, yet, in the back of your mind, you must have sensed that you could never clip your nails, that you could not help but live dragged by the will of the growing nails, pulled into the direction in which the nails grow. I am sorry for you, but there is nothing I could do for you.
>
> Do you remember that train on which you encountered me? It is already more than twenty years ago. Do you remember my face, with the eyes in downcast triangles? You may say you don't remember such a strange face. How many of the faces of people one got to know twenty years earlier does one remember? (ibid., 139)

This mysterious beginning indicates nonetheless that a fate irrevocable has befallen "you." At the same time, it is obvious that "you" here is neither the protagonist nor the focalizer, but the (intended) audience, spoken to by "I"—the first person narrator who has never appeared in the preceding eleven chapters of *Suspects on the Night Train*.

At the end of this penultimate wheel, we learn how the character we have known as "you" in all the preceding 11 wheels has become "you" and can exist only as "you." We also sense that the 12th wheel relates the oldest incident, and that we have been told about more recent journeys that "you" has taken since. As we have seen, "The Eleventh Wheel: To Amsterdam"—newly added when the book was published—asks a most fundamental question about the binary between "I" and "you," and implicates "you" as a criminal suspect of child abuse. This 11th wheel appears to be appropriate for marking the end of her journey.

Yet there is one more wheel, as noted earlier: "The Thirteenth Wheel: To a City That Does Not Exist Anywhere." This wheel is in the format of a play, consisting entirely of utterances of four passengers who happened to be in a same compartment of a night train. They all speak in first person and address others in the second person, using various personal pronouns to indicate gender and social background. Could any of them be the "you" we know? Could the one who speaks only in idioms be Tawada's "you"? Or the one who suffers from leg pain and is looking for missing CT scan prints, though clearly this passenger is male? "You" has indicated her gender ambiguity (as in "To Khabarovsk") and the possibility of being androgynous as a comfortable option.

The question of identification aside, this last "wheel" of *Suspects on the Night Train* superbly articulates the spatial conditions of the compartment as negotiated by passengers, or their body parts, through actions such as sitting or standing, raising their feet so that one of them can look for a missing object in the space under the berth, incidentally smelling exposed socks, and so on. Such choreographic effects illustrate the dynamic relations among the four. Their irritation with one another rises to the level that they somehow think one of them has to leave the compartment. At that point, one of them, apparently a woman who has been polite to the others, offers a verdict[35] there is no need to make one of the four leave because they are not competing with each other for territory in the limited space. Instead, she declares, each of them occupies a separate space-time:

> Isn't every one of us all alone while sleeping? In a dream, some jump out of the train, others have been left behind at the departure point, and yet others have already arrived at the destination. We are not in the same space to begin with. See, can't you hear the roar of the place names rushing past underneath the bed at amazing speed? Each of us is being deprived of land from beneath our feet at a distinct pace. No one needs to get off. Everyone is running separately, while being here yet not here, each on one's own. (ibid., 163)

The heterogeneity of space-time is manifest because each passenger experiences space-time on the train irrelevantly to the experience of each of the others, even though all the passengers on the "same" train are sharing geometrical space and chronological time. Multiplicities of space-time are juxtaposed, as we have seen in Butor's narrative in which different passengers get on and off at different stations, and in Kurahashi's in which different passengers have distinct manners in which they are to experience the space-time of the train carriage, through reading, listening, eating, drinking, smoking, and other activities.

Notes

1. I cite Butor's narrative by its original title of *La Modification* (literally, "The Modification") throughout, instead of the title of any existing English translation, because the original title's less figurative and more graphic nature serves my focus here better. To me, "modification" occurs on many levels and in many ways in the story, not only in terms of the protagonist's mind, emotion, or plan but in terms of physical surroundings that affect his heart or thought and that also exist and operate on equal terms with them. His interiority is not central but is, rather, immersed in the larger context, in which many other people and things are being modified by and modifying others.
2. Since completing this project, I came to know Jason M. Beckman's brilliant article on this anti-novel, "A Virtual You: The Second-Person Narrative as Virtuality," which considers second-person narration in terms of the potential for its evolution in the theory of virtual reality. Beckman (2023) cites *La Modification* and *Suspects on the Night Train*, among others, as second-person narratives.
3. All English extracts from Tawada's *Yōgisha no yakō ressha* are mine unless otherwise noted. Sachiyo Taniguchi (2010) catalogues the use of the second-person pronoun "anata" in many texts by Tawada, including *Suspects on the Night Train*.
4. For a highly informed of the history of technological science and insightful investigation of geographical and optical awareness manifest in this novel as projected onto the protagonist's experience of the train journey, see Rabourdin 2018.
5. The distinctions include their care of their baggage. In *Zone*, Francis locks his briefcase containing highly valuable documents, and even locks it to the bar of the luggage rack—discretely, so as not to attract anyone's attention (Énard 2010, 10; 2008, 15). In contrast, "you" in *La Modification* leaves his bag unlocked. His insouciance is met with the narrator's attention to the fact (Butor 2017, 19; 1957, 23): it is important that the narrator does not think it is unimportant to mention that "you" does not lock his bag.
6. I refer to Kurahashi's narrative throughout by its English title, *Blue Journey*, even though the work remains untranslated at the time of writing, the

English title is used by the author herself, in another novel by her, *Seishōjo* (Divine Maiden, 1965), in which a caricature of "you" appears as a major character.

7. The Larbaud-Butor similarity mentioned earlier concerns their content: in both narratives a man on a long-distance train contemplates his past, present, and future in terms of his relationship with his significant other. The Butor-Kurahashi similarity, in contrast, is not confined to the railway journey setting but includes, and is more significantly about, the use of the second person. Larbaud's narrative, as experimental as it is, is not in the second person but in extended free direct discourse, or "interior monologue."

8. "Deixis is what speakers do to locate themselves in space and time, with respect to things, events, and each other. When speaking, it is impossible not to be deictic, not to 'be in' the context of one's discourse. Not being deictic is not communicating, not being in a situation, not being. This is what happens in some narratives, whose narrator disappears behind the events of the story and which seem to be deploying themselves without the intervention of any speaker. Such narrative, however, is strictly a written achievement, made possible by the fictional space that writing creates" (Bakker 2005, 71).

9. This is the case until "you" resolves to renew his life with his wife Henriette and in his imagination calls to her as "you" (Butor 1958, 248; 1957, 236).

10. Fludernik (1994, 449) declares that the narrator of Butor's *La Modification* cannot be Léon, who is referred to in second person, because the choice of the second-person pronoun is "vous," rather than the "tu" that Léon would use if he were talking to himself. In Larbaud's *My Most Secret Council*, the narrator-protagonist uses "tu" as well as "vous" when talking to himself.

11. Butor's narrative uses "vous" for the second person. Shimizu Tōru, the novel's Japanese translator, adapts "kimi" for "vous," decidedly less formal and more intimate and intrusive than "anata," which is a closest Japanese equivalent for "tu." But perhaps more importantly in our present context, Shimizu all but confirms that the addressor (the invisible and intangible narrator) is male, given the socio-historical circumstances of the late 1950s Japan in which his translation was first published, when male speaker could address either a male or a female "you" as "kimi," whereas a female speaker would not address either as "kimi." This reveals a great deal about the translator's reading of the French anti-novel relevant to points I touch upon later. By choosing "kimi" for "vous," Shimizu effectively denies the possibility of a female gaze upon the male body or female insight into the male consciousness or unconscious. Meanwhile, in English translations,

"you" is used as the only legitimate option, with the obvious effect of losing the implications of Butor's original choice of "vous."

12. In Saeki's letter, however, the second-person address is not "anata" but "kimi," the informal and subordinating pronoun that a man (especially if older) is accustomed to use for a woman, as explained in the previous note.
13. See, for example, Huber 2016.
14. Jason M. Beckman does not dismiss this practice as I do, and sees in it a precursor of virtuality that is extensively practiced in the new media. See Beckman 2023.
15. This may not apply to another second-person narrative by Tawada, *Amerika: Hidō no tairiku* (America: A Continent of No Roads/ Justice), 2005.
16. Butor's "you" is able to anticipate stations without consulting the timetable, make complex judgments for himself, and see through others making experience-based decisions, such as the one Pierre makes and conveys to Agnès that rather than leaving the compartment as soon as the dining car attendant passes through the corridor for the first time to announce the meal, it is best to wait until after the attendant's return to the dining car (Butor 1958, 85; 1957, 88).
17. Perhaps the persistent mention of milk trucks in *La Modification* is a variation on the milk vendor at a station who makes a strong impression on the narrator's mind in the third volume of Marcel Proust's *In Search of Lost Time*.
18. The blue light encapsulates the uncertainty "you" feels about his life plan: "The other light was harsh and fierce, but at least the objects on which it fell offered a hard surface, something to lean on, something to cling to, with which to try to form a rampart against that spreading crack, that insidious questioning which humiliates you, that contagious doubt which is shaking loose more and more pieces of that machine that protects you, of that armour which is proving so much thinner and more fragile than you suspected hitherto, whereas that blueness that seems to hang in the air, making you feel that you have to go right through it to see anything, that blueness, combined with the ceaseless tremor, the noise, your consciousness of other people's breathing, makes things revert to their original uncertainty, and you no longer see them plainly but have to reconstitute them from signs, and so they seem to be looking at you as much as you at them" (Butor 1958, 206–7; 1957, 199).
19. *Blue Journey* simulates the dining car reservation taken by a staff member, asking "you" to choose one of the two seatings, at 11 a.m. or 1 p.m.— exactly the same schedule as in *La Modification*, except that only one lunch reservation is made during the 6.5-hour train ride, as opposed to two meals served during the 25-hour journey in Butor's narrative.

20. In *La Modification*, the futility of checking a wristwatch for the time is compellingly put as follows: "You glance at your watch; it's about a quarter past one; you don't know how fast your watch is now; you've forgotten when you set it right" (Butor 1958, 218; 1957, 209). As seen in Chap. 2, Francis in *Zone* does not wear a wristwatch, and puts its more contemporary equivalent, his smartphone, in his bag, which further helps him lose track of absolute time.
21. It is out of their pockets that Giovanni and Kyra find an eternally valid ticket they did not remember having, as seen in Chap. 4. In Tawada Yōko's "Umi ni otoshita namae" (The Name I Have Dropped to the Sea, 2006), the protagonist who has lost all her memory searches her pockets and tries to reconstruct who she is from receipts, tickets, and other pieces of paper found there (Tawada 2002a, 120–33).
22. This episode appears also in Tawada's "Where Europe Begins," as experienced by a Russian ex-pat female artist who returns home after spending many years in Japan. See Fachinger (consulted in Chap. 4) on this episode in the text and how it has been reincarnated in *The Naked Eye* (Fachinger 2010, 305–6).
23. For more on the use of visual art in this novel, see Lagerwall 2005.
24. For Butor's knowledge of optical devices and its use in this novel, see Rabourdin 2018.
25. This is the case except for the direct (though imagined) calling out to his wife Henriette toward the end of the narrative (Butor 1958, 248; 1957, 236).
26. Freud (1919, 248) depicts an episode of looking at one's own reflection while on the train and mistaking it for an intruder. I thank Darcy Gauthier for referring me to this passage.
27. An exception is, the ticket inspector, who seems surprised to find "you," a frequent passenger in first class, in third class on this occasion (Butor 1958, 187; 1957, 181). On an earlier journey, when traveling with Cécile from Paris to Rome after her visit there, "you" confides in her that the dining room staff know him (Butor 1958, 183; 1957, 178).
28. This paragraph begins without capitalizing the first letter.
29. In *La Modification*, "you" is not an aspiring writer but a typewriter company executive, and thus is connected to the act of writing in quite another way.
30. Reading a book in a lower bunk when the door opens from outside is what Marta in Kawalerowicz's film *Night Train* is seen doing when the female conductor arrives in response to Jerzy's complaint (as discussed in Chap. 1), so as to silently demonstrate her resolve not to relinquish the berth.

31. As seen in Chap. 2, Francis in *Zone* gauges the length of a story to read against the distance of the remaining journey, to decide the pace of reading page per kilometer.
32. In India, toilets are located at each end of the second-class sitting (no sleeper) carriages. See IRFCA Photo Gallery 2003, and Tendulkar n.d. I thank Nisarg Patel for researching the structure of the carriages that "you" is likely taking in this "wheel." For more on cultural representation of the railways in India, see Aguiar 2011.
33. *Blue Journey* has references to toenails being painted and dried by "you's" boyfriend "he," a process that is compared to "a religious rite" (Kurahashi 1969, 221).
34. Another allusion to Miyazawa's narrative in Tawada's *Suspects on the Night Train* in "The Fourth Wheel: To Belgrade": "There must have been many others who got off the train with you. Yet when you stood on the platform, straightened your collar, and looked around, people had already disappeared as if they had been vacuumed into the chilled early morning air" (Tawada 2002a, 47). Cf. "The people who got off the train a while ago must have gone off somewhere, for not one of them was now in sight" (Miyazawa 1992, 37).
35. Ōta Susumu determines without providing any rationale that the fourth passenger, who speaks politely and delivers the final verdict (quoted below) is "you." See Ōta 2004.

CHAPTER 7

Conclusion: Stations as an Extension of the Train Space-Time in the Romantic Narrative "North Station"

This volume has considered the space-time that passengers experience in the carriages of long-distance trains, forming and formed by novelistic and cinematic narrative discourse. To conclude the journey of my literary critical analysis, I would like to ponder railway stations as an extension of the train space-time. I argue that stations are not simply the starting points, destinations, or intermediate stops that demarcate and articulate the fixed and finite, cartographic and chronological course of train travel, but are themselves experienced as space-times: not as neutral functional points, but as space-times that are invested with things and human subjects in motion and in entanglement. Stations are not a "non-place" (Augé 2009) just for certain designated functions but are "lived spaces" (Lefebvre 1991) where "spatial practices" (de Certeau 1984), "affordances" (Gibson 1979), and social relations unfold.

First, I will revisit some key scenes in the narratives discussed in earlier chapters. Some of these scenes have already been brought to the reader's attention, while others are newly mentioned to illustrate my thesis about stations as experienced space-times. Then I will present Bae Suah's short story "Bug-Yeog" (2010; trans., "North Station," 2017), a romance-cum-space-time narrative. It encapsulates and intensifies my arguments here via its most elaborate literary style of narrative fiction, which exemplifies the knot of the station as a space-time and the process of narrative formation.

© The Author(s), under exclusive license to Springer Nature Switzerland AG 2023
A. Sakaki, *Train Travel as Embodied Space-Time in Narrative Theory*, Geocriticism and Spatial Literary Studies, https://doi.org/10.1007/978-3-031-40548-8_7

Stations in romantic narratives are not mere settings or backdrops for dramatic effects but are essential to their storytelling, thereby radicalizing the grammar of the narrative specific to the genre. This makes an intriguing contrast to Chap. 1 of this book, in which I considered three films in the mystery genre (*The Lady Vanishes*, *The Narrow Margin*, and *Night Train*)—a genre that requires watertight coordination of space-time as experienced by bodies in relation to each other and things, and that is thus perfect for conceptual reading of the physical and material conditions to be negotiated in train narratives in general. The short story representing the romance genre, however, undoes (rather than capitalizes on) the hierarchical binaries between interiority (emotion) and exteriority (space), the human and the inanimate, and the dynamic and static. Whereas space-time, with its all materiality and corporeality, is the essential condition in mystery, it is expected to be subordinate in romance—an expectation that will be thwarted in my navigation of romantic narratives that unfold in railway stations.

A station is a peculiar space-time. During a certain span of time, up to the minute of a train's departure or after that train's arrival, it serves as an extension of the train carriage that passengers, railway staff members, and others can move across or occupy for a moment to do various things. It is also an extension of the land (such as urban or suburban space) that surrounds it, and is easily accessed for a good portion of the day and night by anyone who may or may not intend to ride any train. But it is also a gate that shuts or opens to control entries from and into the adjoining space (e.g., a city), and a place where people are united, separated, denied embarkment, or forced to leave. The station can be a stage for dramatic beginnings and endings of relationships between individuals, families, and places of their long-term or temporary attachments, or times spent there.

1   STATIONS IN EARLIER CHAPTERS

The three films examined in Chap. 1 feature stations to some extent. *The Lady Vanishes* includes an incident on the platform of the departing station, where the heroine suffers the fall of a flowerpot onto her head—an attack intended for the older lady, Miss Froy, who is standing next to her. This blow is later used by other passengers, conspirators in the kidnapping of Miss Froy, to discredit the veracity of the heroine's claim that the lady has vanished. Then, at an interim station, a bandaged passenger is brought in, who is swapped with Miss Froy on the train. At the next station, where the bandaged Miss Froy was supposed to be transferred to an ambulance, her escape is noted and some of the train carriages are delinked to follow separate rails. Stations thus perform an important role in the plot, as an extension of space-time for passengers, supplying essential plot elements.

In *The Narrow Margin* an interim station, La Junta, plays a key part for a number of reasons, including that it is the stop where important telegrams are wired, and that some seemingly innocuous conversations, observed on or from the open space of the platform, have consequences for the plot. The closed space of the train carriage and the proximity of passengers' bodies, their belongings, and the train's facilities have been made so obvious that the release of the tension of confinement contributes to a narrative relief, too, albeit a deceptive one, which is in itself a point in the narrative formation.

Night Train opens with a bird's-eye shot of Łódź Station, showing the busy foot traffic of people across a platform. In the current context, however, the ending scene, at a station on the Baltic Coast, is the most revealing. The station is not enclosed by walls, but is open. The sequence has the passengers walk out of the carriages into an extension of land near a coast, without a platform or the roofed structure of the station building. Through the openness, airiness, and osmotic sense of this extension (of water, land, air), passengers disappear into their own worlds of relations and businesses, and, more importantly, out of the cinematic narrative discourse, as if to evaporate into the open space. Horizontal sequences and then layers of train windows receding into the depths of the station space, perhaps in homage to the Victoria Station scene in *The Lady Vanishes*, enhance the feeling of the erosion of the interior/exterior boundary.

The four works discussed in Chap. 2 also involve stations to a degree. In the novel *Sanshirō*, Sanshirō is mindful of which passenger gets on or off the train at which station, yet does not seem to pay much attention to how they experience the space of the station. Even at Hamamatsu, passengers observe Westerners on the platform, not their environment. Stations as locations where passengers buy snacks and begin to eat lunch, and so forth, are well observed through the protagonist's eyes, yet the focus is on the passengers or their purpose, not on the space-time of the station.

Luca in *My Most Secret Council* is keenly aware of the stations and their respective significance: he knows what the effects will be of altering his destination from Messina to Taranto; which station is the point of no return; at which station he should get off to grab some food and possibly purchase some books; from which station the route winds into the interior of the peninsula; and how the landscape changes from station to station. Even though he appears to fall asleep without seeing his destination station (or any further station on the route), he remains alert to stations while awake. The stations are thus mostly noted for their names and locations, though Luca experiences the space-time of the interim station of Salerno on foot, as a place to buy lunch, browse in a bookstall, take in the fresh air, and appreciate sound across the platform. Although factual description is scarce, his navigation of the station is felt in the narrative.

In *Night Train to Lisbon*, the protagonist Gregorius's views of stations are more about what their names evoke in his mind and their locations and potentials to intersect/intercept with the route, rather than about how he may navigate their physical structures. The narrator does not describe the Lisbon railway station in its physical, material detail, which implies a general lack of interest in it on the part of the focalizer Gregorius.

Zone, as noted in Chap. 2, is divided into nine chapters named after the stations along the way (including Milan as the departure point of this leg, and Rome as the destination). However, the narrative is more concerned with what happens in the protagonist's carriage, and also with his interior landscape between stations. As discussed earlier, the narrator-protagonist Francis fights the impulse to change the course of his travel and his life by getting off at one of the stations. He knows Firenze is the penultimate station where he could cancel his whole plan by disembarking. After pulling out of Firenze, he entertains the idea of jumping off the train to free himself of the finitude of the railroad and its timetable, releasing him into an expanse of boundless land in the open air. Francis's reception of train stations is thus ambivalent, yet structurally keen; we need only recall his comparison between Milano Centrale and Bologna stations, one as vertical and the other as horizontal, or between the finality of Venezia St. Lucia and the revocability and openness to options of Venezia Mestre. Such examples of Francis's graphic sensibilities in relation to stations are far more than descriptions of the backdrops for realistic effects but are, instead, formative of *Zone*'s narrative structure.

The three narratives navigated in Chap. 4 feature characters who do not possess the resources to purchase a railway ticket and ride trains in unorthodox ways. Consequently, they do not board trains at stations. Thus, no first or last stations figures into the narratives discussed in Chap. 4.

Giovanni, the protagonist of Miyazawa's "Night," does not remember the Milky Way Station at which Campanella says he caught the train, running at top speed. Although the two boys step out of the train at a few of the stations (all named after constellations) where their train stops, the extended land around them is more focal than are the stations themselves, which are unimpressive. An exception is the Swan Halt (or Cygne Station), an unmanned stop lit in impressive colors:[1]

> [...] the train gradually slowed down, and in no time a platform appeared with an attractive, orderly row of electric lights that gradually got bigger and farther apart till the two boys came directly opposite the big clock of Swan Halt, and stopped precisely in front of it.
> [...]
> "Twenty minutes' stop," said a sign beneath the clock.
> "Shall we get off too?" said Giovanni.
> "Let's." The two of them jumped up together, dashed out through the door, and went running along the ticket barrier. But all they found at the barrier was a single purplish electric lamp; there was no one there. They looked around, but there was no sign of either stationmaster or porters.
> They went into the little square outside the station, surrounded by gingko trees that looked like cut crystal. A broad road led straight from the square into the bluish light of the Milky Way.
> The people who'd got off the train a while ago must have gone off some-where, for no one of them was now in sight. (Miyazawa 1992, 36–37)

Instead of a flow of passengers or other personnel, the station is remarkable for the lack of humans. Rather than human subjects, things like lamps and the big clock command the focalizer's (and the narrator's) attention. This corroborates the story's general posthuman predilection.

Just as Giovanni's ticket is for infinite travel, and he does not have any specific destination in mind ("We are going without limit"), so Trinh's *Night Passage* also lacks the sense of itinerary. Punctuation of the train journey by stations is scarce, except for a couple of stations where Kyra and Nabi get off the train. In this film, stations are only cited as names associated with aesthetic concepts, soon to be left behind for the characters' exploration of their surroundings.

In Tawada's *The Naked Eye*, the narrator-protagonist "I" looks in vain for a station near Bochum. She finally sees a train coming and sneaks aboard during its unscheduled stop. The unofficial and impromptu nature of the stop is critical for a passenger like "I," who is without a ticket. The destination station, which turns out not to be Moscow, as she expected, but Paris, is not described at all.[2]

Thus, in the three Chap. 4 narratives, the stations do not demarcate the routes at the beginning, end, or in the middle. The characters' train experience is boundless, amorphous, and non-geometrical. Their usage of the train extends beyond the control of any administration that maintains a bird's-eye view over the railway system, and instead consists of spatial practices from the worm's-eye view.

In the works discussed in Chap. 6, departure and destination stations are on the minds of the central character, and so are many of the stations in between. Thus, "you" in Butor's *La Modification* gets on the train at Gare de Lyon in Paris, where the narrative begins, and heads for Roma Termini, where the narrative ends. "You" in *Blue Journey* by Kurahashi goes to the Tokyo station at the beginning of Part II of the three-part novel, and ends her trip at the Kyoto station, where Part III begins. Both protagonists pay some attention to stations in between, in part to measure their journey's progress and in part to observe other passengers arrive, leave, and run errands at these interim stations, to the effect of modifying the space of the train carriage they are in.

Suspects on the Night Train by Tawada has chapters ("wheels") each of whose respective title is the destination "you" is leaving for, and the narrative usually begins at the station of her departure point. In some cases—such as "To Paris" (Tawada 2002a, 7), "To Zagreb" (ibid., 41), "To Irkutsk" (ibid., 74), and "To Amsterdam" (ibid., 130)—the station from which "you" is departing receives more attention than in others. In most cases, stations are extensions of the carriage, and hence space-times for passengers to experience. Occasionally, however, stations bear more distinct significance than annexed space-time. Either the departing station or the arrival station is a stage for a drama in itself, a drama that could not have happened during the train ride, precisely because the opening of the station concourse to the surrounding area is essential to what takes place—whether someone emerging from or vanishing into the indistinct space, or the protagonist being at a loss for how to use the time at hand. Once passengers are released from the constraint of the interior space and finite time of the railway journey, stations can be an entry into the great unknown, both thrilling and frightening.

For instance, Tawada's "you" in "The Second Wheel: To Graz" must take an alternative route due to a significant delay of a connecting train in her original plan. She takes the first leg and waits for a night train in Salzburg:

At dawn—or rather in the midnight—"you" got off the train in Salzburg. There was no scent of crime. Rather, there was a sound of breathing by laborers who were about to set out for work. Cold! "You" compressed the front of the coat as tight as if to choke yourself, trembling on. "You" had been thrown into the time unknown. Though the departure and arrival were the same, the time and space in between were crumpled into a mess. (ibid., 33)

In this passage, the multi-sensorial sensations—olfactory (though only figuratively), aural, and then tactile (temperature, clothes)—conjure up the station through the human subject's corporeal experience. Then, the complication of the space-time of the railway itinerary for her trip to Graz via Salzburg, instead of via Singen and Zurich, is compared to a piece of paper that is no longer as smooth and flat as it used to be but "crumpled into a mess." This material vision produces a tactile sensation (and perhaps also an aural sensation, with the reader almost hearing the sound of the paper crumpling).

In another "wheel," "To Belgrade," "you" shares a compartment with a suspicious-looking man who reveals his criminal intention once they arrive in Belgrade. Before that scene and "you's" subsequent escapade, she observes the Belgrade station as follows: "The station was filled with a throng of fur coats wiggling like beasts and with the scent of cigarettes and garlic. The clank of iron and glass crashing against each other and the calls of station staff and vendors crisscrossed with each other. The space was so crowded one could be stifled and cough" (ibid., 57). Here, too, the multi-sensorial sensation is remarkable: from the visual (fur) to the tactile (wiggling) to the olfactory to the aural to the tactile (sense of congestion and air). They are triggering one another, orchestrating the entire scene in synthesis. Together, they form the human subject who, without them, is elusive at best. These sensorial effects are produced by space around the subject. Thus, the subject is not in command of the space—rather, the space, with things and beings in it, is formative of the human subject. By experiencing space with things and other beings, a human subject emerges as such and narrates the experience which becomes a text.

The chapter "To Beijing" grants considerable textual space, or reading time, to the protagonist "you's" experience of the Xi'an Station, while she awaits a night train bound for Beijing. The opening captures the transient, ambiguous, opaque, and uncertain nature of the space around the station in a way that is at once physical and surreal:

The sound of the steel's friction erodes the moon. The station rises to the surface in the middle of the dark universe. Which is up, which is east? You approaches the parked train, maintaining balance with both arms as if to walk on a balance beam. [...] The light from the bare bulb over a vendor soaks into the dusk—just like black ink oozing its way through wet paper. (ibid., 61)

The synthesis of the aural and the visual in the first sentence, the conversion of the solid into the liquid in the second sentence, and the disorientation (not only horizontal but vertical) in the third sentence elaborate upon and orchestrate the sense of ambiguity and uncertainty inherent in the space-time of the station.

The transience of the station space-time is further expanded in the single traveler's experience. Because passenger instruction is sparse at the station, "you" closely observes the carriages from the exterior in hopes of finding some indication that one of them is headed for Beijing. Speaking Chinese, she tries to ask a uniformed person for the platform number from which the train for Beijing is to depart, but is bluntly brushed off. Then she realizes that many people wear uniforms of one kind or another, so that it is impossible to tell which ones are railway staff members. The time at hand for waiting also turns out to be time for doubting. Above all, "you" wonders if the very flimsy-looking ticket she has bought from an unofficial channel is authentic. She explains that she bought it from a young man she met in town who offered to get her an affordable ticket. When he unexpectedly appears at the station, apparently out of pure good will, and shows her which train to take, her recent doubts about his honesty double her guilty conscience. The station is a space for waiting, for spending time in. (And "you" is the kind of person who tends to arrive at stations much sooner than needed.) The extra time in a space where one has nothing to do but wait can enable one to think too much, filling the time with "what ifs" and proliferating narrative potentials into forking paths. The station as space-time thus functions as a paradigmatic expansion of a story into what could be the case, rather than confining one's thoughts to what actually happens.

2 "NORTH STATION"

The story of "North Station" by Bae Suah is about various forms of duration of attention: waiting (e.g., for a train to arrive; for a letter to be written, delivered, read), thinking of taking action, hesitating to take an action, remembering what happened, anticipating what may happen, imagining what could have happened if an alternative action had been taken, regretting what was or was not done, and wondering whether to go back to a moment in time or a place. The story is not made up of actions, events, or situations connected to each other in causal or chronological order. The state of indecision, not passive but loaded with intense thinking and emotions, endures for a considerable length of time—not only until the train arrives at the station and pulls out of it, but for months and years during which the main character ("he") recollects the scene over and again. Narrative and psychic investments in the station as a space-time include potentials and resignations, anxieties and thrills, frustration and relief, regrets and anticipations, and consideration of what-ifs. The station offers a perfect space-time for the interim, transient, suspended state of the narrative; the station is by default a space of the same orientations, being both a static infrastructure and a dynamic turning point of the movement of railway journeys; it is potent both in reality and in the narrative.

It is difficult to deduce the timeline of events in the story of "North Station." The man, the protagonist and focalizer yet not the narrator in this third-person narrative, sees off a woman at the station referred to as "the north station." It remains unclear where the station is located exactly, though it is in India.[3] The woman is taking the last train that arrives at and departs from the north station for her own city, which the man has been to years earlier without knowing he will fall in love with a woman from there. The man's residence is also accessible by train, but is in another city five hours away from the north station. He remembers and imagines the north station as the point where "all the world's trains were bound for a single address" (Bae 2017, 70)—the address of the woman, who has given it to him. The station is also remembered at one point as the place where the man was standing "several months ago" (ibid., 71) from the time he receives her letter entreating him to let her see him one more time—a request he can no longer fulfill due to an unexpected change in his personal life. By the time the narrative closes, "several years" have passed. Yet the man keeps remembering and reinventing the scene of his parting with the woman at the north station:

He, seized with tension, will kiss the woman before the train arrives. But how? She keeps her eyes downturned, flustered and awkward as melted wax dropping messily from a candle, and holds herself perfectly still; the clock on the platform has just passed midnight. Their bodies are angled in the direction from which the train will come; both are so incredibly on edge that if a blind and disoriented pigeon were on nose-dive in front of them, they would mistake it for a passing train—the train they will have missed, the train they will have failed to catch. (ibid., 54)

Anticipation, recognition of the passage of time, supposition, imagination about what could happen—the above passage, soon after the story's beginning, suggests the complexity of temporality in "North Station." Even in the presence of a clock to mark the chronological (absolute) time, the mental time is going back and forth (future perfect), slowing down (wax dropping) and accelerating (pigeon nosedive). Also evident here is the narrator's fixation on the choreographic detail (e.g., direction of the bodies and eyes) and erosive boundaries between humans, inanimate things (wax from a candle), and nonhumans (pigeon). This passage reveals that this narrative does not tell a straightforward story, chronologically or causally, but grows in a non-linear fashion, expanding paradigmatically and proliferating associatively.

Along with the scene of parting on the platform of the north station, a letter that the male protagonist-focalizer receives from his lover is read and recalled many times. The distance produced by the train that will take away the lover is not to be mitigated by letters in those narratives. The fact that they have shared the same space-time of the station is far more comprehensive and irreplaceable than any attempted reiteration of that experience by means of letters. Confessions are indeed impossible once lifted out of the context of the station, in the exteriority of which the interiority of the characters is intrinsically integrated.

And here is how the "North Station" factors in a letter, at the time of parting at the station:

When the train pulled into the station, the woman's hand and his reflexively moved apart. And their hands again verified the feel of the other's palm, in order to shake; a still more formal pose followed this polite gesture, an attempt to conceal the extreme fear and fretfulness which wracked them both—comprising the fear "we might never meet again," the mute questions "will you really write to me?" And its partner "will you really wait for my letter?" And a continuous flood of wordless doubts each following on the heels of the other. The woman's lip quivered as though she might burst into tears. "Are you afraid?" He asked. Without even asking "afraid of what?," the woman hurriedly shook her head. And turned toward the train as she did so, one foot raised to step up into the train. Struggling to conceal a look of frustration, her face contorted into a strange shape. The conductor, wearing a red hat, was standing outside the door to the train and peering at the platform clock. The wind mingled the faint scent of oil with that of coffee from the dining car and of train carpets dirtied by muddy footprints, stimulating their sense of smell. At almost the same time as the conductor's second whistle broke the platform's frozen silence, signaling departure, he bent over the woman's lips in a stiff, hurried movement. And wished her a safe journey. (ibid., 62–63)

The question of letters is not spoken, yet it is assumed—perhaps by both parties, even though the focalizer is firmly the man, and the woman's perspective does not materialize. Still, the dialogism inherent in correspondence is implied in the imagined questions, which zigzag rather than respond to each other, as to whether letters will be written and whether they will be waited for.

Indeed, a letter is not only written but read repeatedly, to the extent that the reader (the man who sees the woman off at the platform) feels he has internalized it:

"Ever since we parted that day at the north station": he reads the passage that begins thus several times, out loud, as though repeating a refrain. After reading it several times back to back, it really does come to feel like a song. Like his own song, which the woman had been pregnant with. Like his song which goes as follows: "It was only our ghosts who parted at the north station that day: the real us left together on the train, and are together even now ..." [...]

"Ever since we parted at the north station that day,"

It had reached the point where he practically knew the letter by heart, could recite large chunks of it with his eyes closed. (ibid., 77–78)

The metaphor of a song for the woman's letter that is apparently delivered to the man is appropriate not only because of his reading it repeatedly, or thinking about the parting referred to in it repeatedly, but also because of her writing the same phrase, "for god's sake," a number of times in the letter. For example, requesting that he should see her again: "For god's sake, don't think about anything, just let me come see you" (ibid., 77).

But the phrase, in fact, is the one that was in his mind, rather than hers, when they were waiting on the platform for the train that would take her away from the north station.

> "For god's sake stay like this!" Just as he, looking up at the platform clock this very moment, longed to command time to stop in its tracks.
>
> The woman has her cold, firm hand resting on the platform bench, and his own palm presses gently down on it. Rigid in these positions, they both face the direction from which the train will come. How he'd longed for a single night's worth of sleep on the woman's balcony. (ibid., 56)

The repetition of the same phrase—across human agencies from the man to the woman, across temporal and spatial distance, and across mediums (silent yet imagined verbal utterance in one instance, written epistolary words in the other)—intensifies not only the impossibility of the lovers' union that is begged for but also, more importantly in our context, the dissolution of subjectivity, cartography, and chronology. The mention of "ghosts" in her letter and in his thoughts is thus appropriate, encapsulating the elusive yet haunting nature of the presence that cannot be named.

Yet the woman's and the man's positioning of "ghosts" is opposite to each other's. The woman fears that their meeting was a meeting of ghosts (ibid., 76–77), whereas the man assures her that their separation was a separation of ghosts. The man's musings on an alternative development of the story, enacted by "the real us" instead of the "ghosts," which he does not seem to write to her, goes as follows:

> At some later date, when the present-now resurfaces in his memory, arriving each time at the memory's end, he would instead take the woman's hand and climb up into the train with her. Passing through the carriages, down the narrow corridor adjoining the passenger compartments, they end up in the dining car, its air sullied with steam. Their bodies vibrate at the same frequency as that of the juddering train. Their wordless whispers, blind stares, and paralyzed lips perform this regular back-and-forth movement, rattling along with the scenery framed by the window, the timetable hanging in the corridor, the cutlery and crockery. [...] Every now and then when the train comes to a stop, a long sharp blast from the conductor's whistle will shatter their restless slumber. This hand and that, these lips and those, that do not pull apart even in a sleep achieved with open eyes, this dream and that, overlapping. This is how the journey goes, for countless weeks and

months. Passing platform after platform, each deserted as a barren steppe, they travel toward the city where the woman lives. (ibid., 63–64)

Instead of the love story ending on the platform of the north station, to be recalled at best or to be revisited for a reunion, it continues, with "the real us" leaving the station behind. The space-time they will share in the carriage is remarkably alive, with multiple sensations: steam, vibration, whispers, stares, rattles, rhythms of things oscillating with the train's movement (recall *The Sad Young Man on the Train* by Marcel Duchamp), and shrills that the train makes at junctures. Dining and drinking and drowsing, the two live as passengers, rather than as those who part and disappear into separate places, for "countless weeks and months." Like Giovanni in "Night" and "you" in *Suspects on the Night Train*, the man and woman in "North Station" obtain an "eternal ticket"—except that it is not for one person but for two, in love, to continue the railway journey infinitely, "passing platform after platform." Instead of making the train serve their life together, the train becomes their new life.

One does not take trains to live. One lives to ride trains.

NOTES

1. Based on his study of timetables and other railway related documents, Terakado (2013, 97–100) hypothesizes that the Toyohara station in Sakhalin may have inspired the Cygne Station.
2. Tawada's "Where Europe Begins" (2002b) describes the Moscow station in some detail, as the Trans-Siberian Railway's "final stop."
3. Tropical elements are occasionally mentioned in the story. The only city name in the story is Chiang Mai (in Thailand), where the story ends, which is specified as elsewhere than where the north station is located.

References

Adelson, Leslie A. 2016. Rusty rails and parallel tracks: Trans-Latin in Yoko Tawada's *Das nackte Auge* (2004). In *Un/translatables: New maps for Germanic literatures*, ed. Bethany Wiggin and Catriona MacLeod, 281–298. Evanston: Northwestern University Press.

Aguiar, Marian. 2011. *Tracking modernity: India's railway and the culture of mobility.* Minneapolis: University of Minnesota Press.

Althusser, Louis. 2006. Philosophy and marxism: Interviews with Fernanda Navarro, 1984–87. In idem, *Philosophy of the encounter: Later writings, 1978–1987,* ed. François Matheron and Olivier Corpet, trans. G.M. Goshgarian, 251–298. London: Verso.

Assayas, Olivier, dir. 2014. *Clouds of Sils Maria.* Toronto: Mongrel Media.

Augé, Marc. 2009. *Non-places: An introduction to supermodernity.* Trans. John Howe. London: Verso.

Bae, Suah. 2017. North station. In idem, *North station,* trans. Deborah Smith, 54–81. Rochester: Open Letter.

Bakhtin, M.M. 1982. *Dialogic imagination: Four essays,* ed. Michael Holquist, trans. Caryl Emerson and Michael Holquist. Austin: University of Texas Press.

Bakker, Egbert J. 2005. *Pointing at the past: From formula to performance in Homeric poetics.* Washington, DC: Center for Hellenic Studies, Trustees for Harvard University.

Bal, Mieke. 1999. Second-person narrative. In idem, *Quoting caravaggio: Contemporary art, preposterous history,* 165–207. Chicago: University of Chicago Press.

© The Author(s), under exclusive license to Springer Nature   263
Switzerland AG 2023
A. Sakaki, *Train Travel as Embodied Space-Time in Narrative Theory,* Geocriticism and Spatial Literary Studies,
https://doi.org/10.1007/978-3-031-40548-8

Barthes, Roland. 1975. *The pleasure of the text*. Trans. Richard Miller. New York: Hill and Wang.

de Bary, Brett. 2012. World literature in the shadow of translation: Reconsidering Tawada Yōko. *Poetica: An International Journal of Linguistic-Literary Studies* 78: 1–16.

Bay, Hansjörg. 2010. "Eyes Wide Shut". Mediale Übersetzungen in Yoko Tawadas *Das Nackte Auge*. *Klincksieck "Études Germanique"* 259 (March): 551–568. https://www.cairn.info/revue-etudes-germaniques-2010-3-page-551.htm. Accessed 2 July 2019.

Beckman, Jason M. 2023. A Virtual You: Reading Kurahashi Yumiko's *Kurai Tabi* through Virtuality. *Literature* 3 (3): 278–295. https://doi.org/10.3390/literature3030019

Benjamin, Walter. 2005. On the image of proust. Trans. Harry Zohn. In idem, *Walter Benjamin: Selected writings, volume 2, part 1: 1927–1930*, 237–247. Cambridge, MA: Belknap Press of Harvard University Press.

———. 2006. The storyteller: Observations on the works of Nikolai Leskov. Trans. Harry Zohn. In *Walter Benjamin: Selected writings, volume 3: 1935–1938*, 143–166. Cambridge, MA: Belknap Press of Harvard University Press.

Benstock, Shari. 1985. From the editor's perspective: 'Reading the signs of women's writing'. *Tulsa Studies in Women's Literature* 4 (1/Spring): 5–15. https://www.jstor.org/stable/463801. Accessed 22 Nov 2021.

Benveniste, Émile. 1973. *Problems in general linguistics*. Trans. Mary Elizabeth Meek. Miami: University of Miami Press.

Biceaga, Victor. 2010. *The concept of passivity in Husserl's phenomenology*. Dordrecht: Springer. https://doi.org/10.1007/978-90-481-3915-6. Accessed 9 May 2022.

Birkholic, Robert. 2013. *Night Train—Jerzy Kawalerowicz*. Trans. Marek Kępa, January. https://culture.pl/en/work/night-train-jerzy-kawalerowicz. Accessed 29 May 2023.

Bissell, David. 2009. Travelling vulnerabilities: Mobile timespaces of quiescence. *Cultural Geographies* 16 (4): 427–445. https://doi.org/10.1177/1474474009340086. Accessed 6 Oct 2021.

———. 2010a. Passenger mobilities: Affective atmospheres and the sociality of public transport. *Environment and Planning D: Society and Space* 28: 270–289. https://doi.org/10.1068/d3909. Accessed 16 July 2020.

———. 2010b. Vibrating materialities: Mobility-body-technology relations. *Area* 42 (4): 479–486. https://doi.org/10.1111/j.1475-4762.2010.00942.x. Accessed 18 June 2021.

Bowen, Elizabeth. 2006. *To the north*. New York: Penguin Random House.

British Film Institute [Signed A. B.]. 1964. POCIAG (Night train), Poland, 1959. *Monthly Film Bulletin* 31 (360): 37. Proquest 2012. http://myaccess.library.utoronto.ca/login?qurl=https%3A%2F%2Fwww.proquest.com%2Fmagazines%2Fnight-train-pociag%2Fdocview%2F1305832365%2Fse-2%3Faccountid%3D14771. Accessed 23 May 2022.

Brogan, Una. 2022. *The alternative modernity of the bicycle in British and French literature, 1880–1920*. Edinburgh: Edinburgh University Press.

Brooke, Michael. 2010. Reviews DVDs: 'Films by Jerzy Kawalerowicz'. *Sight and Sound* 20 (7): 86–87. http://myaccess.library.utoronto.ca/login?qurl=https%3A%2F%2Fwww.proquest.com%2Fmagazines%2Freviews-dvds-films-jerzy-kawalerowicz%2Fdocview%2F753495336%2Fse-2%3Faccountid%3D14771. Accessed 11 Apr 2022.

———. 2015. Magnetic pole. *Sight and Sound* 25 (8): 52–53. Proquest. http://myaccess.library.utoronto.ca/login?qurl=https%3A%2F%2Fwww.proquest.com%2Fmagazines%2Fmagnetic-pole%2Fdocview%2F1701528757%2Fse-2%3Faccountid%3D14771. Accessed 11 Apr 2022.

Brown, Larry A. 2018. Sound. In idem, *How films tell stories: The narratology of film*, 185–197. Nashville: Creative Arts Press.

Butor, Michel. 1957. *La Modification: Roman*. Paris: Les Editions de Miniut.

———. 1958. *Second thoughts*. Trans. Jean Stewart. London: Faber and Faber.

———. 1959. *A change of heart*. Trans. Jean Stewart. New York: Simon and Schuster.

———. 1974. "Travel and Writing." Trans. John Powers and K. Lisker. *Mosaic: A Journal for the Interdisciplinary Study of Literature* 8 (1): 1–16. http://www.jstor.org/stable/24777013. Accessed 12 May 2022.

———. 2005. *Kokoro gawari*. Trans. Shimizu Tōru. Tokyo: Iwanami shoten.

———. 2017. *Changing track*. Trans. Jean Stewart. Surrey: Calder Publications.

Butor, Michel, John Powers, and K. Lisker. 1974. Travel and writing. *Mosaic: A Journal for the Interdisciplinary Study of Literature* 8 (1): 1–16. http://www.jstor.org/stable/24777013. Accessed 12 May 2022.

Caravaggio, Beatriz. 2016. Different trains. Video to music by Steve Reich.

Carroll, Lewis. 1893. *Through the looking-glass: And what Alice found there: By Lewis Carroll*. Illustrated by John Tenniel. Thomas Y. Crowell. Nineteenth century collections online. link.gale.com/apps/doc/CJVERZ028755178/NCCO?u=utoronto_main&sid=bookmark-NCCO&xid=ebfeca5d&pg=61. Accessed 10 Nov 2021.

Carter, Paul. 2002. *Repressed spaces: The poetics of agoraphobia*. London: Reaktion Books.

Cendrars, Blaise. 1972. The prose of the Trans-Siberian and of the Little Jeanne of France. Trans. Roger Kaplan. *Chicago Review* 24 (3): 3–4. Proquest 2003. https://doi.org/10.2307/25294698. Accessed 23 Oct 2021.

———. 1991. The prose of the Trans-Siberian and of Little Jeanne of France; unnatural sonnets. Trans. Ron Padgett. *Sulfur* 28 (Spring): 25–29. Literature Online (LION). http://myaccess.library.utoronto.ca/login?qurl=https%3A%2F%2Fwww.proquest.com%2Fscholarly-journals%2Fprose-trans-siberian-little-jeanne-france%2Fdocview%2F874488168%2Fse-2%3Faccountid%3D14771. Accessed 23 Oct 2021.

Crowell, Steven. 2015. Second Person Phenomenology. In *Phenomenology of Sociality: Discovering the "We".* First edition. Edited by Thomas Szanto and Dermot Moran, 70–89. New York: Routledge. https://doi.org/10.4324/9781315688268.

de Certeau, Michel. 1984. Railway navigation and incarceration. In idem, *The practice of everyday life*, trans. Steven Rendall, 111–114. Berkeley: University of California Press.

Chambers, Ross. 1984. *Story and situation: Narrative seduction and the power of fiction.* Minneapolis: University of Minnesota Press.

Christie, Agatha. 1934. *Murder on the orient express.* London: Collins Crime Club.

Cowan, Robert. 2018. You too: The narratology of apostrophe and second-person narrative in Virgil's *Georgics. Arethusa* 51: 269–298. https://doi.org/10.1353/are.2018.0012. Accessed 17 May 2023.

Cromwell, Steven. 2016. Second-person phenomenology. In *Phenomenology of sociality: Discovering the "We",* ed. Thomas Szanto and Dermot Moran, 70–89. New York: Routledge. https://doi.org/10.4324/9781315688268. Accessed 1 Oct 2021.

Deleuze, Gilles. 1986. *Cinema 1: The movement-image.* Trans. Hugh Tomlinson and Barbara Habberjam. Minneapolis: University of Minnesota Press.

Énard, Mathias. 2008. *Zone: roman.* Arles: Actes sud.

———. 2010. *Zone.* Translated by Charlotte Mandell. First edition. Rochester, NY: Open Letter.

Evenson, Brian. 2010. Introduction. In *Zone*, ed. Mathias Énard, vii–xi. Rochester: Open Letter.

Fachinger, Petra. 2010. Postcolonial/postcommunist picaresque and the logic of 'Trans' in Yoko Tawada's *Das nackte Auge.* In *Yoko Tawada Poetik der Transformation: Beiträge zum Gesamtwerk: Mit dem Stück Sancho Panda von Yoko Tawada*, ed. Christine Ivanovic, 297–308. Tübingen: Stauffenburg Verlag.

Fassbinder, Rainer Werner. 1976. *Die bitterer Tränen der Petra von Kant.* Frankfurt am Main: Suhrkamp Verlag.

———. 1984. The bitter tears of Petra von Kant. In idem, *The bitter tears of Petra von Kant and blood on the neck of the cat*, trans. Anthony Vivis, 13–54. London: Amber Lane Press.

Felton, Earl, Martin Goldsmith, and Jack Leonard. 2004. *The narrow margin (1952): Shooting script.* Alexandria: Alexander Street Press.

Fleischer, Richard, dir. 2005. *The narrow margin.* Atlanta: Turner Entertainment.

Fludernik, Monika. 1994. Second-person narrative as a test case for narratology: The limits of realism. *Style* 28 (3/Fall): 445–479. https://www.jstor.org/stable/42946261. Accessed 19 Apr 2019.

Foucault, Michel. 1986. Of other spaces. Trans. Jay Miskowiec. *Diacritics* 16 (1): 22–27.

———. 2004. Des espaces autres. *Étrès* (54): 12–19. https://www.cairn.info/revue-empan-2004-2-page-12.htm. Accessed 9 Apr 2022.

———. 2008. Of other spaces. Trans. Lieven de Cauter and Michiel Dehaene. In *Heterotopia and the city: Public space in a postcivil society*, ed. Lieven de Cauter and Michiel Dehaene, 13–29. New York: Routledge. https://librarysearch.library.utoronto.ca/permalink/01UTORONTO_INST/14bjeso/alma991105885549706196. Accessed 6 Apr 2022.

———. 2014. Heterotopias. Trans. Pamela Johnston, intro. Anthony Vidler. *AA Files* 69: 18–22. https://librarysearch.library.utoronto.ca/permalink/01UTORONTO_INST/fedca1/cdi_jstor_primary_43202545. Accessed 1 Oct 2018.

Fraser, Benjamin, and Steven D. Spalding, eds. 2012. *Trains, culture, and mobility: Riding the rails*. Lanham: Lexington Books.

Freedman, Alisa. 2011. *Tokyo in transit: Japanese culture on the rails and road*. Stanford: Stanford University Press.

Friedkin, William. 2005. Untitled [commentary]. In *The narrow margin*, dir. Richard Fleischer. Atlanta: Turner Entertainment.

Fujii, James A. 1999. Intimate alienation: Japanese urban rail and the commodification of urban subjects. *Differences (Bloomington, Ind.)* 11 (2): 106–133. https://doi.org/10.1215/10407391-11-2-106. Accessed 14 Aug 2018.

Gavin, Adrienne E., and Andrews F. Humphries. 2015. *Transport in British fiction: Technologies of movement, 1840–1940*. Houndmills/Basingstoke: Palgrave Macmillan.

Gavin, Alice. 2011. 'Around 1910 a certain space shattered': The city and the changing landscape of character. *Critical Inquiry* 53 (2): 46–54. https://doi.org/10.1111/j.1467-8705.2011.01990.x. Accessed 8 July 2019.

Genette, Gérard. 1980. *Narrative discourse: An essay in method*. Trans. Jane E. Lewin. Ithaca: Cornell University Press.

Gibson, James J. 1979. *Ecological approaches to visual perception*. Boston: Houghton Mifflin.

Gorfinkel, Elena. 2012. Weariness, waiting: Enduration and art cinema's tired bodies. *Discourse* 34 (2–3/Spring/Fall): 311–347. https://www.jstor.org/stable/10.13110/discourse.34.2-3.0311. Accessed 8 Feb 2020.

Grunow, Tristan R. 2012. Trains, modernity, and state formation in Meiji Japan. In *Trains, culture, and mobility: Riding the rails*, ed. Benjamin Fraser and Steven D. Spalding, 235–261. Lanham: Lexington Books.

Guèye, Khadidiatou. 2008. Ethnocultural voices and African aesthetics in Trinh Minh-ha's *Reassemblage: From the firelight to the screen*. *Research in African Literatures* 39 (3/Fall): 14–25. https://muse.jhu.edu/article/242669. Accessed 26 May 2019.

Guth, Paul. 1957. Un Révolutionnaire du roman 1926–1957 ou Les Modifications de Michel Butor: Un Portrait-Interview. *Figaro littéraire* 607, décembre 7.

Hirasawa Shin'ichi. 2008. *Miyazawa Kenji "sen'i" no shigaku*. Tokyo: Sōkyū shorin.

Hitchcock, Alfred, dir. 1997. *Strangers on a train*. Burbank: Warner Home Video.

———, dir. 2003. *The lady vanishes*. Irvington: The Criterion Collection.

Hitchcock, Alfred, and John Baxter. 2007. *The lady vanishes*, Special ed.; Fullscreen ed. New York: The Criterion Collection.

Huber, Irmtraud. 2016. *Present-tense narration in contemporary fiction: A narratological overview*. London: Palgrave Macmillan.

Husserl, Edmund. 1964. *The phenomenology of internal time-consciousness*. Trans. James S. Churchill. Bloomington: Indiana University Press.

Hutcheon, Linda. 1980. *Narcissistic narrative: The metafictional paradox*. Waterloo: Wilfrid Laurier University Press.

Iliopoulou, Evgenia. 2019. *Because of you: Understanding second-person storytelling*. Bielfeld: transcript Verlag.

Institut für Bauplanung und Baubetrieb ETH Zürich and Institut für Geotechnik ETH Zürich. 1996. *Historische Alpendurchstiche in der Schweiz: Gotthard Simplon Lötschberg*. Zurich: Gesellschaft für Ingenieurbaukunst.

IRFCA Photo Gallery. 2003. https://www.irfca.org/gallery/Carriages/seating_diagrams.jpg.html? Accessed 28 May 2023.

Irisawa, Yasuo, and Taijirō Amazawa. 1990. *Tōgi: "Ginga tetsudō no yoru" to wa nanika*, Rpt. Tokyo: Seidosha.

Ivanovic, Christine, ed. 2010. *Yoko Tawada Poetik der Transformation: Beiträge zum Gesamtwerk: Mit dem Stück Sancho Panda von Yoko Tawada*. Tübingen: Stauffenburg Verlag.

Jacobowitz, Seth. 2015. *Writing technology in Meiji Japan: A media history of modern Japanese literature and visual culture*. Cambridge, MA: Harvard University Asia Center.

Jensen, Martin Trandberg, Caroline Scarles, and Scott A. Cohen. 2015. A multisensory phenomenology of interrail mobilities. *Annals of Tourism Research* 53: 61–76. https://doi.org/10.1016/j.annals.2015.04.002. Accessed 8 June 2020.

Jones, Ernest. 1953. *The life and work of Sigmund Freud, volume 1, 1856–1900*. New York: Basic Books.

Kacandes, Irene. 1994. Narrative apostrophe: Reading, rhetoric, resistance in Michel Butor's 'La modification' and Julio Cortázar's 'Graffiti'. *Style* 28 (3/Fall): 329–349. https://www.jstor.org/stable/42946255. Accessed 19 Apr 2019.

Katō, Norihiro. 2008. *Sanshirō* wa naze shachū bamen kara hajimaru ka. *Shinchō* 105 (8): 170–171.

Kawabata, Yasunari. 1948. *Yukiguni*. Osaka: Sōgensha.

———. 1957. *Snow country*. Trans. Edward G. Seidensticker. London: Secker & Warburg.

Kawalerowicz, Jerzy, dir. 2005. *Pociąg*. Warszawa: Best Film.

———, dir. 2016. Night train = Pociag. Warszawa: Di Factory.

Khandros, A.G. 2014. The last stop: Jerzy Kawalerowicz's *Night train* (*Pociąg*, 1959). *East European Film Bulletin* 40 (April): 1–7. https://eefb.org/retrospectives/jerzy-kawalerowiczs-night-train-pociag-1959/. Accessed 9 July 2019.

Kiarostami, Abbas, Ken Loach, and Ermanno Olmi, dirs. 2006. *Tickets*. Facets Video.

Knight, James. 2015. Senses of cinema: Jerzy Kawalerowicz's *Night train* (1959). *Cinémathèque Annotations on Film* 76 (September): n.p. http://www.sensesofcinema.com/2015/cteq/night-train/. Accessed 9 July 2019.

Knott, Suzuko Mousel. 2007. Sign language: Reading culture and identity in Tawada Yōko's 'Gotthard Railway'. In *Yōko Tawada: Voices from everywhere*, ed. Doug Slaymaker, 137–151. Lanham: Lexington Books.

Komori, Yōichi. 1996. 'Teikoku' to iu nettowaaku. In *Bungaku no hōhō*, ed. Kawamoto Kōji and Kobayashi Yasuo, 309–326. Tokyo: Tōkyō daigaku shuppankai.

Kraenzle, Christina. 2008. The limits of travel: Yoko Tawada's fictional travelogues. *German Life and Letters* 61 (2): 244–260. https://doi.org/10.1111/j.1468-0483.2008.00422.x. Accessed 16 Nov 2021.

Kurahashi, Yumiko. 1969. *Kurai tabi*. Tokyo: Gakugei shorin.

———. 2008a. *Kurai tabi*. Tokyo: Shinchō bunko.

———. 2008b. *Sei shōjo*. Tokyo: Shinchō bunko.

Kwiatkowska, Paulina. 2013. Rytmy somatograficzne—Lucyna Winnicka w filmach Jerzego Kawalerowicz [Somatographic rhythms: Lucyna Winnicka in films of Jerzy Kawalerowicz]. *Kwartalnik Filmowy* 83–84: 80–98. https://www.ceeol.com/search/article-detail?id=237935. Accessed 9 July 2019.

LaBelle, Brandon. 2010. *Acoustic territories: Sound culture and everyday life*. New York: Continuum.

Lagerwall, Sonia. 2005. A reading of Michel Butor's *La Modification* as an emblematic iconotext. In *Writing and seeing: Essays on word and image*, ed. Rui Carvalho Homem and Maria de Fátima Lambert, 119–129. Leiden/Boston: Brill.

Larbaud, Valery. 1958. Mon plus secret conseil. In idem, *Œuvres*, 647–715. Paris: Gallimard.

Lean, David, dir. 2012. *Brief encounter*. New York: The Criterion Collection.

Lefebvre, Henri. 1991. *Production of space*. Trans. Donald Nicholson-Smith. Oxford: Blackwell.

———. 2013. *Rhythmanalysis*. Trans. Stuart Elden and Gerald Moore. New York: Bloomsbury Academic.

Leff, Leonard. 2007. *Mystery train: Behind The lady vanishes*. New York: The Criterion Collection.

Levinas, Emmanuel. 1987. *Time and the other and additional essays*. Trans. Richard A. Cohen. Pittsburgh: Duquesne University Press.

Macnab, Geoffrey. 2012. Trains of thought. *Sight and Sound* 22 (5): 87. British Film Institute. Proquest. https://www.proquest.com/docview/1017712660?accountid=14771&parentSessionId=2HRjGLHsGLqyzCDLruEFvRYInbNq%2F5VcrQ6XdZItnS0%3D. Accessed 11 Apr 2022.

Maeda, Ai. 1993. Ondoku kara mokudoku e. In *Kindai dokusha no seiritsu*, 167–210. Tokyo: Iwanami shoten.

———. 2004. Communal performance to silent reading: The rise of the modern Japanese reader. Trans. James A. Fujii. In idem, *Text and the city: Essays on Japanese modernity*, ed. James A. Fujii, 223–254. Durham: Duke University Press.

Makimura, Ken'ichirō. 2020. *Sōseki to tetsudō*. Tokyo: Asahi shuppan.

Malabou, Catherine. 2008. *What should we do with our brain?* Trans. Sebastian Rand. New York: Fordham University Press.

Marks, Laura. 2007. Psychoanalytic training: Freud and the railways. In *The railway and modernity: Time, space, and the machine ensemble*, ed. Matthew Beaumont and Michael J. Freeman, 155–175. Oxford: Peter Lang.

Martin, Andrew. 2017. *Night trains: The rise and fall of the sleeper*. London: Profile Books.

Matsunaga, Miho. 2002. Schreiben als Übersetzung. Die Dimension der Übersetzung in den Werken von Yoko Tawada. *Zeitschrift fùr Germanistik* 12 (3): 532–546. http://www.jstor.com/stable/23976357. Accessed 22 May 2022.

Mazdon, Lucy. 2019. Brief encounters: The railway station on film. In *Journeys on screen: Theory, ethics, aesthetics*, ed. Louis Bayman and Natália Pinazza, 36–49. Edinburgh: University of Edinburgh Press.

McCormack, Derek P. 2008. Engineering affective atmospheres on the moving geographies of the 1897 Andrée expedition. *Cultural Geographies* 15 (4): 413–430. https://doi.org/10.1177/1474474008094314. Accessed 12 May 2022.

Medin, Daniel. 2010. The woman who disappeared: Trances of Kafka in Yoko Tawada's Das Nackte Auge. *Klincksieck "Études Germaniques"* 259 (March): 627–636. https://www.cairn.info/revue-etudes-germaniques-2010-3-page-627.htm. Accessed 28 July 2019.

Mercier, Pascal. 2004. *Nachtzug nach Lissabon: Roman*. München: C. Hanser.

———. 2008. *Night train to Lisbon*. Trans. Barbara Harshav. New York: Grove Press.

Misemer, Sarah M. 2010. *Moving forward, looking back: Trains, literature, and the arts in the River Plate*. Lewisburg: Bucknell University Press.

Mitsutani, Margaret. 2010. No one walks here: Tawada Yoko's America. In *Yoko Tawada: Poetik Der Transformation: Beiträge zum Gesamtwerk: Mit dem Stück Sancho Panda von Yoko Tawara*, ed. Christine Ivanovic, 309–322. Tübingen: Stauffenburg Verlag.

Mitchelmore, Stephen. 2015. *This Space of Writing*. Winchester, UK: Zero Books.

Miyazawa, Kenji. 1968. The bears of Mt. Nametoko. Trans. Masako Ohnuki. *Chicago Review* 20 (2): 24–31.

———. 1973. Aomori banka. In idem, *Kōhon Miyazawa Kenji zenshū*, vol. 2, 154–166. Tokyo: Chikuma shobō.

———. 1991. *Night of the milky way railway*. Trans. Sarah Strong. Armonk: M. E. Sharpe.

———. 1992. *Night train to the stars and other stories*. Trans. John Bester. Tokyo: Kodansha International.

———. 1997. The bears of Nametoko. Trans. Karen Colligan-Taylor. In *The Oxford book of Japanese short stories*, ed. Theodore W. Goossen, 103–111. Oxford: Oxford University Press.

———. 2016a. Ginga tetsudō no yoru. In idem, *Miyazawa Kenji korekushon 1: Dōwa I Shōnen shōsetsu hoka*, 88–150. Tokyo: Chikuma shobō.

———. 2016b. Ginga tetsudō no yoru shoki-kei dai-sanji-kō. In idem, *Miyazawa Kenji korekushon 1: Dōwa I Shōnen shōsetsu hoka*, 295–348. Tokyo: Chikuma shobō.

———. 2018. Bears of Nametoko. Trans. John Bester. In idem, *Once and forever: The tales of Miyazawa Kenji*. New York: New York Review Books.

Mottola, Tommaso, dir. 2017. *Karenina & I*. 2017. Produced by Orto Lolare AS. 85 minutes.

Mulvey, Laura. 2006. *Death 24 a second: Stillness and the moving image*. London: Reaktion Books.

Murphy, J.J. 2010. A similar sense of time: The collaboration between writer Jon Raymond and director Kelly Reichardt in *old joy* and *Wendy and Lucy*. In *Analysing the screenplay*, ed. Jill Nelmes, 172–188. New York: Routledge.

Nakagawa, Shigemi. 2008. Kaisetsu: Bungakuteki sōzōryoku to shite no hadaka no me. In *Tabi o suru hadaka no me*, ed. Tawada Yōko, 280–290. Tokyo: Kōdansha bungei bunko.

Nancy, Jean-Luc. 2007. *Listening*. Trans. Charlotte Mandell. New York: Fordham University Press.

Natsume Sōseki [Natsume Kinnosuke]. 1965. *The three-cornered world*. Trans. Alan Turney. London: Peter Owen.

———. 1977. Sanshiro. Trans. Jay Rubin. Seattle: University of Washington Press.

———. 1999. *Sanshiro*. Translated by Jay Rubin. Tokyo: Kodansha International.

———. 2008. *Kusamakura*. Trans. Meredith McKinney. New York: Penguin Books.

———. 2017. *Sanshirō*. In Natsume Kinnosuke, *Teihon Sōseki zenshū 5*, ed. Kōno Kensuke, Yoshida Hiroo, and Munakata Shizue, 271–608, 647–704 (notes). Tokyo: Iwanami shoten.

———. 2018. Sanshirō. In idem, *Sōseki bungaku zenchūshaku 7*, ed. Bandō Maruo Jitsuko, Matsushita Hiroyuki, and Fujii Hidetada. Tokyo: Wakakusa shobō.

Ogawa, Kazusuke. 2001. *"Sanshirō" no Tōkyō gaku*. Tokyo: Nihon Hōsō shuppan kyōkai.

Okazaki, Takeshi. 2014. Kisha wa jōkyō no yokō renshū datta. In *Natsume Sōseki "Sanshirō" o dō yomu ka*, ed. Ishihara Chiaki, 110–115. Tokyo: Kawade shobō shinsha.

Oppenheim, Lois. 1980. *Internationality and intersubjectivity: A phenomenological study of Butor's "La Modification"*. Lexington: French Forum.

Ōta, Susumu. 2004. Anata to watashi to Buraun fujin to: *Yōgisha no yakōressha* no tame no jankushon. *Yuriika [Eureka]* 36 (14): 192–206.

Pearce, Lynne. 2016. *Drivetime: Literary excursions in automotive consciousness.* Edinburgh: Edinburgh University Press.

Peggy Guggenheim Collection. n.d. Marcel Duchamp *Nude (study), sad young man on a train.* https://www.guggenheim-venice.it/en/art/works/nude-study-sad-young-man-on-a-train/. Accessed 22 Mar 2013.

Phelan, James. 1994. 'Self-help' for narratee and narrative audience: How 'I'—and 'you'?—Read 'how'. *Style* 28 (3): 350–365. http://www.jstor.org/stable/42946256. Accessed 19 Apr 2019.

Previšić, Boris. 2016. *Gotthardfantasien: Eine Blütenlese aus Wissenschaft und Literatur.* Baden: Hier und Jetzt.

Prince, Gerald. 1996. Introduction to the study of the narratee. In *Essentials of the theory of fiction,* ed. Michael J. Hoffman and Patrick D. Murphy, 213–233. Durham: Duke University Press.

Pringle, Mary Beth. 1985. Butor's room without a view: The train compartment in 'La Modification'. *Review of Contemporary Fiction* 5 (3/Fall): 112–118. http://myaccess.library.utoronto.ca/login?qurl=https%3A%2F%2Fwww.proquest.com%2Fscholarly-journals%2Ffictions-fiction-henriette-cecile-michel-butors%2Fdocview%2F220501786%2Fse-2%3Faccountid%3D14771. Accessed 17 May 2023.

Rabourdin, Caroline. 2018. The expanding space of the train carriage: A phenomenological reading of Michel Butor's *La modification.* In *Spatial modernities: Geography, narrative, imaginaries,* ed. Johannes Riquet and Elizabeth Kollmann, 176–192. London: Routledge.

Raymond, Jon. 2009. Train choir. In idem, *Livability,* 273–343. London: Bloomsbury.

Reich, Steve. 1989. *Different trains/electric counterpoint.* Musical composition for string quartet and tape. Nonesuch 979176-2.

Reichardt, Kelly, dir. 2008. *Wendy and Lucy.* Portland: Field Guide Films.

Revill, George. 2013. Points of departure: Listening to rhythm in the sonic spaces of the railway station. *The Sociological Review* 61 (suppl. 1): 51–68. https://doi.org/10.1111/1467-954X.12053. Accessed 6 Oct 2021.

———. 2014a. *El tren fantasma*: Arcs of sound and the acoustic spaces of landscape. *Transactions of the Institute of British Geographers* 39: 333–344. https://doi.org/10.1111/tran.12034. Accessed 20 July 2019.

———. 2014b. Reflections on rails and the city. *Transfers* 4 (2/Summer): 124–130. https://doi.org/10.3167/TRANS.2014.040209. Accessed 8 June 2020.

———. 2016. How is space made in sound? Spatial mediation, critical phenomenology and the political agency of sound. *Progress in Human Geography* 40 (2): 240–256. https://doi.org/10.1177/0309132515572271. Accessed 6 Oct 2021.

Rice, Charles. 2007. *The emergence of the interior: Architecture, modernity. Domesticity*: Routledge.

Richter, Amy G. 2005. *Home on the rails: Women, the railroad, and the rise of public domesticity*. Chapel Hill: University of North Carolina Press.

Richter, Gerhard. 2019. *Thinking with Adorno: The uncoercive gaze*. New York: Fordham University Press.

Różycki, Jacek. 1998. „Pociąg" 40 lat później. Program 1, TVP S. A.

Sachs, Hanns. 1945. *Freud: Master and friend*. London: Imago Publishing.

Sakaki, Atsuko. 1999. *Recontextualizing texts: Narrative performance in modern Japanese fiction*, Harvard East Asia monographs no. 180. Cambridge, MA: The Asia Center Publications Program, Harvard University.

———. 2001. Kurahashi Yumiko's negotiations with the fathers. In *The father/daughter plot: Japanese literary women*, ed. Rebecca Copeland and Esperanza Ramirez-Christensen, 292–326. Honolulu: University of Hawai'i Press.

Schivelbusch, Wolfgang. 1986. *The railway journey: The industrialization of space and time in the nineteenth century*. Los Angeles: University of California Press.

Silk, Sally M. 1992. When the writer comes home: Narrative failure in Butor's *La Modification*. *Style* 26 (2): 270–286. http://www.jstor.org/stable/42945972. Accessed 11 May 2022.

Simenon, Georges. 1938. *L'Homme qui regardait passer les trains*. Paris: Gallimard.

———. 1965. *Le Train de Venise: Roman*. Paris: Presses de la Cité.

———. 1974. *The Venice train*. Trans. Alastair Hamilton. London: Hamilton.

———. 2016. *The man who watched the trains go by*. Trans. Siân Reynolds. London: Penguin Books.

Simmel, Georg. 2002. The metropolis and mental life. In idem, *Simmel on culture: Selected writings*, ed. D. Frisby and M. Featherstone, 174–186. London: Sage.

Simon, John K. 1962. View from the train: Butor, Gide, Larbaud. *The French Review* 36 (2): 161–166. https://www.jstor.org/stable/384380. Accessed 19 Apr 2019.

Slaymaker, Doug, ed. 2007. *Yōko Tawada: Voices from everywhere*. Lanham: Lexington Books.

Slaymaker, Douglas. 2010. Traveling without roads: Body and place in Tawada Yōko's fiction. In *Yoko Tawada: Poetik der Transformation Beiträge zum Gesamtwerk Mit dem Stück Sancho Panda von Yoko Tawada*, ed. Christine Ivanovic, 323–328. Tübingen: Stauffenburg.

Spalding, Steven D., and Benjamin Fraser, eds. 2012. *Trains, literature, and culture: Reading/writing the rails*. Lanham: Lexington Books.

Strong, Sarah. 1991. Reader's guide to night of the milky way railway. In *Night of the milky way railway*, ed. Miyazawa Kenji, trans. Sarah Strong, 81–167. Armonk: M. E. Sharpe.

Sugiura, Shizu. Honbun ni suite. In *Miyazawa Kenji korekushon 1: Dōwa I Shōnen shōsetsu hoka*, ed. Miyazawa Kenji, 369–377. Tokyo: Chikuma shobō.

Takeda, Nobuaki. 1999. *Sanshirō no notta kisha.* Tokyo: Kyōiku shuppan.

Taniguchi, Sachiyo. 2010. The personal pronoun anata in the literature of Yoko Tawada. In *Yoko Tawada: Poetik der Transformation Beiträge zum Gesamtwerk Mit dem Stück Sancho Panda von Yoko Tawada*, ed. Christine Ivanovic, 263–276. Tübingen: Stauffenburg.

"Tauchnitz Edition". n.d.. https://sites.owu.edu/seriesofseries/tauchnitz-edition/. Accessed 2 Nov 2021.

Tawada Yōko [Tawada, Yoko]. 1996. Im Bausch des Gotthards. In idem, *Talisman*, 93–99. Tübingen: Konkursbuch.

———. 1998. The Gotthard railway. In idem, *The bridegroom was a dog*, trans. Margaret Mitsutani, 129–165. Tokyo: Kodansha International.

———. 2002a. *Yōgisha no yakō ressha.* Tokyo: Seidosha.

———. 2002b. Where Europe begins. Trans. Susan Bernofsky. In idem, *Where Europe begins*, trans. Susan Bernofsky and Yumi Selden, preface Wim Wenders, 121–146. New York: New Directions.

———. 2004a. *Das Nackte Auge.* Tübingen: Konkursbuch Verlag Claudia Gehrke.

———. 2004b. *Tabi o suru hadaka no me.* Tokyo: Seidosha.

———. 2005. Gottoharuto Tetsudō. In idem, *Gottoharuto tetsudō*, 7–39. Tokyo: Kōdansha bungei bunko.

———. 2006a. *Amerika: Hidō no tairiku.* Tokyo: Seidosha.

———. 2006b. Umi ni otoshita namae. In idem, *Umi ni otoshita namae*, 101–173. Tokyo: Shinchōsha.

———. 2009. *The naked eye.* Trans. Susan Bernofsky. New York: New Directions.

———. 2011/2004. *Das Nackte Auge.* Tübingen: Konkursbuch Verlag Claudia Gehrke.

———. 2012. *Ekusofonī: Bogo no soto e deru tabi.* Tokyo: Iwanami shoten.

———. 2014. Wo Europe anfängt. Erzählung. In idem, *Wo Europa anfängt & Ein Gast*, 7–33. Tübingen: Verlag Claudia Gehrke.

———. 2018. *Chikyū ni chiribamerarete.* Tokyo: Kōdansha.

———. 2022. *Scattered all over the earth.* Trans. Margaret Mitsutani. New York: New Directions.

Tawada, Yoko, Motoyuki Shibata, and Masatsugu Ono. 2007. Shinpojiumu: Hon'yaku no shigaku <ekusufonii> o motomete. *Gunzō* 62 (2): 119–136.

Tendulkar, Prakash. n.d. Coach layout—Broad Gauge. http://trainweb.org/railworld/Coach/coach_layout_-_broad_gauge.htm. Accessed 28 May 2023.

Terakado, Kazuo. 2013. *[Ginga tetsudō no yoru] fiirudo nōto.* Tokyo: Seidosha.

The American Film Institute. 2019. The narrow margin. https://catalog.afi.com/Catalog/MovieDetailsPrintView/50591. Accessed 28 May 2023.

Thomas, Peter. 2014. Railways. In *The Routledge handbook of mobilities*, ed. Peter Edey, David Bissell, Kevin Hannam, Peter Merriman, and Mimi Sheller, 214–224. New York: Routledge.

Thornbury, Barbara. 2014. Tokyo, gender and mobility: Tracking fictional characters on real monorails, trains, subways and trams. *Journal of Urban Cultural Studies* 1 (1): 43–64. https://doi.org/10.1386/jucs.1.1.43_1. Accessed 24 Aug 2018.

———. 2020. *Mapping Tokyo in fiction and film.* Cham: Palgrave Macmillan.

Thrift, Nigel. 2008. *Non-representational theory: Space politics affect.* New York: Routledge.

Tomatsu, Izumi. 1992. Sanshirō. Jojutsu no shiten. *Nihon bungaku* 41 (1): 58–63. https://doi.org/10.20620/nihonbungaku.41.1_58. Accessed 18 May 2022.

Trinh, T. Minh-ha. 1997. Not you/like you: Postcolonial women and the interlocking questions of identity and difference. In *Dangerous liaisons: Gender, nation, and postcolonial perspectives,* ed. Anne McClintock, Aamir Mufti, and Ella Shohat, 415–419. Minneapolis: University of Minnesota Press.

———. 2013a. Lotus eye (Reading Miyazawa Kenji and making *night passage*). In idem, *D-passage: The digital way,* 3–17. Durham: Duke University Press.

———. 2013b. *Night passage* [film script]. In idem, *D-passage: The digital way,* 21–61. Durham: Duke University Press.

Trinh, T. Minh-Ha, and Jean-Paul Bourdier, dirs. 2004. *Night passage.* New York: [Distributed by] Women Make Movies.

Umezu, Tokihiko. 2005. *"Gōshu" to iu namae: "Sero hiki no Gōshu" ron.* Tokyo: Tōkyō shoseki.

Verstraten, Peter. 2009. Sound as a narrative force. In idem, *Film narratology,* trans. Stefan van der Lecq, 146–170. Toronto: University of Toronto Press.

Watts, Laura. 2008. The art and craft of the train travel. *Social & Cultural Geography* 9 (6): 711–726. https://doi.org/10.1080/14649360802292520. Accessed 18 June 2021.

Wells, H.G. 1999. A dream of Armageddon. In idem, *Twelve stories and a dream,* 400–461. Project Gutenberg.

Wilken, Rowan. 2012. Seen from a carriage: A rhythmanalytic study of train travel and mediation. In *Trains, culture, and mobility: Riding the rails,* ed. Benjamin Fraser and Steven D. Spalding, 91–113. Lanham: Lexington Books.

Woolf, Virginia. 1924. *Mr. Bennett and Mrs. Brown.* London: Hogarth Press.

Yonechi, Fumio, and Uwe Richter. 2009. Miyazawa Kenji ga tsukutta 'Kentauru matsuri' no yurai to Gigi: tanka ya 'Ginga tetsudō no your' to Doitsu-go/ Doitsu bunks to no kakawari o megutte [The origin and meaning of Miyazawa Kenji's "Kentaur-Festival": Miyazawa Kenji's *tanka,* His "Night of the Galactic Train," and German language and culture]. *Sōgō seisaku* 11 (1): 13–31. http://id.nii.ac.jp/1318/00001415/. Accessed 26 Oct 2021.

Index[1]

[1] Note: Page numbers followed by 'n' refer to notes.

© The Author(s), under exclusive license to Springer Nature
Switzerland AG 2023
A. Sakaki, *Train Travel as Embodied Space-Time in Narrative Theory*, Geocriticism and Spatial Literary Studies,
https://doi.org/10.1007/978-3-031-40548-8

277

Palimpsest, 16, 38, 51n29, 157, 183
Passenger, 1, 57, 119, 126, 173,
   190, 249
Passive synthesis, 99
Pearce, Lynne, 6
Peggy Guggenheim
   Collection, 1, 46n1
Phelan, James, 187
Phenomenology, 8
Platform, 11, 14, 16, 17, 19, 26,
   28–30, 33, 49n20, 50n26,
   51n30, 51n32, 52n36, 65, 70,
   76, 79, 93, 94, 102, 103, 106,
   109, 112, 203, 215, 231, 238,
   248n34, 250–253, 256, 258–261
Porosity, -rous, 9, 30, 38, 47n5, 113
Pringle, Mary Beth, 218
Prolepsis, 40, 58, 115n20, 131, 138
Public transportation, 5, 121

Q
Qualitative ethnography, 6,
   189–190, 237

R
Rabourdin, Caroline, 244n4
Raymond, Jon, 120, 124n3
Reading, 1, 9, 23, 24, 35, 37, 41,
   42, 49n15, 53n45, 61–63,
   72–74, 81, 82, 84, 86–90, 92,
   97, 99, 100, 115n25, 116n27,
   165, 190, 195, 204, 205, 226,
   231–236, 238, 244, 245n11,
   247n30, 248n31, 250,
   255, 259
Reflexive (surface), 43, 159, 219
Reich, Steve, 117n43
   "Different Trains", 117n43, 133,
      136, 169
Reichardt, Kelly, 119

Wendy and Lucy, 43, 119–124, 132,
   133, 135, 173, 185n8
Relation, 2–7, 9, 12, 22, 23, 29, 31,
   38, 39, 41, 44–46, 46n2, 49n17,
   50n27, 59, 70, 72, 77, 114n12,
   128, 133, 154, 159, 160, 162,
   172n38, 173, 179, 180, 191,
   192, 198, 207, 214, 222, 231,
   243, 250–252
Renoir, Jean, 48n11
Repetition, 1, 2, 26, 40, 67, 87, 97,
   132, 209, 210, 212, 224, 260
Revill, George, 8, 103, 123
Rhythm, 4, 6, 7, 40, 41, 46, 92, 103,
   159, 194, 208, 224, 261
Rhythmscape, 190
Rice, Charles, 47n3
Richter, Amy G, 221
Richter, Gerhard, 189

S
Sakaki, Atsuko, 194
Scarles, Caroline, 190, 191
Scene (narrative), 7, 12, 13, 16, 18,
   20, 23, 26, 38, 45, 46, 63–65,
   71, 73, 131, 137, 173, 189, 219,
   223, 238, 249, 251, 255,
   257, 258
Schivelbusch, Wolfgang, 5
Seat, 4, 20, 21, 39, 63, 64, 66, 68, 70,
   71, 74–80, 82, 98, 99, 115n17,
   120, 130, 143, 145–148, 175,
   178, 183, 185n8, 196, 213, 215,
   216, 223, 224, 226, 231, 238
Second-class, 13, 31, 32, 38, 48n10,
   48n13, 52n38, 52n39, 55n56,
   173, 177, 248n32
Second-person (narration, narrative),
   45, 187–189, 191, 194, 199,
   202, 205–208, 221, 224, 229,
   231, 234, 237

Printed in the USA
CPSIA information can be obtained
at www.ICGtesting.com
LVHW080146221123
764347LV00056B/768